India
Economic Development and Social Opportunity

ONE WEEK LOAN

# India
# Economic Development and
# Social Opportunity

JEAN DRÈZE
and
AMARTYÁ SEN

CLARENDON PRESS · OXFORD

Oxford University Press, Great Clarendon Street, Oxford OX2 6DP

Oxford  New York
Athens  Auckland  Bangkok  Bogotá  Buenos Aires  Calcutta
Cape Town  Chennai  Dar es Salaam  Delhi  Florence  Hong Kong  Istanbul
Karachi  Kuala Lumpur  Madras  Madrid  Melbourne  Mexico City  Mumbai
Nairobi  Paris  São Paulo  Singapore  Taipei  Tokyo  Toronto  Warsaw
and associated companies in
Berlin  Ibadan

Oxford is a registered trade mark of Oxford University Press

Published in the United States
by Oxford University Press Inc., New York

British Library Cataloguing in Publication Data
Data available

Library of Congress Cataloging in Publication Data
Data available

ISBN 0-19-829012-8 (hbk)
ISBN 0-19-829528-6 (pbk)

Printed in Great Britain
on acid-free paper by
Biddles Ltd
Guildford & King's Lynn

# PREFACE

We have tried, in this monograph, to analyse the task of economic development in India in a broad perspective, in which social as well as economic opportunities have central roles. We consider, therefore, not only the facilities offered—important as they are—by well-functioning markets and beneficial exchanges, but also the fundamental role of human capabilities, and their dependence on basic education, health services, ownership patterns, social stratification, gender relations, and the opportunity of social cooperation as well as political protest and opposition. Variations in social opportunities not only lead to diverse achievements in the quality of life, but also influence economic performance, and in particular, the extent to which the facilities offered by functioning markets can be used by the citizens in general.

This general approach is explored fairly extensively, drawing on empirical findings from different parts of India, and also on international comparisons. We outline in particular what can be learned from the experiences of other countries—successful as well as unsuccessful ones—and also from the varieties of experiences *within* India. Special attention is paid to the role of basic education in social transformation as well as economic expansion. The importance of women's agency in bringing about major changes is another central area of investigation in this work. There is also considerable discussion of the role of political and social movements, particularly in confronting deep-seated inequalities.

At the end of the monograph we present a substantial Statistical Appendix, partly as a supplement to the empirical arguments presented here, but also as general information which might be of interest to the reader. Since we do discuss in reasonable detail the nature of the economic challenge faced in India at this time, there is some possibility of treating this book also as an introduction to aspects of the Indian economy (usable even by those readers—those dreadful ones!—who are uninterested in the main theses of this monograph).

The broad perspective presented here, we believe, has some relevance in understanding the obstacles to economic development in India and the basic failure of public policies to remove them. Even though the expansion of social opportunities was very much the central theme in the vision that the leaders of the Indian independence movement had presented to the country at the time the British left, rather little attempt has, in fact, been made to turn that vision into any kind of reality. An opportunity for a break from the past, in this respect, could have been seized when economic reforms were initiated in 1991, but the focus of attention in that programme has been almost exclusively on the opening up of the Indian economy and on broadening the reach of the markets. Those are certainly worthy goals, and the need for reform had been strong for a long time in the over-regulated Indian economy, but the lack of any initiative towards a radical change in social policies, including those in basic education and elementary health care, is a major failure, with deeply negative implications on the prospects of improving living conditions and even on the chances of success of the market reforms themselves. While this book is not primarily a commentary or a critique of contemporary economic policies in India, that subject receives some attention in the general context of diagnosing the roots of India's economic and social backwardness.

The study draws on comparisons of India's achievements with those of other countries, including the ones that have skilfully used market opportunities and international economic integration, such as South Korea and other economies of east Asia and south-east Asia, and more recently post-reform China. In terms of social opportunities, each of these countries had done much more *already* at the time when they were initiating their major economic changes than India has achieved even by *now* (for example, each of them had a much higher level of literacy, already then, than India—still half illiterate—has now). India is in some danger of emulating the divisive pattern of economic growth experienced in countries such as Brazil, with much social inequality, rather than the more participatory development seen in, say, South Korea.[1]

---

[1] The contrast between 'participatory' and 'non-participatory' economic growth was discussed in our previous book, *Hunger and Public Action* (1989).

Expansions of basic human capabilities, including such freedoms as the ability to live long, to read and write, to escape preventable illnesses, to work outside the family irrespective of gender, and to participate in collaborative as well as adversarial politics, not only influence the quality of life that the Indian people can enjoy, but also affect the real opportunities they have to participate in economic expansion. An illustration of the compartmentalized nature of official Indian thinking on this subject is provided by the statement made on behalf of the Government of India to the 'Group of 77' in its meeting at the United Nations in New York last September, asserting that 'the concepts of sustainable human development and of human security' involve a 'conceptual derailment of our basic purpose of development cooperation'. The statement was made precisely at a time when the mini-epidemic of plague in India was frightening foreign tourists and businessmen away from India, and the consequences of neglecting 'sustainable human development and human security' were painfully apparent not only in living conditions in India but also in its impact on India's putative attempt at integration with the world economy.

The policy limitations relate not only to governmental decisions, but also to the nature of public discussion, particularly the potential for criticizing these decisions. So much energy and wrath have been spent on attacking or defending liberalization and deregulation that the monumental neglect of social inequalities and deprivations in public policy has received astonishingly little attention in these debates. The issues underlying liberalization are not, of course, trivial, but engagement on these matters—in opposition or in defence—cannot justify the conformist tranquillity on the neglected provisions of public education, health care, and other direct means of promoting basic human capabilities. In fact, sometimes contentious regulational matters seem to get astonishing priority in political discussions over more foundational concerns related directly to the well-being and freedom of the mass of Indian citizens. Debates on such questions as the details of tax concessions to be given to multinationals, or whether Indians should drink Coca Cola, or whether the private sector should be allowed to operate city buses, tend to 'crowd out' the time that is left to discuss the abysmal situation of basic education and elementary health care, or the persistence of debilitating social in-equalities, or other issues that have a crucial bearing on the well-being and freedom of the population. In a multi-party democracy, there is scope for influencing the agenda of the government through systematic opposition, and the need to examine the priorities of public criticism is as strong as is the necessity that the government should scrutinize its own relative weights and concerns.

The interstate comparisons presented in this monograph draw on more comprehensive studies of the Indian development experience, focusing in particular on three Indian states (Kerala, West Bengal, and Uttar Pradesh), presented in a companion volume, edited by us, and prepared for the World Institute for Development Economics Research.[2] The Kerala study has been prepared by V.K. Ramachandran, the West Bengal study by Sunil Sengupta and Haris Gazdar, and the Uttar Pradesh study by Jean Drèze and Haris Gazdar. We are extremely grateful to Ramachandran, Sengupta, and Gazdar for their contributions. Parts of Chapter 7 of this book also draw on recent research undertaken by Jean Drèze in collaboration with Mamta Murthi and Anne-Catherine Guio.

The work for the present monograph was done at the Delhi School of Economics, at STICERD (London School of Economics), and at Harvard University (particularly the Center for Population and Development Studies), and we would like to acknowledge the facilities offered by these institutions. We would also like to thank the International Development Research Centre (IDRC, Canada) for supporting our collaborative work.

For commenting on parts of the manuscript and for extensive discussions, we are most grateful to Sudhir Anand, Robin Burgess, Robert Cassen, Bhaskar Dutta, Haris Gazdar, Athar Hussain, A.K. Shiva Kumar, Peter Lanjouw, Mamta Murthi, Jenny Olson Lanjouw, V.K. Ramachandran, Carl Riskin, Meera Samson, Sunil Sengupta, Amrit Singh, and Limin Wang. We have been greatly helped by the information and analyses provided to us by the Registrar General, Amulya Nanda, and his colleagues Madan Mohan Jha and K.S. Natarajan. We have also benefited from helpful discussions with Bina Agarwal, Satish Agnihotri, Sanjay Ambatkar, David Archer, Roli Asthana, R.V. Vaidyanatha Ayyar, Amiya Bagchi, Kaushik Basu, Bela Bhatia, Bipul Chattopadhyay, Lincoln Chen, Marty Chen, Ansley Coale, Max Corden, Monica Das Gupta, Gaurav Datt, Angus Deaton, S. Mahendra Dev, Tim Dyson, Fang Jianqun, Michel Garenne, Arun

---

[2] Jean Drèze and Amartya Sen, eds., *Indian Development: Selected Regional Perspectives*, to be published by Oxford University Press, in its series, WIDER Studies in Development Economics.

Ghosh, Debasish Ghosh, Anne-Catherine Guio, Stephen Howes, Praveen Jha, Shikha Jha, Inge Kaul, Stuti Khemani, Sunita Kishor, Stephan Klasen, Atul Kohli, John Kurian, Chris Langford, James Manor, George Matthew, S.S. Meenakshisundaram, Nidhi Mehrotra, Aditi Mehta, Ajay Mehta, Sumati Mehta, Kaivan Munshi, Nirmala Murthy, Sarmistha Pal, S.S. Parmar, Xizhe Peng, Ritu Priya, Ajit Ranade, Sharad Ranjan, Nina Rao, Jon Rohde, Paul Romer, Emma Rothschild, Denzil Saldanha, Sudipta Sarangi, S.K. Shetty, Amarjeet Sinha, E. Somanathan, Rohini Somanathan, P.V. Srinivasan, T.N. Srinivasan, K. Sundaram, Suresh Tendulkar, Sarojini Thakur, J.B.G. Tilak, and John Williamson. For research assistance at different stages of this work, we are indebted to Jason Furman, Jackie Loh, Pia Malaney, Shanti Rabindran, and Snigdha Srivastava. We would also like to thank Meera Samson and Anomita Goswami for invaluable editorial advice. Jackie Jennings kept track of the organizational tasks at the London School of Economics, as did Anna Marie Svedrofsky at Harvard, and to both of them we are most grateful.

J.D.
A.K.S.

# CONTENTS

# FIGURES

# TABLES

# 1

# INTRODUCTION

## 1.1. *India since Independence*

It is nearly half a century now since India achieved independence. On the eve of the departure of the British, on 14 August 1947, Jawaharlal Nehru declared: 'Long years ago we made a tryst with destiny, and now the time comes when we shall redeem our pledge.' 'The achievement we celebrate today,' Nehru went on, 'is but a step, an opening of opportunity, to the great triumphs and achievements that await us.' He reminded the country that the task ahead included 'the ending of poverty and ignorance and disease and inequality of opportunity.'[1] It is with that task that this book is concerned.

It is not hard to notice that the task that Nehru had identified remains, alas, largely unaccomplished. This is not to deny that progress has certainly been made in particular fields. One example is the elimination of substantial famines that continued to wreck the country right up to independence (the last major famine was the Bengal famine in 1943 which killed between 2 and 3 million people). That achievement is far from negligible since many other countries in Asia and Africa have had large famines over this period. Famine has been, for example, a continuing curse in sub-Saharan African countries (Sudan, Somalia, Ethiopia, Nigeria, Mozambique, and others), and even China suffered from a major famine during 1959–61, in which around 23 to 30 million people died. There are also other achievements to which one can point, varying from successful functioning of a multiparty democratic system to the emergence of a

---

[1] Jawaharlal Nehru's speech at the Constituent Assembly, New Delhi, on 14 August 1947; reprinted in Gopal (1983), pp. 76–7.

large scientific community. There are, indeed, many areas of economic and social development in which India's achievements have been quite creditable.

However, the overall success in the task, identified by Nehru, of 'ending of *poverty* and *ignorance* and *disease* and *inequality of opportunity*' has been quite limited. The intensities of many of the deprivations of which Nehru spoke have been considerably reduced, but there is nevertheless a very long way to go before Nehru's objectives can be seen as anywhere near being achieved. For example, while there have been substantial declines in age-specific mortality rates, and the expectation of life at birth in India today (just about 60 years) is certainly a lot higher than at the time of independence in 1947 (around 30 years), many other developing countries that were in a comparable position to India not long ago have meanwhile surged ahead—with life expectancies around or above 70 years in many cases. Similar remarks can be made about other aspects of living conditions, dealing with elementary education, nutritional characteristics, protection from illness, social security, and consumption levels. India's progress over the decades, while far from the worst, has been substantially and systematically outclassed by many other developing countries.

One important point to note here is that these more successful countries, which have left India behind, have pursued very diverse economic policies, from market-oriented capitalism (South Korea, Taiwan, Thailand) to communist-party-led socialism (Cuba, Vietnam, pre-reform China), and also various mixed systems (Costa Rica, Jamaica, Sri Lanka). As far as economic growth is concerned, their records have been extremely diverse, and yet all of them have been able to achieve a radical reduction in human deprivation and insecurity. Despite substantial differences in economic policy, these economically diverse countries have had much in common in terms of social policies, particularly those relating to the expansion of basic education and health care, and India contrasts with all of them in this fundamental respect. There is much to learn from these diverse countries and the commonality of their achievements, even when we might have good reason to shun emulating them in other respects. We shall have more to say on this general contrast in this monograph.

There is one field in which India clearly has done worse than *even* the average of the poorest countries in the world, and that is elementary education. The rate of adult literacy for India has reached only about 50 per cent, which is low not only in comparison with China's 78 per cent, but even compared with the average figure of 55 per cent for all 'low-income economies' excluding China as well as India.[2] India has been left way behind in the field of basic education even by countries which have not done better than India in many other developmental achievements, such as Ghana, Indonesia, Kenya, Myanmar (Burma), Philippines, Zimbabwe, and Zambia.

The comparative perspectives are important in assessing India's performance. The more effective performances (of, say, China, Sri Lanka, Thailand, or South Korea) indicate what has or has not been feasible elsewhere and provide some guidance about the yardstick on the basis of which India's record might be scrutinized. The point is not that there has been no progress in India, nor that other countries are all doing better, but specifically that India's success in removing 'poverty, ignorance, disease, and inequality of opportunity' has been markedly less substantial than that of many other countries. And in one particular field—that of elementary education—India stands considerably behind even the average of the poorest countries in the world. This particular failure will receive considerable attention in this monograph, both because literacy is an important social achievement, and also because it has an important instrumental role in facilitating other achievements.

This monograph is an attempt to understand what has been done and what policy priorities might be helpful in attempting a more rapid elimination of the deprivations identified by Nehru at the time of independence. Just as the yardstick of achievement calls for an international perspective, so does any discussion of policy priorities, since there is so much to be learned from the experience of successes and failures elsewhere.

Another important issue concerns learning from India *itself*. One of the most interesting aspects of India's development record is its remarkable regional diversity in the elimination of basic deprivations. For example, while India's life expectancy figure of around 60 years compares quite unfavourably with China's 69 years, Kerala's life expectancy—about 72 years—appears on the other side of China's achievement. Similarly, the infant mortality rate of 79 per thousand

[2] *World Development Report 1994*, Table 1, p. 162. We have updated the Chinese figure (reported as 73 per cent in *World Development Report 1994*) in the light of the latest census results; see the Statistical Appendix of this book for details.

live births in India is very high indeed in comparison with China's 31, but Kerala's rate of 17 is much better than China's. Again, while India's literacy rate is much lower than that of China, Kerala's is substantially higher than China's. In fact, Kerala's female literacy rate is higher than that of *every individual province* in China (see chapter 4). On the other side, some of the Indian states (for example, Uttar Pradesh, Rajasthan, Madhya Pradesh, Bihar) have much lower achievements than even the low Indian average.

These contrasts *within* India are important to study for their own interest. But there is also much to be learned, we argue, from the light that is thrown by these comparative experiences on what can or cannot be achieved elsewhere in the country. This applies to learning from high achievements in some fields (as in Kerala) as well as from low ones in those very fields (as in Uttar Pradesh), and also from the rather mixed cases (as in West Bengal). One of the main themes of this work is the importance of the lessons to be learned *by* India *from* India, and this can be just as important as learning from the achievements of other countries.[3]

## 1.2. *On Learning from Others*

International comparisons have been much used recently to motivate and defend a programme of economic reforms (involving liberalization of trade, deregulation of some governmental restrictions, encouragement of private enterprise, and so on), citing the achievements of South Korea, Hong Kong, Singapore, Thailand, and other countries that have made splendid use of market-based economic opportunities. Such comparisons are indeed illuminating, but the exercise cannot be sensibly confined only to a few preselected aspects of policies there, related only to one type of institutional reform. Note has to be taken of what the better performing countries did in the fields of education, health services, social security, land reform, gender relations, and generally in the various areas of public action that bear on the identified social goals. The contrast between these countries and India in terms of what has been done in these fields is no

---

[3] The study of the diverse experiences within India is crucial to understanding the role of public action in creating social opportunities. A companion volume of essays, Drèze and Sen (1996), includes case studies of three Indian states: Kerala (by V.K. Ramachandran), Uttar Pradesh (by Jean Drèze and Haris Gazdar), and West Bengal (by Sunil Sengupta and Haris Gazdar).

less striking than the contrasts relating to economic growth and market institutions.

These international comparisons also raise an important general question about the complementarity between the opening up of economic opportunities and the social conditions that facilitate the use of those opportunities (e.g. widespread literacy). There is, in fact, some empirical evidence suggesting that the returns to educational expansion tend to increase with the expansion of market opportunities, and such a complementarity is natural to expect on the basis of general economic reasoning. Education has done much for the quality of life in, say, Sri Lanka, without doing quite so much for economic growth as such.

Similarly, Kerala's poor growth performance despite high educational and social achievements indicates that something more than just education and other social inputs may be needed to accomplish rapid growth of the kind that countries such as South Korea or Thailand (and now China as well) have been experiencing. Kerala's human resources have found plentiful markets outside India, seizing remunerative work in the Gulf and in other countries abroad. The scope for using these human resources at home can certainly be increased to a great extent by expanding economic opportunities within the borders of India.

However, there is also the other side of the complementarity between economic opportunities and social conditions. The effectiveness of the opening up of new economic opportunities and of expanding the possibility of good use of labour and skill may depend greatly on basic educational facilities and related circumstances. This is where a fuller reading of the experiences of the rapidly-growing countries in Asia is badly needed. As will be presently discussed (in chapter 3), India's current level of literacy is not only enormously lower than that of South Korea or China, India's literacy achievements *today* are also very much lower than what South Korea, Thailand, and the other newly industrializing Asian countries had already achieved *by 1960*, when they moved ahead with their rapid economic growth. Since broad-based economic growth in these countries involved using a range of modern industries, and made considerable demand on widely-shared skills and education, the instrumental role of basic education in these development experiences can hardly be overlooked. A similar point can be made about China's recent experience of market-based rapid economic growth, since China too was starting, at the time of its economic reforms, from a much higher base of elementary education than India has achieved so far (see chapter 4). To understand what happened in these countries, it is necessary to take a fairly comprehensive view of their economic and social conditions, rather than just proposing to imitate a specific aspect of their performance, namely their use of market-based incentives. *Learning* from an integrated experience has to be distinguished from simply *copying* some particular features of it.

## 1.3. *Social Opportunity and Public Policy*

Nehru's visionary statement on the elimination of deprivation had identified 'inequality of opportunity' as one of the principal deficiencies that needed to be addressed. The approach used in this study is much concerned with the opportunities that people have to improve the quality of their lives, and with the failures that relate both to the low average level and the high inequality of opportunities that citizens enjoy.[4] The word 'social' in the expression 'social opportunity', which figures even in the title of this book, is mainly a reminder not to view individuals and their opportunities in isolated terms. The options that a person has depend greatly on relations with others and on what the state and other institutions do. We shall be particularly concerned with those opportunities that are strongly influenced by social circumstances and public policy.

The use of the term 'social' is not intended as a contrast with 'economic'. Indeed, it will be argued that various economic arrangements (including the market mechanism) are of central importance to the presence or absence of 'social opportunities', and there is, thus, a deep-seated complementarity here. On the one hand, the opportunities offered by a well-functioning market may be difficult to use when a person is handicapped by, say, illiteracy or ill-health. On the other hand, a person with some education and fine health may still be unable to use his or her abilities because of the limitation of economic opportunities, related to the absence of markets, or overzealous bureaucratic control, or the lack of access to finance, or some other restraint that limits economic initiatives. Social opportunities are, thus, influenced by a variety of factors—among other things, the state of educational and health services (and public policies

---

[4] On different aspects of this approach, see Sen (1987) and Drèze and Sen (1989, 1990).

that deal with them), the nature and availability of finance (and policies that affect them), the presence or absence of markets (and policies that promote or restrict them), and the form and reach of bureaucratic control in general (including the barriers to enterprise imposed by such control). It is right to rail against bureaucratic controls and other barriers that stifle economic activity and individual initiative, but that line of reasoning, which has been—rightly—aired a great deal in India recently has to be seen as one part of a much bigger story about the determination of social opportunities that individuals enjoy. In focusing on social opportunities, we propose a perspective that is substantially *broader* than the narrow view that concentrates simply on promoting markets and competition, as well as the similarly narrow 'contrary' view that just wants to debunk liberalization.

Economic development can, in fact, be seen in terms of expansion of opportunities that the individuals in the society enjoy, and this approach will be briefly discussed in the next chapter. That will also be the occasion to distinguish between (1) the *intrinsic importance* of opportunities (one of the main objectives of economic development is to expand the effective freedom that different individuals enjoy), and (2) the extensive *instrumental role* of individual opportunities in the promotion of other objectives. Opportunities, thus, have both direct and indirect significance.

While Nehru's pointer to the ultimate objectives remains relevant and momentous, we cannot see the challenge *only* in terms of these ultimate goals. Much of economic development consists in bringing these achievements within the realm of possibility, and that requires more instrumental reasoning. We have to pay particular attention to accomplishing those intermediate tasks that would bring the more basic destinations within India's reach. While we can scarcely do better than starting off from where Nehru wanted India to go (to wit, 'the ending of poverty and ignorance and disease and inequality of opportunity'), we are not required—nor particularly well advised—to follow exactly the strategic path that Nehru himself chose. That path has led to some successes but also substantial failures, though the sources of those failures are often misidentified.

The blame for independent India's past failures is often put on the insufficient development of market incentives. We shall argue that while there is considerable truth in that diagnosis, it is quite inadequate as an analysis of what has gone wrong in this country.

There are many failures, particularly in the development of public educational facilities, health care provisions, social security arrangements, local democracy, environmental protection, and so on, and the stifling of market incentives is only one part of that larger picture. The failures can, thus, be scarcely seen simply as the result of an 'overactive' government. What can be justifiably seen as overactivity in some fields has been inseparably accompanied by thoroughgoing *underactivity* in others.

It is not a simple question, we argue, of 'more' or 'less' government. Rather, it is a question of the *type* of governance to have, and of seeing the role of public policies in promoting as well as repressing social opportunities. Indeed, the interrelations between the state, the public, and the market have to be seen in a larger framework, with influences operating in different directions. The recognition of that broader framework does not lend itself to the derivation of simple formulae used by different sides in the contemporary debates (selling liberalization over all else, or rubbishing it forcefully). But that loss of simplicity is a gain as well.

In so far as a general lesson emerges from the diverse investigations undertaken in this book, it may well be the necessity to get the debates on contemporary India's political economy *beyond* the familiar battle-lines around the issues of economic reform, liberalization, and deregulation. There are, of course, things to be discussed there and pros and cons to be assessed, but the main problem with focusing on that question is the resulting neglect of other public policy matters, dealing in particular with education, health, and social security. Both the vigorous defences of economic reforms and the spirited attacks on it contribute to hiding other—basic and urgent—issues.

If the central challenge of economic development in India is understood in terms of the need to expand social opportunities, then liberalization must be seen as occupying only one part of that large stage. By spotlighting that one part, the rest of the stage is left obscure. The limitations of the Indian experience in planning lie as much in omissional errors in the dark part of the stage as it does in the commissioning mistakes in the spotlit section. That uneven concentration extracts a heavy price. The first step is to bring the darker part of the stage more into consideration. The attention needed, as the book argues, is not just from the government, but also from the public at large.

# 2

# ECONOMIC DEVELOPMENT AND SOCIAL OPPORTUNITY

## 2.1. *Development, Freedom and Opportunities*

When the subject of development economics emerged as a distinct field of study, shortly after the second world war, it appeared to be something of a bastard child of growth economics. Some influence other than growth economics was clearly involved in the origin of development economics, but it was not altogether clear what form this influence had taken. In one respect at least, the offspring did not differ from what could be expected from a genuine 'son of growth economics', namely an overarching preoccupation with the growth of real income per head.

Ian Little reflected this understanding very well in his depiction of 'development economics' (in *The Fontana Dictionary of Modern Thought*) as a field that 'in a broad sense comprises all work on *the growth of incomes per head*, including that of the classical economic theorists from Smith to Mill.'[1] The focus of development economics here is uncompromisingly on the growth of incomes. However, while the two classical authors cited by Little, namely Smith and Mill, did indeed write a great deal on the growth of real income per head, they saw income as one of several different means to important ends, and they discussed extensively the nature of these ends—very different as they are from income.

These classical authors were deeply concerned with the recognition that we have reasons to value many things other than income and

---

[1] Little (1977), p. 222. See, however, Little's much broader treatment of development economics in his own major treatise on development economics: Little (1982).

wealth, which relate to the real opportunities to lead the kind of life we would value living. In the writings of Smith, Mill, and other classical political economists, there is much interest in the foundational importance of our ability to do the things we value, so that they saw the freedom to lead valuable lives as intrinsically important—not merely instrumentally so. They did comment fairly extensively on the connection between these matters, on the one hand, and income, wealth, and other economic circumstances, on the other, and they had much to say on economic policies that promote the more basic ends.[2] Neither Smith nor Mill would have had any quarrel with taking a much broader view of the changes that are involved in the process we now call economic development—even with putting into that category Nehru's list of things to do.

In recent years, the profession of development economics has also moved increasingly in that direction, taking a much more inclusive view of the nature of economic development.[3] One way of seeing development is in terms of the expansion of the real freedoms that the citizens enjoy to pursue the objectives they have reason to value, and in this sense the expansion of human capability can be, broadly, seen as the central feature of the process of development.[4]

The 'capability' of a person is a concept that has distinctly Aristotelian roots.[5] The life of a person can be seen as a sequence of things the person does, or states of being he or she achieves, and these constitute a collection of 'functionings'—doings and beings the person achieves. 'Capability' refers to the alternative combinations of functionings from which a person can choose. Thus, the notion

[2] In the case of Smith, see both *The Wealth of Nations* and *The Theory of Moral Sentiments* (Smith, 1776, 1790), and in the case of Mill, *Principles of Political Economy*, *Utilitarianism*, *On Liberty*, and also *The Subjection of Women* (Mill, 1848, 1859, 1861, 1869).

[3] See, for example, Adelman and Morris (1973), Sen (1973, 1984), Grant (1978), Morris (1979), Streeten et al. (1981), Stewart (1985), Chenery and Srinivasan (1988), Desai (1991), Dasgupta (1993), Anand and Ravallion (1993), Kakwani (1993), Toye (1993), Thirlwall (1994); also the *Human Development Reports*, published by UNDP from 1990 onwards.

[4] See Sen (1980, 1985a, 1985b), Desai (1989, 1993b), Drèze and Sen (1989, 1990), Griffin and Knight (1990), UNDP (1990, 1994), Crocker (1991, 1992), Nussbaum (1992, 1993), Anand and Ravallion (1993), Gasper (1993), Lane (1994), Atkinson (1995).

[5] Discussed by Aristotle in *The Nicomachean Ethics* in particular, but also in his *Politics*. On this and on the connection between the Aristotelian focus and the recent analyses of capabilities, see Nussbaum (1993) and the other articles included in Nussbaum and Sen (1993).

of capability is essentially one of freedom—the range of options a person has in deciding what kind of a life to lead. Poverty of a life, in this view, lies not merely in the impoverished state in which the person actually lives, but also in the lack of real opportunity—given by social constraints as well as personal circumstances—to choose other types of living. Even the relevance of low incomes, meagre possessions, and other aspects of what are standardly seen as economic poverty relates ultimately to their role in curtailing capabilities (that is, their role in severely restricting the choices people have to lead valuable and valued lives). Poverty is, thus, ultimately a matter of 'capability deprivation', and note has to be taken of that basic connection not just at the conceptual level, but also in economic investigations and in social or political analyses.[6] This broader and more foundational view of poverty has to be kept in view while concentrating, as we often would in this monograph, on the deprivation of such basic capabilities as the freedom to lead normal spans of life (undiminished by premature mortality), or the freedom to read or write (without being constrained by illiteracy). While the term 'poverty' will typically not be explicitly invoked in such contexts, the underlying concern is one of deprivation and impoverished lives. Even when we focus on economic poverty in the more conventional sense (in the form of insufficient incomes), the basic motivation will be its relevance as a substantial influence on capability deprivation.

The basic objective of development as the expansion of human capabilities was never completely overlooked in the modern development literature, but the focus has been mainly on the generation of economic growth, in the sense of expanding gross national product

---

[6] On this see Sen (1984, 1985a, 1992a). There is an enormous literature on 'poverty in India', which addresses many of the issues taken up in this book, although the general orientation of that literature has been somewhat different, with a more concentrated focus on the specific problem of low income or expenditure. Important contributions to this literature include Dandekar and Rath (1971), Srinivasan and Bardhan (1974), Ahluwalia (1978, 1990), Bardhan (1984a), Ghate (1984), Agarwal (1986), Das (1987), Jain et al. (1988), Srinivasan and Bardhan (1988), Kurian (1989), Kakwani and Subbarao (1990), Krishnaswamy (1990), Saith (1990), I. Singh (1990), Minhas et al. (1991), Nayyar (1991), Osmani (1991), Datt and Ravallion (1992, 1994), Krishnaji (1992), Harriss, Guhan, and Cassen (1992), Mahendra Dev et al. (1992), Ravallion and Subbarao (1992), EPW Research Foundation (1993), Gaiha (1993, 1994b), Parikh and Sudarshan (1993), Roy Choudhury (1993), Tendulkar et al. (1993), Vyas et al. (1993), Beck (1994), Dutta (1994), Dutta et al. (1994), Government of India (1994d), Lipton and Ravallion (1994), Ninan (1994), among others.

and related variables.[7] The expansion of human capabilities can clearly be enhanced by economic growth (even in the limited sense of growth of real income per head), but (1) there are many influences other than economic growth that work in that direction, and (2) the impact of economic growth on human capabilities can be extremely variable, depending on the nature of that growth (for example, how employment-intensive it is, and whether the economic gains from growth are channelled into remedying the deprivations of the most needy).

What is crucial in all this is the need to judge the different policies, ultimately, by their impact on the enhancement of the capabilities that the citizens enjoy (whether or not this comes about through the growth of real incomes). This differs sharply from the more standard practice of judging economic policies by their contribution to the growth of real incomes—seen as a merit in itself. To dispute that practice must not be seen as an invitation to ignore the important instrumental role of economic growth in enhancing basic objectives such as human capabilities; it is mainly a matter of being clear about ends and means.[8]

The recent attempts, in India and elsewhere, to open up market opportunities without being thwarted by bureaucratic barriers has been justified primarily in terms of the expected impact of this change on economic expansion, enhancing outputs and incomes in the economy. To quote the semi-official and distinctly authoritative report by Bhagwati and Srinivasan (1993), 'these structural reforms were necessary because we had evidently failed to generate adequate rates of growth of income and of per capita income' (p. 2). This is indeed a significant direction of causal analysis.[9] On the other side, the

[7] W.A. Lewis, one of the pioneers of development economics, emphasized that the appropriate objective of development is increasing 'the range of human choice', but nevertheless he decided to concentrate specifically on 'the growth of output per head', since that 'gives man greater control over his environment and thereby increases his freedom' (Lewis, 1955, pp. 9–10, 420–1).

[8] On this see Drèze and Sen (1989), and Anand and Ravallion (1993).

[9] For other evaluations of the performance of the Indian economy, and analyses of different approaches to economic policy in India, see Singh (1964), Bhagwati and Desai (1970), Chaudhuri (1971, 1974), Bhagwati and Srinivasan (1975), Nayyar (1976), Cassen (1978), Jha (1980), Bagchi (1982), Alagh (1986), Ahluwalia (1985, 1991, 1992), Chakravarty (1987), Lal (1988), Marathe (1989), Dhar (1990), Guha (1990), Kelkar et al. (1990), Jalan (1991, 1992), Byres (1994), Lewis (1995), Osmani (forthcoming), among others.

justification for focusing on outputs and incomes lies ultimately in the impact that their augmentation may have on the freedoms that people actually enjoy to lead the kind of lives they have reason to value. The analysis of economic development must take note of both the causal connections, and also of other policies and institutional changes that contribute to the enhancement of human capabilities. The success of development programmes cannot be judged merely in terms of their effects on incomes and outputs, and must, at a basic level, focus on the lives that people can lead. This applies as much to the assessment of economic reforms and current economic policies in India today as it does to evaluations of development programmes anywhere else in the world.

## 2.2. *On Education and Health*

Importance has to be attached to the distinct influences that promote or constrain the freedoms that individuals have, including their ability to make use of economic opportunities. As was discussed in the last chapter, education and health can be important 'promoting' factors. The role of these so-called 'social' variables in the fostering of economic progress has recently received much attention in the development literature. But, of course, the subject is of some antiquity, and classical political economists such as Smith or Turgot or Condorcet or Mill or Marx would have seen the recognition of this role as quite non-controversial.[10]

The remarkable neglect of elementary education in India is all the more striking given the widespread recognition, in the contemporary world, of the importance of basic education for economic development. Somehow the educational aspects of economic development have continued to be out of the main focus, and this relative neglect has persisted despite the recent radical changes in economic policy. Similar remarks apply to health care. Even Bhagwati and Srinivasan's (1993) lucid discussion of the challenge of economic reforms is entirely silent on the subject of education and health, and their possible roles in promoting the use of the economic opportunities that may be created by the reforms. Their discussion

[10] Theodore Schultz (1962, 1963, 1971, 1980) has made outstanding contributions in clarifying and emphasizing the importance of the connection between education and economic progress. See also T. Paul Schultz (1988), who provides an excellent account and critique of the relatively recent literature on the subject.

of the problem of 'infrastructure'—fine enough as far as it goes—is confined effectively to transport and power generation (pp. 52–4). An opportunity is missed here to question an old imbalance in Indian planning efforts. The issue relates to the tendency, which was discussed in the last chapter, to see the economic reforms as standing on their own,[11] without linking the case for reform *inter alia* to the failures in social policies (demanding radical changes in social programmes, particularly basic education, *along with* more narrowly economic changes).

Education and health can be seen to be valuable to the freedom of a person in *at least* five distinct ways.

(1) *Intrinsic importance*: Being educated and healthy are valuable achievements in themselves, and the opportunity to have them can be of *direct* importance to a person's effective freedom.

(2) *Instrumental personal roles*: A person's education and health can help him or her to do many things—*other* than just being educated and healthy—that are also valuable. They can, for instance, be important for getting a job and more generally for making use of economic opportunities. The resulting expansion in incomes and economic means can, in turn, add to a person's freedom to achieve functionings that he or she values.

(3) *Instrumental social roles*: Greater literacy and basic education can facilitate public discussion of social needs and encourage informed collective demands (e.g. for health care and social security); these in turn can help expand the facilities that the public enjoys, and contribute to the better utilization of the available services.

(4) *Instrumental process roles*: The process of schooling can have benefits even aside from its explicitly aimed objectives, namely formal education. For example, the incidence of child labour is intimately connected with non-schooling of children, and the expansion of schooling can reduce the distressing phenomenon of child labour so prevalent in India.[12] Schooling also brings young people in touch

[11] Cf. 'Prime Minister Nehru's vision of a strong, independent India, with a sound economy generating rapid growth and reduction of the poverty afflicting many among us, is within our grasp if only the economic reforms are sustained and intensified' (Bhagwati and Srinivasan, 1993, p. 1).

[12] This issue has been extensively discussed by Myron Weiner (1991). On child labour in India, see also Rosenzweig and Evenson (1977), Government of India (1979), Khatu et al. (1983), Naidu and Kapadia (1985), Burra (1986, 1988, forthcoming), A.N. Singh (1990), Kanbargi (1991), Pati (1991).

with others and thereby broadens their horizons, and this can be particularly important for young girls.[13]

(5) *Empowerment and distributive roles*: Greater literacy and educational achievements of disadvantaged groups can increase their ability to resist oppression, to organize politically, and to get a fairer deal. The redistributive effects can be important not only between different social groups or households, but also *within* the family, since there is evidence that better education (particularly female education) contributes to the reduction of gender-based inequalities (see chapter 7 below).

These influences need not work only for the person who receives education or health care. There are also interpersonal effects. For example, one person's educational ability can be of use to another (e.g. to get a pamphlet read, or to have a public announcement explained).[14] The interpersonal connections can be of political significance as well; for example, a community may benefit generally from the civic attention it receives through the educated activism of a particular group within that community. Also, the use of economic opportunity by one person can, in many circumstances, open up further opportunities for others, through backward and forward linkages in supply and demand.[15] It is hard to evaluate the contributions of education except through a broad 'social choice' approach.[16] There are similar interconnections in matters of health because of the obvious importance of externalities in morbidity, preventive care, and curative treatment.[17] Expansion of health and education can have influences that go much beyond the immediate personal effects.

Through these various interconnections, education and health can be variables of great strategic importance in the process of economic development.[18] India's failure to have an adequate public policy in

---

[13] See e.g. Karuna Chanana (1988b).

[14] There are typically significant 'externalities' in the contribution of education to the adoption of innovation, as for example in agriculture, so that one family can benefit from the knowledge and experiences of neighbouring families; on this and related issues, see Chaudhri (1979).

[15] See Hirschman (1958, 1970) on this and related issues.

[16] On the social-choice perspectives in education, see Tapas Majumdar (1983).

[17] This characteristic affects, in many different ways, the nature of 'the health economy' (see Fuchs, 1986).

[18] On various aspects of the relationship between education, health, and economic development, see Behrman and Deolalikar (1988), Psacharopoulos (1988, 1993),

educational and health matters can be, thus, of profound significance in assessing the limited success of Indian development efforts over the last half a century. A policy reform that concentrates just on liberalization and deregulation cannot deal with this part of the failure of past planning.

The removal of counterproductive government controls may indeed expand social opportunities for many people. However, to change the circumstances (such as illiteracy and ill health) that severely constrain the actual social opportunities of a large part of the population, these permissive reforms have to be supplemented by a radical shift in public policy in education and health. If we see economic development in the perspective of social opportunities in general, both for their intrinsic importance and for their instrumental value, we cannot afford to miss this crucial linkage.

## 2.3. *The Government, the State and the Market*

The competing virtues of the market mechanism and governmental action have been much discussed in the literature. But the comparative merits of the two forms of economic decision are so thoroughly context-dependent that it makes little sense to espouse a *general* 'pro state' or 'pro market' view. To illustrate the point at the most obvious level, we could note the simple fact that what a government can do, and will in fact do, must depend on the *nature* of that government. Unfortunately, the history of the modern world is no less full of tales of tyrannies and tortures than the medieval chronicles of the barbarity of those times. The terrifying success that the Khmer Rouge had in Cambodia in quickly disposing off a million people on extraordinary ideological grounds is an obvious example. Idi Amin's Uganda provides an illustration of brutality of another kind—less ideological but not much less vicious. That this is not a simple 'third world' phenomenon is easily illustrated by the enormity of the Nazi atrocities and genocide in twentieth-century Germany. The implicit belief, expressed in some writings, that government interventions are, by and large, guided by the demands of social progress is surely a gigantic folly.

Even when the government's objectives are not as vicious as

---

Osmani (1990, 1992), Summers (1992), Colclough (1993), Dasgupta (1993), among others, and the literature cited in these studies. See also Robert Lane's (1994) discussion of governmental responsibility in developing 'qualities of persons'.

they were in Pol Pot's Cambodia, or in Amin's Uganda, or in Nazi Germany, there is still a question as to who is trying to achieve what through the mechanism of governmental activities. The implicit faith in the goodness and the good sense of the government that underlies much reasoning in favour of government-led economic development cannot, frequently, stand up to scrutiny.

The distinction between the state and the government may be of some significance in this context. The state is, in many ways, a broader concept, which includes the government, but also the legislature that votes on public rules, the political system that regulates elections, the role that is given to opposition parties, and the basic political rights that are upheld by the judiciary. A democratic state makes it that much harder for the ruling government to be unresponsive to the needs and values of the population at large. The nastiness of the Khmer Rouge's governance was sustainable because Pol Pot did not have to face elections or cater to opposition parties, and it is the militarist, undemocratic state that made the genocidal policy of the Khmer Rouge politically feasible. So we have to ask questions not merely about the nature of the actual government in office, but, going beyond that, also about the nature of the state of which the ruling government is only one part.

There is a similar question about the context-dependence of the role of the market mechanism as well.[19] What kinds of markets are we talking about? Most of the theory of efficiency or effectiveness of the market mechanism relates to competitive markets in equilibrium. It is not unreasonable to assume that small violations of those competitive conditions need not alter the results violently (some kind of Leibnizian belief in the 'continuity of nature' is clearly involved in this implicit faith), but actual markets can take very different forms indeed. For example, the cornering by a few operators of goods in short supply—leading to a massive accentuation of shortage and suffering—has happened too often to be dismissed as imaginary nightmares. The recent history of Asia and Africa provides plentiful examples of market exchanges being used to make profits out of the miseries of millions.

There are also cases where the market manages to misjudge the extent of a shortage quite badly, and causes suffering—even chaos—as

[19] The market mechanism also has social influences in the formation of attitudes and ideas, which too can be critically evaluated from alternative perspectives; see e.g. Hirschman (1992), and also Lane (1991).

a result, without this being the result of much wilful manipulation. This happened, for example, in the Bangladesh famine of 1974, when misguided speculation on the part of traders contributed to an enormous hiking of rice prices, followed later by a sharp fall towards pre-hike prices (meanwhile the famine had taken its toll).[20] To take a general 'pro market' view without conditions attached is no less problematic than taking a general 'pro government' view.

The contrast between market-based and government-based economic decisions, thus, requires a clearer understanding of the nature of the markets and the governments involved. These are not, of course, all-or-none questions. There are variations in market forms, in the extent of competition, in the openness of entry, in the actual scope for manipulability, and so on. And there are diversities in the nature of governments, depending on the political system underlying the state, the legal system that sustains political freedom, the power of ruling political groups, the treatment of opposition and dissent, and so on. The assessment of the respective merits of market-based decisions and governmental policies cannot but be thoroughly dependent on the reading of the markets and of the governments involved.

## 2.4. *Interdependence between Markets and Governance*

In assessing the relative merits of the market and the government, note has to be taken of their thoroughgoing interdependence. In particular, the operation and successes of the market mechanism can be deeply influenced by the nature of government actions that go with it. This is so for various reasons—some more obvious than others.

First, it is fairly straightforward to recognize that markets can hardly function in the absence of legal backing of contracts and particular rights. While some of these obligations are carried out automatically (and business ethics can play an important part in the fulfilment of contractual market exchanges), the possibility of legal action in the absence of such compliance is an important background condition for the smooth operation of systems of exchange and production. It is not surprising that the development of the market mechanism

---

[20] See particularly Ravallion (1987) for an econometric study of this process; see also Alamgir (1980). Coles and Hammond (1995) have discussed the operation of markets in the development of famines in general.

during the industrial revolution in Europe closely followed the establishment of law and order that could provide security to business and economic operations. To take a different type of example, it is impossible to understand why the market mechanism is so weak in, say, contemporary Somalia without seeing it in the context of the breakdown of law and order—the form that the 'comeuppance' of the militarist regime has taken in that country. Indeed, the Somalian famine of 1992 was, to a great extent, the result of the breakdown of the market mechanism which in turn had resulted from the breakdown of governance.

Second, the government may have a major role in initiating and facilitating market-reliant economic growth. This has been studied a great deal in the history of such successful capitalist countries as Germany and Japan. More recently, the role of the government has received much attention in interpreting the so-called 'East Asian miracle'—the tremendous success of the newly industrializing countries in east Asia (in particular South Korea, Taiwan, Hong Kong, Singapore, and more recently China and Thailand).[21] This role is easy to understand in the light of economic theory—particularly related to difficulties of initiation, connected with such factors as difficulties of 'tatonnement' (pre-exchange negotiations about market prices, leading to simultaneous production decisions), economies of large scale, importance of technological externalities, and the integral nature of skill formation. The nurturing of an early market mechanism by an active state does not, of course, preclude a more self-sufficient role of the market *later on*.

Third, even the formal theory of achievements of the market mechanism is, implicitly, much dependent on governmental action. Consider the so-called fundamental theorems of welfare economics.[22]

---

[21] Recent studies of the so-called 'East Asian miracle' include Amsden (1989), Wade (1990), Birdsall and Sabot (1993a), Corden (1993), Johansen (1993), Lucas (1993), World Bank (1993c), Fallows (1994), Rodrik (1994a), among others. In this and related contexts, see also Cole and Lyman (1971), Corden (1974), Bhagwati and Krueger (1975), Frank, Kim, and Westphal (1975), Hong and Krueger (1975), Kim (1977), Adelman and Robinson (1978), Westphal (1978), Datta Chaudhuri (1979, 1990), Krueger (1979), Scott (1979), Little (1982, 1994), Chenery et al. (1986), Blomstrom (1989), Wade (1989), Balassa (1991), Dollar (1992), Chowdhury and Islam (1993), Christensen et al. (1993), Fields (1993), Findlay (1993), Findlay and Wallisz (1993), Pack (1993), Stiglitz (1993), Fishlow et al. (1994), Little (1994), Muscat (1994).

[22] See Arrow (1951), Debreu (1959), McKenzie (1959), Arrow and Hahn (1971). For a helpful non-technical introduction, see Koopmans (1957).

The first theorem, which shows that—given some standard conditions—any competitive equilibrium is Pareto efficient, is thought to be less interesting than the second, since a Pareto efficient allocation can be terribly unequal and thoroughly revolting. The second theorem, on the other hand, shows that under some—rather more stringent—assumptions (including the absence of significant economies of large scale), any Pareto efficient allocation is a competitive equilibrium for some set of prices and some initial distribution of resources. If Pareto efficiency is regarded as a necessary condition for overall social optimality, this entails that a socially optimum allocation can be—given the assumed framework—sustained through a competitive equilibrium, provided the initial distribution of resources is appropriately fixed.

The question is: *who* would fix the initial distribution of resources in this way? Here again, the agency of the government would generally be required. Thus, the significance of the so-called 'fundamental theorem of welfare economics' is deeply dependent on governmental action. There may be good reasons for scepticism regarding the political scope, in many societies, for redistributing initial endowments in this way—certainly to the extent that would be needed for social optimality with an equity-sensitive social welfare function. But what can be made achievable by the market in the direction of equity (via the second theorem) would be conditional on appropriate governmental activism.

The interdependence between market and government works, in fact, in the other direction also. It is hard to think of a government achieving anything like an acceptable social arrangement if citizens are prohibited from exchanging commodities, or producing goods and services, on their own initiative. These activities—involving transactions and compacts—form integral parts of the market mechanism, no matter how rudimentary that mechanism might be.

The recent developments in economic theory that have stressed the importance of economies of large scale, and of endogenous growth, have done much to clarify the role of markets and trade.[23] Indeed, as Adam Smith (1776) had argued, markets provide great opportunities

---

[23] See particularly Paul Romer (1986, 1987a, 1987b, 1990, 1993). On related issues, in the context of international trade, see also Krugman (1979, 1986, 1987), Lucas (1988, 1993), Grossman and Helpman (1990, 1991a, 1991b), Helpman and Krugman (1990), Helpman and Razin (1991), Krugman and Smith (1994), and the collection of contributions in Buchanan and Yoon (1994).

for acquiring benefits from trade based on specialization and division of labour, and the recent departures in growth theory and trade theory have involved what Buchanan and Yoon (1994) have aptly called 'the return to increasing returns'.

This line of analysis has also brought out the extent to which the pattern of international division of labour is not given simply by natural blessings and comparative advantages, but is also substantially influenced by the actual history of past experiences and specializations. Thus public policy can have a lasting role in the way the markets are used. The issue of interdependence is, indeed, of even greater significance than a history-free analysis might suggest. While markets must be, in this analysis, an essential vehicle of realizing economic potentials, the long-run influence of active public policy, for example, in initiating particular industries and in providing a wide base of public education (as occurred, say, in Japan or South Korea) can be more easily interpreted and understood in this light.

The wider interdependences discussed here call for a clearer understanding of the relation between government policy and market operations. In particular, it is quite important to distinguish between market-excluding and market-complementary government interventions.

## 2.5. *Market-excluding and Market-complementary Interventions*

The contributions and failures of any social arrangement involve both commission (what it does) and omission (what it fails to do).[24] The markets do certain things, and abstain from doing others. A 'failure' can arise from *either* positively doing something that would have harmful consequences, *or* from not doing something that would have to be done for good results. To illustrate from a different field of ethical judgement, murdering would be an example of harmful commission, whereas failing to stop a preventable murder would be a case of omission.[25]

The market, like other institutions, does certain things, and abstains from doing others. There is a real asymmetry here which is hidden by unclear contrasts between the market mechanism and 'non-market'

[24] The relevance of the distinction in assessing the achievements and failures of the market mechanism has been discussed in Sen (1993a, 1993b).

[25] There are, however, plenty of philosophical difficulties with pressing this distinction very far.

systems. An economic arrangement can be 'non-market' in the sense that markets are not allowed to operate freely or even to operate at all. This can be called a 'market-excluding' arrangement. Or it can be 'non-market' in the sense that many things are done, say, by the state, that the market would not do. Such supplementary operations do not have to prohibit markets and exchanges. This can be called a 'market-complementary' arrangement.

Obviously, it is possible for a system to have a mixture of market-excluding and market-complementary interventions. The respective implications of the two types of 'non-market' arrangements may be very different indeed. The nature of the issue can be usefully illustrated with concrete examples from a particular area of contemporary concern, namely the terrible phenomenon of famine, which continues to plague the modern world. Famines have, of course, occurred in non-market socialist economies as well as in market-based systems. But looking for the moment at famines in market economies, we can ask: why has the market system not been able to avoid them?

It has often been argued that the markets can and do distort food trade. Certainly, examples of markets being manipulated by organized traders are not hard to find. These manipulations have sometimes heightened the suffering and misery associated with famines. On the other hand, it is hard to find evidence to suggest that active trade distortion has been a *primary* cause of famines in market economies. The most obvious failure of the market mechanism lies, in this context, in the things that the market leaves *undone*. If some groups lose their purchasing power and their entitlement to food, say, due to employment loss as a result of a drought or a flood, the market may not do much to regenerate incomes or to recreate their lost command over food. That is an error of *omission*, which has to be distinguished from the positively bad things that the market might do. The remedy in this case need not be sought in 'market-excluding' interventions.

It is not being argued here that *all* the problems associated with the market mechanism in the context of a famine are invariably of the 'omission' type, that is, the result of what the markets do *not* do, rather than of their active presence. The working of the market can positively worsen the situation of particular groups of people, by making things worse through its operation. An example is the role of the market in the decimation of pastoralists when the price of animals and animal products fall in relation to the cost of cheaper staple food, as is common in many famines (for reasons which have been discussed elsewhere; see Sen, 1981, chapters 7 and 8). Pastoralists suffer in this way because their economic existence has come to depend on the way the market functions, due to commercialization. Similarly, the decline in the ratio of wages to food prices that occurs when the demand for labour falls (due to a drought or a flood that affects agricultural activities) can certainly worsen the position of the labourer in an active way, and this vulnerability is related to dependence on market exchange.

Even when there is a problem of market-driven commission, however, the threat of famine cannot be eliminated by outlawing the market, that is, by adopting any *general* 'market-excluding' intervention.[26] Indeed, what is happening in these cases is that the benefits the individuals receive from participating in the market (e.g. by selling labour-power and buying food with one's wage, or by selling animal products and buying cheap food) can suddenly be severely compromised by changed economic circumstances. The process, thus, works through a *reduction of the advantages* of market transaction—advantages that may be vital for survival, and on which people may have come to rely. The process of destitution is sustained by the failure of the market mechanism to provide security of these exchange arrangements and terms of trade.

Lack of clarity about the distinction between market-excluding and market-complementary interventions has been responsible for some misanalysis and misinterpretation. For example, Adam Smith's (1776) defence of private trade in foodgrains and criticism of prohibitory restrictions by the state have often been interpreted as a proposition that state interference can only make a famine worse. But Smith's defence of private trade took the form of disputing the belief that food trades produce serious errors of *commission*. That disputation does not deny in any way the need for state action,

---

[26] In some specific cases, stopping the market from functioning can possibly be useful, for example in preventing 'food countermovements' occurring in certain types of famine situations (see Sen, 1981, Chichilnisky, 1983). Sometimes food can move out from famine-stricken areas to more prosperous regions where people have greater ability to pay for food (for example, from famished Ireland to relatively opulent England during the Irish famines of the 1840s). In such situations, selective restrictions on the market can be useful (in the case of food countermovement, by preventing price increases in the famine-affected food-exporting country or region). But such cases are, on the whole, rather rare.

in tackling a threatening famine, to supplement the operations of the market by creating incomes (e.g. through work programmes) because the market *omits* to do this. Smith's is a rejection of market-excluding systems, but not of public intervention for market-complementary arrangements.

Indeed, Smith's famine analysis is consistent with arguing for a discriminatingly activist government that would create incomes and purchasing power for the disentitled population, and then leave the supply of food to respond to the newly created demand through private trade. There is evidence—both from south Asia and from sub-Saharan Africa—that this combination of (1) undertaking state action to generate incomes and purchasing power of the potential famine victims, and (2) letting private markets respond then to those incomes and demands, often works remarkably well in preventing famines.[27] That combination was explicitly discussed by Smith's friend Condorcet, and Smith's own analysis is entirely consistent with taking that route.[28]

Smith did provide a strong defence of the commissioning aspects of the market mechanism. His famous statement about gains from trade between the butcher, the brewer, and the baker, on the one hand, and the consumer, on the other, points to the advantages that the market positively produces for all the parties involved in the exchange. It does not deny that if we lack the *means* to buy meat, beer, or bread, the butcher, the brewer, and the baker won't do much for us. Stifling that trade would, he argued, be an active mistake, but waiting with hopeful passivity for incomes to be generated that would set the baker et al. to supply the needy can also be a costly error.

The distinction between omission and commission is important in understanding the division between the respective roles of the market and of non-market institutions in modern economies. In fact, it is possible to argue at the same time both (1) for *more* market institutions, and (2) for going *more beyond* the market. Indeed, in the context of the challenges of Indian planning, such a combination may be exactly what is needed. The fact that the form of the Indian political debates has tended to be quite traditional ('pro' or 'against'

---

[27] On the circumstantial and strategic aspects of this combined policy, see Drèze (1990a, 1990b) and Drèze and Sen (1989).

[28] See Rothschild (1992a, 1992b).

the market) has certainly contributed to confounding the nature of the issues. The need for more active use of the market in, say, industrial production and trade does not do away with the need for more state activity in raising India's abysmal level of basic education, health care, and social security. Similarly, on the other side, the recognition of the latter need does nothing to reduce the importance of reforming the over-bureaucratized Indian economy.

The market-complementary arrangements needed to eliminate famines have, on the whole, worked quite well in post-independent India.[29] However, the problem of omission remains a central one in the context of the contemporary Indian economy—not in terms of vulnerability to famine, but in the form of regular undernourishment, widespread illiteracy, and high rates of morbidity and mortality. These are denials of basic freedoms that human beings have reasons to value. Furthermore, these deprivations can also be instrumentally significant by severely constraining the opportunity to participate in the process of economic expansion and social change. In trying to guarantee these freedoms, combining the functionings of markets and those of governments can be critically important. In these circumstances, market-complementary interventions can have favourable effects in a way that neither market-excluding intervention, nor non-intervention, can achieve.

## 2.6. *A Positive Focus*

The literature on freedom in political philosophy is full of discussions that turn on the distinction between 'negative' and 'positive' liberties. That distinction can be interpreted in many different ways, but one way of seeing the contrast is to identify 'negative' liberty with *not being prevented* from doing certain things, while 'positive' liberty also includes those *supportive influences* which actually help a person to do the things that she wants to do.[30] While libertarians have been inclined to stress negative liberty, advocates of public support have tended to concentrate on positive versions of it.

A similar—though not identical—distinction can be made about

---

[29] See Drèze and Sen (1989), chapter 8, Drèze (1990a), and the literature cited there.

[30] For different ways of characterizing the distinction between positive and negative liberty, see Berlin (1969), Nozick (1974), Dworkin (1978, 1981), Sen (1980, 1985b), Roemer (1982), Hamlin and Pettit (1989), Raz (1986), Arneson (1989), Cohen (1990, 1993), Dasgupta (1993), among other contributions.

the readings of the government's 'duties' *vis-à-vis* the citizens. The *negative* roles consist in preventing what are taken to be bad developments (for example, outlawing monopolistic arrangements), whereas *positive* roles concern supporting constructively the efforts of the citizens to help themselves (for example, by arranging public education, by redistributing land, by protecting the legal rights of disadvantaged groups). Leaving out extremist advocacies, most political theories tend to provide room for both positive and negative roles of the government, but the relative importance that is given to the respective spheres can vary greatly.

Much of the debate on liberalization and deregulation is concerned with removing what is diagnosed to be the counterproductive nature of negative operations of the government. This position has been forcefully presented by the central government and the supporters of the new policies. On the other hand, opposition to these types of reforms tends to come from those who see beneficial consequences of these negative governmental functions. The debate on current policy in India has been preoccupied with this battle.

There are certainly issues to be sorted out in this 'negative' sphere, but what the debate neglects altogether is the importance of positive functions, such as provision of public education, health services, and arrangements for social security. There is scope for debate in this field as well (for example, on how, and how much, and how soon), but nothing is sorted out in these matters by concentrating almost completely on the pros and cons of negative roles of the government (and the corresponding advantages and disadvantages of liberalization and deregulation). What is needed most of all at this time is a broadening of focus.

# 3

# INDIA IN
# COMPARATIVE PERSPECTIVE

## 3.1. *India and the World*

In historical terms, the improvement of living conditions that has
taken place in the developing world during the last few decades
has been quite remarkable. To illustrate, it is estimated that, between
1960 and 1992, life expectancy at birth in developing countries has
expanded from 46 to 63 years, infant mortality has declined by
more than 50 per cent, and real per-capita income has almost trebled.[1]
These global *trends* are quite at variance with the gloomy predictions
of famine and chaos that have been regularly made over the same
period, even if absolute levels of deprivation remain intolerably high
in large parts of the world.[2]

The pace of improvement has, of course, been quite uneven
between different countries and regions, and recent decades have
also seen the emergence of striking diversities within the developing
world. In fact, the leading countries in the developing world are
now, in many ways, much closer to industrialized market economies
than to the poorer developing countries. It is not just that real

---

[1] UNDP, *Human Development Report 1994*, p. 207.

[2] For examples of these predictions, see Ehrlich (1968), Paddock and Paddock (1968),
Brown and Eckholm (1974), Ehrlich and Ehrlich (1990), Hardin (1993), and Kaplan
(1994). India has held centre-stage in many of the gloomy prophecies in question,
particularly during the 1960s. To illustrate: 'In thirteen years India is going to add two
hundred million more people to their population. In my opinion, as an old India hand,
I don't see how they can possibly feed two hundred million more people by 1980. They
could if they had the time, say until year 2000. Maybe they could even do it by 1990,
but they can't do it by 1980' (Dr Raymond Ewell, in Ehrlich, 1968, pp. 39–40).

per-capita income is now as high in Hong Kong as in France or Sweden, and quite similar in Saudi Arabia and Ireland. Even countries such as Venezuela and South Korea seem to have more in common with Greece or Portugal, which have comparable levels of real per-capita income, than with Tanzania or Bhutan, where real per-capita income is about 15 times as low. Similarly, the adult literacy rate is a little higher in Jamaica (98 per cent) than in Spain (95 per cent), and quite similar in Uruguay and Italy (about 96 per cent each), but only 18 per cent in Burkina Faso and 26 per cent in Nepal. And the expectation of life at birth is no different in Costa Rica or Cuba (76 years each) from what it is in Germany or Belgium (also 76 years each), while a person born in Afghanistan or Sierra Leone or Uganda can only expect to live for a little over 40 years.[3] While the common division of the world between 'North' and 'South' may have political interest and historical relevance, it is quite misleading in terms of many of the central features of development.

An important aspect of this diverse picture is that elementary deprivation is now heavily concentrated in two particular regions of the world: south Asia and sub-Saharan Africa. Consider, for instance, the set of all countries where the expectation of life at birth is below 60 years. According to recent estimates, there are 52 such countries, with a combined population of 1,685 million.[4] Only 6 of these countries (Afghanistan, Cambodia, Haiti, Laos, Papua New Guinea, and Yemen) are outside south Asia and sub-Saharan Africa; their combined population is only 59 million, or 3.5 per cent of the total population of this set of countries. The remaining 46 countries

[3] The figures mentioned in this paragraph are taken from *World Development Report 1994*, Tables 1, 1a, and 30 (the 'real per-capita income' comparisons are based on purchasing-power-parity estimates of GNP per capita). Some of the figures presented in that report, as well as in *Human Development Report 1994* (also used in this chapter), involve substantial margins of error. This has to be borne in mind when comparing India's reasonably firm estimates with the corresponding—often less reliable—figures for other developing countries. The comparisons presented in this section give a rough idea of where India stands *vis-à-vis* the rest of the developing world, but the detailed inter-country comparisons would, in many cases, call for more scrutiny. For further discussion of the data sources used in this book, see the Statistical Appendix.

[4] The figures cited in this paragraph are calculated from *World Development Report 1994*, Tables 1 and 1a (the reference year is 1992). For India, this report gives a life expectancy estimate of 61 years, but more recent calculations for 1991 by the Office of the Registrar General put life expectancy at birth in India a little below 60 years (59.0 for males and 59.4 years for females). See Statistical Appendix for details.

consist of the whole of south Asia except Sri Lanka (i.e. India, Pakistan, Bangladesh, Nepal, and Bhutan, with a combined population of 1,139 million), and the whole of sub-Saharan Africa except South Africa, Zimbabwe, Lesotho, Botswana, and a collection of tiny islands (e.g. Mauritius and the Seychelles). Of course, even in countries where life expectancy at birth is above 60 on the *average,* it can be well below that figure for particular sections of the population (just as life expectancy can be much above 60 for the more privileged sections of the population in the below-60 countries). But it is clear that there are few regions where elementary deprivation is as endemic as in south Asia and sub-Saharan Africa.

India alone accounts for more than half of the combined population of these 52 deprived countries. It is not the worst performer by any means (in fact, life expectancy in India is very close to 60 years), but this observation has to be interpreted bearing in mind that there are large regional variations in living conditions *within* India. While India is doing significantly better than, say, Ethiopia or Zaire in terms of most development indicators, there are large areas within India where living conditions are not very different from those prevailing in these countries.

To illustrate this point, Table 3.1 compares the levels of infant mortality and adult literacy in the least developed regions of sub-Saharan Africa and India. For each of these two indicators, the table presents 1991 estimates not only for India and sub-Saharan Africa as a whole (first and last rows), but also for the three worst-performing countries of sub-Saharan Africa, the three worst-performing Indian states, and the worst-performing districts of each of these three states. It turns out that there is no country in sub-Saharan Africa—or indeed in the world—where estimated infant mortality rates are as high as in the district of Ganjam in Orissa, or where the adult female literacy rate is as low as in the district of Barmer in Rajasthan. Each of these two districts, incidentally, has a larger population than Botswana or Namibia, and their combined population is larger than that of Sierra Leone, Nicaragua, or Ireland. Even entire states such as Uttar Pradesh (which has a population as large as that of Brazil or Russia) are not doing much better than the least developed among sub-Saharan countries in terms of basic indicators of the kind presented in Table 3.1.[5]

[5]  Shiva Kumar's (1991) estimates of UNDP's 'human development index' (HDI) for

TABLE 3.1. India and Sub-Saharan Africa: Selected Comparisons (1991)

| | Infant mortality rate comparisons | | | Adult literacy rate comparisons | | |
|---|---|---|---|---|---|---|
| | Region | Population (millions) | Infant mortality rate (per 1,000 live births) | Region | Population (millions) | Adult literacy rate[a] (female/male) |
| INDIA | India | 846.3 | 80 | India | 846.3 | 39/64 |
| 'Worst' three Indian states | Orissa | 31.7 | 124 | Rajasthan | 44.0 | 20/55 |
| | Madhya Pradesh | 66.2 | 117 | Bihar | 86.4 | 23/52 |
| | Uttar Pradesh | 139.1 | 97 | Uttar Pradesh | 139.1 | 25/56 |
| 'Worst' district of each of the 'worst' Indian states | Ganjam (Orissa) | 3.2 | 164 | Barmer (Rajasthan) | 1.4 | 8/37 |
| | Tikamgarh (Madhya Pradesh) | 0.9 | 152 | Kishanganj (Bihar) | 1.0 | 10/33 |
| | Hardoi (Uttar Pradesh) | 2.7 | 129 | Bahraich (Uttar Pradesh) | 2.8 | 11/36 |
| 'Worst' three countries of sub-Saharan Africa | Mali | 8.7 | 161 | Burkina Faso | 9.2 | 10/31 |
| | Mozambique | 16.1 | 149 | Sierra Leone | 4.3 | 12/35 |
| | Guinea-Bissau | 1.0 | 148 | Benin | 4.8 | 17/35 |
| SUB-SAHARAN AFRICA | Sub-Saharan Africa | 488.9 | 104 | Sub-Saharan Africa | 488.9 | 40/63 |

Note. [a] The age cut-off is 15 years for African figures, and 7 years for Indian figures. Note that, in India, the 7+ literacy rate is usually a little higher than the 15+ literacy rate (e.g. the all-India 7+ literacy rate in 1981 was 43.6%, compared with 40.8% for the 15+ literacy rate).

Sources. World Development Report 1993, Tables 1 and 28, and Human Development Report 1994, Table 5, for sub-Saharan Africa. Nanda (1992), Tables 2 and 7, Sample Registration Bulletin, January 1994 (Table 8), Tyagi (1993), pp. 24–40 and Government of India (1988), for India (as discussed in the Statistical Appendix, the all-India figures from these sources are broadly consistent with the corresponding figures reported in World Development Report 1993 and Human Development Report 1994). The district-level infant mortality rates (IMR) for India are based on the assumption that, within each state, the ratios of district IMR to state IMR were the same in 1991 as in 1981 (district-level IMR estimates are not available for more recent years than 1981); these figures should be considered as illustrative. All figures relate to 1991, except the African literacy figures, which relate to 1992.

Considering the figures for India and sub-Saharan Africa as a whole, we find that the two regions are not very different in terms of either adult literacy or infant mortality. This is not to say that both regions are generally in the same boat as far as development performance is concerned. As was mentioned already, the expectation of life in India is now around 60 years, while it is still much below that figure in sub-Saharan Africa (averaging about 52 years).[6] Also, since independence, India has been relatively free of the problems of famine and internal armed conflict that periodically ravage a large number of African countries. And many countries of sub-Saharan Africa have had a specific problem of economic *decline* — partly related to these calamities—which makes it particularly hard to improve living standards. On the other side, economic and social inequalities are, in some respects at least, more acute in India. These inequalities, aside from being social failures on their own, also imply much lower levels of well-being for disadvantaged sections of the population than the country or regional aggregates suggest. Gender inequalities, for instance, tend to be larger in India than in sub-Saharan Africa, and are responsible for extremely high levels of female deprivation in India.[7] A comparative assessment of the achievements and failures of the two regions would have to take note of these and other aspects of their respective development experiences.

It is interesting, however, that one problem which India and sub-Saharan Africa have in common is the persistence of endemic illiteracy (a feature which, like low life expectancy, sets south Asia and sub-Saharan Africa apart from most of the rest of the world).

---

Indian states put Uttar Pradesh near the bottom of the international scale, between Ethiopia and Zaire. Uttar Pradesh's performance is even worse in terms of some indicators not included in that HDI index (which is essentially a weighted average of life expectancy, adult literacy, and real income indicators). For instance, it appears that there is no country in the world where the female–male ratio in the population—a useful indicator of basic gender inequality—is as low as in Uttar Pradesh (if one excludes oil-exporting countries such as Kuwait, United Arab Emirates, and Bahrain, where massive male immigration has produced exceptionally low female–male ratios). On this and related issues, see the case study of Uttar Pradesh by Drèze and Gazdar (1996) in the companion volume (Drèze and Sen, 1996).

[6] This figure of 52 years as the weighted average for sub-Saharan Africa is given by *World Development Report 1994* (Table 1, p. 163).

[7] On gender gaps in survival, literacy, and related indicators, see e.g. the data presented in the *Human Development Reports*. For further discussion of this particular contrast between India and sub-Saharan Africa, see Sen (1988).

As Table 3.1 indicates, literacy rates are very similar in the two regions. In India, as in sub-Saharan Africa, every other adult is illiterate.

It is rather striking that India turns out to be doing no better than sub-Saharan Africa in this respect.[8] Unlike many countries of sub-Saharan Africa, India has been relatively protected from the calamities of political instability, military rules, divisive wars, and recurring famines for a period of almost fifty years, but it has failed to take advantage of these favourable circumstances to achieve a breakthrough in the field of basic education. This failure, which stands in sharp contrast with a relatively good record in higher education and scientific research, is one of the most deplorable aspects of India's contemporary development experience.

## 3.2. *Lessons from Other Countries*

The cases of successful economic development in other developing countries are often cited in Indian policy debates. It is, in general, appropriate to do this: many countries have achieved much more than India has been able to do, and it is natural to learn from the accomplishments of these countries. The countries frequently selected for comparison (such as South Korea and the other three of the so-called 'four tigers', and also Thailand and post-reform China) are indeed among the countries from which India can expect to learn greatly, since they have, in different ways, done so very well. To claim that 'India is unique' would be true enough in itself but thoroughly misleading as an alleged ground for refusing to try to learn from other countries.

However, in learning from the experiences of others, we have to be careful to avoid taking an over-simple view of what it is that the 'others' have done, or identifying the relevant 'others' from an over-narrow perspective. First, it would be a great mistake to

---

[8] In fact, if anything, India comes out worse in the comparison, after taking into account differences in age cut-offs. The 1991 census figures for literacy in the 15+ age group in India have not been released at the time of writing, but figures for the 7+ age group are available, and we have used those in Table 3.1 for comparison with the adult literacy figures for sub-Saharan Africa, which relate to the standard 15+ age group. As mentioned in Table 3.1, the use of an age cut-off of 7 years for India—instead of the standard 15 years—has the effect of *raising* the Indian adult literacy rates by a few percentage points. The estimates of 15+ literacy rates in India presented in *World Development Report 1994* (Table 1) and *Human Development Report 1994* (Table 2) are a little lower than the corresponding estimates for sub-Saharan Africa.

assume—as is often done—that all that these successful experiences of, say, the four so-called 'tigers' (South Korea, Hong Kong, Singapore, Taiwan) teach us is the importance of 'freeing' the markets. Much else happened in these countries other than freeing the markets, such as educational expansion, reasonable health care, extensive land reforms, determined governmental leadership in promoting economic growth, and so on.[9] These countries—and also post-reform China—have all been well ahead of India in many 'social' respects that have made it much easier for them to make use of the economic opportunities offered by the expansion of markets, and they have, in fact, been in that 'better prepared' position even at the inception of their market-based leap forward. To overlook these differences on some imagined ground of separating out alleged 'essentials' from other 'ancillary' features would be both mistaken and quite counter-productive in learning from these experiences. We shall examine these issues in the next section.

Second, the 'others' to learn from are not just the countries that have experienced high economic growth (such as the four 'tigers', or Thailand, or post-reform China), but also those that have managed to raise the quality of life through other means (even in the absence of fast economic growth), such as public support for general health care and basic education. It is worth remembering that despite high growth performance, Thailand and even South Korea still have rather lower life expectancy at birth than, say, Sri Lanka or Jamaica, and even Singapore has not yet overtaken Costa Rica in life expectancy, despite large income differences in the opposite direction. China's remarkable success in transforming many aspects of the quality of life during the pre-reform period, at a time of relatively slow economic growth, is also relevant here (we shall have more to say on this, as well as on some of China's failures, in the next chapter). These and other experiences of rapid improvement in living conditions despite slow economic growth are full of important lessons—about the feasibility of achieving radical social progress at an early stage of economic development, about the powerful effects of well-devised

---

[9] Some of these countries—South Korea in particular—have also benefited from low levels of antecedent economic inequality, which helped to make the process of economic expansion more participatory, and also reduced the political pressure for redistribution, with its efficiency costs. Alesina and Rodrik (1994) have investigated the contribution of lesser inequality to economic growth and development; see also Persson and Tabellini (1991), Fishlow et al. (1994), and Rodrik (1994a).

public programmes in the fields of health and education, about the relatively inexpensive nature of labour-intensive public provisions such as primary education in a low-wage economy, about the collaborative and adversarial roles of public action, and so on.[10] It is just as important to identify these lessons as to learn from countries that have achieved rapid economic growth, and succeeded in using rapid growth as a basis for improving the quality of life.

Third, it must be remembered that not all countries with high growth rates have succeeded in translating an expanded command over material resources into a corresponding transformation of living conditions for broad sections of the population. In fact, the development experiences of some fast-growing countries during the last few decades has resembled one of 'unaimed opulence', combining high rates of economic growth with the persistence of widespread poverty, illiteracy, ill health, child labour, criminal violence, and related social failures.[11] Brazil is one widely-discussed example. In many cases (including Brazil itself), the roots of this failure to use economic growth as a basis for transforming the quality of life include high levels of economic and social inequality as well as a lack of public involvement in the protection of basic entitlements. The dangers of unaimed opulence, which may be particularly real for India, form an integral part of the lessons to be learnt from discriminating analyses of the experiences of fast-growing countries.

Fourth, as was argued earlier, given the heterogeneity of India, the question of learning from India itself has to be integrated with learning from others. We cannot, for example, altogether ignore the fact that Kerala, despite its low income level and poor record in generating economic growth, has a higher life expectancy at birth (about 72 years) than what can be found in some of the more economically successful countries further east, such as Indonesia (60 years), or Thailand (69 years), or even South Korea (71), despite per-capita income being a great many times larger in these other countries than in Kerala. We have to learn from the experiences *within* India itself, and this applies to failures as well as successes.

---

[10] We have tried to discuss some of these lessons in Drèze and Sen (1989). For insightful studies of specific country experiences, see also Castaneda (1984, 1985), Alailima (1985), Halstead et al. (1985), Caldwell (1986), Riskin (1987, 1990), Mata and Rosero (1988), Anand and Kanbur (1990), Bruton et al. (1993), among others.

[11] On this phenomenon of unaimed opulence, see Drèze and Sen (1989), chapter 10. On the specific case of Brazil, see Sachs (1990) and Birdsall and Sabot (1993b).

The relevant failures include not only the continued social backwardness of many states (such as Uttar Pradesh), but also the failure of Kerala to achieve reasonable economic growth, despite a remarkably high performance in terms of many aspects of the quality of life.

In an earlier study, we found that, among ten developing countries that had achieved the largest reductions in infant and child mortality rates between 1960 and 1985, five were cases of what we called 'growth-mediated' success, while the other five succeeded in reducing mortality on the basis of organized programmes of public support for health, education, and social security, without fast economic growth and without achieving much increase in average real income.[12] The latter approach—what we called 'support-led' success—proved to be feasible largely because the costs of elementary health care and education tend to be comparatively low in low-wage economies (because of the labour-intensive nature of these activities), so that a poorer economy is not as disadvantaged in providing these services as might be imagined on the basis of considering only their lower ability to pay. In drawing lessons for India from recent development experiences elsewhere in the world, it is important to pay attention to both types of progress, based respectively on economic growth and public support. It is also important to be aware of the possibility of 'unaimed opulence', and to take note of the fact that India could go the way of Brazil rather than of South Korea. We have to discriminate, rather than assume some 'stylized model' of liberalization.

### 3.3. *East Asia and Growth-mediated Progress*

In learning from the experiences of other countries, it is also essential to integrate our 'theory' of what is causing what with an understanding of the facts of the case. The importance of markets and trades in generating economic expansion has been a part of mainstream economic principles for a very long time. Even Adam Smith's (1776) classic analysis of the 'causes' of the wealth of nations dealt precisely with this question, among others. The recent revival of growth-oriented trade theory has done much to bring out the importance of two issues on which Adam Smith himself had much to say, to wit, (1) the importance of economies of large scale, and (2) the

---

[12] Drèze and Sen (1989), chapter 10.

influence of skill formation and human qualities in causing prosperity.[13] The shift in emphasis from seeing the gains from trade primarily in terms of given comparative advantages (the traditional 'Ricardian' focus) is important in interpreting 'the East Asian miracle' and its relevance to India and other countries.

The growing recognition of the role and importance of economies of large scale has also changed one of the intellectual bases of closed-economy planning that was so fashionable—in India as well as else-where—from the nineteen-sixties onwards.[14] Underlying that acceptance of economic autarchy was a sense of export pessimism that made planners in India and elsewhere look for more inter-nally-oriented economic development, aimed at producing within the borders whatever the country needed. The concentration, then common, on 'comparative advantage' as the real source of gainful trade (dependent on differences of factor ratios, natural endowments, etc.) did not persuade those analysts who tended to be sceptical of the possibility of trade expansion, and who underestimated the real gains from trade. Autarchy was, often enough, not so much a policy of jubilant rejection of trade, but the result of a pessimistic perception that the opportunities of trade were severely limited.[15]

With the shifting focus in trade theory, from Ricardo's comparative advantage to Adam Smith's economies of scale, the limits of trade expansion have been substantially reformulated and the grounds for export pessimism have been largely debunked. The limits of trade

[13] See Krugman (1979, 1986, 1987), Romer (1986, 1987b, 1990), Lucas (1988, 1993), Grossman and Helpman (1990, 1991a, 1991b). On different aspects of the lessons to be learned from recent experiences of rapid growth and trade expansion, see also Lucas (1988), Stokey (1988), Helpman and Krugman (1990), Helpman and Razin (1991), Helleiner (1992), Ethier, Helpman, and Neary (1993), Findlay (1993), Krugman and Smith (1994), among other contributions.

[14] For a fine account of the rationale behind planning approaches used in India, see Chakravarty (1987). See also Jalan (1992).

[15] One of the authors of this monograph was, in fact, involved in constructing a model, jointly with K.N. Raj, explicitly assuming this pessimism, entitled 'Alternative Patterns of Growth under Conditions of Stagnant Export Earnings' (Raj and Sen, 1961). While the main interest in that analysis had nothing to do with trade, but with the relations between different sectors in a growth model with constant returns to scale (on this see Atkinson, 1969, and Cooper, 1983), it was the sense—mistaken as it happens—of export pessimism that made models of this kind look at all relevant to Indian planning. Even when export pessimism was not explicitly assumed, it tended to colour the growth scenarios that were explored in development models in that period (see, for example, Chakravarty, 1969).

are not to be seen as being constrained simply by differences in factor ratios and endowments, and what a country loses from autarchy includes the efficiency advantages of a division of labour that uses, *inter alia*, scale advantages and gains from specialization. The need for a radical departure in this respect in Indian economic planning is brought out both by reasoning based on modern growth theory, and by the actual experience of the economies—such as those in east Asia—that have made such excellent use of trade-using patterns of economic growth.

Recent work on economic growth has also brought out sharply the role of labour and the so-called 'human capital'. The economic roles of school education, learning by doing, technical progress, and even economies of large scale can all be seen as contributing—in different ways—to the centrality of direct human agency in generating economic expansion. In terms of economic theory, this shift in emphasis has provided one way of filling the large 'residual' that was identified in the basic neo-classical model of economic growth of Solow (1956), and recent growth theory has done much to bring out the function of direct human agency in economic growth, over and above the contribution made through the accumulation of physical capital.[16] Our attempt to learn from the experiences of 'the East Asian miracle' and other cases of growth-mediated progress cannot ignore the wealth of insights that these analyses have provided.[17]

The crucial role of human capital makes it all the more essential to pay attention to the close relation between sensible public action and economic progress, since public policy has much to contribute to the expansion of education and the promotion of skill formation. The role of widespread basic education in these countries with successful growth-mediated progress cannot be overemphasized.[18] The

[16] There is a vast literature in this field, beginning with Solow's own works that followed his 1956 model (see particularly Solow, 1957). For aspects of the recent revival of the subject, involving 'new' growth theory as well as further exploration of older neo-classical models, see Romer (1986, 1987a, 1987b), Krugman (1987), Barro (1990b), Matsuyama (1991), Stokey (1991a), Young (1992), Mankiw, Romer, and Weil (1992), Barro and Lee (1993a, 1993b), Lucas (1993), among other contributions.

[17] See Rodrik (1994a) for a different reading of 'the East Asian miracle', with more focus on the investment boom in South Korea and Taiwan; see also Fishlow et al. (1994).

[18] On different aspects and interpretations of this role, see Behrman (1987), Behrman and Schneider (1992), Stevenson and Stigler (1992), Barro and Lee (1993a, 1993b), Birdsall and Sabot (1993a), Easterly, Kremer, Pritchett, and Summers (1993), World Bank (1993c), among many other contributions.

modern industries in which these countries have particularly excelled demand many basic skills for which elementary education is essential and secondary education most helpful. While some studies have emphasized the productivity contribution of learning by doing and on-the-job training, rather than the direct impact of formal education, the ability to achieve such training and learning is certainly helped greatly by basic education in schools prior to taking up jobs.[19]

The development of basic education was very much more advanced in all these countries with successful growth-mediated progress at the time of their economic breakthrough compared with India today. Table 3.2 presents some comparative information on this subject. The point to notice is not so much that India's literacy rate *is* far lower than in these countries *today*, nor that India *was* much more backward than these countries in basic education at the time when these countries jumped forward economically, but that India *today* is far behind where these countries *were* when they initiated their rapid economic expansion. The really instructive comparison is between India now and South Korea in 1960 or China in 1980. Despite the passage of time, India's literacy rate now is much below what these countries had achieved many years ago when they began their market-based economic transformation.

In the educational expansion of the high-performing Asian economies, the state has played a major part in every case. An essential

TABLE 3.2. *Adult Literacy Rates in Selected Asian Countries*

|  | 1960 | 1980 | 1992 |
| --- | --- | --- | --- |
| India | 28 | 36 | 50 |
| South Korea | 71 | 93 | 97 |
| Hong Kong | 70 | 90 | ≈ 100 |
| Thailand | 68 | 86 | 94 |
| China | n/a | 69 | 80 |

*Sources. World Development Report 1980*, Table 23, for 1960; *World Development Report 1983*, Table 1, for 1980; *Human Development Report 1994*, Table 2, pp. 132–3, for 1992 (see also the Statistical Appendix of this book).

[19] The World Bank (1993c) study of 'the East Asian miracle', which draws on a wide range of empirical works, has particularly emphasized the importance of this linkage: 'We have shown that the broad base of human capital was critically important to rapid growth in the HPAEs [high-performing Asian economies]. Because the HPAEs attained universal primary education early, literacy was high and cognitive skill levels were substantially above those in other developing economies. Firms therefore had an easier time upgrading the skills of their workers and mastering new technology' (World Bank, 1993c, p. 349).

goal of public policy has been to ensure that the bulk of the young population had the capability to read, write, communicate, and interact in a way that is quite essential for modern industrial production. In India, by contrast, there has been a remarkable apathy towards expanding elementary and secondary education, and certainly 'too little' government action—rather than 'too much'—is the basic failure of Indian planning in this field.[20]

India does, of course, have a large body of people with higher education, and there is certainly an opportunity to use their proficiency to develop skill-centred industries, as has begun to happen to a considerable extent (for example, in and around Bangalore, involving computer software and related industries). These achievements are important and are certainly good signs for the Indian economy. But the abysmal inequalities in India's education system represent a real barrier against widely sharing the fruits of economic progress, in general, and of industrialization, in particular, in the way it has happened in economies like South Korea and China—economies which have succeeded in flooding the world market with goods the making of which requires no great university training, but is helped by widespread basic education that enables people to follow precise guidelines and maintain standards of quality. In contrast, even if India were to take over the bulk of the world's computer software industry, this would still leave its poor, illiterate masses largely untouched. It may be much less glamorous to make simple pocket knives and reliable alarm clocks than to design state-of-the-art computer programmes, but the former gives the Chinese poor a source of income that the latter does not provide—at least not directly—to the Indian poor. It is in the making of these unglamorous products, the market for which is very large across the world, that a high level of basic education is a major asset for China—and for many other high-growth economies of east and south-east Asia.

Despite 'local booms' in a particular range of high-skill industries, the overall growth rate of the Indian economy and that for the industrial sector *as a whole* are still rather low. In fact, taking industrial production as a whole, there has been rather little growth since 1990–1 (Government of India, 1995, p.2). This is not to deny that

---

[20] As argued in chapter 6, this failure reflects not only the low priority given by the state to educational expansion, but also a serious lack of concern for basic education in social and political movements.

India can quite possibly achieve higher rates of growth of GNP or GDP even with present levels of massive illiteracy. But the low coverage and poor quality of basic education in India make it harder to move from the dynamism of a limited range of industries (the expansion of which has been so eulogized in specialist financial journals abroad) to a really broad-based economic advance of a sweeping, shared, and participatory kind that has happened further east. It is a question of the strength and the nature of the economic expansion that can occur in India today, and the extent to which the growth in question can be widely participatory. For reasons presented earlier on in this monograph, the social opportunities offered by market-based economic growth are severely limited in a society in which very large numbers (even majorities in large parts of the country) cannot read or write or count, cannot follow printed or hand-written instructions, cannot operate comfortably in a modern industry, and so on.[21] Inequality in basic education thus translates into inefficiency as well as further inequality in the use of new economic opportunities. The *distributive* failure supplements the effect of educational backwardness in restricting the *overall* scale of expansion of skill-related modern production.

The relationship between education and inequality applies also to gender-based disparities. Again, the high-performing Asian economies have been able to reduce the gender gap in basic education much more rapidly than happened elsewhere, and this achievement has certainly played an important part in reducing the relative disadvantage of women in social opportunities, including economic participation. The growth-mediated success of the east Asian economies has drawn particularly on the expansion of employment options and other opportunities for women. The contrast with India is extremely sharp. In fact, in this respect, south Asia—including India—lags behind every other substantial region of the developing world (including Latin America and Africa, in addition to east Asia).[22]

While the contrast in the field of education is perhaps the most radical difference between India and the high-growth countries in east Asia, there are also other areas in which supportive public policies in social fields have helped these successful Asian economies in a

[21] As noted in chapter 1, there is also considerable evidence that the rate of return to basic education tends to be higher in countries that are more 'open', with less restriction on trade. On this and related issues, see Birdsall and Sabot (1993a).

[22] See World Bank (1993c), pp. 46–7.

way that has not happened in India. These countries have typically had much better levels of health conditions even before their period of rapid economic growth. Greater provision of medical facilities in the east Asian countries, particularly in terms of preventive health care, is an important factor in explaining this contrast. In the case of China, the expansion of rural health care has been one of the most remarkable achievements of the *pre-reform* period.[23] It has proved to be an asset of great value in the economic reforms. This is an important issue not only for the quality of life, but also for economic performance, since morbidity and undernourishment can be serious barriers to productive work and economic performance.[24]

Another area in which many of the great practitioners of growth-mediated progress have done much better than India is that of *land reform*. Land reforms were carried out most extensively in many of the east Asian countries, including Japan, South Korea, Taiwan, and of course China. The advantages of the abolition of landlordism from the point of view of equity are obvious enough, but it also has much to contribute to the general incentive to expand production, and to making it easier for agricultural producers to respond to the opportunities offered by a freer market.[25] Significantly enough, one of the least successful growth performers among the east Asian economies, namely the Philippines, is also an example of an extensive failure to carry out adequate land reforms.[26] The Indian record is even worse than the general situation in the Philippines; some success

[23] On this see Drèze and Sen (1989), chapter 11, and the studies cited there; also chapter 4 of this book.

[24] See Bliss and Stern (1978), Sahn and Alderman (1988), Dasgupta and Ray (1986, 1987, 1990), Osmani (1990, 1992), Dasgupta (1993), among other contributions. The east Asian achievements in this field are reviewed in World Bank (1993c).

[25] It has been argued that sharecropping need not be inefficient when certain conditions are met, for example, when the relative shares can be fully varied and freely negotiated (see, for example, Cheung, 1969). But the assumptions needed are quite strong and seem to be in some conflict with the actual observation of 'lumpiness' in relative shares. On the historical experiences of land reform in some of these east Asian countries, such as Taiwan and South Korea (and their extensive consequences), see Galenson (1979), Kuo (1983), Kim and Leipziger (1993), World Bank (1993c). On the theory of resource allocation under share tenancy, see, among other contributions, Johnson (1950), Cheung (1969), Stiglitz (1974), Newbery (1977), Berry and Cline (1979), Bardhan (1989), and the literature surveys in Bliss and Stern (1982), Binswanger and Rosenzweig (1984), Quibria and Rashid (1984), Otsuka and Hayami (1988), Otsuka et al. (1992).

[26] See World Bank (1993c), p. 169.

in land reforms has been achieved in West Bengal and Kerala, but the overall achievements in most Indian states are quite dismal.

The lessons of successful growth-mediated progress in east Asia include the importance of various areas of state action, including basic education, general—particularly preventive—health care, and land reform. In understanding and interpreting the 'economic miracle' in east Asia, these roles of public action have to be viewed along with the part played by governments in directly promoting industrial expansion and export orientation and in guiding the pattern of in-dustrialization. These directly interventionist functions have been brought out sharply by some—so-called 'revisionist'—studies of the east Asian miracle, which have interpreted the achievements as in-tegrally related to productive public intervention.[27] While other studies have had somewhat different emphases,[28] there is much evidence that the government did play a significant role in directly promoting industrialization in the east Asian success stories, *inter alia* through systematic intervention (for example, through variable financial terms) in advancing particular industries, and in giving priority to chosen directions of international trade (in particular, selective export promo-tion). The special contributions of governmental initiative in educa-tional expansion, general health care, land reforms, etc., can be seen as important examples of this general state activism. It would be quite bizarre to read the east Asian success stories as simple results of liberalization and of the 'freeing' of markets.

## 3.4. *Human Capital and More Basic Values*

While we have been occasionally using the language of 'human capital' in this book, to conform to general practice, that term is somewhat misleading in general, and particularly so in the context of one of the issues on which we want to put some emphasis. This concerns the intrinsic importance of the quality of human life—not seeing it *just* as an instrument for promoting economic growth and success. There is a real asymmetry between what is called 'human capital' (such as education, skill, good health, etc.) and physical capital,

[27] See particularly Amsden (1989), Wade (1990), Kim and Leipziger (1993). See also Westphal et al. (1985) and Datta Chaudhuri (1990).

[28] See World Bank (1993c) and the large literature, cited there, on which it has drawn. See also the critical reviews of Amsden (1994) and Rodrik (1994a), and other contributions to the special section of *World Development,* 22 (4), edited by Alice Amsden.

in that the items covered by the former can have importance of their own (aside from being instrumentally important in production) in a way that does not apply to a piece of machinery. To put it another way, if a machinery did nothing to raise production, it would be quite eccentric to value its existence nevertheless, whereas being educated or being in good health could be valued *even if* it were to do nothing to increase the production of commodities. The constituents of human capital, which are parts of human lives, can be valued for their own sake—above and beyond their instrumental importance as factors of production. Indeed, being a 'component of human capital' cannot be the most fulfilling achievement to which a human being can aspire.

While the distinction between the intrinsic and instrumental importance of human capabilities is of some significance for clarity about means and ends, which is central to rational resource allocation, we should not make heavy weather of this dichotomy. It is important to bear in mind: (1) that health, education, and other features of a good quality of life are of importance on their own (and not just as 'human capital', geared to commodity production), (2) they can also be, in many circumstances, extremely good for promoting commodity production, and (3) they can also have other important personal and social roles (as discussed in chapter 2). There is no particular difficulty in using the language of 'human capital' if it is also recognized that there are other—more direct—rewards of human health, knowledge, and skill.

While human capabilities have both intrinsic and instrumental value, growth of GNP per head must be seen as having only instrumental importance. As discussed in chapter 2, success in economic growth must ultimately be judged by what it does to our lives—the quality of life we can enjoy, and the liberties we can exercise. In general, economic success cannot be dissociated from the 'end' of promoting human capabilities and of enhancing well-being and freedom. The tradition of judging success by the growth of GNP per head, or by some distribution-corrected value of GNP per head, is quite well established in economics. There is no great harm in this so long as the purely instrumental nature of the role of real incomes and commodities is borne in mind—not confusing instrumental effectiveness with intrinsic importance. In this connection, it has been noted that variations in real income per head have considerable explanatory power in accounting for differences in life expectancy, child mortality, literacy, and related indicators of well-being. For example, Anand and Ravallion (1993) find, in regressing proportionate shortfalls of life expectancy from the postulated maximum of 80 years against the logarithm of per-capita GNP, that nearly half the variations in life expectancy can be attributed to differences in GNP per head.[29]

There can be little doubt about the value of higher real income in opening up possibilities of living worthwhile lives that are not available at lower levels of income. On the other hand, it is also interesting to note that the main impact of higher GNP per head on life expectancy seems to work via factors in which public policies play a significant part. Anand and Ravallion (1993) also report that when they relate life expectancy to public health spending per person, the proportion of people below the poverty line (defined in terms of per-capita expenditure), and GNP per head, the significantly positive relationship between GNP and life expectancy entirely vanishes.[30] This need not entail that GNP does not contribute to the raising of longevity. Rather, it would appear that in so far as GNP does contribute to expanding life expectancy, it does this largely through making it possible to have higher public spending (particularly on health care) and through reducing the proportion of people in poverty. The Anand–Ravallion findings are not a denial of the effectiveness of 'growth-mediated' progress, but an argument for seeing the role of growth-mediation through its connection with public services and poverty removal.

This is one illustration of the important interrelations between economic growth, sensible governmental action, and the enhancement of social and economic opportunities for the individuals in the society. These interrelations are particularly crucial in the task of transforming the Indian economy.

## 3.5. *Internal Diversities*

As was mentioned in chapter 1, the relevant comparative lessons for Indian economic development come not only from abroad, but

---

[29] On related matters, see also Anand (1993) and Anand and Kanbur (1993).

[30] Anand and Ravallion's (1993) analysis is based on all the developing countries for which they could find reasonably reliable data on these variables—22 countries in all. Obviously, all such studies need more corroboration and scrutiny, but these results seem to be broadly in line with economic arguments that have been presented elsewhere (see Drèze and Sen, 1989).

also from within the country. Indeed, India is characterized by enormous variations in regional experiences and achievements. Even in terms of the standard economic indicators, these diversities are quite remarkable. Some states, such as Punjab and Haryana, have become much richer than others based on a far better growth performance. Compared with India's gross domestic product per capita of Rs 5,583 in 1991–2, Punjab's figure is Rs 9,643 and Haryana's is Rs 8,690 (Government of India, 1994a). Correspondingly, the proportion of the rural population below the poverty line is only 21 per cent in Punjab and 23 per cent in Haryana, about half the corresponding figure for India as a whole (45 per cent), and one-third of the figure for Bihar and Orissa (66 per cent each).[31]

The contrasts are even sharper in some fields of social development. There are, for example, striking contrasts in literacy levels between different states of India, with the female literacy rate varying from 20 per cent in Rajasthan to 86 per cent in Kerala. These inter-regional contrasts are only one aspect of the internal diversities that characterize India's literacy achievements. A detailed analysis of the literacy situation would have to take note of other types of disparities, e.g. related to gender and caste. While 94 per cent of males in Kerala are literate, for instance, the literacy rate is *well below 10 per cent* among scheduled-caste women in Bihar or Rajasthan.[32]

Remarkable internal diversities can also be seen in other indicators of living conditions, relating to health, nutrition, morbidity, gender inequality, etc. These other indicators tend to be less easy to obtain at a disaggregated level than literacy rates (the latter have nice 'decomposition' properties, in the sense that aggregate literacy rates can be seen as a simple population-weighted average of group-specific literacy rates). But some elementary comparisons of living conditions in different regions are possible, using the relevant state-level indicators.

These state-level indicators remain highly aggregative. The internal diversities within, say, Uttar Pradesh (which had a population of 139 million in 1991) are of much interest in themselves, and cannot

---

[31] See Statistical Appendix, Table A.3 (the figures are based on National Sample Survey data). The reference year is 1987–8, the latest year for which state-specific estimates of the head-count ratio are available.

[32] Tyagi (1993), pp. 26–8, based on the 1991 census. The literacy rates cited here refer to the age group of 7 years and above. For further evidence and discussion of social disparities in educational achievements, see chapter 6.

be fully captured in these broad inter-state comparisons.[33] It must also be remembered that the states in question have very different sizes (even if we restrict ourselves, as we shall do in this section, to states with a population of at least 5 million in 1991), and therefore very different 'weights' in the national indicators. Nevertheless, state-level indicators are of interest in so far as the state is a crucial political and administrative unit. A wide range of relevant fields of action (including health and education) are constitutionally defined as 'state subjects', to be handled at the level of individual states rather than of the central government, or as 'concurrent subjects', involving both state and central governments. This provides a strong motivation for the examination of state-level indicators.

Table 3.3 presents a sample of the available indicators.[34] As this table illustrates, striking contrasts can be observed between the achievements of different states in terms of various indicators of well-being. Female life expectancy at birth varies from 54 years to 74 years between different states; rural female literacy rates in the 10–14 age group range from 22 to 98 per cent; the child death rate is more than ten times as high in Madhya Pradesh as in Kerala; the proportion of the rural population below the poverty line is as high as 66 per cent in Orissa and Bihar, but only 21 per cent in Punjab; the number of women per 1,000 men varies from 865 in Haryana (a level lower than that of any country in the world) to 1,036 in Kerala (a level typical of advanced industrial economies);[35] and so on. There is almost as much diversity within India, in terms of these indicators, as in the rest of the developing world.

While Kerala is an exceptional case of extraordinary achievement in the social field, which broadens the range of regional contrasts within India, it would be a mistake to think that the rest of the country —after taking out Kerala—is mainly homogeneous. The variations

[33] Some of these internal diversities within Uttar Pradesh are discussed in the chapter on this state's experience, authored by Drèze and Gazdar (1996), in the companion volume (Drèze and Sen, 1996).

[34] More detailed information can be found in the Statistical Appendix to this book (particularly Table A.3). For an informative analysis of levels and trends in well-being indicators in different states of India, see Dutta et al. (1994).

[35] The female–male ratio is, in fact, even lower than 865 in a few oil-exporting countries (e.g. Kuwait, United Arab Emirates, Bahrain), but this is mainly due to large-scale immigration of male labourers from abroad; the same explanation would not apply to Haryana or Uttar Pradesh (see e.g. Agnihotri, 1994). On the significance of the female–male ratio as an indicator of basic gender inequality, see chapter 7.

TABLE 3.3. *Selected Indicators for Major Indian States*

| State | Population, 1991 (million) | Life expectancy at birth, 1990–2 | | Death rate for 0–4 age group, 1991 | Total fertility rate, 1991 | Female–male ratio, 1991 | Literacy rate in 7+ age group, 1991 | | Rural literacy rate in 10–14 age group, 1987–8 | | Incidence of poverty, 1987–8 (head-count ratio) | |
|---|---|---|---|---|---|---|---|---|---|---|---|---|
| | | Female | Male | | | | Female | Male | Female | Male | Rural | Urban |
| Kerala | 29.1 | 74.4 | 68.8 | 4.3 | 1.8 | 1,036 | 86 | 94 | 98 | 98 | 44.0 | 44.5 |
| Himachal Pradesh | 5.2 | n/a | n/a | 19.3 | 3.1 | 976 | 52 | 75 | 81 | 95 | 24.8 | 3.3 |
| Maharashtra | 78.9 | 64.7 | 63.1 | 16.3 | 3.0 | 934 | 52 | 77 | 68 | 86 | 54.2 | 35.6 |
| Tamil Nadu | 55.9 | 63.2 | 61.0 | 16.1 | 2.2 | 974 | 51 | 74 | 71 | 85 | 51.3 | 39.2 |
| Punjab | 20.3 | 67.5 | 65.4 | 17.0 | 3.1 | 882 | 50 | 66 | 69 | 76 | 21.0 | 11.2 |
| Gujarat | 41.3 | 61.3 | 59.1 | 23.3 | 3.1 | 934 | 49 | 73 | 61 | 78 | 41.6 | 38.8 |
| West Bengal | 68.1 | 62.0 | 60.5 | 20.6 | 3.2 | 917 | 47 | 68 | 61 | 69 | 57.2 | 30.6 |
| Karnataka | 45.0 | 63.6 | 60.0 | 23.6 | 3.1 | 960 | 44 | 67 | 56 | 74 | 42.3 | 45.0 |
| Assam | 22.4 | n/a | n/a | 32.4 | 3.5 | 923 | 43 | 62 | 78 | 83 | 53.1 | 11.4 |
| Haryana | 16.5 | 63.6 | 62.2 | 23.0 | 4.0 | 865 | 41 | 69 | 63 | 87 | 23.2 | 18.3 |
| Orissa | 31.7 | 54.8 | 55.9 | 39.0 | 3.3 | 971 | 35 | 63 | 51 | 70 | 65.6 | 44.5 |
| Andhra Pradesh | 66.5 | 61.5 | 59.0 | 21.3 | 3.0 | 972 | 33 | 55 | 42 | 66 | 31.6 | 40.0 |
| Madhya Pradesh | 66.2 | 53.5 | 54.1 | 44.5 | 4.6 | 931 | 29 | 58 | 40 | 68 | 49.8 | 46.0 |
| Uttar Pradesh | 139.1 | 54.6 | 56.8 | 35.6 | 5.1 | 879 | 25 | 56 | 39 | 68 | 47.7 | 41.9 |
| Bihar | 86.4 | 58.3 | n/a | 22.8 | 4.4 | 911 | 23 | 52 | 34 | 59 | 66.3 | 56.7 |
| Rajasthan | 44.0 | 57.8 | 57.6 | 30.9 | 4.6 | 910 | 20 | 55 | 22 | 72 | 41.9 | 41.5 |
| INDIA | 846.3 | 59.4 | 59.0 | 26.5 | 3.6 | 927 | 39 | 64 | 52 | 73 | 44.9 | 36.5 |

*Sources.* See Statistical Appendix, which also presents more detailed information on different aspects of living conditions in Indian states. This table includes all states with a population of at least 5 million in 1991, except Jammu and Kashmir (where the 1991 census, on which many of these figures are based, was not conducted). The states have been ranked in descending order of female literacy.

within India are enormous whether or not Kerala is included in these comparisons. For example, while Kerala's fertility rate of 1.8 in 1991 contrasts very powerfully with the rate of 5.1 for Uttar Pradesh, the contrast between Uttar Pradesh and Tamil Nadu is also sharp enough, since the latter's fertility rate of 2.2, though higher than Kerala's 1.8, is much less than half the figure of 5.1 for Uttar Pradesh. To look at these numbers in another way, the fertility rate of Tamil Nadu (2.2) is of a similar order of magnitude as that for the United States and Sweden (2.1), and lower than the rate for *every* 'low income country' in the world, with the exception of China (2.0), whereas the fertility rate of 5.1 in Uttar Pradesh is significantly higher than the average for all 'low income countries' (3.4) and much in excess of the rates for such countries as Sri Lanka (2.5) and Indonesia (2.9), and even Bangladesh (4.0) and Myanmar or Burma (4.2).[36] When we include Kerala in the inter-state comparisons, the contrasts are made sharper, but the divergences are not lost even when Kerala is excluded. Even though we shall often concentrate specifically on Kerala, since there is so much to learn from this very powerful illustration of internal diversity within India, we must nevertheless resist the temptation to see it all as 'Kerala versus the rest'.

In interpreting the picture of internal diversities within India, it is also important to remember that human deprivation has different aspects, involving failures of different kinds of capabilities (see chapter 2). Further, different indicators of deprivation need not be closely correlated with each other, as Table 3.3 brings out clearly enough with respect to the different regions within India. Thus, the relative intensity of deprivation in different parts of the country depends on which aspect or indicator of deprivation we are concerned with. The incidence of rural poverty as measured by the conventional head-count ratio, for instance, is clearly highest in the eastern states, especially Bihar and Orissa, and to a lesser extent West Bengal.[37]

---

[36] These figures for different countries are taken from the *World Development Report 1994*, Table 26 (see World Bank, 1994b). 'Low income countries' are defined here, as in that report, as countries with GNP per capita below $675 in 1992. The figures for the Indian states come from Government of India (1993b).

[37] Independent information on the incidence of hunger seems to conform to this regional pattern. The proportion of rural persons who report that they do not get two square meals a day throughout the year is below 20 per cent in all major Indian states except Orissa, Bihar, and West Bengal, where it is as high as 36.8 per cent, 37.3 per

But child death rates follow quite a different regional pattern, with the central and north-western states of Uttar Pradesh, Madhya Pradesh, and Rajasthan doing considerably worse than West Bengal or Bihar, while Orissa combines a high incidence of poverty with high levels of child mortality. And the female–male ratio figures suggest that gender inequalities are most acute in the north-west, including the relatively prosperous states of Punjab and Haryana—a finding on which there is a good deal of independent evidence.[38] There is, thus, no single 'problem region' within India, and public policy has to be alive to the different kinds of challenges that arise in different parts of the country. In so far as any broad pattern can be identified, it is mainly one of deprivation being endemic in most of north India (except in Punjab and Haryana, where there is a specific problem of gender inequality despite other indicators being relatively favourable), with the south Indian states doing significantly better in most respects, especially in matters of mortality, fertility, literacy, and gender equity.

A related issue is that well-being indicators in different states are poorly correlated with income or expenditure indicators. To illustrate, Figure 3.1 plots the child mortality rate against the incidence of poverty (as measured by the head-count ratio) in different states, for 1987–8. The association between the two is rather weak, to say the least. Some aspects of this weakness of association are indeed rather striking; for instance, child mortality is more than six times as high in Uttar Pradesh as in Kerala even though the head-count measures of poverty are very similar—and quite close to the all-India average— in the two states.[39] This need not be taken to imply that income or

cent, and 39.6 per cent, respectively (Minhas, 1991, p. 28). The robustness of this information requires examination, given the ambiguities that may be attached to the notion of 'getting two square meals a day', but there is some congruence of diagnosis in that the results of this inquiry point in the same direction as those of consumer expenditure surveys so far as the deficiency of purchasing power in eastern India is concerned.

[38] See chapter 7, and the references cited there.

[39] Estimates of the head-count ratio in Kerala in the 1980s seem to be somewhat sensitive to the choice of price indices used to adjust for differences in prices between different states and time periods. The estimates used in Figure 3.1, which suggest that the head-count ratio in Kerala (44.1) is close to the all-India average (42.7), are based on the expert study by Minhas et al. (1991); see also Tendulkar et al. (1993). It may be worth noting that, according to all available studies, the head-count ratio in Kerala was a good deal higher than in India as a whole until the late 1970s (see EPW Research Foundation, 1993). It is clear that Kerala's lead in health, education, and related fields

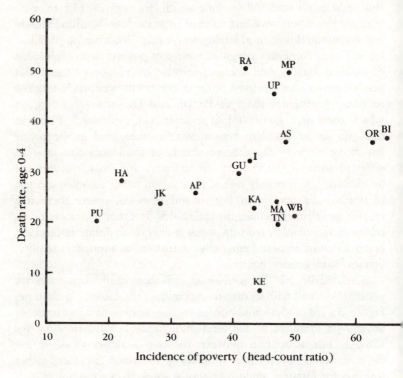

FIG. 3.1. *Indian States: Poverty and Child Mortality, 1987–8*

*Source.* Minhas et al. (1991); *Sample Registration System 1988,* Statement 39 (p. 48).

**I = India**

| | |
|---|---|
| AP = Andhra Pradesh | AS = Assam |
| BI = Bihar | HA = Haryana |
| GU = Gujarat | JK = Jammu & Kashmir |
| KA = Karnataka | KE = Kerala |
| MA = Maharashtra | MP = Madhya Pradesh |
| OR = Orissa | PU = Punjab |
| RA = Rajasthan | TN = Tamil Nadu |
| UP = Uttar Pradesh | WB = West Bengal |

expenditure have no effect on child mortality and related indicators of health or well-being. There is plenty of evidence, in India and in other countries, that health achievements do improve with higher incomes (it is the fast growth of incomes, for instance, that has clearly been the driving force behind the expansion of life expectancy in Punjab). The point is that many *other* factors are involved, which tend to weaken the simple correlation between income and health (or other aspects of well-being), when these other factors are not themselves well correlated with income.

Among the factors (other than private income) that have a strong influence on living conditions, important roles are played by particular kinds of public actions, e.g. those geared to the provision of social services, the removal of traditional inequalities, the promotion of widespread literacy. The contrast between Kerala and Uttar Pradesh, pursued in the next section, provides a useful illustration of this point.

## 3.6. *Studying Indian States*

As discussed earlier, there is much to learn from the diversity of development experiences among different Indian states. In a companion volume of essays (Drèze and Sen, 1996), some of the lessons to be drawn are pursued, based on case studies of Kerala (by V.K. Ramachandran), Uttar Pradesh (by Jean Drèze and Haris Gazdar), and West Bengal (by Sunil Sengupta and Haris Gazdar). In subsequent chapters of this book, we shall make frequent use of the insights arising from these case studies.[40]

The contrast between Kerala and Uttar Pradesh is of particular interest, and we shall have the occasion to refer to that contrast in various contexts. These two states are poles apart in the scales of many indicators of well-being, without being very different—as noted in the preceding section—in terms of conventional measures of the incidence of poverty. As V.K. Ramachandran's case study of Kerala documents in some detail, Kerala's success can be traced to the role of public action in promoting a range of social opportunities relating *inter alia* to elementary education, land reform, the role of women in society, and the widespread and equitable provision of health

---

was achieved at a time when the incidence of poverty, as measured by the head-count ratio, was no lower in Kerala than in India as a whole.

[40] This section itself draws extensively on these case studies.

care and other public services.[41] Interestingly, Uttar Pradesh's *failures* can be plausibly attributed to the public *neglect* of the very same opportunities.[42] The fact that both case studies identify much the same factors of success (in Kerala) and failure (in Uttar Pradesh) is of considerable significance in understanding the diversity of social achievements in different parts of India. Among the identified determinants of social achievements, the following deserve strong emphasis.[43]

First, the role of literacy (and particularly of female literacy) in promoting basic capabilities emerges forcefully in both case studies. One of the distinguishing features of Kerala's development experience is the early promotion of literacy, and this feature has led to important social achievements later on, based on the diverse social and personal roles of literacy (discussed in chapter 2). In Uttar Pradesh, by contrast, the adult female literacy rate is still as low as 25 per cent, and two-thirds of all adolescent girls in rural areas have *never* been to school. This educational backwardness has wide-ranging penalties, including very high mortality and fertility rates.[44]

Second, another element in social success that clearly emerges from both experiences is the agency of women. Uttar Pradesh has a long history of oppressive gender relations, and even now inequalities between men and women in that part of the country are extraordinarily sharp (as we noted earlier, for instance, very few countries in the world have as low a female–male ratio as Uttar Pradesh). As with

---

[41] On these and related aspects of Kerala's development experience, see also Krishnan (1976, 1991, 1994, forthcoming), Mencher (1980), Nair (1981), Nag (1983, 1989), Raj and Tharakan (1983), Panikar and Soman (1984, 1985), Robin Jeffrey (1987, 1992), Franke and Chasin (1989), Mari Bhat and Rajan (1990, 1992), Kannan et al. (1991), Kabir and Krishnan (1992), Sibbons (1992), Kannan (1993), Mahendra Dev (1993c), Oommen (1993a), Prakash (1994), Zachariah et al. (1994), among others, and also the extensive collection of papers summarized in AKG Centre for Research and Studies (1994).

[42] See the case study of Uttar Pradesh by Drèze and Gazdar (1996) in the companion volume.

[43] There are, of course, close interconnections between these different social influences. For instance, the expansion of literacy in Kerala has been both an *outcome* of extensive state involvement in the provision of basic services and a *determinant* of further expansion of social provisions. Public provisioning and widespread literacy have developed together.

[44] On the role of literacy (especially female literacy) in reducing mortality and fertility rates, see chapter 7.

illiteracy, the suppression of women's active and liberated participation in the economy and the society has been a cause of much social backwardness in Uttar Pradesh. In Kerala, by contrast, the position of women in society has been relatively favourable for a long time, and the informed agency of women has played a crucial role in a wide range of social achievements.[45] The expansion of literacy itself owes a great deal to that agency, reflected even in the fact that almost two-thirds of primary-school teachers in Kerala are women (compared with 18 per cent in Uttar Pradesh).

TABLE 3.4. *India, Uttar Pradesh and Kerala: Contrasts in Access to Public Services*

|  | India | Uttar Pradesh | Kerala |
|---|---|---|---|
| Percentage of rural children aged 12–14 who have never been enrolled in a school, 1986–7 | | | |
| Female | 51 | 68 | 1.8 |
| Male | 26 | 27 | 0.4 |
| Proportion of children aged 12–23 months who have not received any vaccination, 1992–3 (%) | 30 | 43 | 11 |
| Percentage of recent births preceded by an antenatal check-up, 1992–3 | 49 | 30 | 97 |
| Proportion of births taking place in medical institutions, 1991 (%) | 24 | 4 | 92 |
| Number of hospital beds per million persons, 1991 | 732 | 340 | 2,418 |
| Proportion of villages with medical facilities, 1981 (%) | 14 | 10 | 96 |
| Proportion of the population receiving subsidized cereals from the public distribution system, 1986–7 (%) | 29 | 3 | 87 |

*Sources.* See Statistical Appendix, and the Explanatory Note in that appendix. Although the contrasts presented here relate primarily to the provision and utilization of *public* services, they may also reflect some differences in the functioning of private services. For further discussion of public services in Uttar Pradesh and Kerala, see Drèze and Gazdar (1996) and Ramachandran (1996) in the companion volume, and the literature cited there.

[45] On this, see particularly Robin Jeffrey (1992).

Third, the contrast between Uttar Pradesh and Kerala brings out the essential role of well-functioning public services in improving living conditions. As we noted earlier in this chapter, the widely divergent levels of well-being in the two states cannot be explained in terms of higher incomes and lower levels of poverty in Kerala (since Uttar Pradesh and Kerala are, in fact, not very different in these respects). If entitlements to basic commodities and services differ so sharply between the two states, it is because of a marked difference in the scope and quality of a wide range of public services such as schooling facilities, basic health care, child immunization, social security arrangements, and public food distribution. In Uttar Pradesh, these public services are comprehensively neglected, sometimes even non-existent, especially in rural areas (Table 3.4 presents some illustrative indications of this particular contrast between Uttar Pradesh and Kerala).

Fourth, both case studies highlight the social influence of public action in a wide sense, going beyond the initiative of the state and involving the public at large. The early promotion of literacy in Kerala has enabled the public to play an active role in state politics and social affairs in a way that has not happened in Uttar Pradesh. Public action in Kerala has been particularly important in orienting the priorities of the state in the direction of a strong commitment to the promotion of social opportunities. Even the expansion of public services has often taken place in response to the organized demands of a well-educated public. The vigilance of the public has also been essential to ensure the adequate *functioning* of public services such as health centres and primary schools in Kerala.[46]

Finally, Uttar Pradesh and Kerala point to the special importance of a particular type of public action—the political organization of deprived sections of the society. In Kerala, informed political activism—building partly on the achievement of mass literacy—has played a crucial role in the reduction of social inequalities based on caste, gender, and (to some extent) class.[47] Political organization has also been important in enabling disadvantaged groups to take an active

---

[46] On this issue, see Mencher (1980), Nag (1989), and Majumdar (1993), and chapter 6 of this book.

[47] The reduction of social and economic inequalities in Kerala is extensively discussed by V.K. Ramachandran (1996) in the companion volume. In tackling class inequalities, land reforms and social security arrangements have played an important part. On the relationship between social security and inequality, see section 5.4.

part in the general processes of economic development, public action, and social change. In Uttar Pradesh, traditional inequalities and social divisions remain extremely powerful, and their persistence hinders many social endeavours.[48] It is still possible, for instance, to find villages in Uttar Pradesh where a powerful landlord has deliberately obstructed the creation of a village school by the government (see section 5.5). More generally, the concentration of political power in the hands of privileged sections of the society has contributed, perhaps more than anything else, to a severe neglect of the basic needs of disadvantaged groups in state and local politics.

Underlying many of these contrasts is the general importance of politics in the development process. Kerala does, of course, possess some special cultural and historical characteristics which may have helped its social transformation. But the political process itself has played an extremely important role in Kerala's development experience, supplementing or supplanting these inherited characteristics.[49] This issue has a strong bearing on the 'replicability' of Kerala's success. Given the role of political movements, there is no reason why Uttar Pradesh—and other states of India where basic deprivations remain endemic—should not be able to emulate many of Kerala's achievements, based on determined and reasoned political activism.

A good illustration of the feasibility of political transformation comes from West Bengal.[50] This is a state where political organization of disadvantaged classes has succeeded in ushering in a significant change in the balance of political power. A concrete expression of this change occurred in 1977, when the Left Front coalition came to office at the state level. The main electoral base of the Left Front, which has retained office since then through successive elections, consists of landless labourers, sharecroppers, slum dwellers, and other disadvantaged groups. This change in the balance of power has made it possible to implement a number of far-reaching social programmes that are often considered 'politically infeasible' in many

[48] On inequality as an obstacle to social progress, see chapter 5.

[49] One important indication of this comes from the comparative experiences of Kerala's three different regions—Travancore, Cochin, and Malabar. We will return to this in the concluding chapter (section 8.6).

[50] For further discussion, see the case study of West Bengal by Sunil Sengupta and Haris Gazdar (1996) in the companion volume.

other states. Two notable examples are land reform and the revitalization of democratic institutions at the village level.[51]

The government of West Bengal has been notably less active in promoting some other types of social opportunities. While issues such as land reform have received high priority in the programme of the Left Front coalition (partly because of the importance of these issues in the political battles that led this coalition to power), public policies concerned with health, education, and related matters have been comparatively neglected. Correspondingly, the improvement of living conditions in West Bengal in recent years has remained relatively slow. An important opportunity has been missed here, since the skills of popular mobilization of the West Bengal government (amply demonstrated in other fields) could have been used with good effect to achieve a real transformation in the fields of education and health.[52] These are serious failures of the West Bengal experience, but they do not detract from the importance of the positive achievements, nor from the general value of that experience as an example of the possibility of radical political change in India today.

[51] See Sengupta and Gazdar (1996), and the literature cited in that study. A number of other public programmes also appear to have been more successful in West Bengal than in most other states, due to the political commitments of the government and the improved scope for collective action at the local level. Examples include public programmes relating to poverty alleviation (see Drèze, 1990d, and Swaminathan, 1990), rural infrastructure (Saha and Swaminathan, 1994, Sengupta and Gazdar, 1996), and paticipatory management of environmental resources (Shah, 1987, Malhotra and Poffenberger, 1989, S.B. Roy, 1992, Gadgil and Guha, 1993).

[52] There have been some important initiatives in that direction during the last few years, e.g. in the context of the Total Literacy Campaign (see C. Sengupta, 1992, S. Banerjee, 1994, Ghosh et al., 1994, and Sengupta and Gazdar, 1996).

# 4

# INDIA AND CHINA

## 4.1. *Perceptions of China*

'An' the dawn comes up like thunder outer China 'crost the Bay!' This isn't politics, but Kipling on nature, on the road to Mandalay. However, following the establishment of the People's Republic of China in 1949, the *political* perceptions of many activists in India began to match this arresting description of the coming dawn from China. Comparison with China and the lessons to be learned from its experience became staple concerns in Indian politics.

Indeed, it is natural to judge Indian successes and failures in comparative terms with China. Some of these comparisons have been academic and scholarly, even distant.[1] Others have been used to precipitate particular political debates in India, with considerable practical impact—in some cases linked to specific revolutionary causes (particularly in giving shape to Maoist political parties). Even non-revolutionary parties of the 'left', which are well integrated in India's parliamentary system of governance, have paid sustained attention to the perceived economic and social achievements of China—looking for lessons and guidance on how to make things move faster in India.

Since the economic reforms introduced around 1979, China's example has been increasingly quoted by quite a different group of political commentators and advocates, to wit, those keen on promoting liberalization—and integration of India into the world economy. China's successful liberalization programmes and its massive entry

[1] Fine examples of academic attempts at comparison can be found in Malenbaum (1956, 1959, 1982), S.J. Patel (1985), Bhalla (1992), Howes (1992), Matson and Selden (1992), Rosen (1992), and Srinivasan (1994), among others.

into international trade has been increasingly projected as a great model for India to act on. The pro-market new 'dawn' may be quite a different event from what the Naxalites dreamed about in their grim struggle, but it too looked to many 'like thunder outer China 'crost the Bay!'

The People's Republic of China was established in October 1949, just a few months before the constitution of the federal Republic of India came into force in January 1950. The Indian leadership—at that stage on good terms with China—tended to underplay the competing importance of China's example, treating the respective efforts at economic development and political emancipation as similar in spirit. As Jawaharlal Nehru put it in a speech in 1954, 'these new and revolutionary changes in China and India, even though they differ in content, symbolize the new spirit of Asia and new vitality which is finding expression in the countries in Asia.'[2]

The sense that there is much to learn from China's experience was immediate and powerful. The radicalism of Chinese politics seemed to many to be deeply relevant to India, given the enormity of its poverty and economic misery. China was the only country in the world comparable with India in terms of population size, and it had similar levels of impoverishment and distress. The fact that as a solution China sought a revolutionary transformation of society had a profound impact on political perceptions in the subcontinent. Similarly, later on, China's choice of market-oriented reform and of a policy of integration with the world economy has given those policies a much wider hearing in India than they could have conceivably had on the basis of what had happened in countries that are much smaller and perceived to be quite dissimilar to India: Hong Kong, Taiwan, Singapore, even South Korea. From revolutionary inspiration to reformist passion, China has got India's ear again and again.

We shall presently argue that there is indeed a great deal to learn from China. For that to happen, however, it is crucial to have a clear view of the roots of Chinese triumphs and successes, and also of the sources of its troubles and failures. It is, of course, first of all necessary to distinguish between—and contrast—the different phases of the Chinese experience, in particular, *before* and *after* the economic reforms initiated in 1979. But going beyond that, it is

---

[2] Speech made on 23 October 1954, reproduced in Gopal (1983), pp. 371–3.

also important to take note of the *interdependence* between the achievements in the different periods. We argue, in particular, that the accomplishments relating to education, health care, land reforms, and social change in the pre-reform period made significantly positive contributions to the achievements of the post-reform period. This is so in terms of their role not only in sustaining high life expectancy and related achievements, but also in providing firm support for economic expansion based on market reforms.

It may have been very far from Mao's own intentions to develop literacy and basic health care in ways that would help to promote market-based, internationally-oriented enterprises (though that dialectical contrariness must have some interest for a Marxist theorist). But these structural achievements in the pre-reform period have certainly served as direct and valuable inputs in fostering economic performance in post-reform China. In drawing lessons from China, these apparently contrary interconnections can be particularly important.

This chapter is much concerned with understanding Chinese political and economic developments (both before and after the reforms of 1979), the interdependence between them, and the lessons that India might draw from what China has or has not done. But we should begin with taking stock of the relative positions of China and India as they are now.

## 4.2. *Conditions of Life and Death*

Living conditions in China at the time of the political transformation in 1949 were probably not radically different from those in India at that time. Both countries were among the poorest in the world and had high levels of mortality, undernutrition, and illiteracy. While generalizations about living standards in India or China of those times are subject to wide margins of error, the available evidence makes it hard to support the idea that a large gap between the two countries already existed in the late forties.[3]

---

[3] *Human Development Report 1994*, Table 4, gives the following estimates for 1960: real GDP per capita: India 617, China 723; life expectancy at birth: India 44, China 47; infant mortality rate: India 165, China 150. These are, of course, just estimates, rather than hard information, but there is also other evidence to suggest that the sharp contrasts in development indicators between the two countries are of relatively recent origin; see Drèze and Sen (1989), chapter 11, and the literature cited there.

TABLE 4.1. *India, China and Kerala: Selected Comparisons*

|  | India | China | Kerala |
|---|---|---|---|
| Real GNP per capita, based on purchasing power parities, 1992 (USA = 100) | 5.2 | 9.1[a] | 4.6[a] |
| Annual growth rate of per-capita GNP, 1980–92 (%) | 3.1 | 7.6 | 0.3[b] |
| Life expectancy at birth, 1992 (years) | 59 | 69 | 72 |
| Infant mortality rate, 1992 (per 1,000 live births) | 79 | 31 | 17 |
| Total fertility rate, 1992 | 3.7 | 2.0 | 1.8 |
| Proportion of low-birthweight babies, 1985–90 (%) | 33 | 9 | n/a |
| Adult literacy rate, 1990–1[c] | | | |
| Female | 39 | 68 | 86 |
| Male | 64 | 87 | 94 |

*Notes.* [a] Subject to a wide margin of error (see text and Statistical Appendix).
[b] Annual growth rate of per-capita 'state domestic product' (at constant prices), 1980–90.
[c] Age 15+ for China; 7+ for India and Kerala. It should be noted that 7+ literacy rates in India are usually a little *higher* than 15+ literacy rates.

*Sources.* The figures for India and China, other than literacy and life expectancy, are compiled from *World Development Report 1994*, Tables 1, 26, 27, and 30; on the literacy and life expectancy figures, see Statistical Appendix. The sources used for the figures relating to Kerala are given in the Statistical Appendix.

Since then, however, a striking contrast has emerged between the two countries. This applies even to per-capita real income. The standard figures of GNP per capita are hard to use for international comparison because of differences in price levels, but recent estimates of gross domestic product per head take note of purchasing power parities and are partly aimed at making such comparisons possible. These estimates suggest that China's GNP per head is about twice as high as India's (see Table 4.1).[4] If China and India were comparably poor in the late forties, they now stand quite far apart.

[4] The Chinese figures relating to per-capita GNP are subject to a wide margin of error. The figures given in *Human Development Report 1994* suggest an even larger gap, with China's GDP per capita more than two and a half times as large as India's. Some figures

The contrasting achievements of India and China can be seen no less forcefully in terms of direct indicators of living standards. Particular aspects of this contrast are summarized in Table 4.1 (Kerala is also included for later reference). While life expectancy at birth in India is still as low as 59 years, the Chinese figure is a decade more (69 years), not very far behind life expectancies in much richer South Korea or in the more advanced countries in Latin America. Infant mortality is two and half times as high in India (79 per thousand live births in comparison with China's 31), and the proportion of low birthweight babies is three and a half times as high (33 per cent in India compared with China's 9). Further evidence based on child anthropometry, disease patterns, and related information support the notion that China is well ahead of India as far as the elimination of health deprivation is concerned.[5]

Another important area in which the contrast is extremely sharp is basic education and literacy. In the next section China and India are compared in this field.

## 4.3. *Contrasts in Basic Education*

As Table 4.1 shows, literacy rates are a good deal higher in China than in India. This particular contrast can be examined more closely, using recent census-based information. Both China and India conducted careful censuses in the early eighties and nineties—in 1981 and 1991 in the case of India, and 1982 and 1990 in the case of China. Each of these four censuses includes detailed information on literacy, which provides a useful basis of comparison.

Table 4.2 presents some relevant figures, derived from these censuses. For convenience, we shall take the reference year '1981–2' to mean 1981 for India and 1982 for China, and '1990–1' to stand for 1991 for India and 1990 for China. In Figures 4.1 and 4.2,

---

published by the World Bank (eg. in *World Development Report 1994*, Table 30, in terms of 'current international dollars') suggest a somewhat smaller gap, with China's GNP per head roughly 50 per cent above India's. There is some uncertainty as to the exact magnitude of the gap in real income per head between the two countries, but what is not in doubt is that China is now well ahead of India in this respect.

[5] See Bumgarner (1992), *World Development Report 1993* (particularly on morbidity), *Human Development Report 1994*, and also the literature cited in Drèze and Sen (1989), chapter 11.

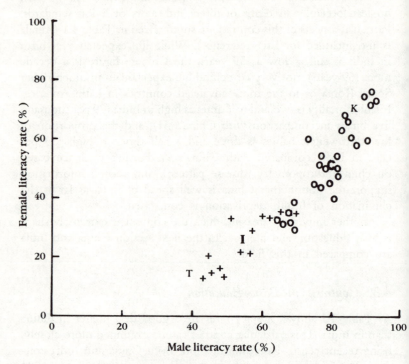

Fig. 4.1. *Adult Literacy Rates in Indian States
and Chinese Provinces (1981 – 2)*

*Source.* Loh (1993) and Drèze and Loh (1995), based on census data. The literacy rates on which this graph is based apply to persons aged 15 and above.

**C = All China**          **I = All India**

**O** = Chinese province          + = Indian state

T = Tibet          K = Kerala

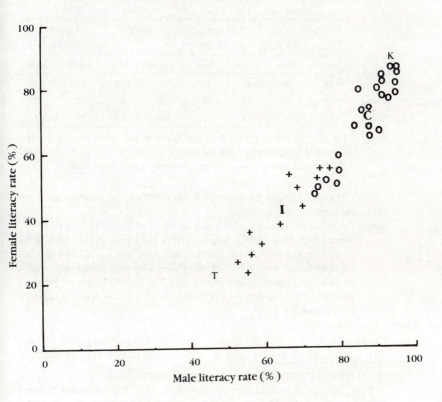

Fig. 4.2. *Adult Literacy Rates in Indian States
and Chinese Provinces (1990 – 1)*

*Source.* Loh (1993) and Dreze and Loh (1995), based on census data. Indian
literacy rates apply to persons aged 7 and above; Chinese literacy rates apply
to persons aged 15 and above. In India, the 7+ literacy rates are usually a little
*higher* than the corresponding 15+ literacy rates.

**C = All China**          **I = All India**

**O** = Chinese province      **+** = Indian state

T = Tibet                 K = Kerala

TABLE 4.2. *Literacy in India, China and Kerala*

| | Literacy rates, 1981–2 | | | | Literacy rates, 1990–1 | | | |
|---|---|---|---|---|---|---|---|---|
| | *Adults* (age 15+) | | *Adolescents* (age 15–19) | | *Adults*[a] | | *Adolescents*[b] (age 15–19) | |
| | Female | Male | Female | Male | Female | Male | Female | Male |
| India | 26 | 55 | 43 | 66 | 39 | 64 | 52 | 74 |
| China | 51 | 79 | 85 | 96 | 68 | 87 | 92 | 97 |
| Kerala | 71 | 86 | 92 | 95 | 86 | 94 | 98 | 98 |

*Notes.* [a] Age 15+ for China, 7+ for India and Kerala (Indian census data for the 15+ age group in 1991 have not been published at the time of writing). As mentioned in Table 4.1, 7+ literacy rates in India are usually a little *higher* than 15+ literacy rates.

[b] The reference year for India and Kerala is 1987–8; the reference age group for Kerala is 10–14.

*Sources.* The Indian figures are compiled from Government of India (1991), Nanda (1992), Verma (1988), Bose (1991a), Sengupta (1991), and Census of India 1981, Series 10 (Kerala), Part IV-A, Social and Cultural Tables; they are all based on 1981 and 1991 census data, except for the 1987–8 adolescent literacy rates, which are based on National Sample Survey data. The Chinese figures are based on 1982 and 1990 census data; see Drèze and Loh (1995) and the Statistical Appendix of this book for details.

we plot male and female literacy rates in 1981–2 and 1990–1 for each province of China and each state of India.[6] The following observations emerge from these basic comparisons.[7]

First, census data unambiguously show that India is well behind China in the field of basic education. Adult literacy rates in India were as low as 39 per cent for women and 64 per cent for men in 1990–1, compared with 68 per cent for Chinese women and 87 per cent for Chinese men.[8]

[6] The literacy figures used in Table 4.2 and Figures 4.1–4.2 are directly compiled from census publications. As explained in the Statistical Appendix, these figures are more reliable than those presented in, say, *World Development Report 1994*; the latter are based on projections made *before* detailed results from the 1990–1 Chinese and Indian censuses were made available (see e.g. *World Development Report 1994*, p. 232). In any case, the two sets of figures are fairly consistent with each other.

[7] For a more detailed discussion, see Drèze and Loh (1995).

[8] As mentioned in Table 4.2, the Indian figures cited here relate to persons aged 7 and above, because 1991 census data for the 15+ age group have not been released at the time of writing. The literacy gap between India and China would look a little *larger* if one were to use the same age cut-off of 15 years for both countries.

Second, age-specific literacy rates bring out a crucial feature of the Chinese advantage. In 1987–8, 26 per cent of adolescent boys in India, and 48 per cent of adolescent girls, were found to be *illiterate*. The corresponding figures for China in 1990 are only 3 per cent for boys and 8 per cent for girls (Table 4.2). In other words, China is now quite close to universal literacy in the younger age groups. In India, by contrast, there is still a massive problem of illiteracy among young boys and—especially—girls.

Third, the 1981–2 census data show that China's lead over India was achieved *before* China embarked on a wide-ranging programme of economic reforms at the end of the seventies. During the eighties, there has been progress in both countries, with no major change in their comparative positions. The Chinese relative advantage over India is, thus, a product of its pre-reform groundwork, rather than its post-reform redirection.

Fourth, female literacy rates are well below male literacy rates in both countries. The gender gap is particularly large in India, where only a little more than half of all adolescent girls are able to read and write. In China, the gender gap in literacy is narrowing quite rapidly, due to near-universal literacy in the younger age groups.

Fifth, there are wide inter-regional disparities in literacy rates in both countries. The regional contrasts are, to a large extent, driven by differences in female literacy. The persistence of high levels of female illiteracy in particular states or provinces is a matter of concern in both countries, but especially so in India.

Sixth, in spite of sharp regional contrasts within each country, most Chinese provinces have much higher literacy rates than every Indian state except Kerala. The state of Kerala in India stands in sharp contrast to the general pattern of Indian disadvantage. With an adult literacy rate of 90 per cent in 1991, and near-universal literacy among adolescent males *and* females, Kerala is not only well ahead of all other Indian states but also in the same league as the most advanced Chinese provinces. In fact, Kerala has a higher female literacy rate than any Chinese province (Figure 4.2), and also a higher male literacy rate for rural areas than every Chinese province (Drèze and Saran, 1995). Furthermore, in Kerala there is no gender bias in literacy rates in the younger age groups, and in that respect too, Kerala does better than all Chinese provinces. As documented in the case study of Kerala by V.K. Ramachandran (1996) in the companion volume, Kerala's remarkable record in the field of literacy is the outcome of more than a hundred years of public action, involving activities of the general public as well as of the state, in the widespread provision of elementary education.

Finally, a prominent exception to the general lead of Chinese provinces over Indian states is Tibet. Literacy rates in Tibet are not only abysmally low (even lower than in the educationally backward states of north India), they also show little sign of significant improvement over time. While the interpretation of census data for Tibet requires further scrutiny, there is a strong possibility of comprehensive neglect of Tibet in the promotion of elementary education.[9] There is an issue here of some importance in linking political freedom with economic and social achievements (see section 4.7).

## 4.4. *Pre-reform Achievements*

If we look at relative rates of growth of GNP per head in pre-reform China and in India over the same period, we do not get any definitive evidence that the Chinese rate of growth was substantially faster than India's. That situation has, of course, changed since the reforms of 1979, which have ushered in a remarkable period of sustained rapid expansion of the Chinese economy. We shall comment on the post-reform experience in the next section, but as far as the pre-reform period is concerned, it is hard to claim that China was really marching ahead in terms of GNP per head, or the related measures of real national income or gross domestic product.

To be sure, the Chinese official statistics claimed high rates of GNP growth over the pre-reform period as well, and organizations such as the World Bank—not to mention the United Nations—went on faithfully reflecting these claims in the statistics distributed in such documents as *World Development Reports*. For example, in the tables included in the Annexe in *World Development Report 1979*, an annual growth rate of 5.1 per cent in GNP per head is attributed to China over 1960–77, compared with India's 1.3 per cent over the same period. But these claims do not square with other statistics that are also available, some of which are, in fact, presented in the

---

[9] It should be mentioned that the Chinese censuses count persons who are able to read and write in *any* local language or script as literate (Dr Peng Xizhe, Institute of Population Research, Shanghai, personal communication). This suggests that census evidence on high levels of illiteracy in Tibet cannot be dismissed as an artificial result of misdefining literacy as command over Chinese.

same documents (on this, see Drèze and Sen, 1989, chapter 11). There is much evidence that if the per-capita growth rate of GNP in China was higher than that in India in the period up to the reforms of 1979, the gap was not especially large.[10]

China's real achievement in this period lies in what it managed to do *despite* poor economic growth, rather than in what it could do *through* high economic growth. For example, the remarkable reduction in chronic undernourishment took place despite the fact that there had been relatively little increase in food availability per person; as Judith Banister (1987) notes, 'annual per capita grain production through 1977 was about the same as in the late 1950's: it averaged 301 kilograms in 1955–57 and 305 kilograms in 1975–77' (p. 354). The causal processes through which the reduction of undernutrition was achieved involved extensive state action including redistributive policies, nutritional support, and of course health care (since undernourishment is frequently caused by parasitic diseases and other illnesses).[11]

China's achievements in the field of health during the pre-reform period include a dramatic reduction of infant and child mortality and a remarkable expansion of longevity. By 1981, the expectation of life at birth was estimated to be already as high as 68 years (compared with 54 years in India), and infant mortality as low as 37 deaths per 1,000 live births (compared with 110 in India).[12] Progress in health and longevity during the eighties has been in the nature of a continuation of these earlier trends, rather than a new departure.

As was noted earlier, China's breakthrough in the field of elementary education had also taken place before the process of economic reform was initiated at the end of the seventies. Census data indicate, for instance, that literacy rates in 1982 for the 15–19 age group were already as high as 96 per cent for males and 85 per cent for females (the corresponding figures for India at that time were 66 per cent

[10] An independent study published by the World Bank (1983), which does not rely on official statistics, estimates that the growth rate of real per-capita GNP in China was 2.7 in 1959–79, compared with 1.4 for India. This is consistent with the available evidence from other independent studies (see Perkins, 1983, 1988, for a review).

[11] On this see Riskin (1987, 1990). On the connection between disease and undernutrition, see also Drèze and Sen (1989, 1990), Tomkins and Watson (1989), Dasgupta and Ray (1990), Osmani (1990).

[12] The figures are from Coale (1993), Tables 1 and 2, and Government of India (1994a), p. 147; see Table 4.3 in the next section.

and 43 per cent—see Table 4.2). The eighties continued that progress and consolidated China's lead, but the relative standings had been decisively established *before* the Chinese reforms.

## 4.5. *Post-reform Records*

The developments that have taken place in China since the reforms of 1979 have been quite remarkable. The rates of economic growth have been outstandingly high. Between 1980 and 1992, the GNP per capita in China seems to have grown at an astonishing 7.6 per cent per year (Table 4.1). Industrial production has grown at more than 11 per cent per year, and even agricultural production—traditionally much more sluggish than industry—has experienced an annual growth rate of 5.4 per cent.[13]

The high rates of growth of output and real income have permitted the use of economic means to reduce poverty and to improve living conditions. The scope for removing poverty is obviously much greater in an economy where per-capita income *doubles every ten years,* as the annual growth rate of 7.6 per cent implies, than in a country where it limps along at 2 or 3 per cent per year, as has been the case in India for much of the last five decades. For China, it is estimated that the proportion of the rural population below the poverty line has fallen from 33 per cent in 1978 to 11 per cent in 1990 (World Bank, 1992). This is a very rapid decline. While India too has achieved a significant reduction of rural poverty in this period, the magnitude of the reduction has been much more modest: a fall from 55 per cent in 1977–8 to 42 per cent in 1988–9.[14] There can be little doubt that China has done much better than India in this particular respect,[15] and in explaining this difference, the much higher growth rate of the Chinese economy must receive

---

[13] *World Development Report 1994*, Table 2. On these and other aspects of economic reform in China, see also Perkins (1988), Hussain (1989), Byrd and Lin (1990), Bhalla (1992), Chen et al. (1992), Lin (1992), Rosen (1992), Riskin (1993), among others.

[14] Tendulkar et al. (1993), Table 4.2.1. The estimates of B.S. Minhas and colleagues, and of the recent report of the Planning Commission's Expert Group on Poverty Estimation, all presented in EPW Research Foundation (1993), suggest a similar pace of decline during the 1980s. See also Statistical Appendix.

[15] The poverty lines used in China and India are not the same, so that what is being compared here are the relative *declines* in poverty during the 1980s, rather than the absolute poverty levels.

the bulk of the credit. Indeed, the post-reform period in China has not been one of substantial redistributive efforts, and the available evidence indicates that income inequality has probably increased rather than decreased since the reforms were initiated.[16] It is participatory growth, rather than radical redistribution, that accounts for the rapid decline of poverty in China in the eighties. In India, the eighties have witnessed some acceleration of economic growth, with little change in economic inequality, and these trends have coincided with the emergence of a marked decline in the head-count index, but the decline of poverty has remained comparatively modest.

This way of evaluating poverty relies on what has been called the head-count index, defined as the proportion of the population with per-capita income (or expenditure) below a specified 'poverty line'. It is based on the notion of poverty as insufficient income or expenditure, and this can be quite inadequate since deprivations can take many different forms—various inadequacies of basic capabilities that relate to many different causal factors (such as public health services and social insurance systems) in addition to private incomes.[17] Further, even within that income-centred perspective, the head-count measure is insensitive to the levels and inequalities of incomes below the poverty line, and a more distribution-sensitive evaluation of poverty may be necessary for a fuller understanding of even income deprivation.[18]

Trends in the head-count ratio do, of course, have obvious informational value, even when we adopt a broader approach to poverty.[19]

---

[16] See A.R. Khan et al. (1992), Bramall and Jones (1993), Griffin and Zhao Renwei (1993), Howes (1993), Knight and Song (1993b), Riskin (1993), Howes and Hussain (1994).

[17] On this, see Sen (1984, 1992a), and chapter 2 of this book. The approach of poverty as capability inadequacy relates to Adam Smith's (1776) treatment of 'necessities', and it treats the lowness of income (such as income levels being below a specified 'poverty line') as being only instrumentally and contingently relevant (with the appropriate poverty line varying between different societies and with diverse individual and social conditions).

[18] See Sen (1976b), Blackorby and Donaldson (1980), Foster, Greer, and Thorbecke (1980), Foster (1984), Kakwani (1986), Atkinson (1989), and Ravallion (1994).

[19] In the literature on poverty in India, the head-count measure has been far more used than any other indicator of poverty, and the rationale for this arises not from any intrinsic importance of this indicator, but rather from the likelihood of its correlation with other—more significant—characterizations of deprivation. On the relationship between different indicators of poverty in the Indian economy, see Tendulkar, Sundaram, and Jain (1993), and Dutta et al. (1994).

The reduction in income poverty in China in the post-reform period is an achievement of great importance, given that lack of income often drastically constrains the lives that people can lead. But this finding needs to be supplemented with further information about what has been happening in matters of living conditions, e.g. mortality rates and related indicators. In fact, while the improvements of living conditions during the pre-reform period, including the expansion of life expectancy and the reduction of infant mortality and illiteracy, have been consolidated and extended in the post-reform period, the rate of progress in these fields since 1979 has been, in some important respects, rather moderate in comparison with (1) the radical transformations of the *pre-reform* period, (2) what has been achieved during the post-reform period in terms of raising *income levels* and reducing head-count measures of poverty, (3) what many *other countries* at a comparable stage of development have achieved since the late seventies.

This statement is illustrated in Table 4.3 with reference to life expectancy and infant mortality. It can be seen that while China achieved an outstanding transformation during the sixties and seventies (starting with levels of infant mortality and life expectancy similar to India's, but catching up with Kerala, Sri Lanka, and South Korea within two decades), the pace of improvement during the post-reform period has been less remarkable.[20] In fact, in comparative international terms, China has not fared particularly well during this period. Life expectancy, for instance, has expanded by only 1.6 years between 1981 and 1991 in China, compared with about 2 years in Sri Lanka, 4 years in South Korea, 4.6 years in Kerala, and 5.3 years in India as a whole.

The comparison with Kerala is especially instructive. At the end of the seventies, China and Kerala had much the same level of infant mortality, and China was a little ahead of Kerala in terms of life expectancy. During the eighties, infant mortality in Kerala further declined from 37 per 1,000 live births to 16.5, and life expectancy increased by another 4.6 years; in China, by contrast, infant mortality only declined from 37 to 31, and life expectancy

---

[20] Some official mortality statistics series even suggest a recorded *increase* in mortality rates in the immediate post-reform years (as discussed in Drèze and Sen, 1989, pp. 215–18). But there are reasons to doubt the accuracy of these statistics. In Table 4.3, we have used the more reliable life tables recently derived from 1982 and 1990 census data (Coale, 1993).

TABLE 4.3 Mortality Decline in China and Selected Economies

| | Infant mortality rate (per 1,000 live births) | | | | Life expectancy at birth (years) | | | |
|---|---|---|---|---|---|---|---|---|
| | 1960 | 1981 | 1991[a] | Percentage decline between 1981 and 1991[a] | 1960 | 1981 | 1991[a] | Expansion between 1981 and 1991[a] (years) |
| China | 150 | 37 | 31 | 16 | 47.1 | 67.7 | 69.3 | 1.6 |
| India | 165 | 110 | 80 | 27 | 44.0 | 53.9[b] | 59.2 | 5.3 |
| Kerala | 93[c] | 37 | 16 | 57 | 50.3[c] | 66.9[b] | 71.5 | 4.6 |
| South Korea | 85 | 33 | 23 | 30 | 53.9 | 66 | 70 | 4 |
| Sri Lanka | 71 | 43 | 26 | 40 | 62.0 | 69 | 71 | 2 |

*Notes.*

[a] 1990, in the case of China.

[b] Unweighted average of SRS-based estimates for 1976–80 and 1981–5.

[c] Unweighted average of census-based estimates for 1951–60 and 1961–70.

*Sources.* Infant mortality rate and life expectancy, 1960 (except Kerala): *Human Development Report 1994*, Table 4 (pp. 136–7). Infant mortality rate and life expectancy, 1981, Sri Lanka and South Korea: *World Development Report 1983*, pp. 148–9 and 192–3. Infant mortality rate and life expectancy, China, 1981 and 1990: Coale (1993). Tables 1–4. Infant mortality rate and life expectancy, 1991, Sri Lanka and South Korea: *World Development Report 1993*, pp. 238–9 and 292–3. Infant mortality rate, 1981 and 1991, India: *Sample Registration Bulletin*, January 1994, Table 1, p. 5. Life expectancy, 1981, India: calculated from Statement 1, *Sample Registration System Abridged Life Table 1986–90* (Office of the Registrar-General, New Delhi). Life expectancy, 1991, India and Kerala: unpublished estimates based on Sample Registration System data, obtained from the Office of the Registrar-General, New Delhi. Infant mortality rate, 1991, Kerala: *Sample Registration Bulletin*, January 1994, Table 8, p. 19. Life expectancy and infant mortality, 1960 and 1981, Kerala: calculated from Ramachandran (1996), based on census and Sample Registration System data. For further comments on the different sources, see the Explanatory Note in the Statistical Appendix of this book.

increased by less than 2 years.[21] This contrast is all the more striking if we remember that China has experienced extraordinary growth of commodity production during the eighties, whereas Kerala's economy has shown remarkable sluggishness.[22]

The preceding observations point to the fact that economic growth is far more effective in expanding some aspects of living standards than in improving others. The difficult areas for post-reform China have been precisely those for which income expansion alone is not a solid basis of rapid progress. While the eighties have witnessed a dramatic expansion of private incomes in China, there seems to have been less success in the further development of public services, particularly in the poorer rural areas. There have been several reasons for this.[23] First, the post-reform period has seen a transition from a system where the collective had the first claim on the products of economic activity (as in the pre-reform commune system) to one where local public services have to be financed by taxing private incomes (a method which raises standard problems of incentives and administrative barriers). This has eroded the financial basis of local public services in some areas, particularly those which have experienced relatively slow economic growth. Second, the rapid expansion of the private economy has tended to drain human resources away from the public sector, where income-earning opportunities (e.g. for teachers and doctors) are far less attractive. Third, there is also some evidence of a reduced state commitment to the widespread and equitable provision of public services. One symptom of this

[21] It is plausible that the slowing down of infant mortality decline in China during the 1980s is partly a reflection of the effects of the 'one-child policy' (see section 4.8). But the same explanation cannot be invoked for the slowing down of mortality decline in other age groups. Even if infant mortality had declined as fast in China as in Kerala during the 1980s, the expansion of life expectancy in China would have been only around 3 years (taking as given the pace of mortality decline in the *other* age groups), compared with 4.6 years in Kerala.

[22] In fact, Kerala's real per-capita 'state domestic product' has remained virtually constant during the 1980s (A.N. Agrawal et al., 1992, p. 49; see also Statistical Appendix). It is right to note that, in Kerala, remittances from abroad are an important source of income, in addition to domestic production. However, recent estimates indicate that the share of remittances in total consumption is below 20 per cent, and has not grown much, if at all, during the 1980s (Krishnan, 1994; see also Ramachandran, 1996).

[23] For further discussion of these diverse developments, see Drèze and Sen (1989), World Bank (1992a), Yu Dezhi (1992), De Geyndt et al. (1992), Bloom (1994), Wong (1994), Drèze and Saran (1995), and the literature cited in these studies.

is the extension of the 'enterprise responsibility' model of public-sector management to social services, leading to widespread introduction of user fees as a means of ensuring cost recovery.

For these and other reasons, public services in large parts of rural China have come under some strain during the post-reform period. Village health services, for instance, have been comprehensively privatized. Whatever adverse effects these developments have had in the post-reform period have clearly been, on balance, outweighed by the favourable impact of rapid growth of private incomes, and the overall progress of living conditions has continued. But the result of this tension has been to moderate China's rate of progress in some social achievements, just when it has done so very well in stimulating economic growth.

This line of reasoning does not dispute the importance of what has been achieved in China in the post-reform period, but it suggests that China's progress on the income front has been diluted in the social field by its changed approach to public services, which could have got more from the expanded resources made available by rapid economic growth. These observations also guard us against 'rubbishing' what China had already done before the reforms. That general conclusion receives further support from the need to consider and scrutinize the factors underlying China's rapid economic growth in the post-reform period.

## 4.6. *Pre-reform and Post-reform Performances*

The spread of basic education across the country is particularly relevant in interpreting the nature of the Chinese economic expansion in the post-reform period. The role of mass education in facilitating fast and widely-shared growth has been much analysed in the recent development literature, particularly in the context of the performance of east Asian economies.[24] In China, the big step in that direction was taken in the pre-reform period. The fact, already noted, that by 1982 literacy rates in China were already as high as 96 per cent for males in the 15–19 age group, and 85 per cent even for females in that age group, made participatory economic expansion possible in a way it would not have been in India *then*—and is very difficult in India even *now*.

---

[24] See chapters 2 and 3 above, and also the works cited there.

Another area in which the post-reform expansions benefited from pre-reform achievements is that of land reforms, which has been identified as an important factor of economic development in east Asia in general.[25] In China, things went, of course, much further than land reforms, and the development of communal agriculture certainly was a considerable handicap for agricultural expansion in the pre-reform period, and indeed had a direct role in precipitating the great famines of 1958–61 (on which more presently). But that process of collectivization had also, *inter alia*, abolished landlordism in China (through a process that had often been quite brutal). When the Chinese government opted for the 'responsibility system' in the late seventies, the country had a land-tenure pattern that could readily support individual farming without the social problems and economic inefficiencies of highly unequal land ownership, in sharp contrast with India.

It is interesting that the institutional developments that have favoured participatory economic growth throughout east Asia (in particular, the spread of basic education and health care, and the abolition of landlordism) had come to different countries in the region in quite different ways. In some cases, even foreign occupation had helped, for example, in the land reforms of Taiwan and South Korea. In the case of China, the pre-reform regime, with its own goals and commitments, carried out some changes that turned out to be immensely useful in the market-based economic expansion of the post-reform period. That connection is extremely important to note for an adequately informed interpretation of the Chinese successes of recent years. If India has to emulate China in market success, it is not adequate just to liberalize economic controls in the way the Chinese have done, without creating the social opportunities that post-reform China inherited from the pre-reform transformation. The 'magic' of China's market rests on the solid foundations of social changes that had occurred earlier, and India cannot simply hope for that magic, without making the enabling social changes—in education, health care, land reforms, etc.—that help make the market function in the way it has in China.

[25] See, for example, Amsden (1989) and Wade (1990), and also World Bank (1993c) and the literature cited there.

## 4.7. *Authoritarianism, Famines and Vulnerability*

In learning from China, it is not enough to look only at positive lessons—what can be fruitfully emulated; it is important to examine the 'non-lessons' as well—what may be best avoided. An obvious instance is the Chinese experience of famine compared with India's better record in that field. The famines of 1958–61 killed, it appears, between 23 and 30 million people.[26] India's performance in famine prevention since independence has been much more successful, and even when a natural calamity like a drought has led to a potential famine situation, the occurrence of an actual famine has been averted through timely government action.[27]

The causation of the Chinese famines can be analysed from different perspectives. First, the disastrous experience of the Great Leap Forward and the related programme of rapid collectivization of agriculture are important elements in this story. The incentive system crashed badly and the organizational base of the Chinese agricultural economy collapsed.

Second, the problem was made worse by the arbitrary nature of some of the distributional policies, including features of communal feeding.[28] There was also an important question of distribution between town and country. The proportion of procurement for the urban areas actually went up precisely when the food output had plummeted.[29]

Third, the Chinese government did not wake up to the nature and magnitude of the calamity for quite a long time, and the disastrous policies were not substantially revised for three years, while the famine raged on. The informational failure was linked to a controlled press, which duped the public in suppressing information about the famine, but in the process deluded the government as well. The local leaders competed with each other to send rosy reports of their alleged success,

[26] Peng's (1987) estimate is 23 million extra deaths, whereas that of Ashton et al. (1984) is close to 30 million.

[27] See Drèze and Sen (1989) and Drèze (1990a). For case studies of famine prevention in post-independence India, see also Ramalingaswami et al. (1971), Choudhary and Bapat (1975), Mathur and Bhattacharya (1975), K.S. Singh (1975), Subramaniam (1975), Desai et al. (1979), Hubbard (1988), Government of India (1989b), Chen (1991), among others.

[28] On this see Peng (1987), who argues that communal kitchens led to over-consumption in some areas while starvation was widespread in others.

[29] See Riskin (1987, 1990).

outdoing their regional rivals, and at one stage the Chinese government was convinced that it had a 100 million more metric tons of foodgrains than it actually had.[30]

Fourth, the government was immune to public pressure, because no opposition party or political dissent was tolerated. There was, thus, no organized demand for the government to resign despite sights of starvation and mortality, and the political leaders could hang on to the disastrous policies for an incredibly long time. This particular aspect of the Chinese famine—its linkage with the lack of democracy in China—fits into a more general pattern of association between democracy and successful prevention of famines, or—seen the other way—between the absence of democracy and the lack of any guarantee that serious attempts to avert famines will be undertaken.[31]

Indeed, it is a remarkable fact that no substantial famine has ever occurred in a democratic country where the government tolerates opposition, accepts the electoral process, and can be publicly criticized. A government which has to deal with opposition parties, to answer unfriendly questions in the parliament, to face condemnation from the public media, and to go to the polls on a regular basis, simply cannot afford *not* to take prompt action to avert a threatening famine. But a non-democratic country has no such guarantee against famines.

In some ways, even the *other* causal factors in the above story of the Chinese famine relate ultimately to the lack of democracy. A policy as disruptive and drastic as the Great Leap Forward could not have been initiated in a pluralist democracy without its being debated extensively. Similarly, government decisions relating to food distribution—between individuals and between town and country— could not have been placed above criticism and public scrutiny. And of course the controlling of news and information would not have been possible in a multiparty democracy in the way it happened routinely in China when it experienced that gigantic famine. In the multi-faceted causal account of the great famine in China, the absence of democracy must be seen as being quite central, with influences on the other elements in the string of causation.

India's democratic system has many flaws, but it certainly is radically more suited to deal with famines. Underlying that specialized point

[30] See Bernstein (1984) and Riskin (1987).

[31] On this see Sen (1982, 1983a) and Drèze and Sen (1989).

about famines and famine prevention, there is a more general issue which is worth considering in this context. The successes of the Chinese economic and social policies have depended crucially on the concerns and commitments of the leadership. Because of its radical commitment to the elimination of poverty and to improving living conditions—a commitment in which Maoist as well as Marxist ideas and ideals played an important part—China did achieve many things that the Indian leadership failed to press for and pursue with any vigour. The elimination of widespread hunger, illiteracy, and ill health falls solidly in this category. When state action operates in the right direction, the results can be quite remarkable, as is illustrated by the social achievements of the pre-reform period.

The fragility of this way of doing things turns on the extreme dependence of the process on the values and politics of the leadership. If and when there is no commitment on the part of the leadership to pursue some particular cause, that cause can be very badly neglected. Also, whenever the leadership is deluded into getting the causal relations wrong, the whole system might still operate as if those mistaken presumptions were exactly right and in no need of exacting scrutiny. When the political leaders, for one reason or another, fail to address a problem, or refuse even to recognize it, there is little scope for public pressure to challenge their inertia or to expose their mistakes. The famines of 1958–61 represent a clear example of this pattern, but there are many others, including the acceptance of endemic illiteracy in Tibet (see section 4.3), the imposition of a draconian one-child policy (discussed in the next section), the excesses of the Cultural Revolution, and the frequent violation of basic human rights. Authoritarianism is an unreliable route to social progress.

## 4.8. *Coercion, Population and Fertility*

One particular field in which the operation of the authoritarianism of contemporary China can be seen in a very clear form is that of population policy, and it is often suggested, particularly in activist international circles, that India should emulate China in this important area. China has adopted fairly draconian measures to force the birth rate down, and its success in this respect has been widely studied and admired, given the alarmist views of the 'world population problem' that are currently shared by many international leaders.

The fear of an impending crisis makes many policy advocates seek forceful measures in the third world for coercing people to have fewer children, and despite criticism from diverse quarters including women's groups, China's attempts in that direction have received much attention and praise.

How alarming the 'population crisis' actually is in a country such as China (or for that matter India) is a debatable question. The case for concern about rapid population has, in fact, involved a combination of excellent arguments with rather misleading interpretations of the nature of the problem. One of these misinterpretations relates to the relationship between population growth and economic growth. It is sometimes thought that restraining population growth is an essential means of raising the rate of growth of per-capita GNP (or of preventing its decline). In fact, however, for countries such as India and China, population policies—important as they may in general be—are likely to make relatively little difference to the rate of per-capita economic growth.

TABLE 4.4. *India and China:*
*Economic Growth and Population Growth*

| Country | Growth rate of population (1980–92) | Growth rate of GDP (1980–92) | Growth rate of GDP per capita, assuming the population growth rate of:[a] | |
|---|---|---|---|---|
| | | | India | China |
| India | 2.1 | 5.2 | 3.1 | 3.8 |
| China | 1.4 | 9.1 | 7.0 | 7.7 |

*Note.* [a] Calculated by subtracting the population growth rate of the country mentioned in the column heading from the GDP growth rate of the country mentioned in the row heading.

*Source.* Calculated from *World Development Report 1994*, Tables 2 and 25.

This point is illustrated in Table 4.4. If China had a population growth rate similar to India's (i.e. 2.1 per cent instead of 1.4 per cent), its growth rate of per-capita GDP—assuming no change in the growth rate of *total* GDP—would only decline from 7.7 per cent per year to 7.0 per cent.[32] Similarly, should India succeed in

[32] The decline would be even smaller under the alternative assumption that a higher rate of population growth raises the growth rate of total GDP. This alternative assumption is rather more plausible than the assumption of unchanged growth of total GDP, which implies that the additional population is totally unproductive.

cutting down the rate of population growth to 1.4 per cent (as in China), its growth rate of per-capita GDP would only increase from 3.1 to 3.8 per cent. The contrast in growth rates of per-capita income between India and China are primarily due to China's much faster growth rate of total income, with differences in population growth rates playing relatively little role in that contrast.

This remark is not intended to dismiss the need for concern about rapid population growth. There are good reasons for such concern, based, for example, on environmental considerations (particularly the impact of population pressure on the local environment),[33] and on the quality of life of women burdened by frequent pregnancies. The point is to recognize that the force and characteristics of the problem are quite different from what are usually stressed in the much-publicized fears about 'the population problem' as a cause of low economic growth.

Coercive methods such as the 'one-child policy' have been tried in large parts of China since the reforms of 1979. Also, the government often refuses to offer housing and related benefits to families with several children—thus penalizing the children as well as the uncon-forming adults. By 1992 the Chinese birth rate had fallen sharply to 19 per thousand, compared with 29 per thousand in India, and 37 per thousand for the average of poor countries other than China and India. China's total fertility rate (a measure of the average number of children born per woman) is now 2.0, just below the 'replacement level' of around 2.1, and much below India's 3.7 or the weighted average of 4.9 for low-income countries other than China and India.[34] This has been seen—understandably—as a story of much success.

The difficulties with this 'solution' of the population problem arise from different sides.[35] First, the lack of freedom associated with this approach is a major social loss in itself. Human rights groups and women's organizations in particular have been especially concerned with the lack of reproductive freedom involved in any coercive system.[36]

Second, apart from the fundamental issue of individual freedom,

---

[33] See Dasgupta (1993).

[34] The figures cited here are from *World Development Report 1994*, Table 26.

[35] On coercive and collaborative approaches to family planning, see Sen (1994a, 1994b).

[36] On the general subject of reproductive freedom and its relation to the population problem, see Sen, Germain, and Chen (1994). This issue is also discussed in chapter 7 of this book, with reference to India.

there are specific consequences to consider in evaluating compulsory birth control. Coercion works by making people do things they would not freely choose to do. The social consequences of such compulsion, including the ways in which an unwilling population tends to react when it is coerced, can be appalling. For example, the demands of a 'one-child family' can lead to the neglect—or worse—of infants, thereby increasing the infant mortality rate. Also, in a country with a strong preference for male children—a characteristic shared by China with India and many other countries in Asia and north Africa—a policy of allowing only one child per family can easily be particularly detrimental for girls, e.g. in the form of fatal neglect of female children. This, it appears, is exactly what has happened on a fairly large scale in China.[37]

Third, it is not at all clear how much additional reduction in the birth rate has actually been achieved through these coercive methods. Many of China's longstanding social and economic programmes have been valuable in reducing fertility, including those that have expanded education (for women as well as men), made health care more generally available, provided more job opportunities for women, and stimulated rapid economic growth. These factors would themselves have reduced the birth rate, and it is not clear how much 'extra lowering' of fertility rates has been achieved in China through compulsion. For example, we can check how many countries in the world which match (or outmatch) China in life expectancy achievements, female literacy rates, and female participation in the labour force, actually have a *higher* fertility rate than China does. Of all the countries in the world for which data are given in the *World Development Report 1994*, there are only three such countries: Jamaica (2.7), Thailand (2.2), and Sweden (2.1)—and the fertility rates of two of these are close enough to China's (2.0). It is, thus, by no means clear what the *extra* contribution of coercion is in reducing fertility in China.

[37] These and other consequences of the one-child policy in China (such as the sharp decline in the female–male ratio at birth, primarily reflecting widespread abortion of female foetuses) have been discussed by Hull (1990), Johansson and Nygren (1991), Banister (1992), Greenhalgh et al. (1993), Zeng Yi et al. (1993), among others. Between 1981 and 1990, male infant mortality in China declined by 10 percentage points (from 38.4 to 28.4 deaths per 1,000 live births), but female infant mortality only declined by 3.5 percentage points, from 36.3 to 32.8 (Coale, 1993). Had infant female mortality declined by 10 percentage points, like male infant mortality, the number of female infant deaths in China would now be below what it actually is by about 78,000 deaths *per year*.

Despite all these problems, many commentators point out that China has nevertheless achieved something in its birth control programme that India has not been able to do. This is indeed the case, and in terms of national averages, it is easy to see that China with its low fertility rate of 2.0 has got population growth under control in a way that India, with its average fertility rate of 3.7, simply has not achieved. However, what is far from clear is the extent to which this contrast can be attributed to the effectiveness of the coercive policies used in China, since we would expect the fertility rate to be much lower in China given its higher level of female literacy (almost twice as high as India's), higher life expectancy (about 10 years more), larger female involvement in gainful employment (fifty per cent higher, in terms of share of the total labour force), and so on.

In order to sort out this issue, it is useful to look at those parts of India which have relatively high literacy rates, and other social features that are associated with voluntary reduction of fertility rates. The state of Kerala does provide an interesting comparison with China, since it too enjoys high levels of basic education, health care, and so on. Kerala's birth rate of 18 per thousand is actually lower than China's 19 per thousand, and this has been achieved without any compulsion by the state. Kerala's fertility rate is 1.8 for 1991, compared with China's 2.0 for 1992. This is in line with what we could expect through progress in factors that help voluntary reduction in birth rates. Kerala has a higher adult female literacy rate—86 per cent—than China (68 per cent). In fact, as was mentioned earlier, the female literacy rate is higher in Kerala than in every single province in China. Also, as was mentioned, in comparison with male and female life expectancies at birth in China of 68 and 71 years, the 1991 figures for Kerala's life expectancy are 69 and 74 years, respectively. Further, women have played an important role in Kerala's economic and political life, and to some extent in property relations and educational movements.[38]

Kerala's success in reducing the birth rate, based on these and other positive achievements, disputes the necessity of coercion for cutting down fertility in poor economies. And since this low fertility has been achieved voluntarily, there is no sign of the adverse effects

---

[38] See Robin Jeffrey (1992), and also V.K. Ramachandran's paper on Kerala in Drèze and Sen (1996).

that were noted in the case of China, e.g. heightened female infant mortality and widespread abortion of female foetuses. As was discussed earlier, Kerala's infant mortality rate (16.5) is now much lower than China's (31), even though both regions had the same infant mortality rate around the time of the introduction of the one-child policy in China. Further, while in China the infant mortality rate is much lower for males (28) than for females (33), in Kerala the opposite is the case, with female infant mortality (16) a little below the male figure (17).[39]

It is sometimes argued that what makes compulsory birth control important and necessary is the speed with which birth rates can be cut down through coercive means, in a way that cannot happen with voluntary processes. However, Kerala's birth rate has fallen from 44 per thousand in the fifties to 18 by 1991—a decline no less fast than that in China. It could, of course, be argued that looking at this very long period does not do justice to the effectiveness of one-child family and other coercive policies that were introduced in 1979, and that we ought really to compare what has happened between 1979 and now.

Table 4.5 presents the comparative picture of fertility rates in China and Kerala in 1979 (when the 'one-child policy' was introduced) and now (to be exact in 1991). The figures for Tamil Nadu are also presented here, since Tamil Nadu has had an active family planning programme (see Antony, 1992), one of the highest literacy rates among the major Indian states, and also relatively high female

TABLE 4.5. *Fertility Rates in China, Kerala and Tamil Nadu*

|  | 1979 | 1991 |
|---|---|---|
| China | 2.8 | 2.0 |
| Kerala | 3.0 | 1.8 |
| Tamil Nadu | 3.5 | 2.2 |

*Sources.* For China, Peng (1991), Li Chengrui (1992), and *World Development Report 1994.* For India, *Sample Registration System 1979–80* and *Sample Registration System 1991.*

[39] The Chinese figures are taken from Coale (1993); the figures from Kerala are derived from India's *Sample Registration System* (Government of India, 1993b, p. 31). It is worth noting that the survival disadvantage of infant females *vis-à-vis* males in China apparently did not exist in the 1970s (before the introduction of the one-child policy). In fact, infant mortality rate estimates for 1981 suggest some female *advantage* at that time (see Coale, 1993, Tables 1 and 2).

participation in gainful employment and low infant mortality (third among major states in both respects), all of which have contributed to a steady reduction of fertility. It appears that both Kerala and Tamil Nadu have achieved much bigger declines in fertility than China has since 1979. Kerala in particular began with a *higher* fertility rate than China in 1979 and ended in 1991 with a fertility rate as much *below* China's as it had been above it in 1979. Despite the added 'advantage' of the one-child policy and other coercive measures, the Chinese fertility rate seems to have fallen much less sharply.

Contrasts between the records of Indian states offer some further insights on this subject. While Kerala, and to a smaller extent Tamil Nadu, have radically reduced fertility rates, other states in the so-called 'northern heartland' (such as Uttar Pradesh, Bihar, Madhya Pradesh, Rajasthan) have much lower levels of education, especially female education, and of general health care. These states all have high fertility rates—between 4.4 and 5.1. This is in spite of a persistent tendency to use heavy-handed methods of family planning in those states (see sections 5.4 and 7.4), in contrast with the more 'collaborative' approach used in Kerala and Tamil Nadu. The regional contrasts within India strongly argue for collaboration (based *inter alia* on the active and educated participation of women), as opposed to coercion.

India has much to learn from China, but the need for coercion and for the violation of democracy is not one of them. India's democracy is faulty in many ways, but the faults are not reduced by making the system *less* democratic. It is possible to admire China's various achievements and to learn from them discriminatingly, *without* emulating its non-democratic features.

## 4.9. *The Real Lessons for India from China*

The 'dawn' may or may not come up 'like thunder outer China', but there are really many things to learn from China's experience, if we take a discriminating approach. Perhaps the first and the most obvious lesson arises from the demonstration of the possibility of making excellent use of the market system in a poor economy without losing the political commitment to economic development and the elimination of mass deprivation. People moved by the intensity of poverty in India often remain sceptical of what the market mechanism can do. To some extent that scepticism is justified, and indeed we have argued that the market mechanism *on its own* may not take us very far in eliminating deprivation in India, if liberalization goes hand in hand with a continued neglect of other conditions of social progress. But the Chinese experience convincingly demonstrates that, properly supplemented, a thriving market economy can help a great deal to lift the masses out of poverty and transform their living conditions. People who have admired China for its other achievements over the decades cannot sensibly shut their eyes to this rather large message.

Second, China's experience also brings out the complementarity between two essential bases of expansion of social opportunities, namely (1) *supportive public intervention*, especially in fields such as education, health care, social security, and land reforms, and (2) *the market mechanism*—an effective basis of trade and production arrangements. We discussed how the achievements of the pre-reform period in the former area have helped China to sustain and promote the market-based opportunities in the post-reform period.

Third, China's liberalization programme has certain pragmatic features that distinguish it from some other attempts at surging towards a market economy. The market mechanism has been used in China to create additional channels of social and economic opportunities, without any attempt to rely on the market itself as a surrogate social system on its own. There has been no breathless attempt at privatization of state enterprises, and no abdication of governance; instead the focus has been on opening up new possibilities for the private sector together with reforming management practices in collectively-owned enterprises. While the privatization attempts in the former Soviet Union and eastern Europe could not but threaten a large section of the established labour force with deep insecurity, the operative mode of the Chinese reforms has been based on a more positive combination of public-sector reform with expansion of private enterprises. There is a great deal to learn from the non-purist pragmatism of the Chinese planners.

Fourth, the pragmatism of the Chinese economic policies has included combining the pursuit of economic growth with continuation of a basic social security system.[40] In urban areas, social security

---

[40] On China's social security system, see Hussain and Liu (1989), Ahmad and Hussain (1991), Hussain (1993, 1994), and the literature cited there.

is based on guaranteed employment, and the continuing social respon-sibilities of the enterprise.[41] In carrying out the rural reforms (based on a new stress on 'household responsibility'), land has been kept under collective ownership, with each adult person in a village—male or female—being entitled to cultivate a given amount of land. The land-based social security arrangements have largely prevented the emergence of a class of dispossessed landless households, and have provided some protection against extreme destitution.[42] This com-bination of collective ownership and individual use rights has been a special feature of Chinese economic reforms.[43]

Fifth, even with that pragmatism, China's market-oriented reforms have been much more successful in raising income levels and in reducing income poverty than in expanding social services (notably in the field of health care) and the social opportunities that depend on these services. While real incomes have galloped forward, life expectancies have moved upwards rather slowly. Oddly enough, China's lead over India in life expectancy has narrowed rather than widened since the reforms began, and despite its massively faster economic growth, China has actually fallen behind Kerala in this field exactly over this period of economic dynamism.

Finally, while India has much to learn from China in the field of economic and social policy, the lessons do not include any over-whelming merit of its more authoritarian system. This is not to deny that the larger success of the Chinese efforts at social progress has been, to a great extent, the result of the stronger political commitment

[41] This 'dual' function of enterprises in urban China (as employers in an economy where markets and competition are increasingly important, and as providers of social security) raises some important issues of enterprise reform, on which see Hussain (1990, 1992, 1993, 1994), Wood (1991), and Hussain and Stern (1992), among others. It should also be mentioned that the 'floating population' of unofficial migrants to urban areas does not enjoy the social protection measures that are available to registered urban residents; the growth of this floating population, too, raises important issues of economic policy (see e.g. World Bank, 1992a).

[42] Additional social security measures in rural areas include (i) collective insistence on support of the elderly by the younger generation, and (ii) unrequited transfers (the *wu bao* or 'five guarantee' system) for those who are deprived of family support and unable to work.

[43] The combination of collective ownership with enterprise responsibility is also a feature of the spectacularly successful 'township and village enterprises' (TVEs). For a good discussion of this aspect of China's TVEs, see Weitzman and Chenggang Xu (1993). See also Byrd and Lin (1990), and the literature cited there.

of its leadership to eliminating poverty and deprivation. But the less challenged powers of the leaders have also left the Chinese economy and society more vulnerable to the kind of crises and disasters of which the famine of 1958–61 is an extreme example. The general problem of lack of democratic control remains, and has manifested itself in different forms. It has also had implications on such subjects as coercive family planning and the loss of reproductive and political freedoms. The fact that India's record is terrible in some related fields does not provide a good reason to be tempted by the political authoritarianism to be found in China.

In learning from China what is needed is neither *piecemeal emulation* (involving liberalization without the supportive social policies), nor indeed *wholesale emulation* (including the loss of democratic features). There is much to learn from causal analyses relating Chinese policies in different periods to the corresponding achievements. The relationships between the accomplishments in China before and after the economic reforms are particularly important to study. There is much for India to learn from China on a *discriminating* basis.

# 5

# PUBLIC ACTION
# AND SOCIAL INEQUALITY

## 5.1. *The Public and Its Role*

'Beware the fury of the patient man,' John Dryden had warned three hundred years ago. Unfortunately, the ruling authorities often have excellent reason to ignore that piece of ancient wisdom. The patient man—or woman—may be much too patient to come into the reckoning of those who are in charge of the levers of control. Successive governments in India have had reason enough to rely on the unending patience of the neglected and deprived millions in India, who have not risen in fury about illiteracy, hunger, illness, or economic insecurity. The stubborn persistence of these deprivations has much to do with that lack of fury.

What the government ends up doing can be deeply influenced by pressures that are put on the government by the public. But much depends on what issues are politicized and which deprivations become widely discussed and electorally momentous. The fact, discussed in the preceding chapter, that major famines have never taken place in a democratic country with a relatively free press and tolerance of opposition parties, indicates the power of public criticism and also the political salience of mass starvation, which receives instant attention in multiparty, electoral politics.[1] A government that has to face criticism from opposition parties and free newspapers, and that has to seek reelection cannot afford to neglect famines, since famines are conspicuous miseries which can be easily brought into

[1] See Sen (1982, 1984), Reddy (1988), Drèze and Sen (1989), Drèze (1990a, 1990b), Ram (1990).

the arena of public discussion by newspapers, opposition parties, and active Parliamentarians. India's success in escaping major famines since the Bengal famine of 1943 (four years *before* independence) has not been unrelated to this feature of public action in the Indian democratic polity.[2]

However, the reach of public criticism can be less effective when the deprivations are less extreme, more complex to analyse, and less easy to remedy, as in the case of regular—but non-extreme—undernourishment and economic insecurity, and of lack of medical care for endemic diseases. Similarly, lack of school facilities or clean water may or may not receive crucially critical attention, depending on the particular nature of politics and journalism in the regions involved. While any responsible editor of a newspaper cannot but write about a famine as and when it begins to emerge, and while the subject of mass starvation is easy to write about politically (even a simple picture of an emaciated mother holding a shrivelled baby speaks volumes as a political statement), journalistic attention on less immediate, less catastrophic deprivations depend much on the skill and political commitment of the practising journalists.[3] Also, what is or is not politicized depends, to a great extent, on the visions and preoccupations of opposition parties. For deprivations less dramatic than famines or catastrophic epidemics, a crucial variable, thus, is the activism of public participation. This depends on a variety of factors, including the nature of the political parties and their leadership, the skill and traditions of investigative journalism, and also the level of literacy and education in the region.[4]

[2] Similar successes in famine prevention have been observed in those sub-Saharan African countries that managed to remain democratic even when democracies were largely wiped out in that broad region. In the 1980s, democratic Zimbabwe and Botswana prevented famines with appropriate and timely public policies despite facing food crises no less severe than those that precipitated famines in dictatorial Ethiopia, Somalia, Sudan, and many other countries there (see Drèze and Sen, 1989, chapter 5).

[3] On this see N. Ram's (1990) analysis of the reach and limitations of the Indian press as it has evolved. A similar point can be made, in the field of health care, about the contrast between the government's swift response to sensational epidemics and its passive acceptance of endemic morbidity. The outbreak of plague in India in September 1994 immediately became a major political issue, lending itself to thundering editorials, and was brought under control within a few days. During the same period, enormous numbers of people died of tuberculosis, hepatitis, tetanus, malaria, diarrhoea, and other endemic diseases, without their plight eliciting anything like the same public response.

[4] See Drèze and Sen (1989), Ram (1990), and Robin Jeffrey (1992).

Public action, in this broad sense, can play a central role in economic development and in bringing social opportunities within the reach of the people as a whole. Sometimes public action is characterized in the economic literature as action by the government, not as action by the public itself. As we have discussed in Drèze and Sen (1989), this interpretation can be seriously misleading, as it draws attention away from the influence that the public can have in determining the direction of governmental action. As we tried to illustrate, actions of the public can be of profound significance to the successes and failures of economic and social change in general, and to development efforts in particular.

The role of public activism in influencing government policy can be particularly important in promoting the positive functions of the government, discussed in the concluding section of chapter 2. These positive functions include the provision of basic public services such as health care, child immunization, primary education, social security, environmental protection, and rural infrastructure. The vigilance and involvement of the public can be quite crucial not only in ensuring an adequate expansion of these essential services, but also in monitoring their functioning. Indeed, the actual reach and effective quality of the services that are meant to be, in principle, available often depends a great deal on the information that the local community gathers and the extent to which it can get its voice heard. The shirking and absenteeism of village teachers, for example, are much more easily observed by the villagers themselves than by government inspectors, and the search for redress can be more effectively achieved with local activism. Similar arguments apply to the diversion of ration supplies from publicly subsidized shops, the misuse of public funds and facilities in rural health centres, the disposal of village trees by local leaders for personal gain, or the stealing of electric wires by enterprising embezzlers. Also, schools, hospitals, etc. can be made more sensitive to public needs if there is local pressure in that direction, in a way that general instructions from high above might not be able to achieve.

Public action can also affect outcomes without having to work through swaying government policy. Public discussions can influence social behaviour, and sometimes even personal behaviour. For example, enlightened public discussion in Kerala clearly has had a considerable role in creating a cultural atmosphere that has acted against the gender bias in the family, and it also seems to have played an important part in spreading the use of birth control in Kerala and thus in the decline in the fertility rate that has been so dramatic there in recent years.[5] Similarly, public action and social movements can do a great deal to challenge social inequalities without necessarily involving the agency of the government. In understanding the process of economic development in India and the barriers that are faced, attention must be paid to the diverse roles and potentially extensive reach of public action.

As far as the influence of public action on governmental decision-making is concerned, attention has to be paid not only to the positive influences that may be exerted on the process of development, but also to negative impacts that particular types of public action might have. Active pressure groups, which too are (in a broad sense) part of the public, can make economic policy severely constrained by extracting concessions for sectarian interests that may divert resources from broad development objectives to narrow pursuit of sectional advantages.[6]

Even the neglect of primary education in governmental planning in India—discussed earlier—has a clear relation with the biased impact of political activism and pressures.[7] On the one hand, the lack of political pressure in favour of elementary education—a deprivation that affects the least powerful sections of the Indian society—has resulted in this need having only a very weak influence on the actual making of public policy. On the other hand, pressure groups in favour of higher education—a subject that directly interests people who are much more dominant in the society—have constituted a powerful force in the direction of giving priority to tertiary education. The neglect of literacy and elementary education relates, to a considerable extent, to the extraordinary priority that has actually been given to expanding higher education.

This is, in fact, an integral component of general *inequality* in India, and it relates to the well-being as well as the agency of the different groups involved. The sections of the population that are most affected by the absence of literacy are typically much worse off than the groups that benefit from higher education. In terms

[5] See T.N. Krishnan (1976, 1991, 1994), Mari Bhat and Rajan (1990, 1992), and Robin Jeffrey (1992).

[6] On this see Myrdal (1968), Olson (1982, 1993), Bardhan (1984b), Datta Chaudhuri (1990), among others.

[7] On this see Sen (1970) and Weiner (1991).

of *consequences*, the bias in educational priorities has tended to reinforce existing inequalities, and has been least kind to the most deprived. But moving from consequences to the *origins*, these iniquitous policies reflect, to a great extent, the pre-existent inequalities in Indian society. The more privileged groups, who clamour for further expansion of higher education, are politically much more powerful and better organized in pressing for what they want.[8] There is, thus, something of a self-sustaining circle here.

To counter this resilient stratification, what is needed is more activism in the political organization of the disadvantaged sections of Indian society.[9] This can be a challenging task, but recent history provides many examples of positive achievements in this field. The immensely impressive expansion of basic education in Kerala, for instance, has been much influenced by the contribution of political organizations working in the direction of more literacy and elementary education.[10] To some extent the lower-caste movements in south and western India, in general, have had this reforming feature.[11] Recently, in other regions as well, the disadvantaged groups (including 'scheduled' and 'backward' castes, and to a lesser extent scheduled tribes) have begun to show their ability to organize and act in a politically decisive manner. There is a great opportunity here for channelling that political activism in the direction of forcefully demanding expansion of basic education for those who are left out of the system, and in asking for greater attention to health care, social

---

[8] On this feature of Indian education, see Sen (1970), Naik (1975c, 1982), Weiner (1991, 1994), Tilak (1993), among others. The traditionally elitist tendencies of the ruling cultural and religious traditions in India may have added to this political problem. Both Hinduism and Islam have, in different ways, had considerable inclination towards religious elitism, with reliance respectively on Brahmin priests and powerful Mullahs, and while there have been many protest movements against each (the medieval poet Kabir fought against both simultaneously), the elitist hold is quite strong in both these religions. This contrasts with the more egalitarian and populist traditions of, say, Buddhism. Indeed, most Buddhist countries have typically had much higher levels of basic literacy than societies dominated by Hinduism or Islam. Thailand, Sri Lanka, and Myanmar (Burma) are good examples.

[9] For different analyses of the political situation in India, and of the prospects for change, see Rudolph and Rudolph (1972, 1987), Frankel (1978), Bardhan (1984b), Dhagamwar (1987), Kohli (1987, 1988, 1990), Frankel and Rao (1989), Vanaik (1991), Brass (1992), Kurrien (1992), Omvedt (1993), among others.

[10] See the chapter on Kerala by V.K. Ramachandran (1996) in the companion volume.

[11] See e.g. Irschick (1969), Rudolph and Rudolph (1972, 1987), Barnett (1976), O'Hanlon (1985), Omvedt (1994).

security, and related forms of public support. The direction of rural politics in India will be particularly important in turning this political evolution into a major force for economic development and the creation of social opportunities. Much would depend on whether the nature of such sectional politics stays confined to narrow issues (such as securing the privilege of guaranteed governmental jobs for a few members of the disadvantaged castes), or whether it can take on broader concerns that affect most people in the deprived categories (such as expansion of education, health care, social security, land reform, and so on). There is a real challenge here for the political parties and movements that claim to represent the underdogs of Indian society.

## 5.2. *The Reach of Inequalities*

India's record in reducing social and economic inequalities since independence has been very disappointing. Despite a virtual consensus about some kind of 'socialism' being a fundamental goal of economic policy, few practical steps have been taken to remove the pervasive inequalities that divide Indian society.

The relevant inequalities take different forms, relating not only to large disparities of income and wealth but also to other bases of advantage such as caste, gender, and education. In so far as it has been concerned with inequality at all, public policy has largely concentrated on the standard economic inequalities (e.g. those relating to income and land ownership), perhaps because these inequalities are particularly conspicuous, and lend themselves to convenient measurement. To a limited extent, there is sense in this, given the extreme nature of these inequalities, which leave some to struggle for their next meal while others lead opulent lives.

It is sometimes argued that the persistence of economic inequality does not matter very much, so long as poverty diminishes.[12] This view might have some plausibility if individual well-being were just a question of income. When, however, well-being is seen in terms

---

[12] This argument is sometimes used to legitimize the current bias of economic policy-making in favour of the so-called 'middle class'. This nebulous entity, most commonly defined as including everyone *above* a certain level of income (there is, it appears, no room for an 'upper class' in India's 'socialist' society), is increasingly regarded as the great engine of future growth in India's economy, with the reduction of poverty being a convenient by-product of a consumerism-driven process of economic expansion.

of basic capabilities, private income must be regarded as one among several relevant means that can be used to enhance well-being. Even if poverty remains unchanged, high levels of economic inequality directly curtail some of the relevant capabilities for the disadvantaged groups; examples of these capabilities include self-esteem, protection from violence, and the ability to participate in society and politics. People have reason to value these equality-related capabilities, even if they are poor and hungry.

Aside from this direct link between inequality and well-being, high levels of economic inequality can also indirectly undermine the ability of a society to promote valued capabilities. Economic disparities affect the character of social life, the nature of the political process, and the priorities of the state. Inequality, for instance, can be a source of social tension and even violence; this may help to explain why levels of violence are so high in, say, Brazil, South Africa, the United States, and the state of Bihar in India (all of which are plagued by persistent inequalities). And, as was discussed in the preceding section, the positive role of the government in expanding social opportunities can be severely undermined by political pressure from privileged groups geared to the protection of sectional interests. On the positive side, low levels of inequality often facilitate cooperative action and the pursuit of collective goals, such as the provision of public services. Even at the village level, it has often been observed that the outcomes of collective action and social provisions are greatly influenced by the nature of economic and social divisions.[13]

In so far as anything has been done to reduce economic inequalities in India, the chosen measures have often consisted of interfering with market transactions that are perceived to generate these inequalities. Examples of such measures include legal controls on share-cropping and moneylending, minimum-wage provisions, restrictions on the scale of private enterprises, rent-control laws, and prohibitions on land sales by tribal people. Some of these measures could be, if appropriately devised, helpful means of reducing inequality. There are persuasive redistributive arguments, for instance, in favour of legislation raising the minimum wage above the market level, and of some forms of positive discrimination in employment policies.

[13] On these issues, see Doherty and Jodha (1979), Wade (1988a, 1988b), Chambers et al. (1989), Platteau (1991), Swamy (1991), Bardhan (1993a), Putnam et al. (1993), Drèze and Gazdar (1996), among others; see also Bardhan (1995), and the empirical and theoretical studies cited there.

At the same time, it must be recognized that interference with market exchange has severe limitations as a redistributive device. The roots of economic inequality in private-ownership market economies lie not in market exchange *per se,* but market exchange based on unequal ownership. Economic or legislative measures that interfere with market exchange without altering the distribution of resources, and without creating an alternative—and more equitable—allocation mechanism, can be quite ineffective and counterproductive. First, such measures sometimes have high efficiency costs, which are borne partly by disadvantaged groups. It is well known, for instance, that extreme rent-control laws supposedly geared to the protection of tenants have often crippled the housing market in urban India, ultimately hurting the interests not only of landlords but also of potential tenants.[14] Second, even the distributive effects of these measures can be quite disappointing. While minimum-wage legislation can be a useful redistributive tool (especially in situations of monopsony), excessive wage demands can lead to labour-saving technological investment and widespread unemployment. The large-scale shift from labour-intensive cultivation to plantations in rural Kerala, where unemployment is now exceptionally high, is often cited as an example of this possibility. Third, it must be borne in mind that market exchange is sometimes a factor of liberation for disadvantaged sections of the population. It is by taking advantage of new opportunities for selling their labour, for instance, that many agricultural labourers in India have managed to free themselves from traditional bonds and feudal oppression.[15] Distributive policies have to take note of these liberating aspects of market exchange, as well as of its potentially exploitative features. Finally, the bureaucratic controls involved in widespread interference with market exchange are often themselves a major source of inequality, and may end

[14] See K. Basu (1994) for a discussion of this point. Instances of this phenomenon can also be found in rural areas. Kapadia (1992), for instance, documents how misguided tenancy legislation has paralysed the lease market, and led to large-scale eviction of landless tenants, in parts of Tamil Nadu.

[15] For reviews of the evidence, see Pal (1994) and Platteau and Baland (1994). For some case studies, see Breman (1974), Ramachandran (1990), and the literature cited in Drèze and Mukherjee (1989). That the market mechanism may serve as an instrument of liberation from traditional inequities was discussed by Karl Marx (1857–8), among others.

up compounding rather than reducing the disparities they are meant to address.

Given these limitations of redistributive measures based on interference with market exchange, it is important to consider alternative (or complementary) means of reducing economic inequalities. An obvious possibility is redistribution of ownership, e.g. through land redistribution. One advantage of ownership-focused redistributive measures is that their adverse effects on efficiency are often less serious than those of exchange-focused redistributive measures. In fact, in the former case, the efficiency effects can even be positive; the high efficiency of small-farm owner-cultivation, for instance, often provides a strong argument for land redistribution on efficiency grounds alone.[16]

Redistributive measures such as land reform, of course, tend to be politically demanding, since privileged classes have a strong interest in resisting them. But the experiences of West Bengal and Kerala, discussed in the papers by V.K. Ramachandran, Sunil Sengupta and Haris Gazdar in the companion volume (Drèze and Sen, 1996), show that a political situation where land reforms are seriously implemented is not impossible to achieve. The reforms that have been implemented in these two states are relatively modest, in terms of total area distributed, but they have succeeded in guaranteeing minimum land entitlements to millions of people, and their benefits in terms of increased economic security, greater self-respect, and improved bargaining power are far from negligible. There is no reason to think that the political conditions that have led to these achievements are impossible to replicate elsewhere in India.

While land is perhaps the most obvious asset to redistribute, it has to be borne in mind that economic opportunities in India depend on a much wider range of endowments. Even in rural areas, land is no longer the overwhelming determinant of economic inequality. The distribution of formal-sector employment, of environmental resources, of educational facilities, and of affordable credit arrangements are examples of other influential factors. Opportunities for redistribution relating to these diverse endowments have to be considered, along with the scope for land redistribution.

No matter how far it will prove possible to go in these directions,

---

[16] See e.g. Bauer (1948), Chayanov (1966), Rao (1966), Berry and Cline (1979), Dasgupta (1993), among many others.

it is important to remember that the standard view of economic inequality (which focuses on income distribution and related issues) only captures a small part of the social inequalities with which we ought to be concerned. The relevant dimensions of inequality include not only income (or expenditure) but also health achievements, literacy rates, self-esteem, and other aspects of well-being. And the social divisions to be considered include not only different income groups but also other divisions, based on caste, gender, age, occupation, education levels, and related attributes. Many of the relevant inequalities are less conspicuous than disparities of purchasing power, but no less perverse.

It is in terms of these broader egalitarian concerns that India's record has been most disappointing, and that the scope for action may be particularly extensive.[17] The reduction of income inequality is a difficult challenge in India as elsewhere, partly due to the incentive problems that tend to arise when there is no strong link between productivity and reward, and partly because of the resistance of privileged classes. But there is no reason to tolerate widespread gender discrimination, the continued oppression of disadvantaged castes, the persistent divide between the literates and the illiterates, the exploitation of child labourers, and other destructive social inequalities. The dilemmas that arise in reducing economic inequality (e.g. the possible conflict between efficiency and equity) often have little force in addressing these inequalities. In fact, in many circumstances, distributional concerns are *congruent* with other social objectives, including economic efficiency. Reduced gender discrimination, for instance, expands the scope of women's agency, which is an important factor of social change and economic success (see chapter 7).

The congruence between distributional concerns and other social objectives is also striking in the context of basic education. As we noted in the preceding section, large disparities of educational achievements are a major form—and cause—of social inequality in India. While higher education is remarkably well developed, a large proportion of the population is still illiterate. Further, these disparities of educational achievements tend to perpetuate and reinforce other kinds of social inequality. The link between caste and literacy, for instance, clearly emerges from a wide range of empirical investigations, including

[17] On the role of India's 'new social movements' in challenging diverse types of social inequalities, see Omvedt (1993).

the case studies presented in the companion volume (Drèze and Sen, 1996). Surveys carried out in Uttar Pradesh and West Bengal show how, in the same village, some privileged castes can be found to have enjoyed near-universal adult literacy for several decades, while literacy rates are still close to zero among disadvantaged castes, particularly for females.[18] Eradicating illiteracy in India would, therefore, not only promote greater equality in educational achievements, but also contribute to the elimination of social inequalities based on caste, gender, and related personal attributes. Widespread literacy would also serve a wide range of other economic and social objectives, given the diverse personal and social roles of education.[19] The compatibility between egalitarian concerns and other social objectives makes the expansion of basic education a particularly important step towards the reduction of inequality in India.

## 5.3. *Social Inequality and Economic Reform*

The preceding discussion has some bearing on the issue of social inequality and economic reform. Opposition to greater reliance on market allocation in India is often based on the fear that such a policy might intensify existing inequalities. This argument deserves serious examination. As we noted earlier, there is a case for considering inequality as a social failure on its own, even when rising inequality goes hand in hand with a decline in poverty. It is right to be concerned about the prospect of further intensification of economic and social inequalities that are already extremely large.

Having said this, apprehensions of rising inequality may be misguided or exaggerated in several distinct ways. First, it is difficult to be sure about the effects of market-oriented reforms on economic inequality. Market allocation can certainly have some unequalizing influences, but so do bureaucratic controls, public-sector inefficiency, and trade restrictions. Some of the effects of reform can certainly be expected to be positive. Trade liberalization, for instance, tilts economic activity towards the production of exportable commodities, which tend to be labour-intensive, and this can be expected to have, often enough, an inequality-reducing influence. These positive

---

[18] See Sengupta and Gazdar (1996) and Drèze and Gazdar (1996).

[19] See chapter 2.

aspects have to be considered along with the unequalizing features of liberalization.

Second, the relationship between market-oriented reforms and social inequality is not just a question of their impact on the distribution of income or expenditure. Their consequences for other kinds of social divisions and inequalities are equally relevant. Here again, some important positive effects can be expected. Many studies have documented, for instance, how the expansion and diversification of employment prospects can undermine the traditional caste hierarchy based on a rigid occupation structure.[20] Similarly, a greater emphasis on economic achievement rather than inherited and immutably ascribed characteristics as a basis of social status can be expected to lead to some dissolution of traditional hierarchies. Women, too, may have much to gain from labour-intensive economic growth, given the positive effects of expanded opportunities for gainful female employment on gender relations and intra-household equity (see chapter 7). These positive links between economic reform and social equality have to be considered together with the equally real fact that privileged social groups are often in a stronger position to take advantage of new economic opportunities.

Third, the impact of market-oriented reforms on social inequality depends a great deal on the precise content of these reforms; and it is also strongly influenced by *other* aspects of social and economic policy. If the reforms in question take the form of simply removing controls, and leaving things to the market, it is difficult to predict in which direction the distributional effects will go. On the other hand, if economic policy involves a strong emphasis on promoting labour-intensive economic activity, on enabling disadvantaged groups to participate in the process of economic growth, on making use of growing resources to expand public services, and on developing social security arrangements, the reform process may provide a real opportunity to achieve greater equity *as well* as to reduce poverty.

In short, there is no predetermined link between economic reform and social inequality. A conscious choice has to be made between participatory growth and unaimed liberalization.

---

[20] For some relevant studies, see Ramachandran (1990), Kapadia (1992), Wadley and Derr (1989), Da Corta (1993), Drèze, Lanjouw, and Sharma (forthcoming), among others.

## 5.4. *Basic Equality, Social Security and Health Care*

One part of the task of reducing social and economic inequalities in India involves the expansion of social security provisions, broadly understood as social arrangements to protect all members of society from extreme deprivation and insecurity.[21] It is, indeed, difficult for persons who live in a condition of acute insecurity and dependence to challenge the inequalities of which they are victims. The availability of independent means of subsistence based on social support makes it that much easier for agricultural labourers to resist exploitative employment relations, for the oppressed castes to rise beyond humiliating occupations, and for women to challenge patriarchal institutions. Also, widespread acceptance of the notion of basic social equality can be much enhanced when some essential entitlements are guaranteed to all citizens as a matter of right. It is difficult to claim that all human beings have equal rights in any substantial sense while the streets are full of unemployed labourers, hungry children, destitute beggars, abandoned widows, and forsaken victims of dreadful diseases. Social security is an essential requirement of social justice.[22]

The case for expanded social security arrangements arises partly from these ethical considerations of basic equality, and partly from the more direct contributions they can make to the well-being of the persons who benefit from them. In devising these arrangements, it is important to take a broad view of the relevant means of intervention. With the help of ample budgetary and administrative resources, many industrialized countries have been able to design effective social security systems based on particular programmes such as unemployment benefits, health insurance, and old-age pensions. In a country such as India, these particular means of intervention raise important problems of financing, administration, and incentives, which severely constrain their effectiveness as tools of social security.

However, alternative means are often available to address the same needs. For instance, even if unemployment insurance is not a feasible

[21] On the strategy of social security in developing countries, see Drèze and Sen (1991), and other contributions in Ahmad et al. (1991). Guhan (1981, 1990, 1992, 1993a, 1993b) has presented pioneering analyses of social security issues in India, and discussed a number of feasible policy initiatives in this field. The large literature on land reform, anti-poverty programmes, famine prevention, employment schemes, food distribution, health care, etc., is also relevant.

[22] See Rawls (1971, 1993), Sen (1980, 1992a), Dworkin (1981), Cohen (1989), van Parijs (1990, 1991), Patnaik (1991).

way of dealing with rural unemployment in India, labour-intensive public works programmes themselves can play a helpful role in addressing that problem. These programmes have less exacting financial requirements than unemployment insurance schemes, have limited disincentive effects, and are comparatively easy to administer (partly because they are based on a simple 'self-selection' mechanism). Public provisions relating to land entitlements, health care, public distribution, water supply, supportive credit, and school meals are other examples of relevant means of intervention in the Indian context.

One particular aspect of social security in which India has been quite successful since independence, as discussed earlier, is that of famine prevention. This achievement reflects, first and foremost, the political compulsion to respond to crisis situations in a democratic society: accountability to the electorate makes it very difficult for the government in office to ignore clamours for action when a famine threatens to develop, or electoral debacles that may follow an unprevented famine. But the successful prevention of famine in India has also involved a well-devised system of public intervention to protect the entitlements of vulnerable groups, chiefly based on large-scale employment programmes. The implementation of these programmes is sometimes quite chaotic, but they have nevertheless been effective, on numerous occasions since independence, in preventing the outbreak of a major famine. This experience illustrates the feasibility of certain kinds of social security arrangements, even in a poor country, when the government has adequate incentives to take action.

Putting in place social security arrangements to deal with chronic deprivation is undoubtedly a more demanding challenge, partly because the political pressures that are easy to mobilize in famine situations are often less immediate in other contexts, and partly because the problem to be addressed is intrinsically more complex. Here too, public employment programmes can be an important means of action, as the experience of Maharashtra's Employment Guarantee Scheme illustrates.[23] But other initiatives of different kinds have also proved helpful in several states. As mentioned earlier, for instance, the land reforms implemented in West Bengal and Kerala can be seen as fulfilling important social security objectives as well as some basic

[23] There is a large literature on Maharashtra's Employment Guarantee Scheme; see Acharya (1990), Bhende et al. (1992), Mahendra Dev (1992, 1993a, 1993b), Ravallion et al. (1993), Mahendra Dev and Ranade (1995), among recent contributions.

egalitarian goals. In recent years, Tamil Nadu has also taken some far-reaching initiatives in the field of social security, involving school meal programmes, innovative pension schemes, improved health care provisions, and related measures.[24] These and other pioneering experiences are highly relevant for other states. Grameen Bank and BRAC in Bangladesh, and SEWA in Gujarat, also provide excellent examples of how imaginative credit arrangements can be used to reduce insecurity.

Among the different forms of intervention that can contribute to the provision of social security, the role of health care deserves forceful emphasis. Illness is, obviously enough, one of the most widespread causes of human deprivation and economic insecurity in India. It affects not only the actual patients and those who depend on them for their subsistence, but also other members of the society, in so far as the *threat* of disease arising from widespread morbidity reduces the quality of life. Further, the limitations of private provision in the domain of health care are well known. A well-developed system of public health is an essential contribution to the fulfilment of social security objectives.

This is one field where there is an overwhelming need for bold initiatives and comprehensive reform. Compared with many other developing countries, India has poor health achievements despite spending a comparatively large part of its GNP on health (if one adds up public and private spending).[25] Much of this mismatch between resources and achievements is due to the poor functioning of the public health care system, especially in rural areas. In some states, this system is little more than a collection of deserted primary health centres, filthy dispensaries, unmotivated doctors, and chaotic hospitals.[26]

There have, in recent years, been some important initiatives geared to better public health provisions. The recent expansion of child

---

[24] For some studies of these different programmes, see Babu and Hallam (1989), Guhan (1990, 1993b), Harriss (1991), Rajivan (1991), Mina Swaminathan (1991), Antony (1992), Mahendra Dev (1993c), Visaria and Visaria (1995), among others.

[25] See e.g. Berman (1992).

[26] On this, see particularly the studies of health care in north India carried out by the Operations Research Group (including Khan and Prasad, 1983, Khan et al., 1980, 1983, 1986, 1987, 1988, 1989) and the Public Systems Group (Indian Institute of Management, 1985, Shah, 1989, Murthy, 1992); also Priya (1987), Budakoti (1988), Prakasamma (1989), Indian Council of Medical Research (1989), among others, for case studies.

immunization programmes, for instance, is certainly a positive (and long-overdue) development, and may have made a significant contribution to the comparatively rapid decline of child death rates during the last few years.[27] But there have also been alarming signs of neglect and deterioration in the basic framework of public health care. One of these signs is the massive displacement of health care activities by family planning programmes (mainly based on female sterilization).

As many field-based investigations have noted, the rural health care system in many states gives overwhelming priority to family planning, to the detriment of other health care services. A recent review of health care policy, for instance, observes that 'the whole rural primary health care system is geared towards family planning work' (Priya, 1990, p. 1820). Similarly, a field study in rural Rajasthan concludes that '[family planning] targets have now become the hallmark of all government activity in the name of health' (Gupta et al., 1992, p. 2330); a survey of 'auxiliary nurse midwives' in rural Maharashtra finds that two-thirds of the respondents regard family planning 'as the top priority work' (Jesani, 1990, p. 1103); a case study of health care in Uttar Pradesh states that 'during the main months for family planning campaigns (usually December to March) virtually all the energies of maternal and child health staff may be directed towards those ends' (Jeffery et al., 1989, p. 216); another study of health and family welfare services in rural Uttar Pradesh reports that 'the sterilization target achievement has the highest priority or rather the single priority' (Maurya, 1989, p. 167); yet another study in Uttar Pradesh found that 'the rampages of the family planning programme are particularly devastating... [the] preoccupation with attaining of the given family planning targets has had devastating effects on the other health activities' (Budakoti, 1988, pp. 153–4); an enquiry made in Andhra Pradesh reveals that 'family planning was taken as the priority function at all levels of health organization and ANMs [Auxiliary Nurse Midwives] would even leave attending delivery for a [sterilization] case' (Raghunandan et al., 1987); a survey

---

[27] For up-to-date information on immunization in India, see International Institute for Population Sciences (1994). Despite some recent progress, the level of child immunization remains very low in many Indian states. As recently as 1992–3, 30 per cent of all Indian children aged 12–23 months had not received *any* vaccine; in states such as Uttar Pradesh, Bihar, and Rajasthan, the corresponding proportion ranged between 43 and 54 per cent; see Statistical Appendix for further details.

of four north Indian states concludes that 'as from the highest level to the lowest everybody is asking regarding sterilization targets... health workers under the pretext of work of motivating sterilization cases neglect other work' (M.H. Shah, 1989, p. 120); a field report from rural Gujarat notes that 'the primary health care machinery, village, taluka and district level machinery including teachers, officials, non-officials, etc., were geared to work for achieving the [family planning] targets' (Iyengar and Bhargava, 1987, p. 1087); and a World Bank assessment of health care policy mentions that 'more than half of all health worker activities are directly associated with family planning' (World Bank, 1989, p. 142).[28] These are highly disturbing findings, which call for a major reassessment of health policy in India.

The record of public involvement in the provision of health care and social security is not similarly poor in all the states of India. Kerala, in fact, has a distinguished record in this respect, which has made a major contribution to the rapid expansion of life expectancy in that state (now around 72 years). But other states have also taken important initiatives in recent years. Nutrition programmes in Tamil Nadu, employment schemes in Maharashtra and Gujarat, primary education in Himachal Pradesh, public distribution in Andhra Pradesh, and land reform in West Bengal are some examples. In contrast, in the large north Indian states (notably Uttar Pradesh, Bihar, Rajasthan, and Madhya Pradesh), where the need for action is in many respects particularly urgent, apathy towards the need to develop social security programmes seems to be most resilient.

In this connection, it is interesting to note that most of the initiatives observed in the more active states have been taken in the context of electoral politics. In some cases, as with school meals in Tamil Nadu, land reforms in West Bengal, and public distribution in Andhra Pradesh, they have even been at the forefront of electoral debates. In the large north Indian states, by contrast, social security and related issues have little place in party programmes and electoral debates;

---

[28] For further reports along the same lines, see Khan, Prasad, and Qaiser (1983), Priya (1987), D. Banerji (1989), Roger Jeffery (1988), pp. 269–73, Prakasamma (1989), Sundari (1993), p. 32, Qadeer and Priya (1992), Rose (1992), p. 246. An important observation made in many of these studies is that family planning targets set by the centre, and the general priority given to family planning in the central government's health policy, are major reasons for this widespread displacement of other health care activities.

there, electoral politics seem to give more room to tactical factionalism, with alliances being made and broken depending on personalities and power bases, and little time being 'wasted' on real issues such as undernutrition, illiteracy, unemployment, or ill health.[29]

There is a plausible connection between this low visibility of basic social issues in north Indian politics and the persistence of widespread illiteracy. Literacy is not a requirement of effective participation in the political process (West Bengal's experience, briefly discussed in chapter 3, is a significant illustration of this point), but it is certainly a useful tool of active involvement. In the more literate states, disadvantaged sections of the population have been relatively successful in putting their needs on the political agenda. The best example is Kerala, where high levels of literacy achieved early on have helped to empower the public to demand extensive state involvement in the provision of health care, public distribution, social security, and, of course, education itself. But the same phenomenon is increasingly important in several other states, particularly in south India.

In the educationally backward states of north India, by contrast, the political agenda is overwhelmingly dominated by the concerns of privileged classes and castes. At the time of elections, the illiterate masses have a reasonable chance to make their voice heard, an opportunity which they have seized with striking sagacity on several occasions (for example in 1977, when the ruling party was massively defeated following the excesses of the Emergency). Between elections, however, the vocal demands of the upper castes, the large farmers, and the urban middle-class receive immensely greater attention than the needs of disadvantaged groups.[30]

These observations bring us back to some general points already raised earlier in this chapter and in chapter 3, including (1) the central role of politics in the development process (of which the expansion of social security arrangements is a crucial aspect), (2) the need for more effective political organization of deprived groups,

---

[29] An interesting symptom of this feature of the political agenda in north India is that even the grants made available by the central government for expanding public services are not fully utilized in some states (see section 6.8).

[30] A related issue is the widely-noted 'criminalization of politics' in many north Indian states. In Uttar Pradesh, for instance, almost half of the 425 Members of Legislative Assembly (MLAs) are known to have a criminal record (T.N. Seshan, Chief Election Commissioner, quoted in *Hindustan Times*, 16 October 1994). This feature of north Indian politics also hinders broad-based participation in the democratic process.

and (3) the importance of basic education as a means of successful participation in political activity.

## 5.5. *Local Governance and Social Reform*

Many of the public provisions that have to be made in order to promote basic equality and ensure minimal social security involve *local* public services. A primary school, for instance, is a public facility available to the local community. The same can be said of primary health care centres, fair price shops, labour-intensive public works schemes, and a whole range of other relevant provisions.

The effective management of these local public services depends crucially on the existence of credible institutions for local governance. To illustrate, it is difficult to see how the endemic problem of teacher absenteeism and shirking in rural India (on which more in the next chapter) can be successfully tackled without involving the proximate and informed agency of village communities. Shirking cannot be easily detected by distant outsiders, and the system of centralized school inspection has proved quite ineffective in much of rural India. It is much easier for the concerned parents, and other local residents, to monitor the behaviour of school teachers; but translating their specific knowledge into remedial action involves a challenging problem of local governance. As things stand, there is no mechanism to ensure any kind of accountability of village teachers to the local community in large parts of India, and this is an important factor in the persistence of endemic dereliction of duty.

Local democracy is a highly neglected institutional base of political participation in India. The case study of Uttar Pradesh by Drèze and Gazdar (1996) in the companion volume brings out how many villages in that state still function in much the same way as in the colonial period, with a single 'headman' acting as an all-purpose intermediary between the local community and the state. An important development, of course, is that the headman is now elected, rather than being selected by the government. In the absence of effective political organization of disadvantaged groups, however, the coveted position of headman is usually seized by some member of the local elite, who often uses his position to further his personal interests much more than to pursue any social goal.[31] This weakness of local

---

[31] One recent survey in eastern Uttar Pradesh, for instance, finds that as many as

democracy, rooted in centralized political institutions and deep social inequalities, has played a major role in the comprehensive breakdown of local public services in Uttar Pradesh. And that failure, in turn, is a chief cause of economic and social backwardness in that state.[32]

The importance of local democracy is not confined, of course, to this issue of public services, or other instrumental roles of participatory politics. Participation also has intrinsic value for the quality of life. Indeed, being able to do something not only for oneself but also for other members of the society is one of the elementary freedoms which people have reason to value. The popular appeal of many social movements in India confirms that this basic capability is highly valued even among people who lead very deprived lives in material terms.

The inadequacies of local governance in rural India have several roots, which call for distinct responses. First, the weakness of democratic institutions at the village level reflects a long tradition of centralized governance. The historical roots of this go back to the colonial period, when hierarchical centralization was crucial in making it possible for a handful of foreigners to administer a large and potentially rebellious population (see e.g. Guha, 1982, 1983, and Guha and Spivak, 1988). But it has been consistently perpetuated by the successive governments of independent India.

Second, the flourishing of local participatory politics has been greatly slowed down by low levels of literacy and basic education. Literacy obviously helps people to understand the functioning of the system, to deal with the government bureaucracy, to be aware of their rights, to understand and tackle new problems, and to achieve other abilities that are important for an effective role in local politics. Also, the possibility of decentralizing particular functions of the government (such as some aspects of school management) depends on adequate expertise being available at the local level. Just as more widespread education has enhanced the quality of *state-level* politics in the more

---

two-thirds of the headmen in 82 surveyed villages belonged to the Thakur caste—the traditional landowning upper caste in that region, notorious for oppressive subjugation of the lower castes. See H.N. Singh (1993).

[32] See Drèze and Gazdar (1996) for further discussion. There is also much evidence that the poor functioning of local public services elsewhere in India relates to the centralized, hierarchical, and non-participatory nature of their management. See, for instance, Robert Wade's (1992) insightful contrast of canal irrigation in India and South Korea, and Somanathan's (1991) analysis of environmental protection in the Himalayan region.

literate states, most notably Kerala, it has also led to more vigorous practice of *local* democracy in those states.

Last but not least, local democracy has often been undermined by acute social inequalities.[33] The low involvement of women in local representative institutions such as village panchayats is a clear illustration of this problem. In large parts of the country, local governance is in the hands of upper-caste men from privileged classes, who are only weakly accountable to the community and often end up using local public services as instruments of patronage. In some cases, the rural elite has been known not only to be indifferent to the general promotion of local public services but even to *obstruct* their expansion, to prevent the empowerment of disadvantaged groups. In Uttar Pradesh, for instance, it is still possible to find villages where a powerful landlord has actively opposed the creation of a village school.[34]

The first of these three reasons for the fragile nature of local democracy in India has recently been addressed in the form of the 73rd and 74th constitutional amendments (the 'Panchayati Raj' amendments), which require all the state governments to introduce certain legislative measures geared to the revitalization of local representative institutions. The measures in question include mandatory elections at regular intervals, reservation of seats in village panchayats for women and members of scheduled castes or tribes, and some devolution of government responsibilities to local authorities. These legislative reforms certainly provide an *opportunity* for correcting the current failures of local governance in rural India. Nevertheless, it would be naive to expect too much from them unless the *other* causes of this problem are also addressed.

Recent experiences in different parts of India bring out these

---

[33] In this connection, it is worth noting that tribal societies in India, which tend to be relatively egalitarian, have a long tradition of participatory local democracy. In some states, notably Nagaland, this tradition has formed a good basis for participatory programmes of economic development and social change. The relatively cohesive nature of many tribal societies in India has also been conducive to diverse types of collective action, ranging from environmental protection to resistance against forced displacement. For some relevant studies, see K.S. Singh (1983, 1985), Delìege (1985), Hardiman (1987), Gokhale (1988), Elwin (1989), Swamy (1991), Baviskar (1992), Brass (1992), Maithani and Rizwana (1992), Drèze, Samson, and Singh (forthcoming), among others.

[34] For an example, see Drèze and Gazdar (1996). This phenomenon of landlord resistance to the spread of elementary education has also been noted elsewhere in north India; see e.g. Wadley and Derr (1989), p. 111, and Banerjee (1994).

opportunities and limitations related to legislative reform. On the positive side, the relatively successful experience of West Bengal discussed by Sengupta and Gazdar (1996) in the companion volume illustrates the scope for radical improvement in local democracy. The formation of all-women panchayats in parts of rural Maharashtra (Omvedt, 1990) is another interesting example of transformation of village politics based on a combination of legislative reform and political organization. On the other side, several empirical studies have underlined the limitations of decentralization in the context of continued inequalities of political power.[35]

The recent legislative reforms hold much promise, but their actual success depends a great deal on other types of public action. If these reforms are not supplemented with a more active programme of social change, they stand in some danger of leading to a proliferation of bureaucracy without any real improvement in local democracy. On the other side, if they go hand in hand with an expansion of public initiatives and social movements aimed at more widespread literacy, a stronger political organization of disadvantaged groups, and a more vigorous challenge to social inequalities, they would represent a real opportunity to transform village politics in rural India.

---

[35] Based on an in-depth study of Karnataka, for instance, Crook and Manor (1994) conclude that, despite many positive achievements, decentralization initiatives in that state have failed to enhance the effectiveness of redistributive poverty alleviation programmes, due to the absence of any commitment to these programmes on the part of the local elites. For a general discussion of the limitations of decentralization in the absence of social change, see Bardhan (1992).

# BASIC EDUCATION
# AS A POLITICAL ISSUE

## 6.1. *Education and Social Change*

The diverse personal and social roles of education were discussed in general terms in chapter 2 of this book. In connection with the issue of social inequality examined in the preceding chapter, the empowerment and redistributive role of education may be worth further exploration. Literacy is a basic tool of self-defence in a society where social interaction often involves the written media. An illiterate person is that much less equipped to defend herself in court, to obtain a bank loan, to enforce her inheritance rights, to take advantage of new technology, to compete for secure employment, to get on the right bus, to take part in political activity, in short, to participate successfully in the modern economy and society. Similar things can be said about numeracy and other skills acquired in the process of basic education.

Basic education is also a catalyst of social change. The contrasts between different states of India, on which we have already commented in chapter 3, provide ample illustration of this elementary fact. For instance, the historical analysis of Kerala's experience presented by V.K. Ramachandran (1996) in the companion volume powerfully brings out the dialectical relationship between educational progress and social change: the spread of education helps to overcome the traditional inequalities of caste, class, and gender, just as the removal of these inequalities contributes to the spread of education. Kerala made an early start down that road, in the nineteenth century, leading to wide-ranging social achievements later on. At the other extreme, the educationally backward states of north India (discussed by Drèze and Gazdar, 1996, in the same volume, with special reference to Uttar Pradesh) have made comparatively little progress in eradicating traditional inequalities, particularly those of caste and gender.

The value of basic education as a tool of social affirmation has not been lost on the Indian people. In fact, a common finding of village studies and household surveys is that education is widely perceived by members of socially or economically disadvantaged groups as the most promising chance of upward mobility for their children.[1] The relationship between education and social change was also well understood by many social leaders during the independence movement. Gokhale, for instance, was a strong advocate of the promotion of basic education, and, as soon as the Indian Councils Act of 1909 made it possible for Indians to propose legislative reforms, he formulated a pioneering Elementary Education Bill (later rejected by the British administration) which would have empowered local authorities to introduce compulsory education. Dr Ambedkar, whose own scholarship helped him to overcome the stigma of low caste (indeed 'untouchability'), saw education as a cornerstone of his strategy for the liberation of oppressed castes—a strategy which has been put to good effect in some parts of India. Education was also of paramount concern to Rammohan Roy, Maharshi Karve, Pandita Ramabai, Swami Vivekananda, Jotirao Phule, Rabindranath Tagore, Mahatma Gandhi, Abdul Ghaffar Khan, Jayaprakash Narayan, and numerous other social reformers and political figures of the pre-independence period.

The empowerment value of basic education is so obvious that there is something puzzling in the fact that the promotion of education has received so little attention from social and political leaders in the post-independence period. One aspect of this neglect is the flagrant inadequacy of government policy in the field of elementary education; we will return to that in section 6.3. But lack of attention to education has not been confined to government circles. It has also been a common attitude of political parties, trade unions, revolutionary organizations, and other social movements.[2]

---

[1] For some relevant empirical studies, see Vlassoff (1980, 1993), Nair et al. (1984), J.C. Caldwell et al. (1985), Bara et al. (1991), Chanana (1988b, 1993), Drèze and Saran (1995), among others. On the relationship between education and social change, see also Nair (1981), Aparna Basu (1988), Karlekar (1988), Nag (1989), Nautiyal (1989), Verma (1989), Raza (1990), Robin Jeffrey (1992), Sengupta (1992), Lieten (1993), Majumdar (1992), Ghosh et al. (1994), and the case studies presented in Drèze and Sen (1996).

[2] This feature of social movements in India stands in sharp contrast with the Latin

Several ideological convictions have contributed to this neglect, including: (1) the conservative upper-caste notion that knowledge is not important or appropriate for the lower castes;[3] (2) a distorted understanding of Gandhi's view that 'literacy in itself is no education';[4] and (3) the belief, held in some radical quarters, that the present educational system is a tool of subjugation of the lower classes or a vestige of the colonial period. It is hard to overstate the need for unequivocal rejection of these and other sceptical views of the value of education. A firm commitment to the widespread and equitable provision of basic education is the first requirement of rapid progress in eradicating educational deprivation in India.

## 6.2. *The State of School Education*

The limited reach of basic education in India has been mentioned on several occasions earlier in this book. Before examining some reasons for these low educational achievements, it may be helpful to recapitulate some essential features of the educational situation in India.

Table 6.1 presents a set of relevant indicators. Aside from reporting the figures for India as a whole, we have added the corresponding figures for Uttar Pradesh and Kerala. This is partly to give an idea of the extent of regional contrasts within India, and partly because the specific contrast between Uttar Pradesh and Kerala receives some attention in this book and the companion volume.[5] The figures

---

American experience, where basic education has often been a cornerstone of popular mobilization and a major focus of radical politics; see e.g. Archer and Costello (1990).

[3] The influence exercised by this traditional view over a long period is evident in a large number of historical documents, from the second-century *Manusmriti* (which forbids the reading of the Vedas to the lower castes) to the writings of the eleventh century Arab traveller Alberuni (who commented on 'those castes who are not allowed to occupy themselves with science'). There are similar traditional attitudes towards the education of women (see e.g. Chanana, 1988b), including 'the prevalent view [in the early nineteenth century] that widowhood would result if women were educated' (Karlekar, 1988, p. 136).

[4] Mahatma Gandhi, cited in Kurrien (1983), p. 45. Gandhi's main concern was that education should go *beyond* literacy, but his emphasis on productive handicraft as the foremost school activity, and the related insistence on the financial self-sufficiency of individual schools, have contributed to some confusion in educational policy in the post-independence period, as Kurrien aptly argues.

[5] See particularly section 3.6 of this book, and Drèze and Sen (1996).

## TABLE 6.1. *Basic Education in India: Achievements and Diversities*

|  | India | Uttar Pradesh | Kerala |
|---|---|---|---|
| **Literacy rates (age 7+) for selected groups, 1991** | | | |
| Total population: | | | |
|   Female | 39 | 25 | 86 |
|   Male | 64 | 56 | 94 |
| Rural scheduled castes: | | | |
|   Female | 19 | 8 | 73 |
|   Male | 46 | 39 | 85 |
| **Literacy rates among children aged 10–14, 1987–8** | | | |
| Rural: Female | 52 | 39 | 98 |
|       Male | 73 | 68 | 98 |
| Urban: Female | 82 | 69 | 98 |
|       Male | 88 | 76 | 97 |
| **Proportion of rural children attending school, 1987–8 (%)** | | | |
| Age 5–9: Female | 40 | 28 | 83 |
|         Male | 52 | 45 | 87 |
| Age 10–14: Female | 42 | 31 | 91 |
|           Male | 66 | 64 | 93 |
| **Percentage of never-enrolled children in the 12–14 age group, 1986–7** | | | |
| Rural: Female | 51 | 68 | 1.8 |
|       Male | 26 | 27 | 0.4 |
| Urban: Female | 19 | 39 | 0.6 |
|       Male | 11 | 19 | 0.0 |
| **Percentage of persons aged 15 and above who have completed primary education, 1981[a]** | | | |
| Female | 21 | 11 | 56 |
| Male | 44 | 37 | 68 |

*Note.* [a] The corresponding census figures for 1991 have not been released at the time of writing.

*Sources.* Calculated from census and National Sample Survey data presented in P. Visaria et al. (1993), pp. 31–3, 53, Sengupta (1991), pp. 15, 28, Nanda (1992), p. 57, Nanda (1993), pp. 22–31, and Census of India 1981, Series-C, Social and Cultural Tables, Table C-2. See also Statistical Appendix.

presented in Table 6.1 are based on two independent and reasonably reliable sources—the census and the National Sample Survey (NSS).

We should mention that Table 6.1 makes no use of official data on 'school enrolment', and related statistics released by the Department of Education. Official school enrolment figures are known to be grossly inflated, partly due to the incentives that government employees at different levels have to report exaggerated figures.[6] According to these figures, for instance, the gross enrolment ratio for boys at the primary level (number of boys enrolled in a primary school as a proportion of the relevant age group) is *above 100 per cent* in all major states except Haryana and Kerala. Even for girls, the gross enrolment ratio is as high as 93 per cent.[7] These cheerful enrolment figures are impossible to reconcile with the survey-based evidence (see Table 6.1). In contrast, the broad consistency between NSS data and independent census data gives additional reason to accept these sources as more authoritative, and to reject the official enrolment figures.[8]

The highly misleading 'official' figures are often reported in international publications that depend on government sources, such as the *Human Development Reports* and *World Development Reports*. According to *Human Development Report 1994,* for instance, India had a gross enrolment ratio of 99 per cent in 1990.[9] Statistics of this kind can easily lead to over-optimistic assessments of India's record in the field of basic education. In their insightful and otherwise illuminating analysis of the Indian economy, for instance, Joshi and Little (1994) give India some credit for the fact that 'school enrolment has risen to 99 per cent' during the eighties (p.17). This statement

---

[6] For further discussion of this issue, see Sen (1970), Prasad (1987), and Drèze and Gazdar (1996).

[7] The figures are from Tyagi (1993), p. 102, and the reference year is 1992–3. It is possible, in principle, for the gross enrolment ratio to exceed 100 per cent, due to the enrolment in primary classes of girls or boys outside the standard age group. But this can hardly explain the enormous discrepancy between official enrolment figures and survey-based data on school enrolment and attendance. Nor can it explain other anomalies of the official enrolment figures, such as the fact that *Kerala* (which has the highest school enrolment rates in the country according to survey data) is one of the only two states with a gross enrolment ratio of boys below 100 per cent.

[8] On the consistency between census and NSS data relating to education, see Sengupta (1991) and P. Visaria et al. (1993).

[9] *Human Development Report 1994*, Table 14, p. 157; *World Development Report 1994* gives a figure of 98 per cent for 1991 (Table 28, p. 216).

corresponds only to the official figures, which do not tally with census and National Sample Survey data.

Coming back to Table 6.1, important features of educational achievements in India include the following. First, average literacy rates are low—64 per cent for males and 39 per cent for females in India as a whole.[10] We have already commented on this on several occasions. We have noted, for instance, how literacy rates in India are much lower than in China (chapter 4), lower than literacy rates in many east and south-east Asian countries 30 years ago (section 3.3), lower than the average literacy rates for 'low-income countries' other than China and India (section 1.1), and also no higher than estimated literacy rates in sub-Saharan Africa (section 3.1).

Second, the problem of low average literacy rates is exacerbated by enormous *inequalities* in educational achievements. One aspect of these inequalities, already mentioned in chapter 3, concerns the existence of large disparities in educational achievements between different states. The female literacy rate, for instance, varies from 20 per cent in Rajasthan and 25 per cent in Uttar Pradesh to 86 per cent in Kerala. This reflects the fact that efforts to expand basic education in different states have enormously varied in strength and effectiveness. As discussed earlier (see particularly chapter 3), there is much to learn from these regional contrasts about the causes of success and failure in the promotion of basic education.

Third, there are also large inequalities in educational achievements between males and females, between urban and rural areas, and between different social groups. These diverse inequalities, combined with low average literacy rates, are responsible for the persistence of extremely low levels of education for disadvantaged sections of the population. To illustrate, the rural female literacy rate is only 19 per cent among scheduled castes (which represent 16 per cent of the Indian population); 16 per cent among scheduled tribes (representing 8 per cent of the population); and below 10 per cent, for *all* females aged 7 and above, in many educationally backward districts of Bihar, Madhya Pradesh, Orissa, Rajasthan, and Uttar Pradesh. When different sources of disadvantage are combined (e.g. the handicap of being female is added to that of belonging to a

---

[10] Unless stated otherwise, all the literacy rates mentioned in this section refer to the age group of 7 years and above, and are based on 1991 census data presented in Tyagi (1993), pp. 24–40. For further information on literacy rates and related indicators of educational achievements, see also the Statistical Appendix of this book.

scheduled caste and living in a backward region), the literacy rates for the most disadvantaged groups come down to minuscule figures. For instance, in 1981 the crude literacy rate among rural scheduled-caste women was below 2.5 per cent in a majority of districts of Uttar Pradesh and Rajasthan (and even below 1 per cent in many districts of those states).[11]

Fourth, illiteracy is widespread not only in the older age groups (as would apply even in, say, China), but also among young boys and girls, particularly in rural areas. For instance, half of all rural females in the 10–14 age group in India (almost two-thirds in Uttar Pradesh) are illiterate. The persistence of endemic illiteracy in the younger age groups is the most distressing aspect of the educational situation in contemporary India.

Fifth, that failure can also be identified using survey-based school enrolment and attendance data. The proportion of rural females aged 12–14 who have never been enrolled in any school is above one-half in India as a whole, above two–thirds in Uttar Pradesh, Madhya Pradesh, and Bihar, and as high as 82 per cent in Rajasthan.[12] Similarly, only 42 per cent of rural females in the 10–14 age group (and 40 per cent in the 5–9 age group) are reported to be attending school. It might be added that these school attendance figures refer to the 'usual' status of a boy or girl at the time of the survey.[13] School attendance figures based on a 'time-rate' notion of school attendance (e.g. the proportion of rural children attending school on an average *day*) would be much lower, given that even children who are reported as usually attending school spend a large proportion of days out of school.[14]

Sixth, an important reason for these low school-attendance figures is a very high drop-out rate. Available information suggests that only half of all children enrolled in Class 1 are still at school four

---

[11] For the last set of figures, we have taken 1981 as the reference year because the corresponding figures for 1991 are still to be published. The figures are from Nuna (1990), pp. 113–14, and based on the 1981 census.

[12] See Statistical Appendix, Table A.3. These four states account for about 40 per cent of the total population of India.

[13] The 1981 census, for instance, has only *one* question on school attendance, which asks whether the person is attending school or not. There is no scope for the investigator to record, say, the number of days of actual attendance during the month or week preceding the survey.

[14] See e.g. Prasad (1987), and Drèze and Gazdar (1996) in the companion volume.

years later.[15] Low levels of basic education in India reflect *both* (1) the low duration of schooling for children who are enrolled at some stage, and (2) the fact that a large proportion of children are *never* enrolled at all.

Seventh, the low enrolment and retention rates imply that the proportion of persons who complete the primary cycle of five classes is extremely low.[16] In 1981, for instance, the proportion of Indian adults who had completed primary education was below one-third (the corresponding figures from the 1991 census are still to be released). In the same year, only one out of nine adult women in Uttar Pradesh had completed the primary cycle.

International comparisons corroborate the diagnosis of low schooling levels in India. We have already discussed this in the context of literacy rates. Further evidence comes from international data on other indicators of educational achievements, such as 'mean years of schooling'. The average number of years of schooling for persons aged 25 and above is only 2.4 in India (1.2 for females and 3.5 for males), compared with 5.0 in China, 7.2 in Sri Lanka, and 9.3 in South Korea.[17] The state of school education in India is indeed dismal.

## 6.3. *Biases and Confounded Strategies*

Education policy in India since independence has suffered from a good deal of inconsistency and confusion.[18] One of the directive

---

[15] Tyagi (1993), p. 100. It should be said that these estimates are based on official enrolment figures (the 'retention rate' is calculated as the ratio of Class-5 enrolment to Class-1 enrolment four years earlier), and it is not clear how the reporting biases mentioned earlier affect these estimates. Interestingly, the available estimates suggest very little difference in retention rates between males and females at the primary level (at higher levels, retention rates are much lower for girls than for boys).

[16] Literacy alone is not, of course, the only educational achievement of importance (even though it has great personal and social significance). With competent teaching, a child can learn to read and write in a few weeks, in most Indian languages. The five years of schooling involved in the full primary cycle provide opportunities for learning many other useful skills.

[17] *Human Development Report 1994*, Table 5, pp. 138–9.

[18] This major problem has been noted in a number of distinguished analyses of educational policy in India, including Naik (1975a, 1975b, 1975c, 1982), Kurrien (1983), K. Kumar (1991), Weiner (1991, 1994), Tilak (1993). On the evolution of educational policy in India, see also Biswas and Agrawal (1986), Agrawal and Aggarwal (1992), Singha (1992), among others.

principles of the Constitution (Article 45) urges the state to provide free and compulsory education up to the age of 14 by 1960. This was an ambitious goal, and the practical measures that were taken to implement it have fallen far short of what was required. To this day, compulsory education has not been actually implemented anywhere in India, even though state governments and even local authorities are empowered to make primary education compulsory. And the provision of educational facilities remains completely out of line with the stated goal of universal school education until the age of 14. There are, for instance, as many as 58 children in the 6–10 age group for each teacher at the primary level (Table 6.2).[19] Even under the unrealistic assumption that teachers are evenly distributed all over the country, in proportion to the number of children in that age group, this overall child–teacher ratio is clearly in conflict with the requirements of universal education in classes of reasonable size up to the age of 10—let alone 14.

Similar inconsistencies of ends and means can be found in a series of commission reports and policy statements that have appeared since 1947. The elusive goal of providing free and compulsory education until the age of 14 within a few years has been regularly reiterated, without any effective steps being taken to reach it. As recently as 1986–7, less than half of all enrolled children managed to complete the initial cycle of 5 years of primary education; barely one-third completed the 8 years corresponding to the stated goal of compulsory and free education; and nearly half of all rural children in the 6–11 age group had never been enrolled in any school.[20] This did not prevent the National Policy on Education of 1986 from declaring with blind optimism that 'by 1995 all children will be provided free and compulsory education up to 14 years of age' (Singha, 1992, p. 12), without giving any sense of the revolutionary policy changes that would be needed to achieve this goal. Not surprisingly, the cheerful expectations of instant success did not materialize. In fact, official figures on retention rates show no improvement after 1986 (see Tyagi, 1993, p. 100).

The revised National Policy on Education, 1992, is in line with

---

[19] The calculations in Table 6.2 *underestimate* the effective child–teacher ratio, since they ignore the fact that some children have to repeat one or more classes.

[20] Tyagi (1993), p. 100, and P. Visaria et al. (1993), p. 53.

TABLE 6.2. *The Child–Teacher Ratio in India, 1991*

| | | |
|---|---:|---|
| *Number of children* | | |
| Total population, 1991 (thousands) | 846,303 | (A) |
| Proportion of population in 6–10 age group, 1981 (%) | 14.6 | |
| Estimated proportion of population in 6–10 age group, 1991[a] (%) | 13.3 | (B) |
| Estimated number of children in 6–10 age group, 1991 (A x B) (thousands) | 112,558 | (C) |
| *Number of teachers* | | |
| Number of primary-school teachers, 1991 (thousands) | 1,637 | (D) |
| Estimated number of teachers in upper-primary and secondary schools who teach primary classes, 1991[b] (thousands) | 312 | (E) |
| Estimated total number of teachers in primary sections, 1991 (D+E) | 1,949 | (F) |
| Number of children in 6–10 age group per primary-section teacher, 1991 (C/F) | 58 | |

*Notes.* [a] Based on assuming that the rate of decline of the proportion of the population in the 6–10 age group between 1981 and 1991 is the same as the rate of decline of the proportion of the population in the 5–9 age group (for the latter group, year-wise estimates are available from *Sample Registration System*).
[b] Based on the assumption that the proportion of primary-section teachers to primary sections in these schools is the same as in primary schools. The precise assumption used here does not make much difference, since the proportion of primary sections located in upper-primary and secondary schools is small (16 per cent in 1986).

*Sources.* Calculated from Nanda (1992), p. 86; Tyagi (1993), p. 82; National Council of Educational Research and Training (1992), p. 34; Census of India 1981, Series 1 (India), Part IV-A, Social and Cultural Tables, Tables C-4 and C-5; *Sample Registration System 1982*, p. 61; *Sample Registration System 1991*, p. 59.

the earlier tradition.[21] Despite stressing that it was 'imperative for the Government to formulate and implement a new Education Policy for the country' (p. 4), the Policy did little more than to repeat the old credo with a different time frame: 'it shall be ensured that free and compulsory education of satisfactory quality is provided to all children up to 14 years of age before we enter the twenty-first century' (p. 20). Once again, the Policy gave no hint of the practical steps that would make this so-called 'resolve' a reality, and did not go much beyond a remarkable collection of platitudes such as 'all

---

[21] All the quotes in this paragraph are from Government of India (1992c). This document spells out the policy of the central government, and leaves room for wide differences in state-level policies, which have indeed varied a great deal in content and effectiveness.

teachers should teach and all students should study' (p. 34), 'the New Education Policy... will adopt an array of meticulously formulated strategies based on micro-planning to ensure children's retention at school' (p. 20), and 'a warm, welcoming and encouraging approach, in which all concerned share a solicitude for the needs of the child, is the best motivation for the child to attend school and learn' (p. 18).[22] Nevertheless, the authors felt able to conclude on an upbeat note:

The future shape of education in India is too complex to envision with precision. Yet, given our tradition which has almost always put high premium on intellectual and spiritual attainment, we are bound to succeed in achieving our objectives.

The main task is to strengthen the base of the pyramid, which might come close to a billion people at the turn of the century. Equally, it is important to ensure that those at the top of the pyramid are among the best in the world. Our cultural well springs had taken good care of both ends in the past; the skew set in with foreign domination and influence. It should now be possible to further intensify the nation-wide effort in Human Resource Development, with Education playing its multifaceted role.[23]

One implication of these vague pieties is that they have opened the door to further inconsistencies between stated goals and actual policy. Since everyone knows that free and compulsory education up to the age of 14 is not going to be achieved by the end of this century (and possibly for long after that), this stated goal provides no concrete guidance. This has made it possible, in particular, to combine the highly egalitarian slogan of free and universal education with extreme inequality in practice. One symptom of this elitism, already noted in the preceding chapter, is the bias against elementary schooling within the educational system. Child labour is considered perfectly acceptable for the boys and girls of poor families, while

---

[22] In a companion document (Government of India, 1992d), an eminent group of educationists and other experts have made a valuable attempt to translate the feeble exhortations of the National Policy on Education into concrete policy guidelines. This 'programme of action', however, only has the status of a set of expert recommendations, and these have, so far, made rather little impact on actual policies at the state level, especially in the educationally backward states. For instance, so far the only states that have implemented the recommendation of framing their own, state-level programme of action are Kerala, Maharashtra, and Tamil Nadu—three of the most advanced states as far as basic education is concerned. (We are grateful to Dr Vaidyanatha Ayyar, Joint Secretary, Department of Education, for a helpful discussion on this.)

[23] Government of India (1992c), p. 50.

the privileged classes enjoy a massively subsidized system of higher education.[24]

In short, the lamentable history of post-independence education policy has suffered from diverse kinds of inconsistencies and con- tradictions, including (1) a confusion of objectives, (2) inconsistencies between stated goals and actual policy, and (3) a specific contradiction between stated goals and resource allocation. The formulation of a more effective policy must begin with the elementary tasks of setting clear goals that are adequately ambitious yet realizable, devising practical measures to meet them, and providing the resources required to implement these measures. This should really go without saying, but, given the failures of earlier policies, there is a case for saying it nevertheless.

## 6.4. *The Role of Expenditure*

The last ten years have seen a growing awareness of India's failures in the field of basic education, and of the inadequacy of existing provisions. The response, as far as the central government is concerned, has mainly taken the form of increasing expenditure on education without really introducing major policy changes.[25]

The expansion of government expenditure on education is certainly a welcome development. Indeed, inadequate public expenditure is one important reason for India's poor educational achievements. Among one hundred and sixteen countries for which the relevant data are available, India ranks as low as eighty-second in terms of

---

[24] Even *within* the field of elementary education, there is a good deal of elitism in educational policy. In particular, the current thrust of official policy for dealing with the non-participation of disadvantaged groups in the elementary education system is mainly to encourage the creation of second-track 'non-formal education' facilities, rather than to affirm an uncompromising commitment to their inclusion in the formal schooling system (see e.g. Government of India, 1992d, chapter 7). Some of these alternative channels of schooling are certainly useful in the short term, but a complacent reliance on this two-track formula as a basis for universalizing elementary education carries the real danger of institutionalizing rather than eliminating the elitist features of Indian education.

[25] There has been a diversity of responses at the level of state governments (which have the primary responsibility for providing education), ranging from bold initiatives in states such as Kerala, Tamil Nadu, and Himachal Pradesh to continued apathy in states such as Uttar Pradesh. Some state-level responses are discussed in the companion volume (Drèze and Sen, 1996).

the proportion of public expenditure on education to GNP.[26] From 1968 onwards, successive versions of the National Policy on Education have 'resolved' to raise this proportion to 6 per cent, but this target has not been approached to this day.[27]

The problem of inadequate aggregate resources is compounded by severe imbalances in allocation. Because education expenditure is borne primarily by individual states, rather than by the central government, there are large inter-state variations in per-capita expenditure on education; and states with lower educational achievements, where the need for public investment is most acute, tend to be those where financial resources are particularly scarce.[28] Another form of imbalance, mentioned earlier, is the relatively low share of elementary education in total education expenditure. This share is not only low (currently less than 50 per cent) in terms of the stated objective of universalizing elementary education, it has also declined significantly from the first Five-Year Plan until the mid-eighties, and, despite some improvement during the last ten years, it remains lower now than in the fifties (Tilak, 1993, pp. 51–9).

If public expenditure on education in India remains low by international standards, recent trends have at least been in the right direction. After stagnating for 25 years, the proportion of public expenditure on education to GNP started increasing noticeably around the mid-eighties, and there has also been some improvement in

[26] *Human Development Report 1994*, Tables 15, 36, and 49 (the reference year is 1990). India's position is even lower (68th from the top among 89 countries for which data are given) in terms of the proportion of education expenditure in total public spending. The expenditure figures used here include outlays of the state governments as well as those of the central government. For a comprehensive analysis of education expenditure in India, see Tilak (1989, 1990, 1993, 1994a, 1994b); also Ghosh (1992).

[27] This does not prevent Government of India (1994a) from making the apparently triumphant statement that public expenditure on education as a proportion of GNP is 'well over 3 per cent now', just after noting that the 6 per cent target has been 'reiterated time and again by committees and experts and also by the Prime Minister' (p. 152). This is another example of the inconsistencies discussed earlier.

[28] Per-capita public expenditure on education in a particular state can be seen as the product of (1) per-capita income in that state, (2) the ratio of government expenditure to state income, and (3) the proportion of state government expenditure allocated to education. By and large, each of these parameters tends to be low in states with high levels of illiteracy. The third one reflects the priority attached by the relevant state government to education (e.g. it is about twice as large in Kerala as in Haryana), but the other two are important constraints on education expenditure in the disadvantaged states.

TABLE 6.3. *Aspects of Government Expenditure on Elementary Education*

| Period | Growth rates of selected variables relating to elementary schools (% per year) | | | |
|---|---|---|---|---|
| | Recurring expenditure, at 1970–1 prices [a] | Number of teachers | Recurring expenditure per teacher [b] | Teacher–population ratio |
| 1950–1 to 1960–1 | 8.5 | 5.6 | 3.0 | 3.6 |
| 1960–1 to 1970–1 | 5.8 | 4.5 | 1.3 | 2.3 |
| 1970–1 to 1980–1 | 2.8 | 2.7 | 0.2 | 0.5 |
| 1980–1 to 1984–5 | 11.1 | 2.1 | 9.0 | 0.0 |
| 1984–5 to 1989–90 | 10.8 | 1.6 | 9.2 | –0.5 |

*Notes.* [a] Recurring expenditure on elementary education accounts for 98 per cent of total government expenditure on elementary education; salaries account for 96 per cent of recurring expenditure; teachers' salaries account for 97 per cent of all salaries (1983–4 figures from Tilak, 1993, p. 60).

[b] This can be taken as a rough index of teachers' real salaries, given that these salaries account for 93 per cent of recurring expenditure.

*Sources.* Calculated from Tilak (1993), p. 57, Tyagi (1993), p. 82, Agrawal et al. (1992), p. 234, and Bose (1991a), p. 48. The wholesale price index (all commodities) has been used to deflate nominal expenditure figures. Elementary schools refer to primary and 'upper primary' schools (classes 1 to 8 in most states).

the share of elementary education (Tilak, 1993), together with some reduction of inter-state disparities (Tyagi, 1993, p. 122).

But where is this extra money going? Table 6.3 provides a clue on this, for elementary education.[29] The table presents figures on the growth rates of government expenditure at 1970–1 prices, of the number of teachers, and of government expenditure per teacher; the latter can be taken as a rough index of teachers' real salaries, given that these salaries absorb well over 90 per cent of recurring expenditure. It can be seen that while the growth rate of expenditure in the eighties has been higher than at any other time since independence (above 10 per cent per year), the increase of expenditure over that period is almost entirely accounted for by sharp increases

[29] The term 'elementary education' officially covers both primary schools (classes 1–5 in most states) and upper primary or 'middle' schools (classes 6–8 in a majority of states).

in teachers' emoluments; these have grown at an extraordinary rate of 9 per cent per year in real terms. The number of teachers, on the other hand, has never grown more slowly. In fact, for the first time, the number of teachers has grown less fast than the population, and much more slowly than the number of children attending primary and upper-primary schools. As a result, there has been a sharp increase in the pupil–teacher ratio during the eighties.[30]

The available evidence indicates no substantial improvement in patterns of education expenditure in the nineties. On the contrary, the growth of education expenditure has slowed down after structural adjustment measures were introduced in 1991, and education expenditure has even declined in real terms in many states (see Gupta and Sarkar, 1994, Jalan and Subbarao, 1995, and table A.4 in the Statistical Appendix of this book). One symptom of these adverse developments is a *decline* in the *absolute number* of teachers in primary and upper-primary schools between 1991–2 and 1992–3 (the latest year for which the relevant data are available).[31] There could hardly be a more inappropriate response to the current failures of basic education in India.

Education expenditure in India needs to be increased, especially at the primary level and in the educationally backward states. At the same time, it would be naive to think that India's educational achievements can be transformed simply by spending more, and especially by spending more on the same—or a smaller number of—teachers. Achieving a real change in the situation of primary education in India is a much more demanding task.

## 6.5. *Priorities and Challenges*

Recent innovations of the central government in the field of education policy have largely consisted of introducing ad hoc 'schemes' to

---

[30] Pupil–teacher ratios have risen in most states over this period (Tyagi, 1993, p. 84), but the increase seems to have been particularly sharp in the educationally backward states. While Kerala has succeeded in preventing any increase in the pupil–teacher ratio during the eighties, Uttar Pradesh has allowed it to increase by *fifty per cent* between 1981–2 and 1992–3.

[31] Tyagi (1993), p. 82. Interestingly, the decline has not been impartial between male and female teachers. In fact, the number of male teachers in primary and upper-primary schools remained virtually unchanged between these two years, while nearly 14,000 female teaching jobs were lost.

address specific problems that happen to come to the attention of policy-makers. In its 350-page annual report for 1993–4 (Government of India, 1994f), the Department of Education provides details of dozens of such schemes, from the sinking 'Operation Blackboard' to the new 'District Primary Education Programme'. By contrast, the same report devotes only one or two pages each to 'universalization of elementary education', 'education of scheduled castes and scheduled tribes' and 'female education'.

Many of the schemes in question are aimed at creating second-track educational facilities such as *shramik vidyapeeths, mahila shikshan kendras, jan shiksha kendras, mahila samakhya, shiksha karmis*, and numerous types of 'non-formal education' centres. Some of these initiatives are undoubtedly useful. Impressive achievements, for instance, have been reported for the recently-launched Total Literacy Campaign, in districts where the local administration and popular organizations have actively seized this opportunity for mass mobilization on the issue of literacy.[32] But as useful as these programmes might be in localized contexts, the basic problem of endemic illiteracy in the younger age groups cannot be solved through such ad hoc schemes and campaigns, many of which represent an over-simple response to a particular—often rather narrow—aspect of the problem of educational backwardness. The priority should be to ensure that every village in the country has a free, functioning, well-staffed, and well-attended regular primary school.

One requirement of this basic objective is the provision of adequate educational facilities within the basic framework of village schools (the issue of child attendance will be taken up further on in this chapter). In this respect, there are no signs of rapid improvement or bold initiatives. In fact, as was discussed earlier, the number of teachers at the elementary level is now growing more slowly than the population, and considerably more slowly than the school-going population at that level. Nor is there much evidence of a sustained improvement in the performance of school teachers. In fact, the problem of teacher absenteeism and shirking seems to be growing rather than declining in some states.

---

[32] On this, see particularly the recent evaluation by Arun Ghosh et al. (1994), who argue that 'for all its deficiencies... [the Total Literacy Campaign] has been among the best things promoted by the government since independence' (p. 37). On the Total Literacy Campaign, see also Ghosh (1991), S. Banerjee (1992), Sengupta (1992), Rao (1993), Rokadiya et al. (1993), Government of India (1994b), Saldanha (1994), among others.

In connection with the last point, some telling findings emerge from a recent field investigation in rural Uttar Pradesh, which covered 15 village schools in four different districts.[33] As a matter of fact, very little teaching activity was observed in the sample schools. Teacher absenteeism was endemic (*two-thirds* of the teachers employed in the sample schools were absent at the time of the investigators' unannounced visits), and the acting teachers did little more than keep a semblance of order among the pupils. In effect, the schools visited were little more than child-minding centres, when they were open at all. Further, it was a virtually unanimous view among residents of the sample villages that the problems of teacher absenteeism and shirking had consistently increased over time.

These field observations are not exceptional. For instance, the main findings of Prasad's (1987) investigation of the functioning of village schools in backward areas of Andhra Pradesh bear striking resemblance with those reported for Uttar Pradesh by Drèze and Gazdar (1996) in the companion volume.[34] Other studies and first-hand reports have also highlighted the pervasive problem of non-functioning or poor functioning of village schools in many parts of the country, especially the large north Indian states.[35] The record of the schooling system is not uniformly poor (some states have done much better than others in this respect), but the deplorable quality of schooling facilities in large parts of rural India is certainly a major issue.

It is tempting to look for increased reliance on private schools as an easy remedy for the inadequacies of the public sector. There is certainly no reason to decry the expansion of private schooling,

[33] See the case study of Uttar Pradesh by Drèze and Gazdar (1996) in the companion volume. The districts included in this field investigation are Moradabad (western UP), Rae Bareli (central UP), Pratapgarh (eastern UP), and Banda (southern UP).

[34] Among the similarities of interest is the widespread prevalence, in both Andhra Pradesh and Uttar Pradesh, of a system of implicit sub-contracting of teaching duties by government teachers to private teachers. See Drèze and Gazdar (1996) for further discussion.

[35] See e.g. Narain (1972) and Ghose (1993) on Rajasthan, Shankari (1993) on Andhra Pradesh, Middleton et al. (1993) on Uttar Pradesh, and Sainath (1993) on Bihar. Anil Bordia, former Education Secretary, takes the view that 'a large proportion of schools do not function in most parts of the country' (Bordia, 1993, p. 8). Even the Government of India (1993d) acknowledges 'the chronic problem of teacher absenteeism' (p. 31) in states such as Rajasthan. See Weiner (1991), chapter 4 for some further testimonies, including that of a senior Education Department official who candidly stated: 'The teachers aren't any good. Often they don't even appear at the school... our schools are trash!'

where such an expansion takes place. Indeed, private schools already make a significant contribution to the availability of schooling facilities in India, even in rural areas. But the private sector has already shown its limitations, as far as basic education in rural areas is concerned, and the reasons are not hard to follow, given the poverty of the potential students. In fact, private schooling facilities are overwhelmingly biased in favour of secondary or tertiary education, urban areas, and male children.[36]

There is, in short, no escape from the need for a major improvement of public schooling facilities in rural India. Two essential steps in that direction are to increase the number of teachers, and to ensure that they teach. While the first step is primarily a matter of financial commitment, the second one raises more difficult organizational issues. Given that school teachers have permanent posts, and a good deal of bureaucratic protection, the basic incentive structure is very weak.

A substantial increase in the number of teachers, by itself, could be expected to lead to better teaching performance of individual teachers. Indeed, field studies suggest that teaching standards tend to be higher in schools with more teachers.[37] As many observers have noted, teaching standards are particularly low in single-teacher schools, which accounted for almost *one-third* of all primary schools in 1986.[38] Work motivation cannot be expected to be very high for a single teacher who acts as his or her own supervisor, and has a guaranteed job irrespective—in practice—of performance. Also, motivation would

---

[36] For further discussion of these issues, see Drèze and Gazdar (1996); also Tilak (1993, 1994a). On the bias of private schooling facilities in favour of higher education levels and urban areas, see the Fifth All-India Education Survey (National Council of Educational Research and Training, 1992), pp. 384–5. According to this survey, the private sector ('aided' and 'unaided' combined) accounted for 54 per cent of all secondary schools in 1986, but only 7 per cent of all primary schools, and barely 3 per cent of primary schools in rural areas. Even after allowing for some underestimation of the number of primary schools in the private sector (given the difficulty of identifying small informal schools in rural areas), the contribution of the private sector to primary schooling appears to be very limited, especially in comparison with its contribution to secondary schooling.

[37] See Drèze and Gazdar (1996). Possible reasons for the positive relationship between teaching standards and the number of teachers include peer monitoring effects, competition between teachers, and greater scope for supervision. Larger schools also tend to be more visible, making it harder to shelter them from public scrutiny.

[38] National Council of Educational Research and Training (1992), p. 895. Here again, there are striking regional variations, with the proportion of single-teacher schools being below 1 per cent in Kerala but well above 50 per cent in Rajasthan.

not be enough: teaching five different grades simultaneously also demands extraordinary skill. Even in two-teacher schools, teaching practices are likely to be poor, if only because frequent absenteeism transforms these schools into single-teacher schools for a large part of the year.[39] In 1986, the proportion of primary schools with only one or two teachers was above 60 per cent in India as a whole.[40] Better staffing of schools is one important means of improving teaching standards.

Other means of improving work incentives and teaching performance require discriminating assessment. The best hope may well be the vigilance of parents. Unlike government inspectors, who seem to prosper by extorting bribes from shirking teachers, parents have a strong personal interest in an improved performance of school teachers.[41] The problem is that, as things stand, they have no easy means of taking action. In most states, teachers are accountable to the Education Department, not to the village community. Official complaints have to go through complicated bureaucratic channels, and are particularly difficult to make for parents who are themselves illiterate. Reforming the chain of accountability, and bringing the levers of control closer to the village community, are important means of improving teaching standards. In fact, this route has already been used with good effect in some parts of the country. In Karnataka, for instance, it is reported that 'after the panchayati raj system was implemented... attendance of primary school teachers and health workers went up by 91 per cent'.[42] In Tamil Nadu, too, it has

---

[39] According to Middleton et al. (1993), school teachers in Uttar Pradesh 'frequently take turns in attending' (p. 11). The same observation is made in the survey of village schools in Uttar Pradesh by Drèze and Gazdar (1996), mentioned earlier.

[40] Tyagi (1993), p. 88. The corresponding figure for Kerala is 1 per cent. In fact, in Kerala, 94 per cent of primary schools have four teachers or more. The figures cited in this paragraph relate to 1986 because more recent figures are not available. Given the slow rate of growth of the number of primary-school teachers in recent years (see section 6.4), it is unlikely that a major improvement in teacher–school ratios has taken place since then.

[41] For a good case study of the ineffectiveness of official school inspection procedures, see Prasad (1987), pp. 75–81.

[42] L.C. Jain, cited in Ford Foundation (1992), and based on the recent Krishnaswamy Report. A more recent study (Crook and Manor, 1994) also finds that the recent decentralization experiment in Karnataka has considerably reduced absenteeism and shirking among teachers, health workers, and other government employees in rural areas. As the authors put it, 'all manner of government employees were now made to work because they were for the first time under the supervision of the questioning public mind' (Crook and Manor, 1994, p. 37). For similar observations, see also Gadgil and

been observed that 'close monitoring by a politically conscious parent community' has been an essential factor in the success of pre-school education and school meal programmes (Swaminathan, 1991, p. 2989). Community institutions and the building up of public accountability have also played a crucial role in the history of Kerala's educational expansion (Krishnan, 1994, Santha, 1994, Ramachandran, 1996).

The recent Panchayati Raj legislation offers new opportunities for extending these experiments elsewhere in India. Given the highly unequal character of the rural society, and the frequent connections between government teachers and local leaders, it would be unwise to expect an automatic transformation of the quality of schooling facilities as a result of the decentralization measures involved in this legislation.[43] But the initiatives that will be taken by different state governments within that framework are worth careful monitoring and evaluation. There may also be much to learn from the experiences of states that have already been relatively successful in improving the performance of village teachers. The first step is to recognize that the poor quality of schooling facilities in rural India is a major social issue, which calls for urgent investigation and action.

## 6.6. *Provision, Utilization and Compulsion*

An expansion of the quantity and quality of schooling facilities in India can be expected to lead, on its own, to a large increase in school attendance and educational achievements. Indeed, empirical studies suggest that popular demand for basic education in India is strong—at least strong enough to induce most parents to send their young children to school in situations where a free and well-functioning school is available close to their homes.[44] One symptom

---

Guha (1993), p. 79, Vyasulu (1993), Aziz (1994), p. 26, Seetharamu (1994), p. 45.

[43] In fact, the results so far have been rather disappointing in most states (this is one of the major conclusions of a recent Seminar on Management of Education under Panchayati Raj held at the National Institute of Educational Planning and Administration; see also NIEPA, 1994). This outcome partly reflects the fact that there has been far more promise than action, as far as decentralization is concerned. It also relates to the point, discussed in section 5.5, that legislative reform alone is not an adequate basis for the promotion of local democracy.

[44] For some empirical studies pointing in this direction, see J.C. Caldwell et al. (1985), Prasad (1987), Nautiyal (1989), Alderman et al. (1993), Drèze and Saran (1995), and the case study of Uttar Pradesh by Drèze and Gazdar (1996) in the companion volume. The specific problem of low parental motivation for female education will be discussed in

of this strong demand for basic education is the fact that, when the local school functions poorly, parents often send their children (especially boys) to study in other villages with better schools, or in private schools where fees have to be paid. While the blame for low attendance levels is often put on reluctant parents, the inadequacy of the schooling establishment may well be the more basic failure.

A good example of what can be achieved on the basis of a sustained expansion of the quantity and quality of schooling facilities is provided by Himachal Pradesh. As recently as 1961, crude literacy rates in Himachal Pradesh (21 per cent for males and 9 per cent for females) were below the corresponding all-India averages.[45] By 1987–8, literacy rates in the 10–14 age group in Himachal Pradesh were as high as 95 per cent for males and 81 per cent for females in rural areas, and even higher in urban areas (96 per cent for males and 97 per cent for females); in that respect, Himachal Pradesh was second to Kerala among the major states.[46] In the same year, 93 per cent of boys aged 10–14 in Himachal Pradesh were attending school—the same figure as in Kerala. For girls in the same age group, Himachal Pradesh did a little better than Kerala in urban areas (95 per cent attendance, compared with 94 per cent in Kerala), but not so in rural areas (91 per cent attendance in Kerala but only 73 per cent in Himachal Pradesh). Even for female attendance in rural areas, Himachal Pradesh was well ahead of all states other than Kerala.[47] The strong commitment of the state government and community institutions to a rapid expansion and improvement of schooling facilities has played a major part in this success.[48]

Aside from this scope for expanding educational achievements by improving the availability and quality of schooling facilities, public

---

section 6.7.

[45] Karkal (1991), Table 5, based on census data.

[46] Sengupta (1991); see also Statistical Appendix.

[47] The school attendance figures are from P. Visaria et al. (1993), based on NSS data; see Statistical Appendix for further details.

[48] On this, see e.g. Goyal and Mehrotra (1995) and Centre for Development Economics (forthcoming). One sign of this commitment is a high level of public expenditure on education. Per-capita government expenditure on education in Himachal Pradesh is about twice as high as the all-India average (Tyagi, 1993, p. 122). The teacher–population ratio is also twice as high as the national average, and a good deal higher than in any of the other major states (calculated from Government of India, 1994f, p. 289).

policy must also seek to promote the *utilization* of existing facilities. The most common reasons for non-attendance or non-enrolment reported in household surveys are, in order of frequency, (1) the high opportunity cost of children's time (in terms of forgone earnings in wage labour, forgone production in household activities, forgone help with minding younger children, etc.), and (2) 'lack of interest in education'.[49] These answers, of course, have to be interpreted in the light of the current functioning of the schooling system in different regions of the country. 'Interest in education', for instance, is likely to be a function of the quality of teaching. Bearing in mind the low standards of teaching in large parts of the country, it is no surprise that many children quickly lose interest in going to school.[50] But these responses also tell us that insufficient valuation of education (relative to child labour, leisure, or other activities) on the part of young children or—more plausibly—their parents may contribute to low attendance levels.

That issue may be particularly relevant in the case of social groups for whom education has traditionally been considered unimportant. We have referred earlier, for instance, to the old notion that education is not important for members of the 'lower' castes. Whatever survives of this notion cannot but affect (1) the educational aspirations of children from these castes, (2) the parental and social support which they receive in pursuit of these aspirations, and (3) the strength of public commitment to the promotion of education among these disadvantaged groups. There is, indeed, some evidence that school attendance levels are particularly low among disadvantaged castes even after controlling for other relevant variables such as household income and educational facilities.[51]

As far as public policy is concerned, there are several ways of addressing the possible problem of inadequate parental motivation and high opportunity cost of schooling. In some parts of India,

---

[49] See e.g. J.C. Caldwell et al. (1985), Prasad (1987), Minhas (1992), P. Visaria et al. (1993), and *Sarvekshana*, January–March 1991; also the earlier literature cited in Patil (1984).

[50] The surveys mentioned here (in particular, the National Sample Survey) make no room for responses such as 'teacher absenteeism', 'lack of learning activities in the school', etc., as possible reasons for non-enrolment.

[51] See the case studies by Drèze and Gazdar (1996) and Sengupta and Gazdar (1996) in the companion volume. Similar considerations apply to female education (on which more in the next section).

notably Tamil Nadu and Kerala, school meals and related incentives have been used with good effect to boost school attendance rates.[52] Popular attitudes to education can also be decisively influenced by active public campaigns; that, indeed, is one of the chief lessons of the recent Total Literacy Campaign.[53] More extensive use can be made of these and other means of promoting school attendance.[54]

Compulsory education is another frequently-advocated means of intervention. On this issue, the inconsistencies of official policy have been particularly flagrant. As was mentioned earlier, official pronouncements urging a rapid introduction of compulsory education until the age of 14 have been made at regular intervals. In contrast to this appearance of official commitment to compulsory education, most policy-makers are of the view that compulsory education is a bad idea, or that it will take many years before compulsory education is feasible or desirable.[55]

It is time to address these inconsistencies, and to initiate a reasoned debate on compulsory education and the forms it might take. The issues involved are quite complex and call for detailed analysis as well as empirical investigation. There is a need to go beyond all-or-nothing positions which fail to do justice to the range of feasible options. For instance, to suggest that compulsory education can be effectively introduced at once in the whole of India and for all children in the 6–14 age group is as counterproductive as the argument that compulsory education is not an issue at all. A concrete proposal has to take into account the inadequacies of the schooling system, the danger of harassment of child labourers, the economic dependence of particular groups (such as young widows) on child labour, and so on. It must also take note of the possibility of perversion of

[52] See e.g. Babu and Hallam (1989), Swaminathan (1991), R. Singh (1994), and Mehrotra (1995). For wide-ranging suggestions of means to improve school attendance in India, see Patil (1984).

[53] See particularly Ghosh et al. (1994), who report that 'tremendous enhancement of demand for primary education and enrolment of children in primary schools have been noticed in many literacy campaign districts' (p. 23).

[54] The feeble nature of earlier campaigns to influence popular perceptions of the value of education contrasts with the extraordinary propaganda efforts that have been made in the field of family planning. These efforts may have contributed to the relatively wide acceptance of a 'small family' norm: according to a recent survey, only 30 per cent of Indian women with two children (and 15 per cent of women with three children) want to have another child (International Institute for Population Sciences, 1994, Table 14).

[55] For a wide range of relevant testimonies, see Weiner (1991).

standards that may result from nominal compliance to overexacting bureaucratic demands.[56] In practice, the desirability and feasibility of introducing compulsory education must depend quite crucially on the proposed time frame, the precise age limits, the enforcement mechanism to be used, the social security arrangements that can be introduced to obviate the need for child labour, and other relevant parameters.

It is also worth remembering that much clarity can be gained on some of these issues on the basis of a *gradual* introduction of compulsory education. Since state governments and local authorities are empowered to introduce compulsory education in the areas under their jurisdiction, there is no need to think only in terms of an all–India policy. The way ahead may well be to begin with compulsory education for the 6–10 age group (corresponding to the primary stage) in the more advanced states, and to expand the scope of compulsory education on the basis of the experiences gained there. Of course, a gradual approach involves some danger of slowing down the whole process. But the process is even slower when it takes the form of setting lofty goals that cannot proceed beyond the stage of pious statements.

Finally, compulsory education *on its own* is obviously not an adequate programme of public action for the promotion of basic education. It can be an important *part* of such a programme, but the more exacting issue is the need for a substantial improvement of the schooling system. Making it legally compulsory for children to attend schools that cannot receive them would not be a great gift.

## 6.7. *On Female Education*

The recognition of female education as a social issue is very recent in India. The dominant Brahminical tradition reserves the study of the Vedas to men of the twice-born castes, and tends to consider female education as a threat to the social order. Female scholars and writers make occasional appearances in Indian history (and there

---

[56] For an example of this phenomenon, see Prasad's (1987) case study of education in Andhra Pradesh, where government pressure to increase enrolment figures at all cost has proved rather counterproductive in a number of ways, aside from failing to lead to a genuine increase in actual attendance: 'the actual attendance during the day(s) of my investigation was between 20–30 per cent of the impressive number of children found in the school records in most of the villages' (Prasad, 1987, p. 76).

are also many examples of remarkable female intellectuals, such as Maitreyi and Gargee, in the ancient scriptures), but widespread female literacy is a twentieth-century phenomenon.[57] In fact, at the end of the nineteenth century, the female literacy rate was still below *one* per cent in every province of British India and every 'native state', with a few exceptions such as Coorg, the Andaman and Nicobar Islands, and the native states of Travancore and Cochin in what is now Kerala.[58] Even in Travancore and Cochin, the female literacy rate was below one per cent as late as 1875, and remained as low as 3 per cent in 1901.[59]

Against this historical background, the expansion of female literacy in the twentieth century (and particularly after independence) is a positive development. In comparative international terms, however, India's record in this respect remains dismal. For instance, as we saw in chapter 3, the available estimates suggest that adult female literacy is higher even in sub-Saharan Africa than in India. A comparison with China (let alone south-east Asia) is even more sobering: in India, half of all females in the 15–19 age group are illiterate, compared with less than 10 per cent in China (see chapter 4).

The poor functioning of India's schooling system, discussed earlier, is one reason for the persistence of endemic female illiteracy. In this connection, it is important to stress that the failure of government primary schools in large parts of the country in not gender-neutral, especially in rural areas. As discussed in the case study of Uttar Pradesh in the companion volume (see Drèze and Gazdar, 1996), a common response of parents to the poor functioning or non-functioning of a government-run village school is to send their sons to study in other villages, or in private schools. But the same response is far less common in the case of girls, because parents are often reluctant to allow their daughters to wander outside the village, or to pay the fees that would be necessary to secure their admission in a private school. The breakdown of a government village school typically affects female children more than male children.[60]

[57] A useful anthology of women's writings in Indian history can be found in Tharu and Lalita (1991).

[58] Census of India, 1901. The female literacy rate was also above 1 per cent in what is now Myanmar (Burma), where it was around 4 per cent.

[59] Census figures on literacy rates in Kerala are presented in the chapter by V.K. Ramachandran (1996) in the companion volume.

[60] Another aspect of the poor quality of the schooling system which may also discourage

This is not say that low levels of female education in India are exclusively due to the poor functioning of the schooling system. Indeed, field investigations indicate that, even when local teaching standards are relatively good, male participation in education is usually much higher than female participation.[61] The problem of low parental motivation for female education needs attention on its own, in addition to the issue of poor functioning of the schooling system.

The low value attached to female education in much of India links with some deep-rooted features of gender relations. Three of these links have been widely observed.[62]

First, the gender division of labour (combined with patrilineal property rights) tends to reduce the perceived benefits of female education. In rural India, a large majority of girls are expected to spend most of their adult life in domestic work and child-rearing (and possibly some family labour in agriculture). It is in the light of these social expectations about the adult life of women that female education appears to many parents to be somewhat 'pointless'. Of course, female education can bring immense benefits even within the limited field of domestic work and child-rearing, but these benefits do not always receive adequate recognition.[63]

Second, the norms of patrilocal residence and village exogamy (requiring a woman to settle in her husband's village at the time of marriage, in effect forcing her to sever most links with her own family), prevalent in large parts of India, have the effect of further undermining the economic incentives which parents might have to

---

female education more than male education is the low number of female teachers in many states. While the proportion of female teachers among primary-school teachers is as high as 63 per cent in Kerala, the corresponding figure is only 29 per cent for India as a whole, 18 per cent in Uttar Pradesh, and 13 per cent in rural Uttar Pradesh (Government of India, 1992b, p. 307). Further, there is considerable evidence that, in north India in particular, daughters are often withdrawn from school due to the absence of female teachers or of separate schools for girls (see Patil, 1984). According to Gupta et al. (1993), p. 55, 'reluctance to have daughters taught by male teachers may begin as early as 7 to 8 years of age'.

[61] See e.g. J.C. Caldwell et al. (1985).

[62] For further discussion, see Drèze and Saran (1995). The focus of the present discussion is primarily on rural areas.

[63] This lack of recognition derives partly from an observational bias (the benefits of female education in household-based activities are less easy to identify than, say, differences in salaries between educated and uneducated men), and partly from the general undervaluation of female activities in a patriarchal society.

send their daughters to school. Since 'an Indian girl is but a sojourner in her own family', as Sudhir Kakar (1979) aptly puts it, the investments that parents make in the education of a daughter primarily 'benefit' other, often distant households. This can strongly reduce the perceived value of female education, at least from the point of view of parental self-interest. The perception is neatly summed up in such popular sayings as 'bringing up a daughter is like watering a plant in another's courtyard'.[64]

Third, the practice of dowry and the ideology of hypergamous marriage (it being thought best that a woman should marry 'up' in the social scale), also influential in large parts of India, can turn female education into a liability. If an educated girl can only marry a *more* educated boy, and if dowry payments increase with the education of the groom, then, given other things, an educated girl is likely to be more expensive to marry off. There is some evidence that this preoccupation is quite real for many parents.[65]

Given these and other links between female education and gender relations, it is not surprising that the twentieth-century progress of female education has been particularly slow in areas of India (such as the large north Indian states) where the gender division of labour, patrilineal inheritance, patrilocal residence, village exogamy, hypergamous marriage, and related patriarchal norms tend to be particularly influential.[66] The positive side of the same coin is that the expansion of female literacy has been comparatively rapid in areas where gender

[64] Quoted by Leela Dube (1988), p. 168. Interestingly, this is a Telugu proverb, confirming the notion that the social influence of patrilocal residence norms is not confined to north India (as Dube herself observes), even though it may be stronger there. For a fine empirical investigation of the relationship between patrilocal residence, village exogamy, and the relative neglect of female children, see Kishor (1993).

[65] The problem has been noted, for instance, in Committee on the Status of Women in India (1974), p. 74, Almeida (1978), p. 264, Seetharamu and Ushadevi (1985), van Bastelaer (1986), p. 61, and Khan (1993). Here again the problem is not confined to north India, even though dowry is more widely practised in that region. In rural Karnataka, for instance, some parents are reported to be worried that education 'would make daughters unmarriageable', because a woman 'must be married to a male with at least as much education' (J.C. Caldwell et al., 1985, pp. 39, 41).

[66] Punjab and Haryana might seem like exceptions to this pattern. But in fact, the record of these two states in the field of female literacy is quite poor, if one controls for their high income levels. While Punjab and Haryana come first and second in the income scale, they only come fifth and tenth, respectively, in the scale of female literacy (see Table 3.3 in chapter 3). Punjab, however, provides a good example of how attitudes to female education can, in some circumstances, change quite rapidly.

relations are less patriarchal. Kerala is the most obvious example, but the same observation applies to much of south India, and also to parts of the Himalayan region in north and north-east India, including Manipur, Meghalaya, and Himachal Pradesh.[67]

Another important corollary of the preceding observations is that the considerations involved in educational decisions are radically different for boys and girls. In the case of male education, the economic incentives are strong, because improved education enhances employment prospects, and parents have a strong stake in the economic advancement of their sons (including—but not exclusively—for reasons of improved old-age security). The influence of these economic motives in educational decisions relating to male children emerges quite clearly in household surveys.[68] Economic returns and parental self-interest, on the other hand, provide very weak incentives for female education, given the prevailing gender division of labour, marriage practices, and property rights. Parental concern for the well-being of a daughter in her own right, and recognition of the contribution which education can make to the quality of her life (and that of others), are more important motivations.

This contrast has strong implications for public policy. As far as male education is concerned, parental motivation is generally high, and can be expected to reinforce any efforts that are made to improve the schooling system. In the case of female education, however, it is particularly important to address the conservatism of social attitudes and parental inertia. As it happens, there is some evidence that the value attached to female education in India can change very substantially over a relatively short period of time under the impact of economic change, public action, and social movements.[69] Even in states such as Rajasthan, where

---

[67] These three states have the highest female literacy rates in the country after Kerala, for the younger age groups (see Sengupta, 1991, pp. 27–8). Several studies have noted the relatively egalitarian character of gender relations in parts of the Himalayan region (Berreman, 1962, 1993, Sopher, 1980a, Miller, 1981, Agnihotri, 1995), some symptoms of which include high female–male ratios in the population, high female labour force participation rates, and a female advantage in child survival (see Nuna, 1990, for some evidence). For Manipur, Meghalaya, and Himachal Pradesh, these features are quite well documented (see e.g. B. Agarwal, 1989, A.K. Shiva Kumar, 1992, Sharma, 1980).

[68] For some relevant studies, see J.C. Caldwell et al. (1985), Raza and Ramachandran (1990), Alderman et al. (1993), Drèze and Saran (1995).

[69] This has been noted in several field studies, including J.C. Caldwell et al. (1985), Chanana (1993), and Vlassoff (1993). The experience of the recent Total Literacy Campaign is particularly instructive in this regard. On the high involvement of women

gender bias in education and related gender inequalities are extremely large, there have been some encouraging cases of rapid change in attitudes to female education, driven by well-planned campaigns.[70] There is a need for more activism in that direction, if the expansion of female education is not to trail well behind that of male education in the future, as in the past.

## 6.8. *Education and Political Action*

In this chapter, we have had occasion to present brief comments on a number of shortcomings of government activity in the field of basic education, including the inconsistencies of official statistics (section 6.2), the confusion of educational policy (section 6.3), the inadequacy and poor use of education expenditure (section 6.4), the mismanagement and lack of accountability of the schooling establishment in rural areas (section 6.5), the absence of a serious debate on compulsory education (section 6.6), the neglect of female education (section 6.7), among others. We have also argued that a deep lack of real commitment to the widespread and equitable provision of basic education lies at the root of these diverse failures (section 6.1).

What is perhaps most striking of all is that the failures of government policy over an extended period have provoked so little political challenge. Had the government shown similar apathy and inconsistency in dealing with, say, the demands of the urban population for basic amenities, or of farmers' organizations for adequately high crop prices, or of the military establishment for modern hardware, or of the World Bank for structural adjustment measures, it is safe to predict that a major political battle would have followed. The fact that the government was able to get away with so much neglect in the field of primary education relates to the lack of political clout of the illiterate masses (we have commented on this issue in section 5.1). It also reflects the fact, discussed at the beginning of this chapter, that the social value of basic education has been neglected not only by government authorities but also in social and political movements.

Much the same remarks also apply at the local level. The case

---

in this campaign (both as learners and as instructors), and the diverse achievements linked with this positive response, see Ghosh et al. (1994); also Sengupta (1992), Agnihotri and Sivaswamy (1993), Saldanha (1994).

[70] See e.g. Ghosh (1991), Rokadiya et al. (1993), Ghosh et al. (1994), and evaluation reports on the Mahila Samakhya programme in different states.

study of Uttar Pradesh by Drèze and Gazdar (1996) in the companion volume, for instance, shows how it is quite possible for a village school to be non-functional for as long as ten years (due to teacher absenteeism and shirking) without any action being taken and any collective protest being organized.[71] There is a crucial contrast to be found here between Uttar Pradesh and Kerala, where a comparable state of affairs would not be passively tolerated.[72] It is, of course, also the case that public expenditure on education is higher in Kerala than in Uttar Pradesh, and this factor is undoubtedly important in Kerala's higher educational achievements. But this difference in expenditure levels is much less striking than the difference relating to the politics of education. In fact, Uttar Pradesh is notorious for having considerably *underutilized* the large grants that have been made available to that state in recent years (by the central government as well as international agencies) for primary education.[73] Similarly, in Uttar Pradesh, very little interest has been taken in the recent Total Literacy Campaign, and, as a result, almost nothing has been gained from it (in contrast with the positive achievements observed in several other states, including Kerala where this campaign was initially launched).[74] The main constraint on educational expansion in Uttar Pradesh is not basically a financial one—it is the low importance attached to basic education in public policy.[75] The responsibility

[71] Similar observations have been made for other states of north India. Narain (1972), for instance, notes that in Rajasthan 'all the villagers may be dissatisfied with a school teacher, yet if he is in the good books of the *sarpanch* and *pradhan* he is not transferred' (p. 152).

[72] The same point has been made with reference to health services; see, for example, Mencher (1980), Nag (1989), and Ramachandran (1996). Mencher, in particular, stresses the role of 'political awareness' in ensuring the effective functioning of health services in Kerala: 'In Kerala, if a PHC was unmanned for a few days, there would be a massive demonstration at the nearest collectorate led by local leftists, who would demand to be given what they knew they were entitled to. This had the effect of making health care much more readily available for the poor in Kerala' (p. 1782). This account is in sharp contrast with the corresponding state of affairs in Uttar Pradesh, where widespread absenteeism of government doctors is passively accepted as a normal state of affairs (see e.g. Khan et al., 1986).

[73] We are grateful to Dr Vaidyanatha Ayyar (Joint Secretary, Department of Education, New Delhi) for drawing our attention to this fact.

[74] See Ghosh et al. (1994), who attribute this poor response in Uttar Pradesh to a 'low political commitment to the eradication of illiteracy' in that state (p. 39).

[75] In the very same state of Uttar Pradesh, students enrolled for higher education are a significant political force. The fact that the first decision taken by the newly-elected

for this failure lies not only with the government, but also with the political movements in this part of India.

Ultimately, the expansion of basic education in India depends a great deal on these political factors. There is no question that, even in a country as poor as India, means can be found to ensure universal attainment of literacy and other basic educational achievements, at least in the younger age groups. There are important strategic questions to consider in implementing that social commitment, but the primary challenge is to make it a more compelling political issue.

government of Uttar Pradesh in December 1993 was to repeal the Anti-Copying Act (sic) is a symptomatic example of their influence. Incidentally, the Anti-Copying Act should not be mistaken for copyright legislation. It is what it says—an act outlawing the practice of copying in higher-education examinations; this restriction has now been largely revoked.

# GENDER INEQUALITY AND WOMEN'S AGENCY

## 7.1. *Female Deprivation and Missing Women*

Inequality between men and women is one of the most crucial disparities in many societies, and this is particularly so in India. Differences in female and male literacy rates, discussed in the last chapter, are one aspect of this broader phenomenon of gender-based inequality in India. In much of the country, women tend in general to fare quite badly in relative terms compared with men, even within the same families. This is reflected not only in such matters as education and opportunity to develop talents, but also in the more elementary fields of nutrition, health, and survival. Indeed, the mortality rates of females tend to exceed those of males until the late twenties, and even the late thirties in some states, and this—as we know from the experiences of other countries—is very much in contrast with what tends to happen when men and women receive similar nutritional and health care.[1] One result is a remarkably low ratio of females to males in the Indian population compared with the corresponding ratio not only in Europe and North America, but also in sub-Saharan Africa. The problem is not, of course, unique to India, but it is particularly serious in this country, and certainly deserves public attention as a matter of major priority.

There are, in fact, striking variations in the ratio of females to males in the population (hereafter 'female–male ratio', or FMR for short) in different regions of the world. While there are important

---

[1] See Sen (1992c), and the literature cited there; see also Kynch (1985).

social and cultural influences on survival rates,[2] there is fairly strong medical evidence to the effect that—given similar care—women tend to have lower age-specific mortality rates than men (indeed, even female foetuses are relatively less prone to miscarriage than their male counterparts). Even though males outnumber females at birth (and even more at conception), women tend to outnumber men substantially in Europe and North America, with an average ratio around 1.05. While that includes some remnant effects of greater male mortality in past wars, the ratio would still be considerably above unity after adjusting for that. In contrast, many parts of the Third World have female–male ratios substantially below unity, for example, 0.96 in North Africa, 0.94 in China, Bangladesh, and West Asia. The average FMR in India is around 0.93—one of the lowest in the world (it is no consolation that Pakistan's ratio of 0.91 is even lower).[3] There is much direct evidence, in India and in the other countries with a sharp 'deficit' of women, of relative neglect of the health and well-being of women (particularly young girls including female infants), leading to survival disadvantage of females *vis-à-vis* males over long periods.

It is easily calculated that no matter what female–male ratio we use as a benchmark for comparison (whether the FMR in contemporary Europe, or in sub-Saharan Africa, or one based on the historical experience of parts of Europe), we would find that there are many millions of 'missing women' in India. The sub-Saharan African ratio had yielded the colossal number of 37 million missing women in India in 1986 (Drèze and Sen, 1989, Table 4.1, p. 52).[4] Klasen's history-based calculation suggests figures closer to 35 million. These are gigantic figures—and again there is no consolation here in the

---

[2] On this see particularly Johansson (1991) and Alaka Basu (1992). See also Sopher (1980b) and Dyson and Moore (1983).

[3] On this see Bardhan (1974, 1984a, 1988), Mitra (1979), Miller (1981), Kynch and Sen (1982), Kynch (1985), Sen (1984, 1985c, 1989, 1992c), Mazumdar (1985), Drèze and Sen (1989), Coale (1992), and Klasen (1994).

[4] It was on the basis of the sub-Saharan African FMR that the figure of 'more than a hundred million missing women' was presented for Asia and north Africa as a whole in Drèze and Sen (1989) and Sen (1989). Coale (1991) suggested a number closer to 60 million, on the basis of the historical experience of Europe, whereas Klasen (1994) arrives at around 90 million missing women on a different reading of the European experience. While refinements of the exact numbers can certainly continue, it is important to emphasize that no matter which standard FMR we use, we do get incredibly large numbers of missing women.

fact that the absolute number of missing women (though not its ratio to the population) in China is estimated to be even higher—between 38 and 40 million. We do have a problem of basic inequality here of extraordinary proportions.

## 7.2. *On the Female–Male Ratio*

We have noted in the preceding section that India has an exceptionally low female–male ratio. This problem is not, of course, equally acute in every region of India. As noted in chapter 3, there are large variations in the female–male ratio between different states. The female–male ratio is particularly low in large parts of north India, especially the north-western states (e.g. 0.87 in Haryana, 0.88 in Punjab and Uttar Pradesh, 0.91 in Rajasthan), and comparatively high in the south (e.g. 0.97 in Tamil Nadu and Andhra Pradesh, 0.96 in Karnataka). In Kerala, the female–male ratio is well above unity; in fact, it is as high as 1.04, a figure comparable to that of Europe and North America.[5]

These regional patterns of female–male ratios are consistent with what is known of the character of gender relations in different parts of the country. The north-western states, for instance, are notorious for highly unequal gender relations, some symptoms of which include the continued practice of female seclusion, very low female labour-force participation rates, a large gender gap in literacy rates, extremely restricted female property rights, strong boy preference in fertility decisions, widespread neglect of female children, and drastic separation of a married woman from her natal family. In all these respects, the social standing of women is somewhat better in south India.[6] And Kerala, of course, has a distinguished history of a more liberated position of women in society.[7] Important aspects of this history include a major success in the expansion of female literacy (see chapter 4), considerable prominence of women in influential social and political

[5] Kerala's high female–male ratio is partly due to high levels of male outmigration, but even the migration-adjusted female–male ratio is well above unity (see e.g. Agnihotri, 1994).

[6] On these regional contrasts in gender relations, see Karve (1965), Bardhan (1974, 1984), Sopher (1980a, 1980b), Miller (1981), Dyson and Moore (1983), Kolenda (1984), Jain and Banerjee (1985), Caldwell and Caldwell (1987), Mandelbaum (1988), Alaka Basu (1992), Gupta, Basu, and Asthana (1993), Agarwal (1994), Agnihotri (1995), among others.

[7] See e.g. Robin Jeffrey (1992).

activities, and a tradition of matrilineal inheritance for an important section of the population.[8]

These regional contrasts, and also changes in the female–male ratio over time, provide a useful means of investigating different aspects of the problem of low female–male ratios in India. This investigation will be pursued a little further in this section and the next one. The motivation for focusing on the female–male ratio is partly that this indicator of gender inequality is important in its own right, and partly that it sheds some interesting light on other aspects of gender relations.

## Two misconceptions

To begin with, we should deal with two misunderstandings that arise from time to time in popular discussions of the issue of low female–male ratios in India.

First, it is sometimes thought that the main cause of the problem is some phenomenon of hidden female infanticide, not captured in reported death statistics. In fact, census figures on female–male ratios are quite consistent with what one would predict based on (1) a standard female–male ratio at birth of about 0.95, and (2) independently recorded age- and sex-specific mortality rates. To illustrate, the predicted female–male ratio at age 5 in India in 1981, using information on age-specific mortality rates from the Sample Registration System, is 0.921.[9] The *actual* female–male ratio at age 5 for that year, obtained from the 1981 census, is 0.920—very close to the predicted value.

It is possible, of course, that recorded child deaths include some female infant deaths due to infanticide, which are reported by the parents as due to some other cause. But the anthropological evidence suggests that female infanticide, when it does occur, takes place very

---

[8] Property has traditionally been inherited through the female line for a powerful community in Kerala—the Nairs. While the Nairs constitute about 20 per cent of the total population, and the practice has changed a good deal in recent years, nevertheless the social and political importance of a long tradition of this kind, which goes against the conventional Indian norms, must not be underestimated.

[9] This predicted female–male ratio at age 5 is calculated using the simple formula $FMR = (0.95) (1-q^f_5) / (1-q^m_5)$, where $q^f_5$ and $q^m_5$ are, respectively, the female and male probability of dying before the fifth birthday. The SRS-based estimates of $q^f_5$ and $q^m_5$ for 1976–80 are taken from Government of India (1988a), p. 3.

soon after birth.[10] The bulk of excess female mortality in childhood, on the other hand, occurs after the age of one, with a less unequal pattern in the first year. In 1981, for instance, 113 out of 1,000 male children born alive died before the age of one, compared with 115 out of 1,000 for female children; in contrast, of the surviving children, another 68 males died before the age of five, compared with as many as 91 females.[11]

The force of excess female mortality, therefore, lies in mortality rates in age groups beyond that of female infanticide. The female disadvantage in these age groups is itself due to a well-documented practice of preferential treatment of boys and neglect of female children in intra-household allocation. There is, indeed, considerable direct evidence of neglect of female children in terms of health care, nutrition, and related needs, particularly in north India.[12]

It may be argued that the deliberate neglect of female children ought to come under the label of infanticide. There might be a case for this, but the point to recognize is that the social practices that lead to excess female mortality are far more subtle and widespread than the graphic stories of infant drowning, poisoning, or asphyxiation that periodically make headlines in the newspapers.[13] This is not to deny that female infanticide, strictly defined, does indeed occur in India today and has done so in the past.[14]

The second misinterpretation concerns some alleged 'Muslim influence'. The reasoning, in so far as there is any, is that female–male

---

[10] See e.g. Panigrahi (1972), Miller (1981), George et al. (1992), and Venkatachalam and Srinivasan (1993).

[11] Calculated from Sample Registration System data presented in Government of India (1988a), p. 3. This pattern of concentration of excess female child mortality in the 1–5 age group is even more pronounced in the states where the problem of excess female mortality in childhood is particularly acute (e.g. Uttar Pradesh, Punjab, Haryana).

[12] See e.g. Chen, Huq, and D'souza (1981), Miller (1981), Kynch and Sen (1983), Sen and Sengupta (1983), Das Gupta (1987, 1994b), Alaka Basu (1989, 1992), M.E. Khan et al. (1989), Chatterjee (1990), Harriss (1990), B. Agarwal (1991), Deolalikar and Vashishta (1992), among many other studies. For a recent review, see Kishor (1994).

[13] A similar point might apply to the tendency to assume too readily that low female–male ratios in the younger age groups in China reflect explicit female infanticide on a large scale.

[14] Female infanticide has a long history in north India, and remains quite common in particular areas or communities; see e.g. Panigrahi (1972) and Miller (1981). See also George et al. (1992) and Venkatachalam and Srinivasan (1993) on the current practice of female infanticide in parts of south India.

ratios in India tend to be particularly low in the north-west of the country, which is geographically close to Islamic countries, has been under Muslim influence for a long time and, even now, has a large Muslim population.[15] But a glance at the figures immediately exposes the fragility of this hypothesis. The state of Kerala, which has the highest female–male ratio among Indian states (1.04 in 1991), comes second in terms of the proportion of Muslims in the population. The state with the lowest proportion of Muslims in the population (1 per cent in 1981) is Punjab, which has had the lowest female–male ratio among all Indian states until it was overtaken by Haryana in 1981. Haryana itself has an extremely small Muslim population (4 per cent of the total population).

We can take a closer look at this whole issue by examining the extent of gender bias in child mortality rates among Hindus and Muslims in different parts of India. The evidence is summarized in Figure 7.1. This diagram shows the ratio of female child mortality to male child mortality in different states, both for the Hindu population (on the horizontal axis) and for the Muslim population (on the vertical axis). The point representing a particular state lies to the right of the point marked '1' on the horizontal axis if and only if female mortality is higher than male mortality among Hindus, and above the point marked '1' on the vertical axis if the same statement applies for Muslims. Further, a state lies above the diagonal if and only if the ratio of female to male child mortality (which can be interpreted as a measure of anti-female bias in child survival) is *higher* among Muslims than among Hindus.[16]

This figure highlights two points. First, *regional* contrasts in the extent of gender bias in child survival are far more striking than the contrast relating to *religious identity*. Specifically, the relative survival chances of girls are low in large parts of north India (including Punjab, Haryana, Uttar Pradesh, Rajasthan, and Bihar), and this applies

---

[15] The political value of this kind of argument has not been lost on either side of the north-western border, judging from a recent report of the Pakistan Institute of Development Economics on the condition of women in Pakistan (Shah, 1986). In its analysis of the 'roots of the Pakistani woman's status' (pp. 19–21), this report primarily blames the historical influence of the 'traditions of the Hindu majority in undivided India' for the deprived condition of women in contemporary Pakistan.

[16] The mortality estimates on which Figure 7.1 is based are indirect estimates grounded on census information, and the individual numbers are subject to some margin of error. The purpose of Figure 7.1 is to highlight a broad pattern, rather than to convey precise estimates for particular states.

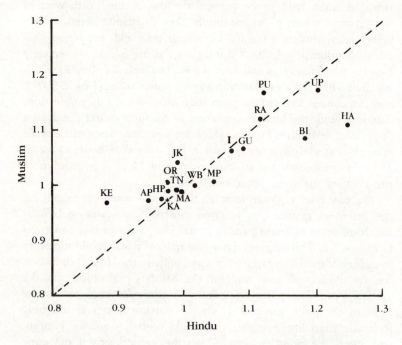

FIG. 7.1. *Ratio of Female to Male Child Mortality Among Hindus and Muslims in Different States, 1981*

*Note.* The horizontal axis indicates the ratio of female child mortality to male child mortality among Hindus in different states; similarly with Muslims on the vertical axis. The child mortality measure used here is '$q_5$', the probability of dying before age 5.

*Source.* Calculated from Government of India (1988a).

**I = India**

| | |
|---|---|
| AP = Andhra Pradesh | HP = Himachal Pradesh |
| BI = Bihar | HA = Haryana |
| GU = Gujarat | JK = Jammu & Kashmir |
| KA = Karnataka | KE = Kerala |
| MA = Maharashtra | MP = Madhya Pradesh |
| OR = Orissa | PU = Punjab |
| RA = Rajasthan | TN = Tamil Nadu |
| UP = Uttar Pradesh | WB = West Bengal |

whether they are Hindus or Muslims. Second, there is no evidence of any overall tendency for the female disadvantage to be particularly large among Muslims.

## Time trends

It is well known that the female–male ratio in India has steadily declined since the beginning of this century. In fact, there has been an almost monotonic decline from 1901 to 1991, when the female–male ratio in India reached its lowest-ever recorded value (927 females per 1,000 males).[17]

The same pattern does not apply at the state level, where a good deal of diversity can be found: since 1901, the female–male ratio has steadily declined in some states (e.g. Bihar, Uttar Pradesh, Orissa), steadily increased in others (e.g. Kerala, Himachal Pradesh), and fluctuated or stagnated in quite a few cases (e.g. West Bengal, Maharashtra).[18]

The root causes of the all-India decline are far from obvious.[19] The fall cannot be explained by sex-selective migration, enumeration biases, or a change in the sex ratio at birth.[20] Nor can it be attributed

[17] The decline of the female–male ratio from 1901 onwards was preceded by a slight rise between 1891 and 1901 (from 963 to 972). This may reflect the demographic effect of the famines of 1896–7 and 1899–1900. Indeed, male mortality typically rises more than female mortality in famine situations (Drèze and Sen, 1989, chapter 4), and this pattern applies in particular to late-nineteenth century famines in India (Maharatna, 1992). Further, the increase of India's female–male ratio between 1891 and 1901 was overwhelmingly concentrated in the districts that now make up the states of Madhya Pradesh, Maharashtra, Orissa, and Rajasthan, and each of these regions was severely affected by the famines of 1896–7 and 1899–1900 (see Bhatia, 1967).

[18] For the latest figures on state-specific female–male ratios since 1901, see Nanda (1992), pp. 102–3. Note that these state-specific female–male ratios, to be used further in this chapter, consistently refer to the 1991 state boundaries.

[19] Important contributions on this subject include P. Visaria (1961, 1967), Mitra (1979), Miller (1981, 1989), Bardhan (1984a, 1988), Dyson (1988), Kanitkar (1991), Kishor (1993), and Agnihotri (1994). It should be mentioned that the focus of this section is primarily on the long-term decline of the female–male ratio since 1901, rather than on the latest developments, which are quite complex and controversial. On the latter, see I. Sen (1986), Karkal (1987), Dyson (1988), Miller (1989), Kundu and Sahu (1991), Rajan et al. (1991, 1992), Srinivas (1991), Nanda (1992), Raju and Premi (1992), among others.

[20] See P. Visaria (1961) and Nanda (1992), pp. 9–14. The female–male ratio at birth has been declining in recent years, possibly due to sex-selective abortion. But this is a

to a change in the age distribution of the population (e.g. due to fertility decline). Indeed, if we combine 1981 age-specific female–male ratios with the 1901 age distribution of the population (available in S.B. Mukherjee, 1976), we obtain an overall female–male ratio of 936, very close to the actual female–male ratio of 934 in 1981. And similarly, combining the 1901 age-specific female–male ratios with the 1981 age distribution of the population, we find an overall female–male ratio of 976, very close to the actual 1901 female–male ratio of 972. The decline of India's female–male ratio over time is overwhelmingly due to the decline of age-specific female–male ratios, rather than to changes in the age distribution of the population.

Another possibility is that states with low initial female–male ratios have tended to experience faster population growth than others, pulling down the all-India average. This has indeed happened to some extent, but it only explains a very small part of the observed decline. In fact, had the 1901 state-specific female–male ratios remained unchanged to 1991, we would now observe an all-India female–male ratio of 970 per thousand (taking as given the current interstate distribution of the population), only 2 points down from the female–male ratio of 972 in 1901.[21]

The contribution of different states to the decline of the female–male ratio at the all-India level is examined in Table 7.1, where we decompose the all-India decline between 1901 and 1991 into: (a) a population-weighted sum of state-specific changes in female–male ratios; (b) a 'differential growth rate effect', which captures the fact that states with different initial female–male ratios grow at different rates (roughly speaking, this term tells us how the all-India female–male ratio would have changed, due to different state-specific population growth rates, had state-specific female–male ratios remained unchanged); and (c) a residual (or 'second-order term') which measures the difference between the actual FMR decline and the linear approximation to this decline obtained by adding up (a) and (b). In this table, the different states are arranged in descending order of female–male ratio in 1901 (except for the residual category of 'other

---

relatively new phenomenon, which cannot explain the sustained decline of the female–male ratio since 1901. In fact, a large-scale survey carried out in the nineteen-fifties in health institutions found a female–male ratio at birth of 942 (Nanda, 1992, p. 11), which is quite standard.

[21] The calculations are based on population figures for 1901 and 1991 presented in Nanda (1992), pp. 86–113.

TABLE 7.1. *Decomposition of the Decline of India's Female–Male Ratio, 1901–91*

| | Share of India's male population | | Female–male ratio | | | Effect of change in state-specific FMR on Indian FMR[a] |
|---|---|---|---|---|---|---|
| | 1901 ($s^0$) | 1991 ($s^1$) | 1901 ($f^0$) | 1991 ($f^1$) | Change ($f^1 - f^0$) | |
| INDIA | 1.000 | 1.000 | 972 | 927 | −45 | – |
| Bihar | 0.111 | 0.104 | 1,054 | 911 | −143 | −15.87 |
| Tamil Nadu | 0.079 | 0.065 | 1,044 | 974 | −70 | −5.50 |
| Orissa | 0.042 | 0.037 | 1,037 | 971 | −66 | −2.79 |
| Kerala | 0.027 | 0.033 | 1,004 | 1,036 | +32 | +0.85 |
| Madhya Pradesh | 0.071 | 0.079 | 990 | 931 | −59 | −4.17 |
| Andhra Pradesh | 0.080 | 0.078 | 985 | 972 | −13 | −1.04 |
| Karnataka | 0.055 | 0.053 | 983 | 960 | −23 | −1.26 |
| Maharashtra | 0.081 | 0.094 | 978 | 934 | −44 | −3.60 |
| Gujarat | 0.039 | 0.049 | 954 | 934 | −20 | −0.78 |
| West Bengal | 0.073 | 0.082 | 945 | 917 | −28 | −2.04 |
| Uttar Pradesh | 0.210 | 0.170 | 937 | 879 | −58 | −12.15 |
| Assam | 0.014 | 0.027 | 919 | 923 | +4 | +0.06 |
| Rajasthan | 0.045 | 0.053 | 905 | 910 | +5 | +0.23 |
| Himachal Pradesh | 0.009 | 0.006 | 884 | 976 | +92 | +0.78 |
| Haryana | 0.021 | 0.020 | 867 | 865 | −2 | −0.04 |
| Punjab | 0.034 | 0.025 | 832 | 882 | +50 | +1.72 |
| Other states/UTs | 0.009 | 0.025 | 943 | 887 | −56 | −0.50 |

Decomposition of the all-India change in FMR

(a) Total effect of changes in state-specific FMRs (column total)    −46.1

(b) 'Differential growth rate effect': $f^0 \star (s^1 - s^0)$    −2.3

(c) Second-order term: $(f^1 - f^0) \star (s^1 - s^0)$    3.4

Change in female–male ratio (a+b+c)    −45.0

*Notes.* [a] Change in state-specific FMR, multiplied by initial share of the male population

UT = Union Territory    $\star$ denotes vector product

*Sources.* Calculated from Nanda (1992), pp. 86–105. All figures exclude Jammu and Kashmir (not covered by the 1991 census).

states/UTs'). It can be seen that the broad regional patterns of female–male ratios that are observed today, and that have been much discussed in the literature, already existed at the beginning of this century. In particular, the north-western region (including Punjab, Haryana, Rajasthan, and Uttar Pradesh) has had the lowest female–male ratios all along, and, similarly, the states of the southern region (Kerala, Andhra Pradesh, Karnataka, and Tamil Nadu) already had above-average female–male ratios in 1901. But there have also been some significant changes in regional patterns. In particular, the relative position of the eastern states (Bihar, Orissa and, to a lesser extent, West Bengal) in the scale of female–male ratios has considerably declined.

Changes in state-specific female–male ratios between 1901 and 1991 have partly taken the form of a 'convergence' effect, with most of the states starting off with a high female–male ratio experiencing a particularly large decline over that period, and some increase taking place in the states with the lowest initial female–male ratios. The main exceptions to this pattern are Kerala (where the female–male ratio increased from a high initial value) and Uttar Pradesh (where there was a large decline despite a low base value). In addition to this convergence pattern, however, there has been a fairly widespread decline of the female–male ratio, not confined to any specific region. The largest absolute declines in female–male ratios have taken place in Bihar, Orissa, Tamil Nadu, Madhya Pradesh, Maharashtra, and Uttar Pradesh. As can be seen from the decomposition in the last column of the table, these six states (which combine large declines in FMR with large populations) account for an overwhelming proportion of the all-India decline in the female–male ratio. Bihar and Uttar Pradesh alone account for about half of the all-India decline.

Figure 7.2 shows the evolution of the female–male ratio in India between 1901 and 1981 (the last census for which age-specific population totals are available), distinguishing between two different age groups: 0–29 and 30+. As this figure suggests, the decline in the overall female–male ratio seems to be driven by a sustained decline in the ratio of women to men in the second age group (this group accounted for about one-third of the population in 1981). The same pattern is observed for each of India's broad geographical regions.[22]

---

[22] The last statement is based on age-specific population totals for the western, northern, southern, central, and eastern 'zones' presented in S.B. Mukherjee (1976). In each of these zones, there has been a sharp and sustained decline in the female–male ratio for

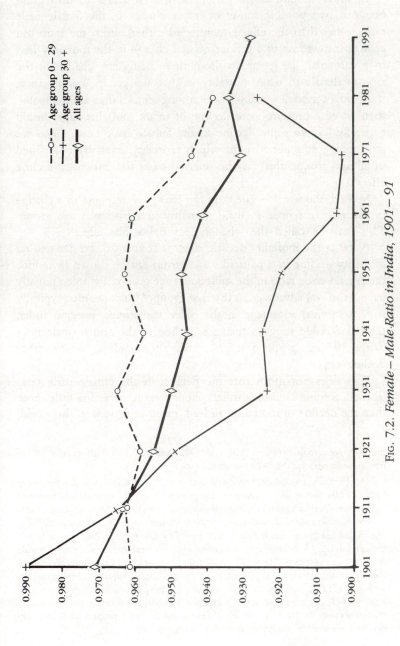

Fig. 7.2. *Female – Male-Ratio in India, 1901 – 91*

In order to understand this pattern, it is useful to distinguish between two possible causes of major change in the female–male ratio (other than the effects mentioned earlier). First, the ratio can change in response to a gender-neutral change in the mortality *level* in a particular age group, without there being any change in the *ratio* of female to male mortality in that age group. For instance, if the infant mortality rate is lower among females than among males, then an equi-proportionate decline of infant mortality rates would generally lead to some decline in the female–male ratio. Since we are looking at a period over which mortality levels have declined in all age groups, this may be referred to as the 'mortality decline effect'.

Second, the female–male ratio can change in response to a change in the *ratio* of female to male mortality in a particular age group. This may be called the 'changing mortality bias effect'.

As far as the mortality decline effect is concerned, gender-neutral mortality decline in a particular age group can be shown to reduce the female–male ratio in the subsequent age groups if women initially have a survival advantage in that age group.[23] Since women typically have a survival advantage in the older age groups, even in India, this relationship suggests that the decline of the female–male ratio in the 30+ age group is at least partly attributable to the mortality decline effect.

This does not mean that the decline in the female–male ratio in India is some kind of 'natural' phenomenon, reflecting little more than the decline of mortality. Indeed, in other regions of the world,

---

the 30+ age group between 1901 and 1981, and relatively little change in the female–male ratio for the 0–29 age group.

[23] More precisely, an equi-proportionate decline of mortality in a particular age group leads to FMR decline in all subsequent age groups if and only if the ratio of female to male mortality in that age group is lower than unity. To see this, let $M_0$ and $F_0$ respectively denote the male and female populations in the reference age group, q the male mortality rate in that age group, and k.q the female mortality rate, where k (the ratio of female to male mortality in the reference age group) can be interpreted as a measure of female disadvantage in survival. The female–male ratio in the next age group (say, $FMR_1$) can then be written as $FMR_1 = [F_0.(1-k.q)]/[M_0.(1-q)]$. The last expression implies that the derivative of $FMR_1$ with respect to q is positive (i.e. equi-proportionate mortality decline leads to FMR decline in the next age group) if and only if k is below unity. A similar reasoning can be used to show that, if k is below unity, then equi-proportionate mortality decline leads to FMR decline in all subsequent age groups.

the decline of mortality in the twentieth century has usually gone hand in hand with an *increase* in the female–male ratio, reflecting a sustained improvement in the survival chances of females relative to males.[24] Even in Kerala and Sri Lanka, recent demographic trends have followed this typical pattern.[25] The all-India FMR decline seems to reflect a combination of the 'mortality decline effect' in the older age groups with a *failure to remove* the anti-female bias in the younger age groups. As Figure 7.2 shows, the female–male ratio in the 0–29 age group has stagnated around 0.96 until 1961; this figure is very close to the typical female–male ratio at birth, indicating roughly equal male and female mortality in that age group.[26] As was mentioned earlier, in countries where young males and females receive similar treatment in terms of food, health care, and related necessities, females have substantial survival advantages. India's female–male ratio of 0.96 in the 0–29 age group suggests some considerable anti-female discrimination, which—in contrast with many other countries—has not gone away with the decline of mortality.[27]

In fact, after 1961, the female–male ratio has declined even in the 0–29 age group, and this cannot be explained in terms of the 'mortality decline effect'. By 1971, female mortality rates were *higher* than male mortality rates throughout that age group (except immediately after birth), and that is still the case today.[28] This development

[24] See e.g. Preston (1976), chapter 6, and Lopez and Ruzicka (1983).

[25] As noted earlier, the female–male ratio in Kerala has steadily increased since 1901 (see also Table 7.1). Similarly, mortality decline in Sri Lanka has gone hand in hand with a major improvement in the relative survival chances of females *vis-à-vis* males; see Nadarajah (1983), Langford (1984, 1988), and Langford and Storey (1993).

[26] This statement does not apply to each age group within the 0–29 age group. In fact, female–male ratios for more narrowly-defined age groups (e.g. 0–4, 5–9, etc.) have followed rather complex patterns over time, which call for more detailed analysis than can be presented in this chapter.

[27] The female–male ratio for the 0–29 age group in, say, Western Europe is also around 0.96 (United Nations, 1993, p. 40), but this is because mortality rates for the younger age groups in that region are very low, so that the female–male ratio in the 0–29 age group remains relatively close to the female–male ratio at birth (around 0.95 in Western Europe). A more relevant comparison may be with sub-Saharan Africa, which has high mortality rates (like India) but relatively little female disadvantage in survival (unlike India). In that region, the female–male ratio for the 0–29 age group was just above unity in 1985 (United Nations, 1993, p. 68).

[28] See e.g the Sample Registration System (SRS) data presented in Karkal (1987), and in the annual SRS publications. It should be mentioned that, since 1971, there has been a consolidation of female survival advantage in the older age groups, and the age at which

is in sharp contrast with the typical pattern of reduced female disadvantage in the younger age groups as mortality declines.

The preceding discussion does not rule out the possibility that, even in the older age groups, the decline in the female–male ratio reflects some adverse change in the relative survival chances of women *vis-à-vis* men. Since 1971, the trend has been in the direction of an increase in female survival advantage in these age groups, but this does not rule out a contrary trend earlier on. The FMR decline, in fact, is most pronounced in the pre-1971 period (Figure 7.2), and for that period there is no reliable evidence of the direction of change in the relative survival rates of adult men and women.

If it is the case that the relative survival rates of men and women in the older age groups were changing in favour of men at one stage, contrary to the usual pattern in a phase of longevity expansion, the main explanation may simply be that adult men disproportionately benefited from improvements in living conditions and medical care. Such a phenomenon is quite plausible, given the tendency of economic development to affect men more rapidly than women: the current lifestyle of women in, say, rural Bihar or Uttar Pradesh is probably much closer to what it was at the beginning of this century than in the case of men. The fact that professional attendance at birth remains so rare in these states, while modern medical treatment is very often used to cure diseases that are not specific to women, is a good illustration of this point.[29]

A further possibility is that, aside from men benefiting more than women from medical advances and related improvements, there has also been a more basic change in gender relations, leading to a shift in the distribution of resources in favour of men. An example of this possibility is considered presently.

---

this advantage begins has also come down (see e.g. Karkal, 1987, Dyson, 1988, and Rajan et al., 1992). As a result, female life expectancy has overtaken male life expectancy. These developments will get reflected, in due course, in the female–male ratio, which may start rising as a result (unless other developments, such as the spread of sex-selective abortion, work in the other direction).

[29] In 1991, the proportion of all births taking place in medical institutions was as low as 4 per cent in Uttar Pradesh and 12 per cent in Bihar, compared with 92 per cent in Kerala (see Statistical Appendix, Table A.3). Maternal health, in general, remains one of the most neglected areas of health policy in India; see Karkal (1985), M.E. Khan et al. (1986), Bang et al. (1989), Sundari (1993, 1994), Das Gupta (1994b), Germain (1994), Jejeebhoy and Rama Rao (1994), and Mari Bhat et al. (1994).

## Gender and caste

The decline of the female–male ratio in India has not been at all even between different castes and religious communities. Specifically, the decline appears to have been significantly more pronounced among disadvantaged castes.[30]

Many census reports of the pre-independence period have noted that the female–male ratio tends to be considerably higher among the 'lower' castes than in the population as a whole.[31] This is no longer the case: in 1991, the female–male ratio among scheduled castes was 922 per thousand, compared with 927 in the population as a whole.[32] As far as the female–male ratio is concerned, the scheduled castes are now much like the rest of the population, in contrast with the earlier pattern.

A detailed examination of this development is complicated by the fact that pre-independence and post-independence census reports use different caste classifications. Pre-independence census reports give caste-specific population totals (for males and females), but post-independence reports do not provide a caste breakdown, except among the scheduled castes. A further difficulty is that the names under which particular castes are recorded often change over time.

In order to keep things reasonably simple, we shall restrict our discussion of the relationship between female–male ratios and caste to the state of Uttar Pradesh (as we saw earlier, Uttar Pradesh accounts for a large part of the all-India decline in the female–male ratio since 1901). For this state, the 1981 census lists 66 'scheduled castes', of which 47 can be readily identified in the 1901 census volumes. Assuming that these 47 castes are more or less representative of the whole group of scheduled castes, we can reconstruct the 1901 female–male ratio for this group. The results are presented in Table 7.2.

As the table indicates, castes that are now classified as scheduled castes (previously often referred to simply as 'untouchables') had

[30] For a pioneering discussion of this issue with reference to the post-independence period, see Agnihotri (1994).

[31] See e.g. Census of India, 1931, United Provinces of Agra and Oudh, vol. XVIII, part I, p. 278.

[32] Nanda (1993), p. 12, based on 1991 census data. The female–male ratio remains higher among scheduled tribes (972 per thousand in 1991) than in the population as a whole, but that gap too is slowly narrowing over time (Agnihotri, 1994).

TABLE 7.2. *Female–Male Ratio and Caste in Uttar Pradesh,*
*1901 and 1981*

| | Total population, 1901 (thousands) | Female–male ratio, 1901 | Female–male ratio, 1981[a] |
|---|---|---|---|
| (i) Scheduled castes (SC) | | | |
| Chamar | 5,891 | 986 | 880 |
| All SCs[b] | 9,821 | 970 | 892 |
| (ii) Kshatriya, Rajput, Thakur | 3,354 | 887 | 878[c] |
| (iii) Other Hindu | 27,517 | 929 | |
| Hindu (i + ii + iii) | 40,692 | 935 | 881 |
| Muslim | 6,731 | 957 | 903 |
| Other | 269 | 783 | 884 |
| Total | 47,692 | 937 | 885 |

*Note.* [a] The corresponding 1991 figures are still to be published.

[b] Only 47 of the 66 castes listed as 'scheduled castes' in the 1981 census could be confidently identified in the 1901 census; the 1901 figures in this row apply to these 47 castes. The 1981 figures include a tiny proportion (about 1 per cent) of scheduled-caste persons who were not counted as 'Hindus' in that census.

[c] Female–male ratio for all Hindus not belonging to a scheduled caste (post-independence censuses provide no information on the caste composition of the population outside the scheduled castes).

*Sources.* Calculated from Census of India 1901, North-West Provinces and Oudh (Allahabad, 1902), volume 16A; Census of India 1981, Series 22, Uttar Pradesh, Parts IX-i and IX-vii; Census of India 1981, Series 22, Uttar Pradesh, Paper 1 of 1985. The list of scheduled castes is from Census of India 1981, Series 22, Uttar Pradesh, Paper 2 of 1982.

much above average female–male ratios in 1901. The Chamars, for instance, who are by far the largest scheduled caste in Uttar Pradesh, had a female–male ratio of 986 in 1901, compared with 937 for the state population as a whole. By 1981, however, the female–male ratio among scheduled castes (including the Chamars) was very close to the UP average. This is one indication that, as far as gender relations are concerned, the scheduled castes in Uttar Pradesh are now more like the 'higher' castes than they used to be.[33]

---

[33] The female–male ratio among Muslims in Uttar Pradesh has also declined a good deal since the beginning of the century (from 957 in 1901 to 903 in 1981), but remains higher than the female–male ratio for the Hindu population in that state.

The contrast between the scheduled castes and the martial castes (Kshatriya et al.) is particularly interesting. The martial castes, which have a high rank in the caste hierarchy, and an important place in the history and culture of large parts of north India (including Uttar Pradesh), have a long tradition of fierce patriarchy. In fact, the martial castes in north India have played a leading role in the history of female infanticide, child marriage, seclusion, dowry, *sati, johar,* levirate, polygamy, and related patriarchal practices.[34] Among these castes, in Uttar Pradesh, the female–male ratio was already very low at the beginning of the period under consideration (887 in 1901). Further, it has changed little over the years, at least during the pre-independence period (the relevant caste-specific figures are not available for the post-independence period). This is an important indication, suggesting that whatever factors led to a decline in the female–male ratio among other castes did not operate among the martial castes over this period—or had already operated earlier.

This pattern is consistent with the hypothesis, widely discussed in the literature on social anthropology, that the patriarchal norms of the higher castes are gradually spreading to other castes. The most common interpretation of this phenomenon is that it reflects a process of emulation of the higher castes by the lower castes, with the lifestyle of women playing a central role in this process as a symbol of social status.[35] This process is likely to be particularly strong when the disadvantaged castes experience upward economic mobility. That the norms of the martial castes should often have been taken as the 'model' in Uttar Pradesh is not surprising, given the dominant position which these castes have occupied in that region for a long time.[36]

---

[34] See e.g. Tod (1929), Altekar (1956), Karve (1965), Panigrahi (1972), Hitchcock (1975), Bahadur (1978), Miller (1981), Kolenda (1984), Singh (1988).

[35] The notion of 'Sanskritization' was developed by M.N. Srinivas (1962, 1965, 1967, 1989); see also Berreman (1993), and the more recent studies cited there. Increased resistance to widow remarriage among upwardly-mobile castes (the prohibition of widow remarriage being widely perceived as an upper-caste norm) is a well-documented example of how restrictions on the lifestyle of women often play an important role in the Sanskritization process. On this, see Kolenda (1983), Drèze (1990c), Chen and Drèze (1994), Chen (forthcoming, a), and the literature cited there.

[36] On the long-standing dominance of martial castes in rural Uttar Pradesh, see Drèze and Gazdar (1996), and the literature cited there. It should be mentioned that the dominant position of these castes in the rural society of Uttar Pradesh derives less from their martial activities as such (which are now largely confined to local feuds and fist

The observed convergence of female–male ratios among scheduled castes and higher castes may have causes other than this process of emulation. It has often been suggested, for instance, that gender inequality in India tends to be relatively low among poorer households.[37] In the cross-section analysis of district female–male ratios discussed further in this chapter, it is also found that higher levels of poverty tend to go with higher female–male ratios, for a *given* composition of the population in terms of the proportion of scheduled castes and scheduled tribes. It is, in fact, plausible that the partnership aspect of gender relations is stronger in poorer households, where survival depends on effective cooperation, than among privileged households, where women tend to have a more dependent and symbolic position. And this feature of gender relations within the household, in turn, may affect the general status of women in different classes. If there is a causal association of this kind between poverty and gender inequality, then economic growth and poverty reduction may, in some respects at least, be a source of intensified female disadvantage. The sharp decline of female–male ratios among scheduled castes may be a manifestation of this economic process, rather than being directly related to caste as such.

What is not in doubt is that the convergence effect has taken place (not only in Uttar Pradesh but also in India as a whole), and that it has made some contribution to the overall decline of the female–male ratio in India since 1901.[38] The time pattern of this convergence is also interesting. Specifically, the decline of the female–male ratio among scheduled castes seems to have been particularly dramatic after 1961. In Uttar Pradesh, for instance, the female–male ratio in 1961 was not yet terribly low for the scheduled castes—941 to be exact, compared with 909 for the population as a whole. Thirty years later, the corresponding values were 877 and

---

fights) than from their temporal power as traditional landowners.

[37] For some relevant studies, see Miller (1981, 1993a), Das Gupta (1987), Krishnaji (1987), Alaka Basu (1992), Dasgupta (1993), Rogaly (1994), Murthi, Guio, and Drèze (1995).

[38] The FMR decline among scheduled castes, on its own, must have made a relatively modest contribution to the overall FMR decline in India, given the small share of this group in the total population (about 16 per cent in 1991). But the process of diffusion of the patriarchal culture of the higher castes, and related causal antecedents of the convergence effect, may have affected a broader section of the population. The widespread transition from bride-price to dowry among large parts of the population in south India illustrates this possibility.

879, indicating a massive decline of the female–male ratio among scheduled castes after 1961.[39] A similar pattern applies in India as a whole, with the female–male ratio among scheduled castes falling from 957 in 1961 (compared with 941 for the population as a whole) to 922 in 1991 (compared with 927 for the whole population). It is quite possible that the post-1961 decline of the female–male ratio in the 0–29 age group at the all-India level, noted earlier in this section, relates at least partly to the convergence effects we have just discussed.

All this is a useful reminder of the fact that economic progress on its own does not necessarily do very much to reduce gender inequalities. In fact, in so far as the convergent decline of the female–male ratio among scheduled castes is due to some process of emulation linked with their upward economic mobility, or to some other causal process related to the expansion of the economy, this seems to be a case where economic growth leads to some *intensification* of gender bias. The fact that higher levels of poverty are associated with higher female–male ratios in cross-section analysis reinforces these observations based on time trends. Clearly, the removal of gender inequalities cannot be based on some presumption that the problem will resolve itself on its own in the process of economic expansion. Punjab and Haryana are good illustrations of this point: both states have experienced rapid economic growth since independence, and are now far ahead of all other Indian states in terms of per-capita income, but they still have lower female–male ratios than any other state except Uttar Pradesh. Achieving greater gender equality involves a process of active social change which has no obvious link with economic growth.

## 7.3. *Women's Agency and Child Survival*

A number of empirical studies indicate that the extent of anti-female bias in survival is substantially reduced by various influences that give women more voice and agency within the family. One of these influences is female education, and this consideration adds to those already presented in earlier chapters on the crucial role of basic education in general and female education in particular. Another

---

[39] See Agnihotri (1994), who also presents an excellent analysis of the phenomenon of accelerated FMR decline, after 1961, among the scheduled castes in many Indian states.

factor of importance is women's ability to earn an independent income through paid employment.[40] This opportunity tends to enhance the social standing of a woman in the household and the society. Her contribution to the prosperity of the family is, then, more visible, and she also has more voice, because of being less dependent on others. Further, outside employment often has useful 'educational' effects, in terms of exposure to the world outside the family. These positive links between gainful female employment and the status of women are also relevant to the female child, in so far as they affect the importance that is attached to her development and well-being.[41]

It is worth examining more closely how these and other aspects of female agency influence male and female mortality rates, and the extent of gender bias in survival. The age patterns of male and female mortality are complex (Kynch and Sen, 1983), and the discussion in this section will be confined to mortality in the 0–4 age group— hereafter 'under-five mortality'. Countries with basic gender in-equality—including India, Pakistan, Bangladesh, China, West Asia, and so on—tend to have a high ratio of female to male mortality even in this age group, in contrast with the situation in Europe or America or sub-Saharan Africa, where female children typically have a substantial survival advantage. In India itself, male and female death rates in the 0–4 age group are now quite close to each other in terms of averages for the country as a whole, but a strong female disadvantage persists in regions where gender inequality is particularly pronounced, including most states of north India.[42]

---

[40] A higher participation rate of women in so-called 'gainful' activities in sub-Saharan Africa seems to play a major role in placing women there at a less disadvantaged position compared with their counterparts in north Africa and Asia. On this see Boserup (1970), Kynch and Sen (1983), Bardhan (1984a, 1988), Sen (1984, 1989). Within India, high rates of female labour-force participation among tribal communities, and in the Himalayan region, also help to explain the comparatively favourable status of women (and relatively high female–male ratio) in these societies.

[41] See Miller (1981), Rosenzweig and Schultz (1982), Kynch and Sen (1983), Sen (1985c, 1990), Alaka Basu (1992), Guio (1994), Murthi, Guio, and Drèze (1995); also Kishor (1993, 1994), and the literature cited there. The strength of these relations, however, depends on the nature of the female employment, its social standing, and economic rewards. For further discussion of this issue, see Ursula Sharma (1980, 1986), Kalpana Bardhan (1985), Bina Agarwal (1986), Desai and Jain (1992), among others, and also Nirmala Banerjee's (1982) illuminating study of the condition of 'unorganised women workers' in Calcutta.

[42] In 1991, the death rate in the 0–4 age group (per thousand) was 25.6 for males and 27.5 for females at the all-India level. The female mortality rate in that age group was

In a recent study, Murthi, Guio, and Drèze (1995) present an analysis of variations in under-five mortality rates between different districts of India in 1981 (the latest year for which adequately detailed data are available). One aspect of this analysis is an examination of the relationship between an index of female disadvantage in child survival (reflecting the *ratio* of female to male mortality in the 0–4 age group at the district level) and a number of other district-level variables such as the female literacy rate, female labour-force participation, the incidence of poverty, the level of urbanization, the availability of medical facilities, and the proportion of scheduled castes and scheduled tribes in the population. The basic results are presented in the first column of Table 7.3.[43]

As discussed in Murthi, Guio, and Drèze (1995), what is rather striking is that the variables directly relating to women's agency (in particular, the female labour-force participation rate and the female literacy rate) have strong effects on the extent of female disadvantage in child survival, and go in the expected direction, i.e. higher levels of female literacy and labour-force participation are associated with lower levels of female disadvantage in child survival. By contrast, variables that relate to the *general* level of development and modernization either turn out to have no statistically significant effect, or suggest that modernization, if anything, *amplifies* the gender bias in child survival. This applies *inter alia* to urbanization, male literacy, the availability of medical facilities, and the level of poverty (with lower levels of poverty being associated with a *larger* female disadvantage). These results, based on cross-section evidence, reinforce an observation made earlier in connection with the decline of the female–male ratio over time: on their own, the forces of development and modernization do not necessarily lead to a rapid reduction in gender inequalities. In so far as a positive connection does exist in India between the level of development and reduced gender bias in survival,

---

lower than the male mortality rate in Andhra Pradesh, Assam, Himachal Pradesh, Kerala, and Tamil Nadu, but higher in all other major states. The female disadvantage was most pronounced in Bihar, Haryana, Madhya Pradesh, Punjab, Rajasthan, and Uttar Pradesh. See the Statistical Appendix for further details.

[43] For a detailed discussion of these results, see Drèze, Guio, and Murthi (1995) and Murthi, Guio, and Drèze (1995). Some of the findings presented there have much in common with those of an independent study carried out earlier by Sunita Kishor (1993). For related analyses based on Indian district data, see also Rosenzweig and Schultz (1982), Gulati (1992), and Khemani (1994).

TABLE 7.3. *Basic Results of a Cross-section Analysis of the Determinants of Child Mortality, Fertility and Gender Bias in Indian Districts (1981)*

| Independent variable | Dependent variable | | |
|---|---|---|---|
| | Female disadvantage in child survival (FD) | Under-five mortality rate, male and female combined (Q5) | Total fertility rate (TFR) |
| Constant | 0.86 (3.00)* | 205.82 (14.37)* | 6.594 (23.10)* |
| Female labour-force participation (proportion of 'main workers' in the female population) | −0.02 (−3.85)* | 0.44 (1.82) | −0.017 (−3.57)* |
| Female literacy rate (proportion of literate women in the female population) | −0.04 (−4.46)* | −0.87 (−2.45)* | −0.031 (−4.28)* |
| Male literacy rate (proportion of literate men in the male population) | 0.015 (1.97)* | −0.49 (−1.40) | −0.005 (−0.70) |
| Level of urbanization (proportion of the population living in urban areas) | 0.005 (1.73) | −0.31 (−2.40)* | −0.0004 (−0.15) |
| Availability of medical facilities (proportion of villages with some medical facilities) | 0.005 (1.84) | −0.25 (−2.23)* | −0.002 (−1.04) |
| Level of rural poverty ('Sen index') | −0.02 (−3.13)* | 0.54 (1.76) | 0.007 (1.14) |
| Scheduled castes (proportion of scheduled-caste persons in the population) | −0.01 (−1.13) | 0.55 (1.89) | −0.007 (−1.23) |
| Scheduled tribes (proportion of scheduled-tribe persons in the population) | −0.01 (−3.96)* | −0.60 (−3.57)* | −0.011 (−3.40)* |
| Dummy variables for different regions[a] | | | |
| South | −0.82 (−4.91)* | −41.50 (−3.85)* | −0.548 (2.60)* |
| East | 0.154 (0.81) | −38.08 (−2.91)* | −0.254 (−0.99) |
| West | −0.15 (−0.87) | −12.35 (−1.32) | −0.379 (−2.06)* |

*Notes.* [a] The different regions are defined as follows: South = Andhra Pradesh, Karnataka, Kerala, and Tamil Nadu; East = Bihar, Orissa, and West Bengal; West = Gujarat and Maharashtra. The 'control region', for which no dummy variable is included, consists of the northern and central states of Haryana, Madhya Pradesh, Punjab, Rajasthan, and Uttar Pradesh.

[*] Significant at 5% level (asymptotic t-ratios in brackets).

*Source.* Drèze, Guio, and Murthi (1995).

*Explanatory Note.* The observations on which these regressions are based consist of 296 districts for which the relevant data are available. All the variables relate to 1981, and are based on the 1981 census, except for the 'poverty' indicator. The poverty indicator used for each district is the Sen index of rural poverty in 1972–3 for the National Sample Survey 'region' in which the district in question is situated (the 296 districts are located in 51 different NSS regions). The regressions are based on maximum-likelihood estimation, in a model which takes into account spatial correlation in the error terms. These regressions can be interpreted as the 'reduced form' of a system of simultaneous equations which determines three endogenous variables: the total fertility rate (TFR), the level of child mortality for both sexes combined (Q5), and the extent of female disadvantage in child survival (FD), as measured by the proportionate difference between female and male child mortality (or, more precisely, by $FD = [Q5_f - Q5_m]/Q5_f$, where $Q5_f$ and $Q5_m$ are the levels of female and male child mortality, respectively). For further details on definitions, sources, estimation, diagnostics, and related issues, and a detailed discussion of the results, see Murthi, Guio, and Drèze (1995).

it seems to work *through* variables that are directly related to women's agency, such as female literacy and female labour-force participation.[44]

The analysis also includes dummy variables for different regions, and it turns out that at least some of these regional dummies (particularly the 'South India' dummy) are statistically significant even after the other variables are included. In other words, the sharp contrasts that are observed between different regions of India, in terms of the relative survival chances of male and female children, are only partly explained by differences in female literacy, female labour-force participation, and other variables included in this analysis. This suggests that other variables, which may be hard to quantify, also have an important influence. Women's property rights, cultural or ideological

---

[44] There is also some evidence, from the same study, of high fertility rates being associated with low survival chances of female children *vis-à-vis* male children. This is consistent with the fact that the survival disadvantages of female children progressively worsen as we consider children of higher 'parity', that is, the second girl in a family tends to do worse than the first, and so on. On this, see particularly Das Gupta's (1987) pioneering work on rural Punjab; also M.E. Khan et al. (1989) on rural Uttar Pradesh.

influences, and some aspects of the kinship system (e.g. the rules of exogamy and patrilocality) are plausible examples of such variables.[45]

A similar analysis can be used to examine the effects of different variables on the *level* of under-five mortality for males and females combined. We have already noted that higher female labour-force participation improves the *relative* survival chances of girls *vis-à-vis* boys. But this does not tell us how female labour-force participation affects the absolute levels of under-five mortality. It is, in fact, difficult to predict whether the effect of higher female labour-force participation on child survival is positive or negative.[46] There are at least two important effects to consider, working in opposite directions. First, as was discussed earlier, involvement in gainful employment has many positive effects on a woman's agency roles, which often include child-care. Second, the 'double burden' of household work and outside employment can impair women's ability to ensure the good health of their children, if only by reducing the time available for child-care activities (since men typically show great reluctance to share the domestic chores).[47] In the case of girls, a third consideration is that higher levels of female labour-force participation in the society may enhance the importance attached to the survival of a female child. The net result of these different effects is a matter of empirical investigation. The analysis of district-level data summarized in Table 7.3 (second column) suggests a positive association between female

[45] On these different influences, see the studies cited in Drèze and Sen (1989), D.B. Gupta et al. (1993), and Dasgupta (1993); also Das Gupta (1990, 1994b), Alaka Basu (1992), Sunita Kishor (1993), Bina Agarwal (1994), and Satish Agnihotri (1994, 1995), among other recent contributions. The persistence of regional influences on relative survival chances, even after controlling for a wide range of district characteristics on which quantitative data are available, has been noted earlier by Kishor (1993).

[46] The variable used to measure female labour-force participation is the ratio of female 'main workers' (women engaged in 'economically productive work' for at least 183 days in the year) to the total female population. The instructions to census investigators make it clear that unpaid 'household duties' are not to be counted as economically productive work (Government of India, 1981, pp. 106–7). The census definition of 'economically productive work' is questionable, but it serves our purpose, since we are interested in the relationship between child survival and women's independent income-earning opportunities (rather than their economic contribution generally—whether or not rewarded).

[47] For useful empirical analyses of this 'maternal dilemma' in the Indian context, see Alaka Basu (1992) and Gillespie and McNeill (1992). On the related issue of the relationship between maternal labour-force participation and child nutrition, see Leslie (1988), Leslie and Paolisso (1989), and the literature cited there.

labour-force participation and under-five mortality, but this association is not statistically significant.[48]

Female literacy, on the other hand, is unambiguously found to have a negative and statistically significant impact on under-five mortality, even after controlling for male literacy. This is consistent with growing evidence of a close relationship between female literacy and child survival in many countries, including India.[49] Further, the authors find that female literacy has a larger effect on female under-five mortality than on male under-five mortality; this is why the *ratio* of female to male mortality is lower at higher levels of female literacy, even though mortality rates fall for both male and female children as female literacy increases.

It is worth adding that, in quantitative terms, the effect of female literacy on child mortality is quite large. This point is illustrated in Table 7.4, which shows how the predicted values of the 'dependent variables' in this analysis (the extent of female disadvantage in child survival, the level of under-five mortality, and the total fertility rate) respond to changes in female literacy when the *other* exogenous variables are kept at their mean value, and similarly with male literacy and poverty. For instance, keeping other variables constant, an increase in the crude female literacy rate from, say, 22 per cent (the actual 1981 figure) to 75 per cent reduces the predicted value of under-five mortality for males and females combined from 156 per thousand (again, the actual 1981 figure) to 110 per thousand. The powerful effect of female literacy contrasts with the comparatively ineffective roles of, say, male literacy or general poverty reduction as instruments of child mortality reduction. An increase in male literacy over the same range (from 22 to 75 per cent) only reduces under-five mortality from 167 per thousand to 141 per thousand. And a 50 per cent

---

[48] As discussed in Murthi, Guio, and Drèze (1995), there is a real possibility of this association being, in fact, negative after controlling more carefully for the economic and social disadvantages that often motivate Indian women to seek paid employment. That possibility is consistent with international evidence on the relationship between female employment and child nutrition. Based on a review of 50 relevant studies, for instance, Joanne Leslie (1988) concludes that 'overall there is little evidence of a negative effect of maternal employment on child nutrition' (p. 1341).

[49] On this, see J.C. Caldwell (1979, 1986), Behrman and Wolfe (1984, 1987), Ware (1984), A.K. Jain (1985), Cleland and van Ginneken (1987, 1988), Nag (1989), Beenstock and Sturdy (1990), Cleland (1990), Das Gupta (1990), Bhuiya and Streatfield (1991), Bourne and Walker (1991), Thomas et al. (1991), Alaka Basu (1992), Barro and Lee (1993a, 1993b), D.B. Gupta et al. (1993), Subbarao and Raney (1994), among others.

TABLE 7.4. *Effects of Selected Independent Variables (Female Literacy, Male Literacy and Poverty) on Child Mortality (Q5), Female Disadvantage (FD) and Fertility (TFR)*

| Assumed level of the independent variable (%) | Predicted values of Q5, FD and TFR when the female literacy rate takes the value indicated in the first column | | | Predicted values of Q5, FD and TFR when the male literacy rate takes the value indicated in the first column | | | Predicted values of Q5, FD and TFR when the proportion of the population below the poverty line takes the value indicated in the first column[a] | | |
|---|---|---|---|---|---|---|---|---|---|
| | Q5 | FD | TFR | Q5 | FD | TFR | Q5 | FD | TFR |
| 10 | 166.4 | 10.7 | 5.38 | 172.9 | −2.0 | 5.18 | 151.5 | 9.8 | 4.79 |
| 20 | 157.7 | 5.9 | 5.07 | 168.0 | −0.1 | 5.13 | 152.7 | 8.5 | 4.85 |
| 30 | 149.0 | 1.1 | 4.76 | 163.1 | 1.8 | 5.08 | 153.8 | 7.1 | 4.91 |
| 40 | 140.2 | −3.3 | 4.45 | 158.2 | 3.9 | 5.03 | 154.9 | 5.8 | 4.97 |
| 50 | 131.5 | −7.1 | 4.15 | 153.3 | 5.9 | 4.98 | 156.0 | 4.4 | 5.03 |
| 60 | 122.8 | −10.3 | 3.84 | 148.4 | 8.0 | 4.93 | 157.2 | 3.1 | 5.09 |
| 70 | 114.0 | −12.8 | 3.53 | 143.5 | 10.1 | 4.88 | 158.3 | 1.8 | 5.15 |
| 80 | 105.3 | −14.8 | 3.22 | 138.7 | 12.2 | 4.83 | 159.5 | 0.5 | 5.21 |

*Note.* [a] For convenience of interpretation, the 'Sen index' of poverty has been replaced, in this table, by the 'head-count ratio' (i.e. the proportion of the population below the poverty line). The figures presented in the last three columns are based on the same regressions as in Table 7.3, with the Sen index replaced by the head-count ratio.

*Source.* Drèze, Guio, and Murthi (1995), based on the regressions presented in Table 7.3. The variables Q5, FD, and TFR are defined as in that table.

reduction in the incidence of poverty (from the actual 1981 level) only reduces the predicted value of under-five mortality from 156 per thousand to 153 per thousand.

Here again, the message seems to be that some variables relating to women's agency (in this case, female literacy) often play a much more important role in promoting social well-being (in particular, child survival) than variables relating to the general level of opulence in the society. These findings have important practical implications, given that both types of variables can be influenced through public action, but require very different forms of intervention.

## 7.4. *Fertility and Women's Emancipation*

It is not surprising that the agency of women is also particularly important for achievements in population policy. The serious adverse effects of high birth rates include their impact on the lives women can lead, and the drudgery of continuous child bearing and rearing, which is routinely imposed on many Asian and African women. There is, as a result, a close connection between women's *well-being* and women's *agency* in bringing about a change in the fertility pattern. Women in India have to face the lack of freedom to do other things that goes with a high frequency of births, not to mention the dangers of repeated pregnancy and high maternal mortality. It is, thus, understandable that reductions in birth rates have often been associated with enhancement of women's status and voice.

These connections are indeed reflected in inter-district variations of the total fertility rate, as Tables 7.3 and 7.4 indicate. In fact, among all the variables included in the analysis, other than regional dummies and ethnic composition, the only ones that have a statistically significant effect on fertility are female literacy and female labour-force participation. Once again, the importance of women's agency emerges forcefully from this analysis, especially in comparison with the weaker effects of variables relating to general economic progress.

The link between female literacy and fertility is particularly clear. This connection has been widely observed in other countries, and it is not surprising that it should emerge in India too.[50] The un-

---

[50] For recent empirical analyses of this connection at the international level, see Barro and Lee (1993a, 1993b), Cassen (1994), and Subbarao and Raney (1994). On the connection between fertility and female education in India, see Vlassoff (1980), Jain and Nag (1985, 1986), J.C. Caldwell et al. (1989), Satia and Jejeebhoy (1991), Alaka Basu

willingness of educated women to be shackled to continuous child-rearing clearly plays a role in bringing about this change. Education also makes the horizon of vision wider, and, at a more mundane level, helps to disseminate the knowledge of family planning.

As we discussed in chapter 4, Kerala's particular experience of fertility reduction based on women's agency is quite remarkable, and has extremely important lessons for the rest of India. While the total fertility rate for India as a whole is still as high as 3.7, that rate in Kerala has now fallen below the 'replacement level' of 2.1 to 1.8. Kerala's high level of female education has been particularly influential in bringing about this decline in the birth rate.[51]

There is also some demographic evidence to indicate that birth rates tend to go down following the decline of death rates. This is partly because the need for having many children to ensure some survivors goes down with lower mortality rates, but also because of the complementarity between the respective means of birth control and death control (giving people access to contraception can be effectively combined with delivery of medical attention and health care). In Kerala, the sharp reduction of death rates has been followed by a rapid decline of fertility, with the birth rate falling from 44 per thousand in 1951–61 to 18 by 1991. Since female agency and literacy are important in the reduction of mortality rates (as was discussed in the last section), this is another—more indirect—route through which women's agency, in general, and female literacy, in particular, can reduce birth rates (in addition to the direct impacts mentioned earlier).

Recently, there has been a good deal of discussion of the imperative need to reduce birth rates in the world, and those in India in particular. China's achievement in cutting down birth rates over a short period through rather draconian measures has suggested to many the need for India to emulate China in this respect. As was discussed in chapter 4, however, the coercive methods do involve many social costs, including the direct one of the loss of the effective freedom of people—in particular, women—to decide themselves on matters that are clearly rather personal. That aspect of the problem is often dismissed, especially in the West, on the grounds that cultural differences between

---

(1992, 1993), Das Gupta (1994a), Egerö et al. (1994), Parikh (1995), Visaria and Visaria (1994); also Alaka Basu and Roger Jeffery (forthcoming) and the literature cited there.

[51] On these issues, see also Krishnan (1976, 1991, 1994), Kabir and Krishnan (1992), Mari Bhat and Rajan (1990, 1992), Zachariah et al. (1994).

Asia and the West make such policies acceptable in the Third World in a way they would not be in the West.[52] Cultural relativism is a tricky terrain, and while it is easy enough to refer to despotic Oriental traditions, that line of reasoning would be no more convincing than making judgements on what to do in the Western societies today on the basis of the history of Spanish inquisitions or Nazi concentration camps.

It is not clear how the acceptability of coercion can be tested except through democratic confrontation. While that testing has not occurred in China, it was indeed attempted in India during the Emergency period in the seventies when compulsory birth control was tried by Mrs Gandhi's government, along with suspending various legal rights and civil liberties. The policy of coercion in general—including that in birth control—was overwhelmingly defeated in the general elections that followed. Furthermore, family-planning experts have noted how voluntary birth-control programmes received a severe set-back from that brief programme of compulsory sterilization, as people had become deeply suspicious of the entire movement. The coercive measures of the Emergency period, in fact, aside from having little immediate impact on fertility rates, were followed by a long period of *stagnation* in the birth rate, which only ended in 1985.[53]

There is evidence that some forms of compulsion or forceful pressure to accept birth control (especially sterilization) continue to be used in some Indian states, particularly in the north, where fertility rates tend to be high. Even when coercion is not part of official policy, the government's firm insistence on 'meeting the family-planning targets' often leads administrators and health-care personnel at different levels to resort to all kinds of pressure tactics that come close to compulsion.[54] Examples of such tactics include verbal threats, making sterilization a condition of eligibility for anti-poverty programmes,

[52] See, for example, Hardin (1993).

[53] See Bose (1991a), pp. 67–8. The Emergency period also caused a substantial *decline* in medical attendance at birth, and a large *increase* in neo-natal mortality rates, and it took five years for the pre-Emergency levels of these variables to be restored; on this, see Tulasidhar and Sarma (1993).

[54] This phenomenon is mentioned in many field-based studies recently carried out in north India; see e.g. Iyengar and Bhargava (1987), p. 1087, D. Banerji (1989), p. 1477, P. Jeffery et al. (1989), p. 216, H.N. Singh (1993), p. 35, Gidwani (1994), p. 40, Drèze, Lanjouw, and Sharma (forthcoming). It is no consolation that family-planning targets are apparently being replaced, in official parlance, by 'expected levels of achievement' (see Visaria and Visaria, 1994).

depriving mothers of more than two children from maternity benefits, reserving certain kinds of health care services to persons who have been sterilized, and forbidding persons who have more than two children from contesting panchayat elections.[55] The long-run consequences of these practices can be quite disastrous both for health care and for the consensual emergence of social norms favouring smaller families.

What also has to be borne in mind is the fact, discussed in chapter 4, that compulsion has not produced a lower birth rate in China compared with what Kerala has already achieved entirely through voluntary channels, relying on the educated agency of women. In fact, it is not at all clear (for reasons discussed earlier) exactly how much of *extra* reduction in birth rate China has been able to achieve by resorting to coercive methods. What must be taken into account in trying to assess the contribution of compulsion is that China has had many social and economic attainments that are favourable to fertility reduction, including expansion of education in general and female education in particular, augmentation of health care, enhancement of employment opportunities for women, and, recently, rapid economic development. These factors would themselves have reduced the birth rates (well below that of the Indian average, for example). While China seems to get too much credit for its authoritarian measures, it gets far too little credit for other—supportive—policies that have helped to cut down the birth rate.

Kerala's low birth rate—lower than China's—also suggests that these supportive influences may be effective enough to render compulsion quite redundant, even if it were acceptable otherwise. As has been noted before, Kerala not only has a much higher level of female literacy (86 per cent) than India as a whole (39 per cent), it is also well ahead of China's female literacy rate (68 per cent).[56] The fact that the ranking of female literacy is exactly the same as that

[55] It is quite extraordinary that the last measure (recently introduced in Rajasthan and Haryana) has been widely praised, even though it involves a strong violation not only of personal liberty but also of basic democratic values. Even the government's draft National Population Policy, despite placing emphasis on the need to reject coercive methods, gives full support to this measure as one means of meeting the overriding goal of bringing the total fertility rate down to 2.1 by the year 2010 (Government of India, 1994c, p. 40). At the time of writing, there is a strong possibility of the proposed measure being adopted at the all-India level, and extended to diverse forms of political participation other than the contesting of panchayat elections.

[56] See Table 4.2 in chapter 4.

of birth rates is in line with other evidence for the close connection between the two. It might also be mentioned here, in passing, that the increasing popularity of sex-selective abortion of female foetuses in China, as well as parts of India, contrasts sharply with the absence of such a practice in Kerala. While the solution of this problem has been sought in India through banning sex-selective abortion—a ban that may well be evaded easily enough—the real resolution of the problem must lie ultimately in a shift in family preference away from the rejection of female children.

As we saw in chapter 4, Kerala is not alone in having achieved a rapid reduction of the birth rate without compulsion. A similar—if not equally rapid—success has also occurred in Tamil Nadu, where the total fertility rate (2.2 in 1991) is now very close to the replacement level. A significant acceleration of fertility decline has also occurred during the eighties in a number of other states.[57] Further, what is rather striking is that the states where fertility decline remains extremely slow (including Uttar Pradesh, Bihar, Rajasthan, and Madhya Pradesh) are precisely those where coercive methods, by all available accounts, have been most extensively used.

These diverse experiences reinforce the general arguments presented earlier in favour of a collaborative approach to fertility reduction, based on due recognition of the agency of women in bringing down fertility and mortality rates. An unequivocal rejection of all coercive and heavy-handed methods (including those that are currently being used) is essential from many points of view, including those of fertility reduction, mortality reduction, women's well-being, and elementary freedom.[58]

[57] See Visaria and Visaria (1994).

[58] Aside from the imperative need to reject coercive methods, it is also important to promote the *quality* and diversity of non-coercive means of family planning. As things stand, family planning in India is overwhelmingly dominated by female sterilization, even in the southern states. To illustrate, while nearly 40 per cent of currently-married women aged 13–49 in south India are sterilized, only 14 per cent of women in that group have *ever* used a non-terminal, modern contraception method. Even the *knowledge* of modern methods of family planning other than sterilization is extraordinarily limited in India. Only half of rural married women aged 13–49, for instance, seem to know what a condom or IUD is. On these matters, see International Institute for Population Sciences (1994), and also Table A.3 in the Statistical Appendix of this book.

## 7.5. *Widowhood and Gender Relations*

One consequence of the low participation of Indian women in public life and political activity is that many social issues relating to women and gender relations receive far too little attention. In recent years, there has been improved awareness of some specific aspects of gender inequality and female deprivation, such as the problem of low female–male ratios and the anti-female bias in child survival. But many other issues continue to get low social recognition; they apparently haven't yet caught the attention of the male-dominated society. Examples include the problem of reproductive health and maternal mortality (severely neglected in health research and policy), the widespread violation of women's legal property rights (aside from the persistence of continued anti-female bias in the law itself), and the general acceptance of endemic violence against women.

Another striking example of the low social visibility of some important aspects of the condition of women concerns the well-being of widows.[59] There are about 33 million widows in India, representing 8 per cent of the female population—a proportion similar to that of agricultural labourers in the male population.[60] Further, there is a good deal of evidence of the deprived condition of many widows in India. A recent demographic study, for instance, concludes that mortality rates are, on average, 86 per cent higher among elderly widows than among married women of the same age.[61] Similarly, economic surveys indicate that the loss of one's husband often leads to a sharp decline of household income. Anthropological studies have also highlighted the fact that many widows suffer from social marginalization and psychological hardship, in addition to being particularly vulnerable to poverty.

It should be added that the *prospect* of widowhood reduces the quality of life of most Indian women, even if only a minority of

[59] On this, see Drèze (1990c), Chen and Drèze (1994, 1995) Chen (forthcoming, a), and the literature cited there. This section draws extensively on these studies. It should be mentioned that, while widows represent the vast majority of single adult women in India, other single women (e.g. those who are divorced or separated) also tend to experience major social disadvantages. For some relevant studies, see Krishnakumari (1987) and Dandavate et al. (1989).

[60] See Government of India (1993b), p. 71, and Nanda (1992), pp. 115, 155. The reference year is 1991.

[61] See Mari Bhat (1994). These results corroborate earlier findings for Bangladesh (see Rahman et al., 1992).

them are actually widowed at any particular point in time. The proportion of widows in the female population rises sharply with age, reaching 63 per cent among women aged 60 and above, and close to 80 per cent among women aged 70 and above. In other words, an Indian woman who survives to old age is most likely to become a widow. The prospect of losing their husband at some stage cannot but affect the lives of Indian women even before that event. For instance, there is a close relationship between widowhood, old-age insecurity, and fertility decisions in the early stages of married life.

In spite of their magnitude and significance, the deprivations of widows rarely feature in public debates, in the media, or even in social science research, except when—in a small number of cases—they take a sensational form, such as *sati*. This fact relates to the general point, made in section 5.1, that endemic but quiet deprivations are often much harder to bring to public attention than sensational events such as a famine or natural disaster. A similar point can be made in relation to other aspects of women's deprivation. The frequent media focus on rape, for instance, contrasts with the quiet acceptance of widespread domestic violence against women.

If widowhood is such a neglected social issue, it is partly because the experience of losing one's spouse is, overwhelmingly, a woman's experience. Only 2.5 per cent of all Indian men are widowed, compared with 8.1 per cent of women.[62] Further, the consequences of losing one's spouse are very different for men and women. A widower not only has greater freedom to remarry than his female counterpart, he also has more extensive property rights, wider opportunities for remunerative employment, and a more authoritative claim on economic support from his children. Had the living conditions of widowers been as precarious as those of widows, it is likely that widowed persons would have attracted far more attention.

The circumstances of widows vary a great deal between different regions, communities, classes, and age groups. Nevertheless, it is possible to identify some basic factors of disadvantage and insecurity experienced by many Indian widows. The following considerations emerge with particular force from recent surveys carried out in north India.[63]

---

[62] Government of India (1993b), p. 71. This large gender gap primarily reflects a high incidence of remarriage among widowers.

[63] For the evidence, and further discussion, see Drèze (1990c) and Chen and Drèze (1994, 1995).

First, a strong tradition of patrilineal ownership, which modern legislation has only begun to challenge, makes it hard for many widows to defend their legal inheritance rights. Formally, according to contemporary Indian law, a widow has an unequivocal right to a share of her husband's property, including his land.[64] This is in addition to the legal rights she has—irrespective of her marital status—to a share of her parents' property. Field studies, however, indicate that these legal rights are comprehensively violated, and that a large majority of widows have very limited and insecure property rights. This deprivation of property rights not only represents the loss of a potential source of independent income, but also diminishes the bargaining power of a widow *vis-à-vis* her in-laws, sons, and other potential supporters.

Second, the norms of patrilocal residence are an important cause of social isolation. In north India, widows are expected to remain in their husband's village, and most of them do so. At the same time, they are unlikely to receive much support from their in-laws. On the contrary, the relationship between a widow and her in-laws is typically quite tense (property rights being one of the most common sources of tension). Widows are thus denied both the freedom to leave their husband's village, and the support they need to live there happily.

Third, widows have a limited freedom to remarry. In some communities, particularly in north-west India, ascriptive leviratic unions (e.g. between a widow and her brother-in-law) remain quite common. Elsewhere, the standard pattern is that most childless widows remarry, but only a small proportion of widowed mothers do so.

Fourth, the gender division of labour severely restricts employment opportunities for widows. Census data indicate that age-specific labour-force participation rates are a little higher for widows than for married women. But the low involvement of north Indian women in gainful employment—irrespective of marital status—is the basic problem. Further, because widows tend to be concentrated in the older age groups, their average labour-force participation rate is lower than that of married women.

Fifth, most widows can expect little economic support from their

[64] According to the Hindu Succession Act of 1956, for instance, a widow is entitled to the same share of her husband's land as other 'Class 1' heirs (these also include the deceased person's children and widowed mother, if alive). On the general issue of women's land rights in India, see Bina Agarwal (1988, 1994).

family or community, except possibly in the form of co-residence with one of their adult sons. In particular, the notion that the joint family provides economic security to widows in rural India is little more than a myth. Most surveys find that co-residence of a widow with her in-laws is rare in north India (except in cases of leviratic unions), and that the relationship between a widow and her deceased husband's family is often far from harmonious. An overwhelming majority of widows live on their own, with their unmarried children, or as a dependent in the household of one of their adult sons.

As these observations illustrate, there are close links between the position of widows in society and a whole range of patriarchal institutions such as patrilineal inheritance, patrilocal residence, remarriage norms, and the gender division of labour. In that sense, the cause of widows must be seen as an integral part of the larger battle against gender inequalities.

Taking effective action (e.g. aimed at expanding women's land rights) requires a combination of public pressure and state response. The first task is to bring the issue closer to the centre of public attention. The agency of the women's movement is central to this challenge, and so is that of widows themselves.[65]

## 7.6. *Gender Equality and Social Progress*

Earlier in this chapter, we have had several occasions to note the role of women's agency in social progress. In particular, we have discussed the connections between women's agency and child survival, and also between women's agency and fertility, based on an analysis of inter-district variations in under-five mortality. These connections also show up in more aggregative comparisons of different regions in India. In fact, it is rather striking that the demographically 'backward' regions of India (where mortality, and also fertility, are particularly

---

[65] Many Indian widows—and other single women—have shown that they are not just victims of the existing social order, but also spirited agents of change; see e.g. Bhatia (forthcoming), Chen (forthcoming, b), and Omvedt (1989a). The last author, in a very enlightening account of collective action by single women in Sangli district (Maharashtra), emphasizes 'the militancy of these women, who tend to provide the vanguard of toiling women's struggles everywhere' (p. 911). It is, in fact, not surprising that single women have often been found at the forefront of social and political movements. Indeed, freedom from conjugal control and the need to earn an independent living often lead single women to adopt a more autonomous and assertive lifestyle than their married sisters.

high) tend to be those where gender relations are highly unequal. This applies particularly to the large north Indian states (Uttar Pradesh, Bihar, Madhya Pradesh, and Rajasthan). Even in Punjab and Haryana, mortality and fertility rates are not much lower than the all-India averages (in fact, the fertility rate in Haryana is higher than the Indian average), despite very high levels of per-capita income in comparison with other Indian states, and this may have something to do with the comprehensive subordination of women in these two states.

Conversely, states which have experienced rapid progress in improving health and reducing mortality and fertility are often those where women play an important social or economic role. Two striking examples are Kerala and Manipur.[66] The empowerment of women has had a different basis in each case: the early promotion of female literacy (and, perhaps, the influence of matrilineal communities) has played a crucial role in Kerala, while other sources of female emancipation (including the economic roles of women) appear to have been more central in the case of Manipur. But the common feature is that, in both cases, women have ended up with a far more equal and active role in the society than their sisters in, say, the large north Indian states. And, correspondingly, there has been far more progress in the fields of health and mortality reduction, not just in terms of reducing the female disadvantage in survival, but also in improving survival chances for *everyone*.

There is a sense in which this connection is quite obvious. Given the gender division of labour that prevails in most of India, nutrition, child health, and related matters typically depend primarily on women's decisions and actions. It is hardly surprising that social achievements in this domain are more impressive where women are better educated, more resourceful, more valued, more influential, and generally more equal agents within the household and in society.

The importance of women's agency, of course, is not confined to the field of demographic change. When the creative abilities and personal contributions of one half of the society are stifled by constant subjugation, in addition to the drudgery of constant domestic work and child-bearing, social opportunities are suppressed in a wide range of domains. Even the level of economic production is likely to

[66] On Kerala, see the case study by V.K. Ramachandran (1996) in the companion volume, and the literature cited there. The case of Manipur, where birth and death rates are comparable to those of Kerala, is examined in A.K. Shiva Kumar (1992, 1994).

be higher, other things being equal, in a society where women are able to engage in a diverse range of activities compared with that in a society where their life is confined to domestic work. The realms of politics and social reform can also be considerably enriched by the active participation of women.

This general connection, too, emerges from broad inter-regional comparisons. Kerala not only has much lower levels of mortality and fertility than, say, Uttar Pradesh or Rajasthan, it has also made far more progress in removing traditional social inequalities, in using public services as a basis for enhancing the quality of life, and in evolving a vigorous civil society. By comparison, the large north Indian states are notorious for the persistence of feudal agrarian relations, for the continued oppression of disadvantaged castes, for chaotic public services, and for the comprehensive corruption of political institutions. Even in comparison with south India as a whole (not just Kerala), these north Indian states present a picture of resilient social backwardness. If one were to look for the deep historical roots of these inter-regional contrasts in the nature of society and politics, the position of women in society is certainly one of the influences that would command attention.

What is also striking is how the gender factor can overpower many other influences that often receive more attention, such as religious identity and national boundaries. We have already seen that the extent of anti-female bias in child survival does not vary much, if at all, between Hindus and Muslims in north India. Nor does it vary much between north India and Pakistan. The entire northern region is one where the agency of women has been comprehensively repressed, among Hindus as much as among Muslims or Sikhs, leading not only to a severe female disadvantage in child survival but also to the persistence of very high levels of mortality and fertility. Similarly, it is remarkable that Kerala and Sri Lanka have so much in common in terms of social achievements, cutting across the religious, cultural, and national boundaries. Here again, the common heritage of less unequal gender relations (which includes less patriarchal kinship systems, less male-dominated property rights, and a greater prominence of women in influential economic, social, and political activities) appears to be a causal factor of major importance.

By way of conclusion, we would like to focus on four elementary points. First, the persistence of extraordinarily high levels of gender inequality and female deprivation are among India's most serious social failures. Few other regions in the world have achieved so little in promoting gender justice.

Second, gender inequality does not decline automatically with the process of economic growth. In fact, we have seen that some important forces operate in the reverse direction (e.g. the tendency of upwardly-mobile castes to restrict the lifestyle of women in order to achieve a higher social status). Even where economic growth has a positive influence on the status of women, e.g. by expanding female employment opportunities or literacy rates, this influence tends to be slow and indirect. It is important to aim at more radical and rapid social change based on public action.

Third, gender inequality is not only a social failure in itself, it also leads to other social failures. We have illustrated this link in some detail with particular reference to child mortality and general fertility, but have also pointed to similar links that apply in other fields where the agency of women is important.

Finally, the agency of women as a force for change is one of the most neglected aspects of the development literature, and this neglect applies as forcefully—or more—in India as anywhere else. There has, happily, been a growing awareness in recent years of the disadvantaged predicament of women in Indian society. That understanding of the victimization of women has to be supplemented by a recognition of women as agents of social change. It is not merely that more justice must be received by women, but also that social justice can be achieved only through the active agency of women. The suppression of women from participation in social, political, and economic life hurts the people as a whole, not just women. Those regions in India, such as Kerala, which have moved in the direction of more gender equality have received more for all from that move. The emancipation of women is an integral part of social progress, not just a 'women's issue'.

# 8

# WELL BEYOND LIBERALIZATION

## 8.1 *What is the Cage?*

A tiger in a cage adorned the cover of the informative survey of
the Indian economy that *The Economist* published on 4 May 1991.[1]
The Indian economy was then in deep trouble, and the special
report began with a crisp diagnosis: 'The future of India looks more
threatened than for many years'. The analysis put much of the blame
for India's economic predicament on its 'ever-proliferating
bureaucracy' and its 'licence raj', and expressed the dialectic hope
that with the election then due, 'the new government will immediately
face a fiscal crisis' and as a consequence it 'might—just might—start
a reappraisal of the economic role of government that is so long
overdue'. The events that ushered in the economic reforms after
the new elections did not depart very far from that scenario.

The analogy of the caged tiger was an appropriate one in many
ways (even if *The Economist* might have been over-kind in referring
to 'India's boundless potential'). India does have a long history of
commerce, trade, and sophisticated industrial production; even at
the time of the industrial revolution, Lancashire had to resort to
rather wily tactics to compete with India's unpowered but refined
cotton textile industry. It has had a labour force of talent which
has shown the ability to adapt to new technical challenges given
the opportunity to do so. And Indian entrepreneurs and professionals
have been remarkably successful in a variety of economic operations
outside India, varying from running neighbourhood grocery stores

---

[1] 'A Survey of India', *The Economist*, 4 May 1991. The report was prepared by Clive
Crook.

(outdoing, for example, 'the nation of shopkeepers' in efficient shop-keeping) to making industrial and trading fortunes (taking an ell whenever they have been given an inch). There certainly is some animal in the cage.

The reforms that were introduced by the end of 1991 have indeed concentrated on removing the 'licence raj' and the 'ever-proliferating bureaucracy'. While the reforms have not moved as fast as was anticipated, there have been serious attempts in that general direction, and a promise of furtherance as and when circumstances permit. The liberalization that has occurred has led to a considerable expansion of exports in some sectors and a substantial improvement in the foreign exchange balance. It also has already led to a remarkable international response—involving a buoyant investment interest and high financial rating of the new economic policies. The appreciation has not been confined only to financial commentators with a long-standing interest in the Indian economy (such as *The Economist*), but has also included the normally more aloof American business interest groups, with the redoubtable *Forbes* magazine picturing India on the cover (23 May 1994), with the note: 'India may be the best emerging market of all'.

Yet the development performance of the Indian economy remains quite moderate. Even in terms of just the growth of GNP, GDP, and industrial production, the annual rates of expansion during 1991–4 (since the reforms) are all significantly *lower* than those achieved in the previous decade.[2] While the growth rate of GDP has risen over time from the first year of reform (a point that is often repeated by the government), it has not so far caught up with the pre-reform average growth of the eighties. The 'uncaging of the tiger' has not—at least not yet—led to any dynamic animal springing out and sprinting ahead.

The central issue, however, is not the moderate performance in overall economic growth. Rather, it is a question of the preparedness of the country for large-scale *participatory* growth, an issue to which we shall return presently. The year-to-year growth of GNP and GDP can, quite possibly, move up rapidly (as it is already doing to some extent), but the country remains handicapped economically and socially by its overwhelming illiteracy, backwardness in health

[2] See the Government of India's (1995) latest *Economic Survey* (p. 2 and Appendix); also Table A.4 in the Statistical Appendix of this book.

care, and other crucial deprivations. The hesitancy of the overall growth rate may well be cured soon enough, but these limitations would still continue to restrain the participatory possibilities of the growth process. As was argued earlier, the cage that keeps the Indian economy well tamed is not only that of bureaucracy and governmental overactivity, but also that of illiteracy, undernourishment, ill health, and social inequalities, and their causal antecedents: governmental neglect and public apathy.[3]

This recognition does not entail a dismissal of the diagnosis of bureaucratic overactivity, or a disputation of the need for basic economic reforms. In this monograph we have tried to argue for a broader view of economic development, which has to be seen in terms of expanding social opportunities.[4] While the removal of barriers to using markets can significantly enhance such opportunities, the practical usability of these opportunities requires the sharing of certain basic capabilities—including those associated particularly with literacy and education (and also those connected with basic health, social security, gender equality, land rights, local democracy). The rapid expansion of these capabilities depends crucially on public action of a kind that has been severely neglected in India—both before and after the recent reforms. The real issue in 'uncaging' the tiger is the need to go *well beyond* liberalization.

In principle, the social role of the government seems to be widely accepted by all. In particular, the rhetoric of every Indian government—without exception—has included handsome tribute to the importance of basic education. The real issue is not rhetorical acceptability, but the willingness to put actual—not imagined—emphasis on this particular requirement for the transformation of the Indian economy. This simply has not happened. While India has a highly developed—if overextended—higher education sector (sending nearly six times as many people to the universities and institutions of higher learning as China does, compared with its population), it remains one of the most backward countries in the world in terms of elementary education.[5] Its literacy rates are low in the Asian

---

[3] See chapters 3–6.

[4] See chapters 1–3.

[5] This was already beginning to be the case in 1970 when one of the authors of this monograph gave the Lal Bahadur Shastri Memorial Lecture on this subject, under the title 'The Crisis in Indian Education' (Sen, 1970), but all the criticisms then made are even more true today—25 years further on.

context (though higher in comparison with its like-minded neighbours, Pakistan and Bangladesh), and they are well behind the achievements of the more forward-looking countries in sub-Saharan Africa.[6]

With nearly half the people—and close to two-thirds of the women—illiterate, the transformation of the Indian economy is no easy task.[7] Even an efficient utilization of the world market requires production to specification, needs quality control, and depends on an informed consciousness of the economic tasks involved. The success of the east Asian 'tigers', and more recently of China, has been based on a much higher level of literacy and basic education than India has. This is one layer of the 'cage' that incarcerates the Indian economy and society.

This diagnosis is not concerned primarily with the overall rate of growth of GNP per head, even though it is hard to assume that illiteracy and ill health are not barriers to achieving high economic performance. India has had comparatively high rates of growth of per capita GNP in the eighties (before the reforms), and can achieve that again—and much more—in the future. The overall growth rate can be pushed up by rapid expansion of some favourably placed sectors. It is also quite possible, as many commentators have argued, that the slowness of the economic reforms is holding things up, and that a quickening of essential reforms would speed up the average growth rate of the Indian economy. Some sectors of the economy, especially those that rely on high skills of the kind that India already has plentifully (such as basic computer proficiency), have already been growing fast and can expand a lot faster. But, to have an impact on India's widespread poverty, what is needed is an expansion on a much wider basis (as has happened in, say, South Korea or China), and this would be extremely difficult to achieve without a much more inclusive base of basic education.[8]

The central issue, as was already stated, is not just the overall growth rate, and the reasons for concern go much beyond the current 'growth frustration', which could well change in the near future. We have particularly emphasized the need for *participatory* economic expansion, which is not the same thing as high achievement in

---

[6] Chapters 3 and 6.

[7] *The Economist* in its 'caged tiger' report had also, in fact, noted the need for public programmes of elementary education.

[8] See chapters 3 and 4.

some particular sectors (oriented to more specialized—and more mid-dle-class—skills), nor just the same as a high rate of growth of aggregate GNP per head.[9] For example, in the sixties and seventies, the Brazilian economy grew very fast but achieved rather little reduction of poverty, particularly in terms of social backwardness and sectional deprivation. The lack of participatory nature of that growth was extremely important in that outcome. Comparing Brazil's problems with patterns of more inclusive growth processes in east Asia tends to bring out the big difference made by a process of widely-shared, participatory growth, and the specific role of widespread basic education in fostering growth of this kind.[10] There is something quite important in this choice.[11] India stands in some danger of going Brazil's way, rather than South Korea's.

This does not affect in any way the diagnosis that India offers great investment opportunities in particular sectors even without any further expansion of basic education and health care. The *Forbes* magazine could well be exactly right in identifying India as 'the best emerging market of all' (India's middle class is probably larger than that of any other country), and yet this does not entail—and *Forbes* had not suggested it would—that this is a big force in eliminating poverty and deprivation of the Indian masses. The lessons from east Asia and China are not just about growth, but about widely-shared growth, assisted by careful social support.

## 8.2. *People as Ends and as Means*

We began this monograph by quoting Nehru's speech at the eve of independence, when he identified the 'tasks ahead' as 'the ending of poverty and ignorance and disease and inequality of opportunity'. The elimination of ignorance, of illiteracy, of remediable poverty, of preventable disease, and of needless inequalities in opportunities

[9] On this see also Drèze and Sen (1989), Part iii, and particularly the analysis of what was called 'unaimed opulence'.

[10] See particularly Birdsall and Sabot (1993a, 1993b). On aspects of the Brazilian experience, see also Sachs (1990). On aspects of Korean economic development, see also Amsden (1989), Wade (1990), and the earlier studies of Hong and Krueger (1975), Adelman and Robinson (1978), Datta Chaudhuri (1979), and Westphal et al. (1988).

[11] On the contrast between growth in Brazil and South Korea, and more generally between Latin American and east Asian patterns of economic expansion, see also McGuire (1994).

were to be seen as objectives that are valued for their own sake. They expand our freedom to lead the lives we have reason to value, and these elementary capabilities are of importance on their own.[12]

These capabilities can and do also contribute much to economic growth and to making the growth process participatory (as was discussed in the earlier chapters of this book), and human capabilities are among the chief means of economic success. But this excellence as means should not overshadow the *intrinsic* importance of human capabilities and effective freedom as the ends of social and political organization. We must not make the mistake—common in some circles—of taking the growth rate of GNP to be the ultimate test of success, and of treating the removal of illiteracy, ill health, etc., as—at best—possible means to that hallowed end. The first and the most important aspect of Nehru's listing of what we have to do is to make clear that the elimination of illiteracy, ill health and other avoidable deprivations are valuable for their own sake—they are 'the tasks' that we face.

In this sense, it is perhaps a mistake to see the development of education, health care, and other basic achievements *only* or *primarily* as expansions of 'human resources'—the accumulation of 'human capital'—as if people were just the *means* of production and not its ultimate *end*. The bettering of human life does not have to be justified by showing that a person with a better life is also a better producer. As Kant had noted, there is a categorical need to 'treat humanity, whether in their own person or in that of any other, in every case as an end withal, never as means only'. In arguing for a view of economic development that focuses on human capabilities, we are not just arguing for giving importance to so-called 'human capital'.

However, after noting this basic point, and getting our ends and means sorted out, we have every reason to pay full attention to the importance of human capabilities *also as instruments* for economic and social performance. A quality that is of intrinsic importance can, in addition, also be instrumentally momentous, without compromising its intrinsic value. Basic education, good health, and other human attainments are not only directly valuable as constituent elements of our basic capabilities, these capabilities can also help in

---

[12] See chapter 2 and the literature cited there.

generating economic success of a more standard kind, which in turn can contribute to enhancing the quality of human life in other ways.

The instrumental analysis has to be integrated with the intrinsic importance of human capabilities and effective freedoms. There are, thus, two distinct elements in this view of economic development: (1) the intrinsic and inalienable eminence of basic capabilities and the quality of life, and (2) the contingent but significant practical importance of many of these capabilities (especially those related to education, health, and elementary freedoms) in promoting participatory economic growth and, through it, further advancing the quality of life that people can enjoy. It is this dual concern that has largely motivated the approach we have tried to present in this work—a 'people-centred' approach, which puts human agency (rather than organizations such as markets or governments) at the centre of the stage.

## 8.3. *Radical Needs and Moderate Reforms*

The concentration on participatory growth calls for an integrated view of the process of economic expansion—focusing on the significance of economic growth, on the one hand, and on the importance of the participatory character of that growth, on the other. The crucial role of wide participation is central to this approach, and in so far as this requirement is missed out in policy discussions, that omission calls for rectification. At the same time, we must not confound that requirement with a rejection of the importance of economic growth itself. There has to be growth for it to be participatory.

While the neglect of social opportunities through the lack of adequate progress in basic education, health care, social security, land reforms, and similar fields has been detrimental to economic and social development in India, so has been the neglect of the appropriate incentives for economic efficiency and expansion. In pointing to the part of the 'cage' that the reformers often tend to ignore, we have no intention of dismissing the other part of the 'cage' that does motivate them. We are arguing for a more complete view of the difficulties that the Indian economy faces, not for shifting our diagnosis from one lopsided view to another. The fact that the boat of Indian officialdom has managed, in the past, to crash on both Scylla and Charybdis at the same time (a feat unknown to Ulysses) does not tell us to avoid only one of these dangers, overlooking the other.

There is scope for serious debate about many aspects of the economic reforms that are currently being introduced in India, and specific arguments have been presented in different directions.[13] Both the exact content of the reforms, and the policy approach in which they are embedded, call for much scrutiny. But these questions do not undermine the general necessity and desirability of removing counterproductive regulations and restrictions, nor of allowing greater use of the opportunities of international exchange. India has paid a heavy price for its overregulated and dysfunctional rules of economic governance, and there is a clear case for removing that handicap.

The counterproductive effects of many governmental restrictions, controls, and regulations in India have been clear for a long time, and have indeed been denounced by scholars and observers of many different persuasions. This problem has not been confined to India only, and has been a general feature of a number of developing countries, including India's neighbours in south Asia.[14] But the limitations have been particularly strong and resilient in India, and have survived many other changes of economic policies. The rhetoric of 'equity' has often been invoked to justify governmental interventions without any scrutinized political assessment of how those powers will be exercised and what actual effects they will have. In practice, these ill-directed regulations have not only interfered often enough with the efficiency of economic operations (especially of modern industries), they have also failed fairly comprehensively to promote any kind of real equity in distributional matters. Typically, the bureaucracy's rewards from being able to control economic operations,

---

[13] For some important contributions to this debate, on different sides, see Rudra (1991), Srinivasan (1991a, 1991b, 1993), Ahluwalia (1992), Desai (1992, 1993a), Parikh (1992, 1995), Patel (1992), Ravallion and Subbarao (1992), Kaushik Basu (1993, 1994), Bhagwati (1993), Bhagwati and Srinivasan (1993), Bhattacharya and Mitra (1993), Chandrasekhar and Ghosh (1993), Harriss (1993), Joshi and Little (1993, 1994), A. Mukherjee (1993), Mundle (1993), Oommen (1993), Parikh and Sudarshan (1993), A. Singh (1993), Toye (1993), Bagchi (1994), EPW Research Foundation (1994), Eswaran and Kotwal (1994), Gaiha (1994a), Ghosh (1994), Indira Gandhi Institute of Development Research (1994), Krishnaswamy (1994), Nayyar (1994), Patnaik (1994), S.L. Rao (1994), Sau (1994), S. Sen (1994), Cassen and Joshi (1995), among others.

[14] For an early analysis of the negative role of counterproductive regulations in a number of developing countries, see Little, Scitovsky, and Scott (1970). See also Corden (1974), Krueger (1974), and Bhagwati and Srinivasan (1975), among other contributions.

distribute favours, or cause (or threaten to cause) obstructions, have been exploited by those who were already in privileged positions. While a lot of all this was done in the name of the Indian poor, that hapless creature has got very little from it.

Similar remarks apply to the need for making better use of the opportunities offered by international trade. Many countries have made excellent use of these opportunities, and India too can reap much more fully the benefits of economies of scale and efficient division of labour.[15] While greater involvement in trade is sometimes seen as something that compromises the country's economic independence, or that jeopardizes India's sovereignty, there is little objective basis for such fears. Given the diversity of trading partners, the worry that India would be an economic prisoner in the international world of open exchange is quite unfounded. This does not deny the importance of getting the terms and conditions of trade right, including having fair regulations from GATT (or its successor) and other international institutions, which have often been far from even-handed. But in general there is little reason for fearfully abstaining from the benefits offered by international trade and exchange. In fact, it is worth recalling that India's share of international trade used to be about four times as high, forty years ago, as it is now, so that an expansion of India's involvement in international trade, far from putting the country in a new and uncertain position, would merely help to restore its position prior to decades of spiralling decline in the world economy.[16] On this whole issue, India has much to learn from China, which has boldly seized the opportunities of international trade in recent years, with remarkable results in terms of broad-based expansion of living standards, and without much sign of its economic or political sovereignty being compromised.[17]

While much energy has been spent on sorting out these issues, too little attention has been paid to what is *lacking* in the current

---

[15] See chapter 3. The dynamic role of trade as an aspect of economic change applies to national as well as international trade; on this see Bauer and Yamey (1957) and Bauer (1972, 1991). The restrictions imposed by interstate fiscal barriers in India (e.g. through the 'octroi') have recently led to protests by lorry drivers because of the harassment and delays involved, but there is here a more general economic issue as well.

[16] On 'India's regression in the world economy', see S.J. Patel (1985, 1994).

[17] The 'open door' policy of the Chinese government involved eschewing one of the most cherished principles of the Mao era, i.e. that of self- sufficiency. This is another illustration of the pragmatism of economic policy in China, discussed in chapter 4.

orientation of economic policy in India. The removal of counter-productive regulations on domestic production and international trade can form a helpful *part* of a programme of participatory and wide-ly-shared growth, but it may achieve relatively little in the absence of more active public policy aimed at removing the other social handicaps that shackle the Indian economy and reduce the well-being of the population. The absence of real reform in the field of basic education is a telling illustration of the government's neglect of that part of the agenda. There has been much talk, in recent years, about the importance of basic education and the need to give it a 'high priority'. Many official pronouncements in this direction have been made, many new 'schemes' have been launched, and many glossy publications extolling the virtues of these initiatives have been produced. But, as we saw in chapter 6, this rhetoric has gone hand in hand with a remarkably slow actual expansion of basic schooling facilities, and even falling teaching inputs in per capita terms. We have also discussed how the dismal functioning of the schooling system, and related failures of education policy, contribute to the persistence of widespread illiteracy in much of the country, especially north India. To illustrate, the fact that, according to a recent survey of 15 primary schools in rural Uttar Pradesh, two-thirds of the village teachers were absent from the school at the time of the investigators' unannounced visit is another remarkable example of the gap between rhetoric and reality in the field of basic education.

In the field of health care, too, there is little sign of any determination to address the tragic limitations of current policy. As we noted in chapter 5, health care facilities in many parts of rural India have been extensively diverted to forceful programmes of family planning (mainly based on female sterilization), compounding the problem of persistently high levels of morbidity and mortality. Similarly, a recent survey of family health in India reveals that 30 per cent of all children aged 12–23 months have never received *any* vaccination, that only half of all pregnant women go through some kind of antenatal check-up, and that only a tiny minority of married women have convenient access to non-terminal methods of modern con-traception (with much worse figures in rural areas, among disad-vantaged social groups, and in states where health policy has been particularly neglected).[18] These failures in a crucially important field

18 These figures are derived from the National Family Health Survey, as reported in

of government action receive extraordinarily little attention in current debates. Similar things can be said of recent trends in many other areas of social and economic policy.

The absence of any real commitment to social reform fits into that general pattern. We have discussed, in chapter 7, how the persistence of extraordinary gender inequalities in India is a major obstacle to social progress. There has been no decisive attempt on the part of the government, before or after the reforms, to challenge these inequalities. The general attitude of the administration, the courts, the police, and other government institutions has rather been to endorse and enforce the traditional view of Indian women as subordinate members of society. Similarly, there has been little real challenge to caste-based inequalities, and the somewhat checkered introduction of reservation policies for disadvantaged castes has gone hand in hand with a tacit acceptance of a caste hierarchy in the Indian society. As we saw in chapter 5, these and other traditional inequalities are resilient factors of economic and social backwardness in India, particularly in rural areas.

In earlier chapters of this book, we have discussed how policy developments in India, including those since the 'reforms', have continued the tradition of neglecting the fundamental importance of basic capabilities in economic development, and of the positive role of the state in promoting these capabilities.[19] Judged in that perspective, the current reorientation of economic policy is much less of a radical departure from the past than it is often considered to be, and it leaves unaddressed some of the most debilitating biases of earlier regimes. Correcting these biases—not just in political rhetoric but in practical action—calls for a major shift of emphasis in policy-making. There is also an acute need to pay more attention to these issues in public debates and social and political movements, involving the opposition as well as the government.

## 8.4. *Governance and Public Action*

The positive roles of the state in economic development span a

---

International Institute for Population Sciences (1994); some further results of this survey are given in the Statistical Appendix of this book. The inter-state contrasts suggest a clear relation between health achievements and public initiatives in this field. Here again, the large north Indian states stand out with a particularly poor record in both respects.

[19] See particularly chapters 2 and 5–7.

wide range of activities. In this book, we have paid particular attention to specific activities that demand priority attention at this stage, such as the expansion of basic education. But there are many other relevant fields of action, including not only those which we have had occasion to discuss (e.g. health care, social security, population policy, land reform, local democracy, women's rights), but also others which are less closely related to the central concerns of this book (e.g. the need for sound environmental policies, for improved rural infrastructure, or for a credible legal system). The key issue is that many of the basic entitlements that people need in order to improve their lives (e.g. to primary education, child vaccination, safe contraception, clean water, social security, environmental resources, legal protection) depend to varying extents on some form of positive government activity. The positive role of the state is, thus, potentially quite extensive.

At the same time, the standards of government activity in many of these fields are, as things stand, abysmally low (and, in some cases, deteriorating). The task of making the positive role of the state more effective in India is, therefore, extremely challenging.

The quality of governance ultimately relates, to a considerable extent, to the practice of domestic politics and to 'public action' in the broad sense of action *by* the public (rather than just *for* the public, by the government).[20] Even though many of the weighty decisions that have to be taken are ultimately settled by the government in office (in New Delhi or in the respective state capitals), they are, to varying extents, influenced by the actions and demands of the public. Thus, political parties and public activists have an important role in the emergence and survival of particular policies and economic strategies. The democratic framework of the Indian polity permits this exercise in ways that are not open in many other developing economies.

The role of the public is not confined to influencing or challenging the decisions of the government. The agency of the public is also directly important in many fields of economic and social activity. There are, indeed, many different types of community-based action where public activism can be very rewarding.[21] The monitoring of

[20] See chapters 5–7; also Drèze and Sen (1989).

[21] Robert Putnam (1993) has brought out the importance of 'civic traditions' and non-governmental public action for successful political, economic, and social life, in the specific context of Italy, with important general lessons for other countries as well.

school education, including the prevention of large-scale absenteeism on the part of rural teachers (common in many parts of India), is a good illustration (this was discussed in chapter 5). To cite another example, recent experiences in different parts of India have also shown that community management can, in some circumstances, provide an excellent institutional basis for the protection of local environmental resources.[22]

The agency of the public can also play an essential part in the task of reducing social inequalities. As discussed in chapter 5, there are many good reasons to be concerned about the persistence of extraordinary inequalities in Indian society. We have argued for taking a broad view of inequality, which pays attention not only to the standard economic inequalities but also to other relevant social divisions based on gender, caste, literacy, and other characteristics. In combating these diverse inequalities, social movements and collective action have a crucial role to play.[23]

Whether the involvement of the public at large takes the form of pressing for particular forms of government action, or of working for social change outside the sphere of government activity, the results can depend a great deal on effective political organization of disadvantaged groups. India's democratic institutions provide many potential bases of public action (including not only the electoral process but also the news media, the legal system, village panchayats, etc.), but an important organizational task is involved in seizing these opportunities. The extent to which this process of political organization of disadvantaged groups has occurred has varied a great deal between different parts of India. Kerala stands out as a case of early success, but there have also been commendable achievements elsewhere. In West Bengal, for instance, effective organization of disadvantaged groups under the leadership of the 'left front' parties has led to a significant change in the balance of political power, and this, in turn, has provided the basis for important social achievements, notably land reform.[24] In some states of south and western

---

[22] See e.g. Agarwal and Narain (1989), Gadgil and Guha (1993), and the literature cited there.

[23] V.K. Ramachandran's chapter in the companion volume (Drèze and Sen, 1996) extensively discusses the role of social movements in breaking the old inequalities of class, caste, and gender in Kerala. Other examples, elsewhere in India, are discussed by Fernandes (1985), Shah (1990), and Omvedt (1993); see also the literature cited there.

[24] See chapter 3, and also the case study of West Bengal by Sunil Sengupta and Haris

India, the ability of disadvantaged groups to organize and participate in the political process has also significantly improved in recent years. Consolidating these achievements (and extending them to states where government institutions and the political process are still comprehensively dominated by privileged groups) is one of the major challenges ahead.

Both the state and the public have central roles to play in economic development. While different schools of thought tend to place different emphasis on their respective roles, it is hard to avoid seeing them as thoroughly interdependent. Just as the nature of state activities depends a great deal on public demands and pressures, the actions of the public—both collaborative and adversarial—are all the more effective when the state plays its part in helping to empower the citizens by guaranteeing basic democratic freedoms, ensuring widespread literacy, protecting the legal rights of disadvantaged groups, and providing some security against extreme destitution. There is, in this sense, a deeply complementary relationship between state action and public action.

This dialectical feature of the relationship between state action and public action makes it possible for a society to be caught in a vicious circle of (1) government apathy towards the needs of the citizens, and (2) public inability to challenge that apathy, as has happened in states such as Uttar Pradesh.[25] On the positive side, it also means that the rewards of efforts aimed at breaking that vicious circle (e.g. based on the political organization of disadvantaged groups, or on the promotion of widespread literacy) can be very large, as Kerala's experience illustrates. This is one reason why the promotion of literacy—to which both state action and public action have much to contribute—is so central to the transformation of Indian politics. Among the many adverse effects of illiteracy and educational backwardness in India are their role in muting public pressure for social change and governmental responsibility. The rewards of

---

Gazdar (1996) in the companion volume. As discussed in that study, political developments in West Bengal have provided an improved basis for many social reforms, but there has been uneven success in actually using this opportunity. In particular, while issues of land reform and local democracy have been addressed with relatively good effect, public policies dealing with health, education, and related matters have been—so far—largely neglected.

[25] On this reading of Uttar Pradesh's development experience, see Drèze and Gazdar (1996) in the companion volume.

expanding basic education include its impact on the nature and force of public action. In arguing for greater attention to the role of social opportunities in economic development, we have tried to emphasize not only the use of these opportunities to generate higher earnings and better lives for the individuals directly involved, but also the social use of these freedoms to influence the government and the society at large.

## 8.5. *Women's Agency and Social Change*

In the course of different arguments in this monograph, we have had the occasion to comment on the importance of women's agency for social progress.[26] The focus on women's agency has to be distinguished from the more usual concentration on women's well-being. There are good reasons to pay particular attention to each in examining the requirements of economic development and social change in India. The persistence of sharp gender inequalities in many different forms is one of the most striking aspects of the Indian economy, and it yields disparities in well-being as well as differences in power and decision-making authority.

Perhaps the most telling expression of gender inequality of well-being is to be found in the low female–male ratio in India, and the high proportion of 'missing women' whose absence can be attributed to differential care, including medical attention.[27] Unequal sharing of the rewards of family life is one of the prominent features of gender relations in India. In remedying these inequalities, the activities of women's organizations and other forms of agency can be of crucial importance, and in several different contexts, the effectiveness of such activities has already been well demonstrated.[28]

The first reason for the importance of women's agency is, thus, the persistence of gender-based inequalities of well-being, and the relevance of women's actions and movements in bringing about a change in this field. The need for women's own agency in securing gender justice arises partly from the fact that gender inequality does

[26] See chapters 3–7.

[27] See chapter 7.

[28] See Omvedt (1980, 1989a, 1993), K. Bardhan (1985), Poitevin and Rairkar (1985), Desai (1988), Duvvury (1989), Stree Shakti Sanghatana (1989), Kishwar and Vanita (1991), Dietrich (1992), Rose (1992), D.K.S. Roy (1992), Chaudhuri (1993), among others.

not decline automatically with the process of economic growth. In fact, as we saw in chapter 7, in some respects economic progress can even lead to an actual deterioration in the position of women in society. In so far as economic expansion does reduce gender inequality, this happens mainly *through* other variables that relate more closely to women's agency, such as female labour-force participation and female literacy. Economic growth, for instance, can positively influence the status of women through expanding opportunities for remunerative female employment, which often results in an improvement in the 'deal' that a woman receives within the family. But even these influences, though fairly extensive in some cases, can be slow, and in great need of supplementation by more direct public action in pursuit of gender equity, focusing for instance on educational transformation, women's ownership rights, and political activism.

Second, women's empowerment can positively influence the lives not only of women themselves but also of men, and of course those of children. There is much evidence, for instance, that women's education tends to reduce child mortality rates, for both boys and girls. In fact, there is good reason to relate the remarkably high life-expectancy levels in Kerala to its educational achievements, particularly of women, and on the other side, to relate the low life expectancies of some of the northern states to backwardness in female education.[29] The subordination of women in Indian society tends to impair their effectiveness in reducing deprivation in general, and it is not only the well-being of female children or adult women which is improved by the enhanced agency of women.

Third, as we have also seen (chapter 7), women's emancipation, in the form of basic education and economic independence, tends

[29] See section 7.3, and the studies cited there. It is worth emphasizing that the positive link between female education and child survival is likely to relate not only to the agency of women *within* the family, but also to their role in politics and public life. In particular, a more active and informed public role of women in society tends to be associated with greater pressure in the direction of expanding health care and related public services, and with an improved use of these services. After noting that 'women have invariably been the large majority of the participants' (p. 22) in the Total Literacy Campaign, for instance, Ghosh et al. (1994) observe that the campaign has led to 'greater and more vociferous demand for [education and] other services to meet [the participants'] basic needs in regard to employment, housing, health, etc.' (p. 38). Similarly, according to a recent study of the renowned Self-Employed Women's Association based in Ahmedabad, 'SEWA found that health care was the most urgent need after economic issues that the women wanted to organize around' (Rose, 1992, p. 249).

to have quite a strong impact on fertility rates. This linkage has been widely observed in international comparisons, but it is consistent also with Kerala's remarkable reduction of fertility rates, and to some extent, with Tamil Nadu's recent success in that direction.[30] On the other side, the low position of women in the 'northern heartland' clearly does contribute not a little to the high fertility rates that are found in such states as Uttar Pradesh, Madhya Pradesh, Rajasthan, and Bihar. Through this connection with demographic change, the role of women's agency extends well beyond the interests of today's women, and even beyond the interests of all living people today, and has a significant impact on the lives of future generations.

Fourth, aside from specialized roles, women's agency is important as a part of the agency of all people. Women's decisions and actions can have a profound impact on the policies that the government decides to pursue and the lives that people can lead. Women have often been very active in demanding and working for basic social change, and the discussion in the last section on the importance of actions of the public applies particularly to women. In much of India, women tend to remain rather homebound and politically unassertive, and given the critical importance of political action and pressure, a real difference can be made by women taking an active role in these activities.[31] The effectiveness of public action and the expansion of social opportunities depend a great deal on the effective freedom of women to exercise their reasoned agency.

## 8.6. *Comparative Perspectives*

International comparisons have been used fairly extensively in this book, in a variety of contexts. We have invoked them, for instance, in discussing the intrinsic as well as instrumental roles of human capabilities in economic development, the respective contributions of economic growth and public support in expanding social opportunities, the role of markets in fostering economic growth, and the enormity of India's failures in areas such as basic education and gender inequality.[32]

---

[30] See chapter 7, and also Sen (1994b).

[31] See, for example, Robin Jeffrey (1987, 1992), including his account of 'how women made Kerala literate'.

[32] See particularly chapters 3, 4, and 7.

We have paid special attention to the contrast between India and China, not only because of the obvious relevance of the Chinese experience for India, but also because of the sustained influence of that particular comparison in Indian political debates (see section 4.1). In interpreting China's experience (particularly involving a much more radical elimination of endemic deprivations than India has been able to achieve so far), we have emphasized the complementarities between the *pre-reform* achievements and the *post-reform* success in promoting rapid economic expansion on a widespread basis.[33] When China adopted its programme of market-oriented economic reforms in the late seventies, it had already gone a long way towards achieving the conditions that facilitate broad-based involvement of people in the process of economic expansion. The relevant achievements include (1) land reform, (2) near-universal literacy in the younger age groups, (3) a radical reduction of endemic morbidity and undernutrition, (4) the foundations of a social security system, (5) a functioning system of local governance, and (6) a major expansion of the basis of high participation of women in the labour force. India is nowhere near achieving these solid foundations of broad-based economic expansion, and the challenges of economic and social reform in India have to be seen in that light.

At the same time, we have also guarded against the temptation of advocating imitative emulation of the Chinese experience. China's experience of expanding social opportunities, while most impressive in many respects, has included some failures of monumental proportions. As was discussed in chapter 4, many of these failures reflect China's authoritarian system of governance, which keeps government policies outside the reach of public scrutiny and popular challenge. The famines of 1958–61, the excesses of the Cultural Revolution, the widespread and continuing violation of elementary freedoms, and the devastating human consequences of coercive population policies, are telling illustrations of that pattern. Just as China's positive achievements provide a powerful illustration of the scope for positive government activity in economic development, its failures clearly point to the dangers of authoritarian governance—and that, too, is a lesson of major importance for India.

These basic lessons from China's experience are, to a great extent, reinforced by a consideration of regional diversities within India.

---

[33] See chapter 4.

As we have discussed on several occasions, India has much to learn not only from China and other countries but also from its own experience. This is particularly so given that India is a most diverse country, and that the records of different regions and states are extremely disparate. The diversity of experiences within India relates especially to the varieties of public policies pursued in the respective states, and, in particular, to the dissimilar use of public action to enhance the quality of life and to expand basic human capabilities.[34]

Kerala's experience is particularly instructive in that respect, and has received sustained attention in this book. There is, indeed, much evidence of the extensive links between Kerala's outstanding social achievements (including a life expectancy of 72 years, a fertility rate below the replacement level, near-universal literacy in the younger age groups, a virtual absence of child labour, and relatively low levels of gender inequality) and its rich history of public action (involving early state initiatives and social movements for the promotion of literacy, the implementation of land reforms, the elimination of traditional inequalities, the provision of wide-ranging public services, and related goals).[35] Kerala's experience of early promotion of social opportunities based on public action is of far-reaching significance for other Indian states, and indeed for other countries also.

Kerala's record includes some failures as well, and we have noted in particular how Kerala's performance in generating economic growth has been very moderate indeed. In fact, there has been virtually no growth of the domestic economy in Kerala during the eighties (see Statistical Appendix). While the social opportunities of living long, healthy, and literate lives have been radically enhanced in an exemplary manner, the opportunities that depend on economic success have been more stagnant.

This contrast raises interesting issues concerning the causal antecedents of participatory growth. Kerala has been very successful in developing the social opportunities (related to widespread education, health care, land reforms, social security, etc.) that constitute the centrally important *social* conditions for having participatory economic growth. And yet Kerala has had, in fact, little participatory economic growth at home. The failure in this case has arisen not from any

---

[34] See particularly chapter 3.
[35] See the study by V.K. Ramachandran (1996) in the companion volume, and also the literature cited there and in section 3.6 of this book.

lack of participation but from the low growth of Kerala's domestic economy; as we have argued earlier, there has to be growth for it to be participatory. The roots of this failure include the continuation of overregulated economic governance that has blighted the prospects of economic expansion all over India for many decades, the removal of which has met more resistance in Kerala than in most other Indian states.

The radical commitments of left-leaning governments, on the one hand, and of activist general politics, on the other, have done much in Kerala to guarantee widespread social opportunities in many crucial fields. But that political climate has also tended to encourage economic policies that are extremely hostile to the market mechanism, even in areas where this hostility—and the excessive reliance on government regulation that goes with it—is quite counterproductive. This has made it harder to change the overregulated economy of Kerala, even in comparison with the situation in other Indian states. As was argued earlier, programmes of positive public action need not be combined with a general rejection of the economic advantages of the market. Kerala's experience illustrates the need for a discriminating choice of public intervention, which is one of the central themes of this monograph.

The contrast between (1) the advantages of Kerala's radical social preparedness, and (2) the handicaps of its essentially conservative economic policies (often clinging forcefully to old-fashioned bureaucratic regulations), has tended to produce an odd mismatch. As a result, the people of Kerala have been much more inclined to make use of economic opportunities outside the state than at home. While Kerala's domestic economy has continued to stagnate over the decades, its 'outside incomes' (including remittances) have been very large over that same period, reflecting extensive use by the people of Kerala of economic opportunities elsewhere, often in other countries.[36]

Kerala, it would appear, has to learn as well as teach. But while Kerala's *learning* can be easily integrated into the contemporary reformist focus on incentives, economic growth, and deregulation, what it has to *teach* takes us well beyond these concerns. As far as these positive lessons are concerned, however, there is a tendency to dismiss

---

[36] On the role of migration and remittances in Kerala's economy, see Krishnan (1994, forthcoming).

the exemplary force of Kerala's achievements as those of 'merely a state, not a country'. Since intercountry comparisons for policy analysis typically focus on nations as a whole, Kerala's experience tends not to receive the international attention that is given to the achievements of particular countries—from Sri Lanka and Costa Rica to South Korea and Hong Kong. This is not a sensible neglect for several distinct reasons.

First, with its 29 million people, Kerala has a larger population than most countries in the world (even Canada), including many from which comparative lessons are often drawn, such as Sri Lanka (17.4 million) and Costa Rica (3.2 million), and, of course, the primarily city states of Hong Kong (5.8 million) and Singapore (2.8 million). Even South Korea, which receives a great deal of attention in the development literature and is often seen as a development 'model', had about the same population size in the early sixties (when its rapid transformation began) as Kerala has now. To achieve as much as Kerala has done for a population of its size is no mean record in world history.

Second, given the political federalism of the Indian union, each state has considerable autonomy in such fields as school education and health care. To be sure, an initiative of the central government can be extremely powerful in its impact on state policies, partly through fiscal linkages (a large proportion of each state's resources comes from allocation of central revenue such as income tax collections), but also through political connections and party contacts that operate between the centre and the states. But this does not prevent a state from taking a bold initiative in matters of education and health care, and to go well forward on its own if it so chooses. This is what Kerala has done with remarkable canniness and determination.

There is a different kind of objection that could be a more legitimate reason for doubting that Kerala's experience can be emulated. Kerala has been fortunate with its past. For one thing, the bulk of what is now Kerala consisted of two 'native states'—Travancore and Cochin —formally outside British India. They were not subjected to the general shortage of official interest of Whitehall in Indian elementary education (as opposed to higher education). When Rani Gouri Parvathi Bai, the young queen of Travancore, made her pioneering statement in 1817 on the importance of basic education, there was no need to bring that policy initiative in line with what was happening in the rest of India, under the Raj.[37]

Kerala has also been fortunate in having strong social movements that concentrated on educational advancement—along with general emancipation—of the lower castes, and this has been a special feature of left-wing and radical political movements in Kerala. It has also profited from a tradition of openness to the world, which has included welcoming early Christians (at least from the fourth century), Jews (from shortly after the fall of Jerusalem), and Muslims (from the days of Arab trading, as settlers rather than as conquerors). Into this rather open and receptive environment, the extensive educational efforts of Christian missionaries in the nineteenth century fitted comfortably. Kerala has also benefited from the matrilineal tradition of property inheritance for an important part of the community (the Nairs), which has contributed to giving women in Kerala a better social position, even in the past.

Having good luck in one's history is not, however, a policy parameter that one can adjust. Those who see a unique and unrepeatable pattern in Kerala's remarkable record in educational expansion can point to the very special nature of its past, and suggest that other states can learn rather little from it. This, however, would be quite the wrong conclusion to draw from Kerala's heterogeneous history. When the state of Kerala was created in independent India, it was made up, on linguistic grounds, of the erstwhile native states of Travancore and Cochin, and the region of Malabar from the old province of Madras in British India (later Tamil Nadu). The Malabar region, transferred from the Raj, was very much behind Travancore and Cochin in terms of literacy, life expectancy, and other achievements that make Kerala so special. But by the eighties, Malabar had 'caught up' to such an extent with the rest of Kerala that it could no longer be seen in divergent terms.[38] The initiatives

---

[37] The independence from general British Indian policy applied not only to the princely rulers of these states, but also to the British 'Residents' in Trivandrum. The Residents could consider independent initiatives, and indeed in the big move in Travancore in the direction of elementary education in the early nineteenth century, the Resident Mr Munro played an extremely supportive—and possibly even catalytic—role. There is some evidence that he drafted Rani Parvathi Bai's 1817 statement, whether or not the initiative was also his (on this, see Ramachandran, 1996).

[38] On this see Kabir and Krishnan (1992), George (1994), Krishnan (1994), and Ramachandran (1996).

that the state governments of Kerala took, under different 'manage-ments' (led by the Communist Party as well as by the Congress), succeeded in bringing Malabar rather at par with the rest of Kerala over a short period of time. So there is a lesson here that is not imprisoned in the fixity of history. Other parts of India can indeed learn a lot from Kerala's experience on what can be done here and now through determined public action.

It is also worth noting that while Kerala was already very advanced compared with British India at the time of independence, much of the great achievements of Kerala that are so admired now are the results of post-independence public policies. In fact, in the fifties Kerala's adult literacy rate was around 50 per cent compared with 90 now, its life expectancy at birth was 44 years *vis-à-vis* 72 now, and its birth rate was 32 as opposed to 18.5 now.[39] Kerala did have a good start, but the policies that have made its achievements so extraordinary are the products of more recent political initiatives and public action. In fact, as we showed in chapter 4, it is only over the last decade or so that Kerala has actually overtaken China with considerable rapidity in raising life expectancy, reducing infant mortality, cutting down fertility rates, and so on.

As was discussed earlier, there are also other states in India which indicate that substantial rewards can be obtained from serious public efforts in raising human capabilities. West Bengal provides a good example of the possibility and rewards of land reform programmes (enhancing equity as well as the efficiency of local agriculture).[40] Tamil Nadu shows how the fertility rate can be quite dramatically reduced through well-coordinated family planning programmes, making good use of its base of comparatively favourable social back-ground (being among the top three major states in primary education, in female participation in outside employment, and in low infant mortality, along with having a traditionally higher age at marriage).[41] Himachal Pradesh provides a helpful example of rapid reduction of illiteracy among children, partly based on a relatively bold schooling programme. Punjab illustrates the possibility of encouraging economic growth through infrastructural development (though its economic

---

[39] On these figures and the general history that they represent, see Ramachandran (1996).

[40] See chapter 3, and the paper by Sunil Sengupta and Haris Gazdar (1996) in the companion volume.

[41] See chapters 4 and 7, and the Statistical Appendix.

success has been hit hard recently by conflict and violence). There are other examples of this kind, from which lessons can be drawn and used. While Kerala stands out as the leader in social developments, it does not stand alone.

On the other side, the penalties of governmental neglect and public inertia are well illustrated by a number of other states, such as Uttar Pradesh, where basic deprivations remain endemic. In fact, as we saw in chapter 3, there is an interesting complementarity between the lessons emerging from positive and negative experiences. Just as Kerala's achievements richly illustrate the positive influences of widespread literacy, public services, women's agency, adversarial politics, collective organization, and related factors of social progress, the failures of Uttar Pradesh illustrate the tremendous stifling of social opportunities that often results from neglecting these positive influences.

## 8.7. *A Concluding Remark*

Economic policies in India have undergone much change over the last few years, and more changes are in the process of being implemented. The debate surrounding these reforms has mobilized enormous attention and energy, and the arguments presented on each side have been quite forceful and firm, even acrimonious.

In this monograph, we have emphasized the need to take the debates on economic policy well *beyond* the issue of economic reforms in their present form. This is not because we see particularly great merit in avoiding acrimonious debates (a bit of healthy mud-slinging might indeed have something to commend in making people take an interest in complex and apparently dull problems), but because we believe that the concentration on attacking or defending economic reforms as the central policy issue distracts attention from a broader view of social opportunities of which the use of the market can be *an important yet quite incomplete* part. The economic reforms do constitute an important departure, but there are many other issues of great importance which have been thoroughly overshadowed by the focus on arguments—both *for* and *against*—the reforms. This has also led to summary assessments—both championing and dismissal—of economic policies that cannot really be judged adequately without placing them in a much broader context.

We have argued for the necessity of asking—and addressing—a

very different set of questions, rather than confining the analysis to examining different answers to the old familiar questions. The central issue, we have argued, is to expand the social opportunities open to the people. In so far as these opportunities are compromised—directly or indirectly—by counterproductive regulations and controls, by restrictions on economic initiatives, by the stifling of competition and its efficiency-generating advantages, and so on, the removal of these hindrances must be seen as extremely important. But we have also discussed why the creation and use of social opportunities for all require much more than the 'freeing' of markets. While the case for economic reforms may take good note of the diagnosis that India has too much government interference in some fields, it ignores the fact that India also has insufficient and ineffective government activity in many other fields, including basic education, health care, social security, land reform, and the promotion of social change. This inertia, too, contributes to the persistence of widespread deprivation, economic stagnation, and social inequality.

What needs curing is not just 'too little market' or 'too much market'. The expansion of markets is *among* the instruments that can help to promote human capabilities, and, given the imperative need for rapid elimination of endemic deprivation in India, it would be irresponsible to ignore that opportunity. But much more is involved in freeing the Indian economy from the cage in which it has been confined, and many of the relevant tasks call for more—not less—government activity and public action.

The distinction between market-complementary and market-excluding governmental activities—discussed in chapter 2—is central to this proposition. Many of the traditional government interventions in India have tended to take a market-excluding form: for example, regulations and controls that stifle economic initiatives in certain areas, the prohibition of trade that shuts out economic options in particular fields, and so on. And at the same time, some types of supportive—as opposed to negative and restrictive—government activities (such as a comprehensive policy of basic education for all, an adequately widespread programme of health care, and so on) have been systematically neglected. It is possible to go more beyond the market in rectifying the latter neglect, while giving greater scope to the market in curing the former transgression.

Policy debates in India have to be taken away from the narrow concentration on issues of liberalization. The nostalgia of the old debates 'Are you *pro* or *anti* market?', or 'Are you *in favour* or *against* state activities?' seems to have an odd 'hold' on all sides, so that we concentrate only on some issues and ignore many—often more important—ones. The focus of government policy at this time seems to be overwhelmingly concerned with the need to remove counterproductive regulations, while continuing the traditional neglect of positive activities. We have also argued that there is a strong case for reorienting public discussion and criticism from the merits and demerits of liberalization towards taking adequate note of the tremendous social and economic deprivations that blight living conditions in India and limit the actual prospects of participatory economic expansion. The terms of the debate need radical change.

# STATISTICAL APPENDIX

# EXPLANATORY NOTE

This Appendix presents statistical information on aspects of Indian economic and social development. Table A.1 focuses on international comparisons of development indicators for selected Asian countries. Table A.2 attempts to integrate some of these comparisons with internal contrasts within India. The Indian states appearing in Table A.2 are those for which case studies are presented in the companion volume (Drèze and Sen, 1996). Table A.3 gives a more detailed picture of economic development and social opportunity in different Indian states. This table presents information on: per-capita income and related indicators; mortality and fertility; literacy and related educational achievements; school attendance and enrolment; gender-related indicators; maternal health and related matters; and social infrastructure. Table A.4 provides some information relating to trends over time.

## 1. *Sources*

In constructing the tables included in this Appendix as well as in the text, we have tried to concentrate on indicators for which the informational basis is relatively reliable. Even for these indicators, there are occasional difficulties, including minor discrepancies between different statistical sources. For the purpose of international comparisons (such as those presented in Table A.1), we have typically used *World Development Report 1994* (and earlier issues of that Report, when applicable). When the relevant indicator is not available in that publication, we have used *Human Development Report 1994*. The main exceptions to this procedure concern (1) literacy figures, and (2) longevity indicators for India and China. These exceptions are discussed in the next section.

For state-specific indicators within India, we have relied, in each case, on the most appropriate national statistical source, e.g. the 1991 census for literacy rates, the National Sample Survey for per-capita expenditure, the Sample Registration System for mortality and fertility rates, and so on. In some tables (e.g. Table A.3), we have also made use of the all-India figure from the same source. It is worth mentioning that, in most cases, these all-India figures from national statistical sources are very close to the corresponding figures given in *World Development Report 1994,* which are used here for the purposes of international comparisons.

Some figures are quite sensitive to the choice of reference year. Generally, we have used the most recent year for which the relevant information is available as the reference year, unless there were specific reasons to use some other year. There are also cases where different issues of an annual statistical publication give different figures for the same indicator and the same reference year. In these cases, we have used the most recent issue of the publication in question, on the assumption that these changes reflect a refinement rather than a deterioration of the estimation methods used to produce these figures.

## 2. *Comments on Specific Indicators*

### *Literacy rates in India and China*

The literacy rates for India and China used in chapter 4, and in this Appendix, are taken directly from the relevant census volumes, rather than from international publications such as *World Development Report.* The results of the most recent censuses in India and China, it appears, are yet to be incorporated in these international publications. For instance, the adult literacy rate figures presented in *World Development Report 1994,* Table 1, are based on 'projections prepared in 1989 by UNESCO' (p. 232), and these figures are obviously out of date compared with the more recent figures made available by the 1990 census in China and the 1991 census in India. We have, therefore, preferred to use the census figures, and, for consistency, we have also used census figures from direct sources for earlier years.[1]

[1] For a more detailed discussion of the different sources, and of the methodological issues arising in comparisons of literacy rates in India and China, see Drèze and Loh (1995). The literacy figures derived from India's 1991 census can be found in Nanda (1992). The 1990 census figures for China can be found in State Statistical Bureau of

At the time of writing, the only age groups for which literacy figures are available from the 1991 census in India are those of 'all ages combined' and '7 years and above'. The latter age group has frequently been used in this book for comparison with 'adult literacy rates' in other countries, which usually refer to the age group of 15 years and above (see, for example, Tables 3.1, 4.1, and 4.2). This is not particularly misleading, since 7+ literacy rates in India tend to be very close to (though usually a little *higher* than) the 15+ literacy rates.

## Literacy rates in other countries

As mentioned above, the literacy figures given in *World Development Report 1994* (with 1990 as reference year) are rather out of date. The same literacy figures are given in *Human Development Report 1993*, but *Human Development Report 1994* presents an updated series, with 1992 as the reference year. This updated series is also based on UNESCO projections, but it appears to incorporate more recent information. For instance, the literacy figures given for China in this new series are much closer to the 1990 census figures than those given in the old series.[2] Since the literacy figures given in *Human Development Report 1994* seem to be more up to date, we have used these figures, rather than those given in *World Development Report 1994*, for purposes of international comparison (e.g. in Table A.1, for countries other than India and China).

## Life expectancy in India and China

*World Development Report 1994* and *Human Development Report 1994* give figures for life expectancy at birth in India (1992) of 61 years and 60 years, respectively. These figures appear to be projections based on published estimates of the Office of the Registrar General, which relate to 1986–90, and place life expectancy for that period at 57.7 years for males and 58.1 years for females. In this book, we have used more recent, unpublished estimates of life expectancy calculated by the Office of the Registrar General from Sample Registration System data. According to these estimates, life expectancy at

---

the People's Republic of China (1992, 1993a, 1993b).

[2] A personal communication from the UNDP office confirms that the Chinese literacy figures reported in *Human Development Report 1994* incorporate some information based on the 1990 census. We are grateful to Inge Kaul for this clarification.

birth in India in 1990–2 (with 1991 as the mid-point of the reference period) was 59.0 for males and 59.4 for females. These recent estimates are not very different from the projected figures presented in *World Development Report 1994* and *Human Development Report 1994*.

For life expectancy in China, the estimates presented in *World Development Report 1994* are consistent with those calculated by Ansley Coale (1993) based on the 1990 census. Both sources suggest that life expectancy in China was around 69 years in 1992. We have used this estimate, rather than the somewhat higher figure (71 years) given in *Human Development Report 1994*. We have also used Ansley Coale's census-based estimates for life expectancy in China in 1981 (see e.g. Table 4.3 in chapter 4).

*Estimates of purchasing-power-parity income in Indian states*

Table A.2 presents some tentative estimates of real per-capita income in three Indian states (Kerala, Uttar Pradesh, and West Bengal), relative to the United States. These estimates attempt to measure the state-level equivalent of the familiar 'PPP–GNP' indicator (a measure of real Gross National Product based on 'purchasing-power-parity') used in international comparisons. The estimate for each state is calculated by multiplying the all-India figure (namely 5.2, with USA = 100), obtained from *World Development Report 1994*, by a state-specific coefficient $c$ defined as $c = SDP/(p. GDP)$, where SDP denotes per-capita 'state domestic product' at current prices, GDP is all-India gross domestic product per capita at current prices, and $p$ is an index of state-level prices relative to all-India prices.[3]

To ensure internal consistency of the calculations, the all-India per-capita GDP figure was calculated as a population-weighted average of the state-specific per-capita SDP figures. The latter are given in *Economic Survey 1994–95* (Government of India, 1995), Appendix, Table 1.8. The reference year for these figures is 1991–2.

Minhas et al. (1991) give estimates of the index $p$ for 1970–1, 1983, and 1987–8.[4] These estimates suggest that this index is fairly

---

[3] In the case of Kerala, we have multiplied the estimate so obtained by 1.2, to account for remittances from outside the state (the total value of these remittances is estimated at roughly 20 per cent of Kerala's domestic product; see Krishnan, 1994).

[4] See Minhas et al. (1991), Table 1. The authors give separate indices for rural and urban areas. We have calculated the state price index $p$ as an average of the rural and urban indices.

stable over time, at least for the states we are concerned with in this table (Kerala, Uttar Pradesh, and West Bengal). In order to calculate the 1991–2 value of the coefficient $c$, we have assumed that $p$ remained constant between 1987–8 and 1991–2.

Obviously, a substantial margin of error is involved in these calculations, given the difficulties involved in estimating state domestic products as well as relative price levels. The resulting estimates presented in Table A.2 should be considered as tentative.

## 3. *Poverty Estimates for India*

The estimates of poverty indices in India (and in different Indian states) presented earlier in this book, and in Tables A.3 and A.4 of this Appendix, are based on a study by Tendulkar, Sundaram, and Jain (1993), which covers the period 1970–1 to 1988–9. In Table A.4, we also present another series of estimates, based on recent work by Gaurav Datt (1995), who has calculated estimates of different poverty indices for the entire 1951–91 period. Although there are methodological differences between the two studies, their results are broadly consistent. In addition to the 'head-count ratio' indices calculated by Tendulkar, Sundaram, and Jain (1993), we present two alternative poverty indices: the 'Sen index' (from Tendulkar et al., 1993) and the 'squared poverty gap' index (from Datt, 1995).[5] All these poverty estimates are based on National Sample Survey data.

Preliminary results from the 48th round of the National Sample Survey suggest that the incidence of poverty in India in 1992–3 (in terms of the head–count ratio) was somewhat higher than at the end of the eighties.[6] Although this phenomenon partly reflects short-run factors of a transient kind (particularly the sharp increase in foodgrain prices in that year), it also reinforces the considerations presented earlier in this book on the overarching need for economic growth to be participatory and widely-shared, in a way that the

[5] The head-count ratio simply indicates the proportion of the population below the poverty line. The other two indices, unlike the head-count ratio, are sensitive to the distribution of consumer expenditure below the poverty line. The Sen index also takes note of *relative* deprivations below the poverty line (since the weights given to different households reflect their *rank* in the scale of per-capita expenditure). On the definitions and properties of these different poverty indices, see Sen (1976b, 1983b), Foster (1984), Foster and Shorrocks (1991), Ravallion (1994).

[6] Suresh Tendulkar, Delhi School of Economics, personal communication.

experience of Indian economic expansion has not been, *either* before *or* after the reforms.

## 4. *Sources Used in Table A.3*

For convenience, the sources used in Table A.3 (which provides state-specific information on a range of social and economic indicators), along with brief explanatory remarks, are listed in a chart at the end of this appendix.

TABLE A.1. *Economic and Social Indicators in India and Selected Asian Countries*

| | India | Bangladesh | Nepal | Pakistan | Sri Lanka | China | South Korea | Indonesia | Thailand |
|---|---|---|---|---|---|---|---|---|---|
| POPULATION, mid-1992 (millions) | 883.6 | 114.4 | 19.9 | 119.3 | 17.4 | 1,162.2 | 43.7 | 184.3 | 58.0 |
| **PER-CAPITA INCOME AND RELATED INDICATORS** | | | | | | | | | |
| GNP per capita, 1992 (US$) | 310 | 220 | 170 | 420 | 540 | 470 | 6,790 | 670 | 1,840 |
| PPP estimates of GNP per capita, 1992 (1992 international dollars) | 1,210 | 1,230 | 1,100 | 2,130 | 2,810 | 1,910[a] | 8,950 | 2,970 | 5,890 |
| PPP estimates of GNP per capita, 1992 (USA = 100) | 5.2 | 5.3 | 4.8 | 9.2 | 12.2 | 9.1[a] | 38.7 | 12.8 | 25.5 |
| Average annual growth rate of per-capita GNP, 1980–92 (%) | 3.1 | 1.8 | 2 | 3.1 | 2.6 | 7.6 | 8.5 | 4 | 6 |
| **LONGEVITY, MORTALITY AND FERTILITY** | | | | | | | | | |
| Life expectancy at birth, 1992[b] (years) | | | | | | | | | |
| Female | 59 | 56 | 53 | 59 | 74 | 71 | 75 | 62 | 72 |
| Male | 59 | 55 | 54 | 59 | 70 | 68 | 67 | 59 | 67 |
| Persons | 59 | 55 | 54 | 59 | 72 | 69 | 71 | 60 | 69 |
| Crude death rate, 1992 (per 1,000) | 10 | 11 | 13 | 10 | 6 | 8 | 6 | 10 | 6 |
| Infant mortality rate, 1992 (per 1,000 live births) | 79 | 91 | 99[a] | 95 | 18 | 31 | 13 | 66 | 26 |
| Proportion of low-birthweight babies, 1990 (%) | 33 | 50 | n/a | 25 | 25 | 9 | 9 | 14 | 13 |
| Crude birth rate, 1992 (per 1,000) | 29 | 31 | 38 | 40 | 21 | 19 | 16 | 25 | 20 |
| Total fertility rate, 1992 | 3.7 | 4.0 | 5.5[a] | 5.6 | 2.5 | 2.0 | 1.8 | 2.9 | 2.2[a] |
| **LITERACY AND EDUCATION** | | | | | | | | | |
| Adult literacy rate (age 15+)[c], 1992 (%) | | | | | | | | | |
| Female | 39 | 23 | 14 | 22 | 85 | 68 | 95 | 77 | 92 |
| Male | 64 | 49 | 39 | 49 | 94 | 87 | 99 | 91 | 96 |
| Persons | 52 | 37 | 27 | 36 | 89 | 78 | 97 | 84 | 94 |

Table A.1 (contd.)

| | India | Bangladesh | Nepal | Pakistan | Sri Lanka | China | South Korea | Indonesia | Thailand |
|---|---|---|---|---|---|---|---|---|---|
| Mean years of schooling (age 25+), 1992 | 2.4 | 2 | 2.1 | 1.9 | 7.2 | 5 | 9.3 | 4.1 | 3.9 |
| Proportion of first-grade entrants who complete the primary cycle of school education (%) | 62 | 47 | n/a | 48 | 97 | 85 | 99 | 77 | 87 |
| OTHER GENDER-RELATED INDICATORS | | | | | | | | | |
| Female–male ratio (ratio of females to males in the population), 1992 (%) | 93 | 94 | 95 | 92 | 99 | 94 | 100 | 101 | 99 |
| Female share of the labour force, 1990–2 (%) | 29 | 41 | 34 | 14 | 33 | 43 | 40 | 40 | 47 |
| SAVINGS, INVESTMENT AND TRADE | | | | | | | | | |
| Gross domestic savings as proportion of GDP, 1992[d] (%) | 22 | 6 | 12 | 14 | 15 | 43 | 37 | 37 | 35 |
| Gross domestic investment as proportion of GDP, 1992[d] (%) | 23 | 12 | 22 | 21 | 23 | 39 | 37 | 35 | 40 |
| Exports of goods and non-factor services as proportion of GDP, 1992[d] (%) | 10 | 10 | 19 | 17 | 32 | 18 | 32 | 29 | 36 |
| Average annual growth rate of exports, 1980–92 (%) | 5.9 | 7.6 | 9.7 | 11.1 | 6.5 | 11.9 | 11.9 | 5.6 | 14.7 |
| Net present value of total external debt as proportion of GNP, 1992 (%) | 26 | 29 | 29 | 37 | 41 | 13 | 14 | 62 | 35 |
| Total debt service as proportion of exports, 1992 (%) | 25 | 17 | 12 | 24 | 14 | 10 | 7 | 32 | 14 |

Notes. [a] Subject to more than the usual margin or error. [b] 1991 for India, 1990 for China. [c] Age 7+, in the case of India (see Explanatory Note). [d] 1990 for China and South Korea.

Sources. *World Development Report 1994*, Tables 1, 9, 13, 23, 26–30 (pp. 162–221), *World Development Report 1992*, Table 9, and *Human Development Report 1994*, Tables 5, 9, 14, 15, 18, 21 (pp. 130–83). On the literacy and life expectancy figures for India and China, see the Explanatory Note in this Appendix.

TABLE A.2. *India in Comparative Perspective*

| Country/ state | Population, 1992 (millions) | Estimated PPP per-capita GNP, 1992 (USA=100) | Growth rate of per-capita GDP, 1980–92 (% per year) | Adult literacy rate, 1992 (%) | | Life expectancy at birth, 1992 (years) | | Crude death rate, 1992 (per 1,000) | Infant mortality rate, 1992 (per 1,000 live births) | Total fertility rate, 1992 | Female-male ratio, 1992 |
|---|---|---|---|---|---|---|---|---|---|---|---|
| | | | | Female | Male | Female | Male | | | | |
| Bangladesh | 114 | 5.3 | 1.9 | 23 | 49 | 56 | 55 | 11 | 91 | 4.0 | 94 |
| Pakistan | 119 | 9.2 | 3.0 | 22 | 49 | 59 | 59 | 10 | 95 | 5.6 | 92 |
| Sri Lanka | 17 | 12.2 | 2.6 | 85 | 94 | 74 | 70 | 6 | 18 | 2.5 | 99 |
| Kerala[a] | 29 | 4.6[b] | 0.3[c] | 86 | 94 | 74 | 69 | 6 | 17 | 1.8 | 104 |
| West Bengal[a] | 68 | 5.1[b] | 2.5[c] | 47 | 68 | 62 | 61 | 8 | 66 | 3.2 | 92 |
| Uttar Pradesh[a] | 139 | 4.1[b] | 2.2[c] | 25 | 56 | 55 | 57 | 12 | 98 | 5.1 | 88 |
| INDIA | 884 | 5.2 | 3.1 | 39 | 64 | 59 | 59 | 10 | 79 | 3.7 | 93 |
| China | 1,162 | 9.1 | 7.7 | 68 | 87 | 71 | 68 | 8 | 31 | 2.0 | 94 |
| South Korea | 44 | 38.7 | 8.3 | 95 | 99 | 75 | 67 | 6 | 13 | 1.8 | 100 |
| Thailand | 58 | 25.5 | 6.4 | 92 | 96 | 72 | 67 | 6 | 26 | 2.2 | 99 |

*Notes.* [a] In the case of Indian states, figures mentioned in the column heading as applying to 1992 apply, in fact, to 1991, or (in the case of IMR and CDR) to 1990–2.
[b] Tentative estimates (see Explanatory Note).
[c] 1980–90.

*Sources.* For countries: see Table A.1 (also *World Development Report 1994*, Table 2, for growth rate of per-capita GDP). For Indian states: see Table A.3 and the Explanatory Note.

TABLE A.3. Selected Indicators for Indian States

PART 1. Per-capita income and related indicators

| State | Population, 1991 (millions) | Per-capita net state domestic product at current prices, 1991–2 (Rs/year) | Growth rate of per-capita SDP, 1980–90 (% per year) | Average per-capita consumer expenditure, 1987–8 (Rs/month at 1970–1 prices) | | Measures of poverty, 1987–8 | | | | Gini coefficient of per-capita consumer expenditure, 1987–8 | |
| | | | | | | Head-count ratio (%) | | Sen index | | | |
| | | | | Rural | Urban | Rural | Urban | Rural | Urban | Rural | Urban |
|---|---|---|---|---|---|---|---|---|---|---|---|
| Andhra Pradesh | 67 | 5,570 | 1.7 | 44.7 | 57.9 | 31.6 | 40.0 | 9.5 | 14.2 | 0.31 | 0.36 |
| Assam | 22 | 4,230 | 2.9 | 41.7 | 73.9 | 53.1 | 11.4 | 16.0 | 2.3 | 0.23 | 0.31 |
| Bihar | 86 | 2,904 | 1.8 | 37.2 | 47.4 | 66.3 | 56.7 | 25.0 | 20.0 | 0.26 | 0.31 |
| Gujarat | 41 | 6,425 | 2.2 | 40.8 | 57.4 | 41.6 | 38.8 | 11.4 | 12.1 | 0.26 | 0.28 |
| Haryana | 16 | 8,690 | 3.2 | 56.8 | 65.3 | 23.2 | 18.3 | 6.7 | 5.2 | 0.29 | 0.28 |
| Himachal Pradesh | 5 | 5,355 | 2.0 | 54.2 | 96.1 | 24.8 | 3.3 | 6.7 | 3.3 | 0.28 | 0.28 |
| Jammu & Kashmir | 8[a] | 4,051 | -0.1 | 47.6 | 63.0 | 33.1 | 11.0 | 8.9 | 2.3 | 0.30 | 0.28 |
| Karnataka | 45 | 5,555 | 3.0 | 39.9 | 53.2 | 42.3 | 45.0 | 15.3 | 17.0 | 0.30 | 0.34 |
| Kerala | 29 | 4,618 | 0.3 | 52.2 | 64.4 | 44.0 | 44.5 | 15.4 | 16.9 | 0.32 | 0.36 |
| Madhya Pradesh | 66 | 4,077 | 3.1 | 37.2 | 57.3 | 49.8 | 46.0 | 17.9 | 17.4 | 0.29 | 0.33 |
| Maharashtra | 79 | 8,180 | 2.8 | 42.6 | 66.5 | 54.2 | 35.6 | 19.9 | 14.1 | 0.32 | 0.34 |
| Orissa | 32 | 4,068 | 2.7 | 33.4 | 58.1 | 65.6 | 44.5 | 26.8 | 17.4 | 0.27 | 0.31 |
| Punjab | 20 | 9,643 | 3.2 | 63.1 | 73.3 | 21.0 | 11.2 | 4.9 | 2.6 | 0.30 | 0.28 |
| Rajasthan | 44 | 4,361 | 2.4 | 40.7 | 57.6 | 41.9 | 41.5 | 17.1 | 14.0 | 0.32 | 0.35 |
| Tamil Nadu | 56 | 5,078 | 2.5 | 38.7 | 55.5 | 51.3 | 39.2 | 20.2 | 14.5 | 0.33 | 0.36 |
| Uttar Pradesh | 139 | 4,012 | 2.2 | 37.7 | 55.1 | 47.7 | 41.9 | 16.2 | 14.8 | 0.29 | 0.33 |
| West Bengal | 68 | 5,383 | 2.5 | 40.5 | 65.1 | 57.2 | 30.6 | 20.1 | 9.1 | 0.26 | 0.35 |
| INDIA | 846[b] | 5,583[c] | 3.1 | 41.2 | 61.2 | 44.9 | 36.5 | 15.5 | 12.8 | n/a | n/a |

Notes.  [a] Projection from earlier censuses.
  [b] Including the estimated population of Jammu and Kashmir.
  [c] Per-capita net national product at current prices.

Table A.3 (contd.)

PART 2. Mortality and Fertility

| State | Life expectancy at birth, 1990–2 (years) | | Infant mortality rate, 1990–2 (per 1,000 live births) | Death rate, age 0–4, 1991 (per 1,000) | | Estimated maternal mortality rate, 1982–6 (per 100,000 live births) | Death rate, 1990–2 (per 1,000) | Birth rate, 1990–2 (per 1,000) | Total fertility rate, 1991 |
|---|---|---|---|---|---|---|---|---|---|
| | Female | Male | | Female | Male | | | | |
| Andhra Pradesh | 61.5 | 59.0 | 71 | 20.2 | 22.3 | 402 | 9.3 | 25.5 | 3.0 |
| Assam | n/a | n/a | 76 | 30.4 | 34.4 | 1,028 | 10.8 | 30.4 | 3.5 |
| Bihar | 58.3 | n/a | 72 | 24.8 | 20.9 | 813 | 10.4 | 31.9 | 4.4 |
| Gujarat | 61.3 | 59.1 | 69 | 23.5 | 23.1 | 355 | 8.8 | 28.3 | 3.1 |
| Haryana | 63.6 | 62.2 | 71 | 23.8 | 22.3 | 435 | 8.4 | 32.3 | 4.0 |
| Himachal Pradesh | n/a | n/a | 70 | 18.0 | 20.4 | n/a | 8.7 | 27.9 | 3.1 |
| Jammu & Kashmir | n/a | n/a | 69[a] | n/a | n/a | n/a | 8.0[a] | 31.5[a] | 3.3[a] |
| Karnataka | 63.6 | 60.0 | 73 | 23.9 | 23.4 | 415 | 8.5 | 27.0 | 3.1 |
| Kerala | 74.4 | 68.8 | 17 | 4.1 | 4.5 | 234 | 6.1 | 18.5 | 1.8 |
| Madhya Pradesh | 53.5 | 54.1 | 111 | 46.6 | 42.4 | 535 | 13.0 | 35.7 | 4.6 |
| Maharashtra | 64.7 | 63.1 | 59 | 16.7 | 15.9 | 393 | 7.8 | 26.3 | 3.0 |
| Orissa | 54.8 | 55.9 | 120 | 39.2 | 38.8 | 778 | 12.1 | 28.9 | 3.3 |
| Punjab | 67.5 | 65.4 | 57 | 18.4 | 15.6 | n/a | 7.9 | 27.5 | 3.1 |
| Rajasthan | 57.8 | 57.6 | 84 | 33.8 | 28.4 | 938 | 10.1 | 34.4 | 4.6 |
| Tamil Nadu | 63.2 | 61.0 | 58 | 15.3 | 16.9 | 319 | 8.6 | 21.0 | 2.2 |
| Uttar Pradesh | 54.6 | 56.8 | 98 | 38.4 | 33.2 | 931 | 12.1 | 35.8 | 5.1 |
| West Bengal | 62.0 | 60.5 | 66 | 20.8 | 20.4 | 551 | 8.3 | 26.6 | 3.2 |
| INDIA | 59.4 | 59.0 | 80 | 27.5 | 25.6 | 555 | 9.8 | 29.5 | 3.6 |

Note.  [a] 1989 (or 1988–90, for three-year averages).

Table A.3 (contd.)

PART 3. Literacy and Education

| State | Literacy rate, age 7+, 1991 (%) | | Literacy rate, age 10–14, 1987–8 (%) | | | | Proportion of persons aged 6 and above who have completed primary education, 1992–3 (%) | |
| | | | Rural | | Urban | | | |
| | Female | Male | Female | Male | Female | Male | Female | Male |
|---|---|---|---|---|---|---|---|---|
| Andhra Pradesh | 32.7 | 55.1 | 42.3 | 65.7 | 80.0 | 87.7 | 26.4 | 45.3 |
| Assam | 43.0 | 61.9 | 78.1 | 82.5 | 86.8 | 92.9 | 28.5 | 41.2 |
| Bihar | 22.9 | 52.5 | 34.1 | 59.5 | 71.0 | 80.5 | 17.4 | 42.9 |
| Gujarat | 48.6 | 73.1 | 60.9 | 78.2 | 83.3 | 87.5 | 33.5 | 53.6 |
| Haryana | 40.5 | 69.1 | 63.5 | 87.3 | 88.6 | 93.4 | 30.9 | 53.5 |
| Himachal Pradesh | 52.1 | 75.4 | 80.7 | 95.1 | 97.2 | 96.0 | 39.2 | 56.8 |
| Jammu & Kashmir | n/a | n/a | 49.7 | 78.7 | 79.5 | 83.6 | 37.7[a] | 56.3[a] |
| Karnataka | 44.3 | 67.3 | 55.8 | 74.2 | 85.9 | 86.8 | 30.4 | 46.8 |
| Kerala | 86.2 | 93.6 | 98.2 | 98.1 | 97.8 | 97.3 | 60.5 | 65.8 |
| Madhya Pradesh | 28.9 | 58.4 | 40.0 | 67.8 | 85.5 | 92.3 | 21.0 | 44.6 |
| Maharashtra | 52.3 | 76.6 | 68.2 | 86.3 | 90.7 | 94.7 | 35.9 | 55.1 |
| Orissa | 34.7 | 63.1 | 51.4 | 70.0 | 79.4 | 89.6 | 23.0 | 42.8 |
| Punjab | 50.4 | 65.7 | 68.8 | 76.5 | 87.3 | 89.5 | 41.0 | 51.6 |
| Rajasthan | 20.4 | 55.0 | 22.2 | 71.6 | 62.5 | 89.1 | 15.6 | 41.8 |
| Tamil Nadu | 51.3 | 73.8 | 70.8 | 85.1 | 85.6 | 91.7 | 40.1 | 58.7 |
| Uttar Pradesh | 25.3 | 55.7 | 39.0 | 68.0 | 68.8 | 76.0 | 21.4 | 47.3 |
| West Bengal | 46.6 | 67.8 | 60.7 | 69.0 | 82.2 | 87.4 | 29.2 | 47.4 |
| INDIA | 39.3 | 64.1 | 51.7 | 72.9 | 81.6 | 87.9 | 28.1 | 48.6 |

Note.  [a] Jammu region only.

Table A.3 (contd.)

PART 4. School Attendance and Enrolment

| State | Proportion of rural children attending school, 1987–8 (%) | | | | Proportion of never-enrolled children in 12–14 age group, 1986–7 (%) | | | |
| | age 5–9 | | age 10–14 | | Rural | | Urban | |
| | Female | Male | Female | Male | Female | Male | Female | Male |
|---|---|---|---|---|---|---|---|---|
| Andhra Pradesh | 45.2 | 63.3 | 30.9 | 57.0 | 59.7 | 32.7 | 18.9 | 9.4 |
| Assam | 47.8 | 48.6 | 70.9 | 76.1 | 28.5 | 22.9 | 18.0 | 5.1 |
| Bihar | 19.7 | 33.0 | 28.7 | 54.6 | 67.3 | 41.9 | 38.0 | 19.5 |
| Gujarat | 52.1 | 63.1 | 52.2 | 76.5 | 38.7 | 22.5 | 17.7 | 10.2 |
| Haryana | 53.8 | 60.2 | 51.6 | 81.8 | 42.4 | 12.9 | 14.6 | 6.2 |
| Himachal Pradesh | 63.3 | 73.6 | 73.0 | 92.5 | n/a | n/a | n/a | n/a |
| Jammu & Kashmir | 40.3 | 53.4 | 45.8 | 77.5 | 47.6 | 21.5 | 29.3 | 18.9 |
| Karnataka | 50.6 | 57.0 | 45.5 | 65.0 | 46.5 | 26.0 | 17.4 | 11.7 |
| Kerala | 82.8 | 86.9 | 91.2 | 93.3 | 1.8 | 0.4 | 0.6 | 0.1 |
| Madhya Pradesh | 26.3 | 43.9 | 29.9 | 61.6 | 66.4 | 30.6 | 18.1 | 6.6 |
| Maharashtra | 54.4 | 64.0 | 59.3 | 72.1 | 27.7 | 12.6 | 12.4 | 4.6 |
| Orissa | 44.9 | 55.4 | 19.2 | 69.6 | 54.7 | 34.0 | 20.3 | 20.2 |
| Punjab | 59.1 | 66.3 | 59.3 | 72.1 | 33.3 | 22.6 | 7.9 | 7.9 |
| Rajasthan | 25.5 | 47.8 | 19.2 | 69.6 | 81.7 | 26.1 | 36.0 | 12.5 |
| Tamil Nadu | 77.7 | 84.9 | 48.7 | 70.7 | 26.3 | 11.5 | 5.6 | 3.7 |
| Uttar Pradesh | 28.2 | 45.4 | 30.7 | 63.8 | 68.0 | 27.2 | 38.8 | 19.2 |
| West Bengal | 40.9 | 44.8 | 52.8 | 64.3 | 45.9 | 34.6 | 15.2 | 13.0 |
| INDIA | 40.4 | 52.5 | 41.9 | 66.1 | 50.7 | 26.4 | 19.3 | 10.9 |

Table A.3 (contd.)

PART 5. Other Gender-related Indicators

| State | Female–male ratio, 1991 | Ratio of female death rate to male death rate, age 0–4, 1991 (%) | Married women as percentage of all women in 15–19 age group, 1981 | Female labour-force participation rate, 1991 (%) | Female employment as percentage of total public-sector employment, 1989 |
|---|---|---|---|---|---|
| Andhra Pradesh | 972 | 90.6 | 56 | 30.1 | 10.2 |
| Assam | 923 | 88.4 | n/a | 12.6 | n/a |
| Bihar | 911 | 118.7 | 64 | 10.0 | 6.8 |
| Gujarat | 934 | 101.7 | 27 | 13.7 | 14.4 |
| Haryana | 865 | 106.7 | 48 | 6.0 | 13.4 |
| Himachal Pradesh | 976 | 88.2 | 32 | 19.4 | 11.1 |
| Jammu & Kashmir | n/a | n/a | 28 | n/a | 9.5 |
| Karnataka | 960 | 102.1 | 36 | 22.7 | 14.8 |
| Kerala | 1036 | 91.1 | 14 | 12.8 | 29.5 |
| Madhya Pradesh | 931 | 109.9 | 62 | 22.8 | 9.5 |
| Maharashtra | 934 | 105.0 | 38 | 26.5 | 13.1 |
| Orissa | 971 | 101.0 | 31 | 12.1 | 7.4 |
| Punjab | 882 | 117.9 | 13 | 2.8 | 14.8 |
| Rajasthan | 910 | 119.0 | 64 | 13.0 | 10.9 |
| Tamil Nadu | 974 | 90.5 | 23 | 25.1 | 19.0 |
| Uttar Pradesh | 879 | 115.7 | 61 | 7.5 | 7.7 |
| West Bengal | 917 | 102.0 | 38 | 8.0 | 9.9 |
| INDIA | 927 | 107.4 | 46 | 16.0 | n/a |

Table A.3 (contd.)

PART 6. Maternal Health and Related Matters

| State | Percentage of currently-married women aged 13–49 who are aware of, have ever used, are currently using any modern non-terminal method of contraception, 1992–3 | | | Proportion of currently-married women below 49 who are sterilized, 1992–3 (%) | Percentage of recent births preceded by different kinds of maternal care, 1992–3 | | Proportion of births taking place in medical institutions, 1991 (%) | Proportion of children aged 12–23 months who have not received any vaccination, 1992–3 (%) |
| --- | --- | --- | --- | --- | --- | --- | --- | --- |
| | aware of | ever used | currently using | | tetanus vaccine | antenatal check-up | | |
| Andhra Pradesh | 61 | 6 | 2 | 38 | 81 | 66 | 38 | 18 |
| Assam | 82 | 18 | 5 | 12 | 44 | 47 | 18 | 44 |
| Bihar | 68 | 6 | 3 | 17 | 37 | 27 | 12 | 54 |
| Gujarat | 77 | 14 | 6 | 38 | 70 | 50 | 24 | 19 |
| Haryana | 91 | 23 | 10 | 30 | 70 | 67 | 20 | 18 |
| Himachal Pradesh | 88 | 25 | 9 | 33 | 71 | 74 | 22 | 9 |
| Jammu & Kashmir | 89[a] | 24[a] | 10[a] | 25[a] | 78[a] | 79[a] | 15[b] | 16[a] |
| Karnataka | 84 | 14 | 5 | 41 | 77 | 65 | 41 | 15 |
| Kerala | 97 | 27 | 6 | 42 | 94 | 97 | 92 | 11 |
| Madhya Pradesh | 57 | 12 | 6 | 26 | 51 | 36 | 13 | 34 |
| Maharashtra | 77 | 16 | 6 | 40 | 82 | 70 | 34 | 8 |
| Orissa | 61 | 8 | 3 | 28 | 63 | 39 | 10 | 28 |
| Punjab | 94 | 32 | 17 | 32 | 87 | 86 | 7 | 18 |
| Rajasthan | 59 | 7 | 3 | 25 | 35 | 23 | 5 | 49 |
| Tamil Nadu | 86 | 16 | 6 | 38 | 94 | 78 | 57 | 3 |
| Uttar Pradesh | 80 | 11 | 6 | 12 | 44 | 30 | 4 | 43 |
| West Bengal | 91 | 23 | 7 | 26 | 78 | 69 | 31 | 22 |
| INDIA | 76 | 14 | 5.5 | 27 | 61 | 49 | 24 | 30 |

Notes.   [a] Jammu region only.   [b] 1989.

Table A.3 (contd.)

PART 7. Public Services and Social Infrastructure

| State | Proportion of villages with medical facilities, 1981 (%) | Per-capita supply of foodgrains through the public distribution system, 1986–7 (kg/year) | Proportion of the population receiving subsidized foodgrains from the public distribution system, 1986–7 | | Proportion of households having access to safe drinking water, 1991 (%) | | Number of hospital beds per million persons, 1991 | | Proportion of households with electricity connection, 1991 | |
|---|---|---|---|---|---|---|---|---|---|---|
| | | | Rural | Urban | Rural | Urban | Rural | Urban | Rural | Urban |
| Andhra Pradesh | 23.0 | 22.8 | 59.7 | 51.4 | 57.4 | 87.1 | 76 | 1,827 | 37.5 | 73.3 |
| Assam | n/a | 30.5 | 24.6 | 43.0 | 60.9 | 88.2 | 175 | 4,414 | 12.4 | 63.2 |
| Bihar | 13.8 | 6.5 | 1.7 | 7.1 | 62.4 | 85.5 | 31 | 2,276 | 5.6 | 58.8 |
| Gujarat | 26.2 | 24.5 | 44.5 | 32.0 | 67.0 | 93.1 | 185 | 2,904 | 56.4 | 83.0 |
| Haryana | 57.1 | 6.2 | 3.1 | 7.1 | 68.3 | 95.5 | 44 | 1,593 | 63.2 | 89.1 |
| Himachal Pradesh | 13.4 | 25.0 | 28.2 | 25.3 | 76.7 | 94.2 | 102 | 1,871 | 85.9 | 96.2 |
| Jammu & Kashmir | 17.9 | 34.6 | 23.3 | 78.6 | n/a | n/a | 77 | 4,215 | n/a | n/a |
| Karnataka | 10.8 | 19.9 | 61.9 | 62.7 | 73.2 | 90.3 | 81 | 2,297 | 41.8 | 76.3 |
| Kerala | 96.3 | 60.2 | 87.7 | 87.0 | 71.2 | 85.1 | 1,768 | 4,230 | 42.0 | 67.7 |
| Madhya Pradesh | 5.6 | 7.4 | 9.1 | 17.4 | 54.4 | 87.0 | 39 | 1,313 | 34.5 | 72.5 |
| Maharashtra | 17.6 | 22.4 | 47.7 | 43.8 | 62.0 | 95.2 | 250 | 3,251 | 58.5 | 86.1 |
| Orissa | 10.6 | 7.1 | 1.7 | 13.8 | 46.8 | 81.2 | 107 | 2,610 | 17.5 | 62.1 |
| Punjab | 24.3 | 4.7 | 0.1 | 4.6 | 94.3 | 98.0 | 196 | 2,040 | 77.0 | 94.6 |
| Rajasthan | 13.2 | 17.4 | 8.8 | 5.6 | 53.0 | 91.2 | 38 | 2,039 | 22.4 | 76.7 |
| Tamil Nadu | 23.4 | 25.4 | 53.5 | 55.4 | 67.7 | 87.7 | 115 | 2,336 | 44.5 | 76.8 |
| Uttar Pradesh | 9.6 | 2.9 | 2.1 | 7.0 | 60.1 | 90.7 | 23 | 1,619 | 11.0 | 67.8 |
| West Bengal | 13.2 | 26.1 | 26.9 | 59.8 | 84.1 | 94.8 | 154 | 2,479 | 17.8 | 70.2 |
| INDIA | 14.0 | 18.1 | 26.8[a] | 35.5[a] | 63.6 | 90.7 | 152 | 2,409 | 30.5 | 75.8 |

Note.  [a] Calculated as a weighted average of the state-specific figures.

TABLE A.4. Time Trends for Selected Indicators (India)

| | 1950–1 | 1960–1 | 1970–1 | 1973–4 | 1977–8 | 1980–1 | 1983–4 | 1987–8 | 1990–1 | 1991–2 | 1992–3 | 1993–4 | Index of annual rate of change, 1970–1 to 1990–1 [a] (%) |
|---|---|---|---|---|---|---|---|---|---|---|---|---|---|
| Per-capita net national product at constant prices[b] (1950–1 = 100) | 100 | 120 | 135 | 132 | 145 | 145 | 159 | 169 | 197 | 193 | 198 | 203[c] | 1.8 |
| Index of agricultural production[b] (1950–1 = 100) | 100 | 148 | 191 | 192 | 228 | 231 | 266 | 259 | 328 | 319 | 335[c] | 342[c] | 2.5 |
| Index of industrial production[b] (1950–1 = 100) | 100 | 198 | 357 | 396 | 533 | 546 | 658 | 909 | 1,162 | 1,161 | 1,195 | 1,244[c] | 5.8 |
| Gross domestic capital formation (as % of GDP) | 10.2 | 15.7 | 16.6 | 19.1 | 19.5 | 22.7 | 20.1 | 22.9 | 27.1 | 23.6 | 22.0 | 20.4[c] | 2.0 |
| 'Volume index' of foreign trade (1978–9 = 100) | | | | | | | | | | | | | |
| Exports | – | – | 59.0 | 69.5 | 93.2 | 108.1 | 113.0 | 140.0 | 194.1 | 208.6 | 222.9 | 272.4 | 5.5 |
| Imports | – | – | 67.2 | 87.2 | 100.0 | 137.9 | 185.4 | 204.8 | 237.7 | 228.0 | 282.0 | 329.1 | 6.5 |
| Employment in organized private sector[d] (thousand persons) | – | 5,040 | 6,742 | 6,794 | 7,043 | 7,395 | 7,346 | 7,392 | 7,677 | 7,846 | – | – | 0.6 |
| Employment in the public sector (thousand persons) | – | 7,050 | 10,731 | 12,486 | 14,200 | 15,484 | 16,869 | 18,320 | 19,058 | 19,210 | – | – | 2.8 |

Table A.4. (contd.)

| | 1950–1 | 1960–1 | 1970–1 | 1973–4 | 1977–8 | 1980–1 | 1983–4 | 1987–8 | 1990–1 | 1991–2 | 1992–3 | 1993–4 | Index of annual rate of change, 1970–1 to 1990–1ᵃ (%) |
|---|---|---|---|---|---|---|---|---|---|---|---|---|---|
| Per-capita earnings of public-sector employees (Rs/year at 1960 prices) | – | – | – | 2,229 | 3,101 | 3,551 | 3,939 | 4,421 | 5,171 | 5,237 | 5,484 | 5,672 | 4.6 |
| Real wages of agricultural labourers (Rs/day at 1960 prices) | – | – | 1.52 | 1.37 | 1.74 | 1.65 | 1.71 | 2.36 | 2.57 | 2.44 | – | – | 2.9 |
| Per-capita net availability of cereals and pulses (grams/day) | 395 | 469 | 469 | 451 | 468 | 455 | 480 | 449 | 510 | 469ᶜ | 464ᶜ | 474ᶜ | 0.3 |
| Head-count index of poverty (%) | | | | | | | | | | | | | |
| Rural | – | – | 57.3 | 56.2 | 54.5 | – | 49.0 | 44.9 | – | – | – | – | -1.4 |
| Urban | – | – | 45.9 | 49.2 | 43.0 | – | 38.3 | 36.5 | – | – | – | – | -1.7 |
| 'Sen index' of poverty | | | | | | | | | | | | | |
| Rural | – | – | 23.6 | 22.4 | 22.3 | – | 18.8 | 15.5 | – | – | – | – | -2.3 |
| Urban | – | – | 18.0 | 18.6 | 16.5 | – | 13.6 | 12.8 | – | – | – | – | -2.3 |
| 'Squared poverty gap' index of poverty | | | | | | | | | | | | | |
| Rural | 7.5 | 5.5 | 6.8 | 7.1 | 6.1 | – | 4.8 | 3.4 | 2.9 | – | – | – | -4.6 |
| Urban | 4.8 | 5.8 | 5.4 | 5.2 | 4.5 | – | 3.6 | 3.3 | 3.1 | – | – | – | -2.9 |

*Table A.4. (contd.)*

| | 1950–1 | 1960–1 | 1970–1 | 1973–4 | 1977–8 | 1980–1 | 1983–4 | 1987–8 | 1990–1 | 1991–2 | 1992–3 | 1993–4 | Index of annual rate of change, 1970–1 to 1990–1[a] (%) |
|---|---|---|---|---|---|---|---|---|---|---|---|---|---|
| Gini coefficient of per-capita consumer expenditure | | | | | | | | | | | | | |
| Rural | 33.7 | 32.5 | 28.8 | 28.5 | 30.9 | – | 30.1 | 30.1 | 27.7 | – | – | – | 0.0 |
| Urban | 40.0 | 35.6 | 34.7 | 30.8 | 34.7 | – | 34.1 | 35.6 | 34.0 | – | – | – | 0.2 |
| Literacy rate[e] (%) | | | | | | | | | | | | | |
| Female | 9 | 15 | 22 | – | – | 30 | – | – | 39 | – | – | – | 2.9 |
| Male | 27 | 40 | 46 | – | – | 56 | – | – | 64 | – | – | – | 1.7 |
| Birth rate[f] (per 1,000) | 39.9 | 41.7 | 36.9 | 34.5 | 33.3 | 33.9 | 33.9 | 31.5 | 29.5 | 29.2 | 28.7 | – | –0.9 |
| Life expectancy at birth[g] (years) | 32.1 | 41.3 | 45.6 | – | – | 50.4 | – | – | 59.2 | – | – | – | 1.3 |
| Government expenditure on education, health, and defence[h] (Rs per person per year, at constant 1981–2 prices) | | | | | | | | | | | | | |
| Education | 10.2 | 29.2 | 47.6 | 46.3 | 56.0 | 57.1 | 68.2 | 97.4 | 115.4 | 109.5 | 111.9 | 112.5 | 4.6 |
| Health | 4.8 | 11.9 | 18.5 | 18.8 | 25.5 | 28.9 | 37.9 | 47.6 | 49.0 | 47.2 | 47.4 | 46.6 | 5.5 |
| Defence and police | n/a | 45.8 | 80.8 | 76.0 | 82.6 | 78.1 | 94.6 | 136.9 | 137.7 | 128.8 | 125.8 | 123.0 | 3.1 |

*Notes.* [a] Annual growth rate, calculated by OLS regression of the logarithm of the relevant variable on time, based on the available observations for the 1970–91 period.

b The original figures are based on different 'base years' (1980–1, in the case of per-capita net national product and industrial production, and 'triennium ending 1969–70', in the case of agricultural production), and have been normalized by simple division of the original figure for each year by the original 1950–1 figure.

c Provisional estimates, from Government of India (1995).

d Non-agricultural establishments employing 10 persons or more.

e Age 7 and above for 1981 and 1991, 5 and above for other years.

f Data for 1950–1 and 1960–1 relate to the decades 1941–50 and 1951–60, respectively (census estimates).

g Data for 1950–1, 1960–1, 1970–1, and 1980–1 relate to the decades 1941–50, 1951–60, 1961–70, and 1971–80, respectively (census estimates).

h Central and state governments combined.

Sources. Government of India, *Economic Survey 1980–81* (pp. 69, 98, 99), *Economic Survey 1984–85* (pp. 94, 166–7), *Economic Survey 1987–88* (p. S-79), *Economic Survey 1990–91* (p. S-38), *Economic Survey 1991–92* (p. S-91), *Economic Survey 1993–94*, (pp. 2, S-1, S-2, S-9, S-13, S-24, S-39, S-53 to S-55, S-98), *Economic Survey 1994–95*, (pp. S-3, S-7, S-13, S-24, S-39, S-54, S-55, S-56, S-99, S-100). The following sources have also been used: Tendulkar, Sundaram, and Jain (1993) and Datt (1995) for estimates of poverty indices and Gini coefficients; *Sample Registration Bulletin*, July 1993, Table 1 (p. 5), for birth rates from 1970–1 to 1990–1; Chandhok (1990), p. 1072; unpublished estimates from the Office of the Registrar-General, for birth rates in 1992 and 1993, and life expectancy in 1991. The index of real wages for (male) agricultural labourers was calculated by Bipul Chattopadhyay (Institute of Economic Growth, New Delhi), from data published in various issues of *Agricultural Wages in India*, based on the method described in Acharya (1989). The figures on government expenditure (last row) are calculated from Centre for Monitoring the Indian Economy (1994a), *Basic Statistics Relating to the Indian Economy*, Tables 2.3, 2.8, 17.2, 22.2 (we have used the Wholesale Price Index to deflate expenditure figures at current prices). In cases where the original source gives figures for *calendar* years, we have placed the figure for a particular year in the column corresponding to the pair of years *ending* in that year (e.g. the 1991 literacy rate estimate appears in the 1990–1 column, etc.).

## Sources Used in Table A.3

| Indicator | Source and Remarks |
|---|---|
| Population, 1991 | Census of India 1991, 'final population totals', as reported in Nanda (1992), pp. 86–95. |
| Per-capita state domestic product, 1991–2 | *Economic Survey 1993–94* (Government of India, 1994a), Tables 1.1 and 1.8, pp. S-3 and S-12. |
| Growth rate of per-capita SDP, 1980–90 | Calculated (by OLS regression of the logarithm of per-capita SDP at constant prices on time) from Central Statistical Organisation (1991a, 1991b). |
| Average per-capita consumer expenditure, 1987–8 | Tendulkar et al. (1993), Table A.5, based on the 43rd round of the National Sample Survey, 1987–8. |
| Measures of poverty | Tendulkar et al. (1993), Table A.5, based on the 43rd round of the National Sample Survey, 1987–8. Some of these estimates are also presented in Minhas et al. (1991). |
| Gini coefficient of per-capita consumer expenditure, 1987–8 | National Sample Survey, 43rd round, 1987–8, special tabulation by Dr P.V. Srinivasan, Indira Gandhi Institute of Development Research, Bombay. |
| Life expectancy at birth, 1991 | Unpublished estimates based on Sample Registration System data, supplied by the Office of the Registrar-General, New Delhi. |
| Infant mortality rate, 1990–2 | Three-year average based on Sample Registration System, presented in *Sample Registration Bulletin,* January 1994, Tables 14 and 17 (pp. 46–53 and 62–4). |
| Death rate, age 0–4, 1991 | *Sample Registration System: Fertility and Mortality Indicators 1991* (Government of India, 1993b), Table 7, pp. 152–74. |
| Estimated maternal mortality rate | Mari Bhat et al. (1992), Table 4. |
| Death rate, 1990–2 | Three-year average based on Sample Registration System, presented in *Sample Registration Bulletin,* January 1994, pp. 22–9 and 58–61. |
| Birth rate, 1990–2 | Three-year average based on Sample Registration System, presented in *Sample Registration Bulletin,* January 1994, pp. 22–9 and 54–7. |
| Total fertility rate, 1991 | *Sample Registration System: Fertility and Mortality Indicators 1991* (Government of India, 1993b), pp. 94–105. |
| Literacy rates, age 7 and above, 1991 | Census of India 1991, 'final population totals', as reported in Nanda (1992), pp. 210–17. |
| Literacy rates, age 10–14, 1987–8 | Sengupta (1991), Statements 2.3, 3.5, and 3.6 (pp. 17 and 28), based on National Sample Survey data. |

| Indicator | Source and Remarks |
|---|---|
| Proportion of persons aged 6 and above who have completed primary education, 1992–3 | International Institute for Population Sciences (1994), Tables 6 and 7. The IIPS survey (1992–3) was not aimed at collecting data on education, but the broad consistency between the literacy figures derived from this survey and those obtained from the 1991 census suggests that the IIPS figures on completion of primary education, too, are reasonably accurate. |
| School attendance, 1987–8 | Visaria et al. (1993), Tables 5 and 6 (pp. 31–4), based on National Sample Survey data. |
| School enrolment, 1986–7 | Visaria et al. (1993), Table 15, p.53, based on National Sample Survey data. |
| Female–male ratio, 1991 | Census of India (1991), 'final population totals', as reported in Nanda (1992), Tables 5.3 and 6 (pp. 206–17). |
| Ratio of female to male death rate, age 0–4, 1991 | Calculated from *Sample Registration System: Fertility and Mortality Indicators 1991* (Government of India, 1993b), Table 7, pp. 152–74. |
| Proportion of married women in the 15–19 age group, 1981 | Nuna (1990), p. 98, based on 1981 census data. |
| Female labour-force participation rate, 1991 | Nanda (1992), Table 3.1, pp. 115–23, based on 1991 census data. |
| Female employment in the public sector, 1989 | Nuna (1990), p. 99. |
| Awareness and use of contraception, 1992–3 | International Institute for Population Sciences (1994), Tables 15, 17, and 18. |
| Incidence of female sterilization, 1992–3 | International Institute for Population Sciences (1994), Table 18. |
| Antenatal care, 1992–3 | International Institute for Population Sciences (1994), Table 24. |
| Birth attendance, 1991 | *Sample Registration System: Fertility and Mortality Indicators 1991* (Government of India, 1993b), Statement 25, p. 27. |
| Child vaccination, 1992–3 | International Institute for Population Sciences (1994), Table 28. |
| Medical facilities in rural areas, 1981 | Calculated from district-level data on medical facilities available in the *District Census Handbooks* of the 1981 census. |
| Supply of foodgrains through the public distribution system, 1986–7 | Jha (1994), based on special tabulations of the 42nd round of the National Sample Survey. |
| Coverage of public distribution system, 1986–7 | Parikh (1994), based on special tabulations of the 42nd round of the National Sample Survey. |

| Indicator | Source and Remarks |
|---|---|
| Access to safe drinking water, 1991 | Sundaram and Tendulkar (1994), based on 1991 census data. |
| Availability of hospital beds, 1991 | Calculated from Government of India (1992e), Table 8.01, p. 117. |
| Electrification, 1991 | Government of India (1993e), Table 3.3, based on 1991 census data. |

*Note.* Some of the demographic statistics for 'India' (last row in Table A.3) exclude Jammu and Kashmir, where the 1991 census was not conducted, and where the Sample Registration System (SRS) has also been inoperative in recent years. In Table A.3, SRS-based data for Jammu and Kashmir relate to the latest year for which information is available (as specified in the tables), and are taken from the relevant issues of *Sample Registration System* and *Sample Registration Bulletin*.

# REFERENCES

Acharya, Sarthi (1989), 'Agricultural Wages in India: A Disaggregated Analysis', *Indian Journal of Agricultural Economics*, 44.

—— (1990), *Maharashtra Employment Guarantee Scheme: A Study of Labour Market Intervention* (Delhi: ILO-ARTEP).

Adelman, Irma, and Morris, Cynthia T. (1973), *Economic Growth and Social Equity in Developing Countries* (Stanford: Stanford University Press).

Adelman, Irma, and Robinson, Sherman (1978), *Income Distribution Policy in Developing Countries: A Case Study of Korea* (Oxford: Clarendon Press).

Agarwal, Anil, and Narain, Sunita (1989), *Towards Green Villages* (New Delhi: Centre for Science and Environment).

Agarwal, Bina (1986), 'Women, Poverty and Agricultural Growth in India', *Journal of Peasant Studies*, 13.

—— (1988), 'Who Sows? Who Reaps? Women and Land Rights in India', *Journal of Peasant Studies,* 15.

—— (1989), 'Tribal Matriliny in Transition: The Garos, Khasis and Lalungs of North-East India', mimeo, Institute of Economic Growth, New Delhi.

—— (1991), 'Social Security and the Family: Coping with Seasonality and Calamity in Rural India', in Ahmad et al. (1991).

—— (1994), *A Field of One's Own: Gender and Land Rights in South Asia* (Cambridge: Cambridge University Press).

Agnihotri, Anita, and Sivaswamy, G. (1993), *Total Literacy Campaign in the Sundergarh District of Orissa* (New Delhi: Directorate of Adult Education).

Agnihotri, Satish (1994), 'Missing Females: A Disaggregated Analysis', mimeo, University of East Anglia; forthcoming in *Economic and Political Weekly*.

—— (1995), 'Sex Ratio Variations in India: What Do Languages Tell Us?', mimeo, University of East Anglia.

Agrawal, A.N., Varma, H.O., and Gupta, R.C. (1992), *India: Economic Information Yearbook 1991–92* (New Delhi: National Publishing House).

Agrawal, S.P., and Aggarwal, J.C. (1992), *Women's Education in India* (New Delhi: Concept).

Ahluwalia, Isher Judge (1985), *Industrial Growth in India* (New Delhi: Oxford University Press).

Ahluwalia, Isher Judge (1991), *Productivity and Growth in Indian Manufacturing* (New Delhi: Oxford University Press).

—— (1992), *Trade Policy and Industrialisation in India* (Bombay: Export-Import Bank of India).

Ahluwalia, Montek S. (1978), 'Rural Poverty and Agricultural Performance in India', *Journal of Development Studies*, 14.

—— (1990), 'Policies for Poverty Alleviation', *Asian Development Review*, 8.

Ahmad, E., Drèze, J.P., Hills, J., and Sen, A.K. (eds.) (1991), *Social Security in Developing Countries* (Oxford: Oxford University Press).

Ahmad, E., and Hussain, A. (1991), 'Social Security in China: A Historical Perspective', in Ahmad et al. (1991).

AKG Centre for Research and Studies (1994), *International Congress on Kerala Studies: Abstracts*, 5 volumes (Thiruvananthapuram: AKG Centre for Research and Studies).

Alagh, Yoginder K. (1986), *Some Aspects of Planning Policies in India* (Allahabad: Vohra Publishers).

Alailima, Patricia (1985), 'Evolution of Government Policies and Expenditure on Social Welfare in Sri Lanka during the 20th Century', mimeo, Colombo.

Alamgir, Mohiuddin (1980), *Famine in South Asia* (Boston: Oelgeschlager, Gunn and Hain).

Alderman, H., Behrman, J.R., Khan, S., Ross, D.R., and Sabot, R. (1993), 'Public School Expenditures in Rural Pakistan: Efficiently Targeting Girls in a Lagging Region', mimeo, World Bank, Washington, DC.

Alesina, Alberto, and Rodrik, Dani (1994), 'Distributive Politics and Economic Growth', *Quarterly Journal of Economics,* 109.

Almeida, A. (1978), 'The Gift of a Bride: Sociological Implications of the Dowry System in Goa', mimeo, Université Catholique de Louvain, Louvain-la-Neuve, Belgium.

Altekar, A.S. (1956), *The Position of Women in Hindu Civilization* (Delhi: Motilal Banarsidass).

Amsden, Alice H. (1989), *Asia's Next Giant: Late Industrialization in South Korea* (Oxford: Clarendon Press).

—— (1994), 'Why Isn't the Whole World Experimenting with the East Asian Model to Develop?', *World Development*, 22.

Anand, Sudhir (1993), 'Inequality between and within Nations', mimeo, Center for Population and Development Studies, Harvard University.

Anand, Sudhir, and Kanbur, S.M. Ravi (1990), 'Public Policy and Basic Needs Provision: Intervention and Achievement in Sri Lanka', in Drèze and Sen (1990), vol. III.

—— (1993), 'Inequality and Development: A Critique', *Journal of Development Economics*, 40.

Anand, Sudhir, and Ravallion, Martin (1993), 'Human Development in Poor Countries: On the Role of Private Incomes and Public Services', *Journal of Economic Perspectives,* 7 (Winter).

Anand, Sudhir, and Sen, Amartya (1994), 'Sustainable Human Development', UNDP Working Paper; forthcoming in *World Development.*

Antony, T.V. (1992), 'The Family Planning Programme: Lessons from Tamil Nadu's Experience', *The Indian Journal of Social Science,* 5(3).

Archer, David, and Costello, Patrick (1990), *Literacy and Power: The Latin American Battleground* (London: Earthscan Publications).

Arneson, R. (1989), 'Equality and Equality of Opportunity for Welfare', *Philosophical Studies,* 56.

—— (1990), 'Liberalism, Distributive Subjectivism, and Equal Opportunity for Welfare', *Philosophy and Public Affairs,* 19.

Arrow, Kenneth J. (1951), 'An Extension of the Basic Theorems of Classical Welfare Economics', in J. Neyman (ed.), *Proceedings of the Second Berkeley Symposium on Mathematical Economics* (Berkeley, CA: University of California Press).

Arrow, Kenneth J., and Hahn, Frank (1971), *General Competitive Analysis* (San Francisco: Holden-Day).

Ashton, B., Hill, K., Piazza, A., and Zeitz, R. (1984), 'Famine in China, 1958–61', *Population and Development Review,* 10.

Atkinson, A.B. (1969), 'Import Strategy and Growth under Conditions of Stagnant Export Earnings', *Oxford Economic Papers,* 21.

—— (1989), *Poverty and Social Security* (New York: Harvester and Wheatsheaf).

—— (1995), 'Capabilities, Exclusion, and the Supply of Goods', in Basu et al. (1995).

Aziz, Abdul (1994), 'History of Panchayat Reforms in Karnataka', paper presented at a Seminar on Management of Education under Panchayati Raj held at the National Institute of Educational Planning and Administration, 27–8 October, 1994.

Babu, S.C., and Hallam, J.A. (1989), 'Socioeconomic Impacts of School Feeding Programmes: Empirical Evidence from a South Indian Village', *Food Policy,* 14.

Bagchi, Amiya K. (1982), *The Political Economy of Underdevelopment* (Cambridge: Cambridge University Press).

—— (1994), 'Making Sense of Government's Macroeconomic Stabilization Strategy', *Economic and Political Weekly,* April 30.

Bahadur, K.P. (1978), *History, Caste and Culture of the Rajputs* (Delhi: Ess Publications).

Balassa, Bela (1991), *Economic Policies in the Pacific Area Developing Countries* (New York: New York University Press).

Bandyopadhyay, R.(1991), 'Education for an Enlightened Society: A Review', *Economic and Political Weekly*, February 16.

Banerjee, Nirmala (1982), *Unorganised Women Workers: The Calcutta Experience* (Calcutta: Centre for Studies in Social Sciences).

—— (1985), 'Women's Work and Discrimination', in Jain and Banerjee (1985).

Banerjee, Sumanta (1992), ' "Uses of Literacy": Total Literacy Campaign in Three West Bengal Districts', *Economic and Political Weekly*, February 29.

—— (1994), 'Obstacles to Change', *Economic and Political Weekly*, March 26.

Banerji, Debabar (1985), *Health and Family Planning Services in India* (New Delhi: Lok Paksh).

—— (1989), 'Rural Social Transformation and Change in Health Behaviour', *Economic and Political Weekly*, July 1.

Bang, R.A., et al. (1989), 'High Prevalence of Gynaecological Diseases in Rural Indian Women', *The Lancet*, January 14.

Banister, Judith (1992), 'Demographic Aspects of Poverty in China', background paper prepared for the World Bank (1992) report *China: Strategies for Reducing Poverty in the 1990s* (Washington, DC: World Bank).

Bara, D., Bhengra, R., and Minz, B. (1991), 'Tribal Female Literacy: Factors in Differentiation among Munda Religious Communities', *Social Action*, 41.

Bardhan, Kalpana (1985), 'Womens' Work, Welfare and Status', *Economic and Political Weekly*, 20 (50–52).

Bardhan, Pranab (1974), 'On Life and Death Questions', *Economic and Political Weekly*, 9 (Special Number).

—— (1984a), *Land, Labor and Rural Poverty* (New York: Columbia University Press).

—— (1984b), *The Political Economy of Development in India* (Oxford: Blackwell).

—— (1988), 'Sex Disparity in Child Survival in Rural India', in Srinivasan and Bardhan (1988).

—— (1992), 'The State Against Society: The Great Divide in Indian Social Science Discourse', paper presented at a workshop on 'Production Units in Micro and Macrostructural Perspectives' held at the School of Oriental and African Studies, London, 12–18 July 1992.

—— (1993a), 'Symposium on Management of Local Commons', *Journal of Economic Perspectives,* 7 (4).

—— (1993b), 'Economics of Development and the Development of Economics', *Journal of Economic Perspectives*, 7 (Spring).

—— (1995), 'Rational Fools and Cooperation in a Poor Hydraulic Economy', in Basu et al. (1995).

Bardhan, Pranab (ed.) (1989), *The Economic Theory of Agrarian Institutions* (Oxford: Clarendon Press).

Barnett, Marguerite Ross (1976), *The Politics of Cultural Nationalism in South India* (Princeton: Princeton University Press).

Barro, Robert J. (1990a), 'Government Spending in a Simple Model of Endogenous Growth', *Journal of Political Economy*, 98.

—— (1990b), 'Economic Growth in a Cross Section of Countries', *Quarterly Journal of Economics*, 105.

Barro, Robert J., and Lee, Jong-Wha (1993a), 'Losers and Winners in Economic Growth', Working Paper 4341, National Bureau of Economic Research.

—— (1993b), 'International Comparisons of Educational Attainment', paper presented at a conference on 'How Do National Policies Affect Long-Run Growth?', World Bank, Washington, DC.

Basu, Alaka Malwade (1989), 'Is Discrimination in Food Really Necessary for Explaining Sex Differentials in Childhood Mortality?', *Population Studies*, 43 (2).

—— (1991), 'Demand and its Sociocultural Context', in Satia and Jejeebhoy (1991).

—— (1992), *Culture, the Status of Women and Demographic Behaviour* (Oxford: Clarendon Press).

—— (1993), 'Fertility Decline and Increasing Gender Imbalances in India: Including the South Indian Turnaround', mimeo, Institute of Economic Growth, Delhi University.

Basu, Alaka M., and Jeffery, Roger (eds.) (forthcoming), *Girls' Schooling, Women's Autonomy and Fertility Change in South Asia* (New Delhi: Sage).

Basu, Aparna (1988), 'A Century's Journey: Women's Education in Western India, 1820–1920', in Chanana (1988b).

Basu, Kaushik (1993), 'Structural Reform in India, 1991–93: Experience and Agenda', *Economic and Political Weekly*, November 27.

—— (1994), 'Where There is no Economist: Some Institutional and Legal Prerequisites of Economic Reforms in India', Working Paper No. 6, Centre for Development Economics, Delhi School of Economics.

Basu, K., Pattanaik, P., and Suzumura, K. (eds.) (1995), *Choice, Welfare, and Development* (Oxford: Clarendon).

Bauer, Peter (1948), *The Rubber Industry* (London: Longmans).

—— (1972), *Dissent on Development* (London: Weidenfeld).

—— (1991), *The Development Frontier* (Cambridge, MA: Harvard University Press).

Bauer, Peter, and Yamey, Basil (1957), *The Economics of Underdeveloped Countries* (Cambridge: Cambridge University Press).

Baviskar, Amita (1992), 'Development, Nature and Resistance: The Case of Bhilala Tribals in the Narmada Valley', unpublished Ph.D. thesis, Cornell University.

Beck, Tony (1994), *The Experience of Poverty: Fighting for Respect and Resources in Village India* (London: Intermediate Technology Publications).

Beenstock, M., and Sturdy, P. (1990), 'The Determinants of Infant Mortality in Regional India', *World Development*, 18.

Behrman, Jere R. (1987), 'Schooling in Developing Countries: Which Countries Are the Under- and Over-Achievers and What Is the Schooling Impact?', *Economics of Education Review*, 6.

Behrman, Jere R., and Deolalikar, Anil B. (1988), 'Health and Nutrition', in Chenery and Srinivasan (1988).

Behrman, Jere R., and Schneider, Ryan (1992), 'An International Perspective on Schooling Investment in the Last Quarter Century in Some Fast-Growing Eastern and Southeastern Countries', mimeo, World Bank, Washington, DC.

Behrman, Jere R., and Srinivasan, T.N. (eds.) (1994), *Handbook of Development Economics*, vol. III (Amsterdam: North-Holland).

Behrman, J.R., and Wolfe, B.L. (1984), 'More Evidence on Nutrition Demand: Income Seems Overrated and Women's Schooling Underemphasized', *Journal of Development Economics*, 14.

—— (1987), 'How Does Mother's Schooling Affect Family Health, Nutrition, Medical Care Usage, and Household Sanitation?', *Journal of Econometrics*, 36.

Berlin, I. (1969), *Four Essays on Liberty*, 2nd edition (Oxford: Oxford University Press).

Berman, Peter (1992), 'Health Care Expenditure in India', paper presented at a workshop on 'Health and Development in India', 2–4 January, 1992; to be published in M. Das Gupta et al. (forthcoming).

Berman, Peter, and Khan, M.E. (eds.) (1993), *Paying for India's Health Care* (New Delhi: Sage).

Bernstein, T.P. (1984), 'Stalinism, Famine, and Chinese Peasants', *Theory and Society*, 13.

Berreman, Gerald D. (1962), 'Village Exogamy in Northernmost India', *Southwestern Journal of Anthropology*, 18.

—— (1993), 'Sanskritization as Female Oppression in India', in Miller (1993b).

Berry, R. Albert, and Cline, William (1979), *Agrarian Structure and Productivity in Developing Countries* (Baltimore, MD: Johns Hopkins University Press).

Bhagwati, Jagdish (1993), *India in Transition* (Oxford: Clarendon Press).

Bhagwati, Jagdish, and Desai, Padma (1970), *India: Planning for Industrialization* (Oxford: Oxford University Press).

Bhagwati, Jagdish, and Krueger, Anne O. (eds.) (1975), *Trade Strategies for Economic Development* (New York: National Bureau of Economic Research).

Bhagwati, Jagdish, and Srinivasan, T.N. (1975), *Foreign Trade Regimes and Economic Development: India* (New York: National Bureau of Economic Research).

—— (1993), *India's Economic Reforms*, with a 'Preface' by the Finance Minister, Manmohan Singh (New Delhi: Ministry of Finance, Government of India).

Bhalla, A.S. (1992), *Uneven Development in the Third World: A Study of India and China* (London: Macmillan).

Bhatia, Bela (forthcoming), 'Social Action with Rural Widows in Gujarat', in Chen (forthcoming, b).

Bhatia, B.M. (1967), *Famines in India* (Bombay: Asia Publishing House).

Bhattacharya, B.B., and Mitra, Arup (1993), 'Employment and Structural Adjustment', *Economic and Political Weekly*, September 18.

Bhende, M.J., Walker, T.S., Lieberman, S.S., and Venkataram, J.V. (1992), 'EGS and the Poor: Evidence from Longitudinal Village Studies', *Economic and Political Weekly*, March 28.

Bhuiya, A., and Streatfield, K.(1991), 'Mothers' Education and Survival of Female Children in a Rural Area of Bangladesh', *Population Studies*, 45.

Binswanger, Hans, and Rosenzweig, Mark (1984), *Contractual Arrangements, Employment and Wages in Rural Labor Markets in Asia* (New Haven: Yale University Press).

Birdsall, Nancy (1993), 'Social Development Is Economic Development', Policy Research Working Paper 1123, World Bank, Washington, DC.

Birdsall, Nancy, and Sabot, Richard H. (1993a), 'Virtuous Circles: Human Capital, Growth and Equity in East Asia', mimeo, World Bank, Washington, DC.

Birdsall, Nancy, and Sabot, Richard H. (eds.) (1993b), *Opportunity Forgone: Education, Growth and Inequality in Brazil* (Washington, DC: World Bank).

Biswas, A., and Agrawal, S.P. (1986), *Development of Education in India: A Historical Survey of Educational Documents Before and After Independence* (New Delhi: Concept).

Blackorby, Charles, and Donaldson, David (1980), 'Ethical Indices for the Measurement of Poverty', *Econometrica*, 48.

Bliss, Christopher, and Stern, Nicholas (1978), 'Productivity, Wages and Nutrition', *Journal of Development Economics*, 5.

——— (1982), *Palanpur: The Economy of an Indian Village* (Oxford: Oxford University Press).

Blomstrom, Magnus (1989), *Foreign Investments and Spillovers* (London: Routledge).

Bloom, Gerald (1994), 'Financing Rural Health Services: Lessons from China', mimeo, Institute of Development Studies, University of Sussex.

Bordia, Anil (1993), 'Universalization of Primary Education in India: Is Compulsion the Answer?', mimeo, New Delhi.

Bose, Ashish (1991a), *Demographic Diversity of India* (Delhi: B.R. Publishing).

——— (1991b), *Population of India: 1991 Census Results and Methodology* (Delhi: B.R. Publishing).

Boserup, Ester (1970), *Women's Role in Economic Development* (New York: St Martin's).

Bourne, K., and Walker, G.M.(1991), 'The Differential Effect of Mothers' Education on Mortality of Boys and Girls in India', *Population Studies*, 45.

Bramall, Chris, and Jones, Marion (1993), 'Rural Income Inequality in China since 1978', *Journal of Peasant Studies*, 21(1).

Brass, Paul R. (1992), *The Political Economy of India since Independence*, first corrected Indian edition (New Delhi: Cambridge University Press).

Breman, Jan (1974), *Patronage and Exploitation* (Berkeley, CA: University of California Press).

Brown, Lester R., and Eckholm, Erik P. (1974), *By Bread Alone* (Oxford: Pergamon).

Bruton, Henry, with Abeyesekara, G., Sanderatne, N., and Yusof, Z.A. (1993), *The Political Economy of Poverty, Equity, and Growth: Sri Lanka and Malaysia* (New York: Oxford University Press).

Buchanan, James M., and Yoon, Yong J. (1994), *The Return to Increasing Returns* (Ann Arbor: University of Michigan Press).

Budakoti, D.K. (1988), 'Study of the Community and Community Health Work in Two Primary Health Centres in Chamoli District of Uttar Pradesh', M.Phil. dissertation, Centre for Social Medicine and Community Health, Jawaharlal Nehru University, New Delhi.

Bumgarner, R. (1992), 'China: Long-Term Issues in Options for the Health Transition', World Bank Country Study, World Bank, Washington, DC.

Burra, Neera (1986), 'Child Labour in India: Poverty, Exploitation and Vested Interests', *Social Action*, 36.

—— (1988), *Child Labour Health Hazards* (New Delhi: Seminar Publications).

—— (forthcoming), *Born to Work: Child Labour in India* (Delhi: Oxford University Press).

Byrd, W., and Lin, Q. (eds.) (1990), *China's Rural Industry: Structure, Development, and Reform* (Oxford: Oxford University Press).

Byres, T. (ed.) (1994), *The State and Development Planning in India* (Oxford: Oxford University Press).

Cain, Mead (1981), 'Risk and Insurance: Perspectives on Fertility and Agrarian Change in India and Bangladesh', *Population and Development Review*, 7.

Caldwell, J.C. (1979), 'Education as a Factor in Mortality Decline: An Examination of Nigerian Data', *Population Studies*, 33.

—— (1986), 'Routes to Low Mortality in Poor Countries', *Population and Development Review*, 12.

Caldwell, J.C., Reddy, P.H., and Caldwell, P. (1985), 'Educational Transition in Rural South India', *Population and Development Review*, 11 (1).

—— (1989), *The Causes of Demographic Change* (Madison: University of Wisconsin Press).

Caldwell, Pat, and Caldwell, John (1987), 'Where There is a Narrower Gap between Female and Male Situations: Lessons from South India and Sri Lanka', paper presented at a workshop on 'Differentials in Mortality and Health Care', BAMANEH/SSRC, Dhaka.

Cassen, Robert (1978), *India: Population, Economy, Society* (London: Macmillan).

Cassen, Robert, with contributors (1994), *Population and Development: Old Debates, New Conclusions* (Washington, DC: Transaction Books for Overseas Development Council).

Cassen, Robert, and Joshi, Vijay (eds.) (1995), *India: The Future of Economic Reform* (Delhi: Oxford University Press).

Castaneda, T. (1984), 'Contexto Socioeconómico y Causas del Descenso de la Mortalidad Infantil en Chile', Documento de Trabajo No. 28, Centro de Estudios Públicos, Santiago, Chile.

—— (1985), 'Determinantes del Descenso de la Mortalidad Infantil en Chile 1975–1983', *Cuadernos de Economía*, 22.

Central Statistical Organisation (1991a), *Estimates of State Domestic Product and Gross Fixed Capital Formation* (New Delhi: CSO).

—— (1991b), *National Accounts Statistics* (New Delhi: CSO).

—— (1994), *National Accounts Statistics* (New Delhi: CSO).

Centre for Development Economics (forthcoming), *Public Report on Basic Education* (Delhi: Oxford University Press).

Centre for Monitoring the Indian Economy (1994a), *Basic Statistics Relating to the Indian Economy* (Bombay: CMIE).

—— (1994b), *Basic Statistics Relating to States of India* (Bombay: CMIE).

Chakravarty, Sukhamoy (1969), *Capital and Development Planning* (Cambridge, MA: MIT Press).

—— (1987), *Development Planning: The Indian Experience* (Oxford: Oxford University Press).

Chambers, Robert, Saxena, N.C., and Shah, Tushaar (1989), *To the Hands of the Poor: Water and Trees* (New Delhi: Oxford and IBH).

Chanana, Karuna (1988a), 'Social Change or Social Reform: The Education of Women in Pre-Independence India', in Chanana (1988b).

—— (1993), 'Educational Attainment, Status Reproduction and Female Autonomy: Case Studies of Punjabi Women', paper presented at a workshop on 'Female Education, Autonomy and Fertility Change in South Asia', New Delhi, 8–10 April 1993.

Chanana, Karuna (ed.) (1988b), *Socialisation, Education and Women: Explorations in Gender Identity* (New Delhi: Orient Longman).

Chandhok, H.L. (1990), *Indian Database*, vol. II (New Delhi: The Policy Group).

Chandrasekhar, C.P., and Ghosh, Jayati (1993), 'Economic Discipline and External Vulnerability: A Comment on Fiscal and Adjustment Strategies', *Economic and Political Weekly*, April 10.

Chatterjee, Meera (1990), 'Indian Women: Their Health and Productivity', Discussion Paper No. 109, World Bank, Washington, DC.

Chaudhri, D.P. (1979), *Education, Innovations, and Agricultural Development* (London: Croom Helm).

Chaudhuri, M. (1993), *Indian Women's Movement* (New Delhi: Radiant).

Chaudhuri, Pramit (1974), *The Indian Economy* (London: Crosby, Lockwood and Staples).

Chaudhuri, Pramit (ed.) (1971), *Aspects of Indian Economic Development* (London: Allen & Unwin).

Chayanov, A.V. (1966), *The Theory of the Peasant Economy*, English translation, edited by D. Thorner, B. Kerblay, and R.E.F. Smith (Homewood, IL: Irwin).

Chen, Kang, Jefferson, Gary H., and Singh, Inderjit (1992), 'Lessons from China's Economic Reform', *Journal of Comparative Economics*, 16.

Chen, Lincoln, Huq, E., and D'Souza, S. (1981), 'Sex Bias in the Family Allocation of Food and Health Care in Rural Bangladesh', *Population and Development Review*, 7.

Chen, Marty (1991), *Coping with Seasonality and Drought* (London: Sage).

Chen, Marty (forthcoming, a), *The Lives of Widows in Rural India*, to be published as a monograph.

Chen, Marty (ed.) (forthcoming, b), Proceedings of a conference on 'Widows in India' held in Bangalore, March 1994, to be published as a monograph.

Chen, Marty, and Drèze, Jean (1994), 'Widowhood and Well-being in Rural North India', in M. Das Gupta et al. (1994).

——— (1995), 'Recent Research on Widows in India: A Workshop and Conference Report', mimeo, Delhi School of Economics; forthcoming in *Economic and Political Weekly*.

Chenery, Hollis, Robinson, Sherman, and Syrquin, Moshe (eds.) (1986), *Industrialization and Growth: A Comparative Study* (New York: Oxford University Press).

Chenery, Hollis, and Srinivasan, T.N. (eds.) (1988), *Handbook of Development Economics*, vol. I (Amsterdam: North-Holland).

Cheung, S.N.S. (1969), *The Theory of Share Tenancy* (Chicago: University of Chicago Press).

Chichilnisky, Graciela (1983), 'North–South Trade with Export Enclaves: Food Consumption and Food Exports', mimeo, Columbia University.

Chinese Academy of Social Sciences (1987), *Almanac of China's Population 1986* (Beijing: Population Research Centre).

Choudhary, K.M., and Bapat, M.T. (1975), 'A Study of Impact of Famine and Relief Measures in Gujarat and Rajasthan', mimeo, Agricultural Economics Research Centre, Sardar Patel University.

Chowdhury, Anis, and Islam, Iyanatul (1993), *The Newly-Industrialising Economies of East Asia* (London and New York: Routledge).

Christensen, Scott, Dollar, David, and Siamwalla, Ammar (1993), 'Thailand: The Institutional and Political Underpinnings of Growth', mimeo, World Bank, Washington, DC.

Cleland, J. (1990), 'Maternal Education and Child Survival: Further Evidence and Explanations', in J. Caldwell et al. (eds.), *What We Know About Health Transition: The Cultural, Social and Behavioural Determinants of Health* (Canberra: Health Transition Centre, Australian National University).

Cleland, J., and van Ginneken, J. (1987), 'The Effect of Maternal Schooling on Childhood Mortality: The Search for an Explanation', paper presented at a conference on 'Health Intervention and Mortality Change in Developing Countries', University of Sheffield, September 1987.

—— (1988), 'Maternal Education and Child Survival in Developing Countries: The Search for Pathways of Influence', *Social Science and Medicine*, 27 (12).

Coale, Ansley J. (1991), 'Excess Female Mortality and the Balance of the Sexes: An Estimate of the Number of "Missing Females"', *Population and Development Review*, 17.

—— (1993), 'Mortality Schedules in China Derived from Data in the 1982 and 1990 Censuses', Working Paper No. 93–7, Office of Population Research, Princeton University.

Cohen, G.A. (1989), 'On the Currency of Egalitarian Justice', *Ethics*, 99.

—— (1990), 'Equality of What? On Welfare, Goods and Capabilities', *Recherches Economiques de Louvain*, 56.

—— (1993), 'Equality of What? On Welfare, Resources and Capabilities', in Nussbaum and Sen (1993).

Colclough, Christopher, with Lewin, Keith (1993), *Educating All the Children* (Oxford: Oxford University Press).

Cole, D.C., and Lyman, P.N. (1971), *Korean Development: The Interplay of Politics and Economics* (Cambridge, MA: Harvard University Press).

Coles, J.L., and Hammond, P.J. (1995), 'Walrasian Equilibrium without Survival: Existence, Efficiency, and Remedial Policy', in Basu et al. (1995).

Committee on the Status of Women in India (1974), *Towards Equality* (New Delhi: Ministry of Education and Social Welfare).

Cooper, Charles (1983), 'Extensions of the Raj–Sen Model of Economic Growth', *Oxford Economic Papers*, 35.

Corden, W. Max (1974), *Trade Policy and Economic Welfare* (Oxford: Clarendon Press).

—— (1993), 'Seven Asian Miracle Economies: Overview of Macroeconomic Policies', mimeo, World Bank, Washington, DC.

Crocker, D.A. (1991), 'Toward Development Ethics', *World Development*, 19.

—— (1992), 'Functioning and Capability: The Foundations of Sen's and Nussbaum's Development Ethics', *Political Theory*, 20.

Crook, R.C., and Manor, J. (1994), 'Enhancing Participation and Institutional Performance: Democratic Decentralisation in South Asia and West Africa', report to the Overseas Development Administration, January 1994.

Da Corta, Lucia (1993), 'Inequality, Household Mobility and Class Differentiation in South Indian Villages: A Study in Method', unpublished D.Phil. thesis, University of Oxford.

Dandavate, P., Kumari, R., and Verghese, J. (eds.) (1989), *Widows, Abandoned and Destitute Women in India* (New Delhi: Radiant Publishers).

Dandekar, V.M., and Rath, N. (1971), *Poverty in India* (Bombay: Sameeksha Trust).

Das, Arvind (1987), 'Changel: Three Centuries of an Indian Village', *Journal of Peasant Studies,* 15 (1).

—— (1995), 'One from the Wild Heart', *The Telegraph*, March 27.

Das Gupta, Monica (1987), 'Selective Discrimination against Female Children in Rural Punjab', *Population and Development Review*, 13.

—— (1990), 'Death Clustering, Mother's Education and the Determinants of Child Mortality in Rural Punjab, India', *Population Studies*, 44.

—— (1993), 'Fertility Decline in Punjab, India: Parallels with Historical Europe', mimeo, Center for Population and Development Studies, Harvard University.

—— (1994a), 'What Motivates Fertility Decline? Lessons from a Case Study of Punjab, India', mimeo, Center for Population and Development Studies, Harvard University.

—— (1994b), 'Life Course Perspectives on Women's Autonomy and Health Outcomes', paper presented at a meeting of the Population Association of America, Miami, May 1994.

Das Gupta, Monica, Krishnan, T.N., and Chen, Lincoln (eds.) (1994), *Women's Health in India: Risk and Vulnerability* (Bombay: Oxford University Press).

—— (forthcoming) *Health, Poverty and Development in India* (Bombay: Oxford University Press).

Dasgupta, Partha (1993), *An Inquiry into Well-being and Destitution* (Oxford: Clarendon Press).

Dasgupta, Partha, and Ray, Debraj (1986), 'Inequality as a Determinant of Malnutrition and Unemployment: Theory', *Economic Journal,* 96.

—— (1987), 'Inequality as a Determinant of Malnutrition and Unemployment: Policy', *Economic Journal*, 97.

—— (1990), 'Adapting to Undernourishment: The Biological Evidence and Its Implications', in Drèze and Sen (1990), vol. I.

Datt, Gaurav (1995), 'Poverty in India: 1951–1991', mimeo, World Bank, Washington, DC.

Datt, Gaurav, and Ravallion, Martin (1992), 'Regional Disparities, Targetting, and Poverty in India', in M. Lipton and J. van der Gaag (eds.), *Including the Poor* (Washington, DC: World Bank).

—— (1994), 'Growth and Poverty in Rural India', mimeo, World Bank.

Datta Chaudhuri, Mrinal K. (1979), *Industrialization and Foreign Trade: An Analysis*

*Based on the Development Experience of the Republic of Korea and the Philippines,* ILO Working Paper II-4 (Bangkok: ARTEP, ILO).

Datta Chaudhuri, Mrinal K. (1990), 'Market Failure and Government Failure', *Journal of Economic Perspectives,* 4.

Debreu, Gérard (1959), *Theory of Value* (New York: Wiley).

De Geyndt, W., Zhao Xiyan, and Liu Shunli (1992), 'From Barefoot Doctor to Village Doctor in Rural China', World Bank Technical Paper No. 187, Asia Technical Department Series, World Bank, Washington, DC.

Deliège, Robert (1985), *The Bhils of Western India* (New Delhi: National Publishing House).

Deolalikar, Anil, and Vashishtha, Prem (1992), 'The Utilization of Government and Private Health Services in India', mimeo, National Council of Applied Economic Research, New Delhi.

Desai, G.M., Singh, G., and Sah, D.C. (1979), 'Impact of Scarcity on Farm Economy and Significance of Relief Operations', CMA Monograph No. 84, Indian Institute of Management, Ahmedabad.

Desai, Meghnad (1989), 'Poverty and Capability: Towards an Empirically Implementable Measure', in F. Bracho (ed.), *Towards a New Way to Measure Development* (Caracao: Office of the High Commission, Venezuela, 1989).

—— (1991) 'Human Development: Concepts and Measurement', *European Economic Review,* 35.

—— (1992), 'Is There Life After Mahalanobis? The Political Economy of India's New Economic Policy', *Indian Economic Review,* special number in memory of Sukhamoy Chakravarty.

—— (1993a), *Capitalism, Socialism and the Indian Economy* (Bombay: Export–Import Bank of India).

—— (1993b), 'The Measurement Problem in Economics', Invited Lecture at the Annual Conference of the Scottish Economics Association; forthcoming in the *Scottish Journal of Political Economy.*

Desai, Neera (ed.) (1988), *A Decade of Women's Movement in India* (Bombay: Himalaya Publishing House).

Desai, Sonalde, and Jain, Devaki (1992), 'Maternal Employment and Changes in Family Dynamics: The Social Context of Women's Work in Rural South India', Working Paper No. 39, The Population Council, New York.

Deshpande, L.K., and Rodgers, G. (eds.) (1992), 'The Indian Labour Market in the Face of Structural Economic Change', special issue of the *Indian Journal of Labour Economics.*

Dhagamwar, Vasudha (1987), 'The Disadvantaged and the Law', paper presented at a workshop on 'Poverty in India', Queen Elizabeth House, Oxford, October 1–6, 1987.

Dhar, P.N. (1990), *Constraints on Growth: Reflections on the Indian Experience* (Delhi: Oxford University Press).

Dietrich, Gabriele (1992), *Reflections on the Women's Movement in India: Religion, Ecology, Development* (New Delhi: Horizon India Books).

Dixit, Avinash K., and Norman, Victor (1980), *Theory of International Trade* (Cambridge: Cambridge University Press).

Doherty, V.S., and Jodha, N.S. (1979), 'Conditions for Group Action among Farmers', in J. Wong (ed.), *Group Farming in Asia*, (Singapore: Singapore University Press).

Dollar, David (1992), 'Outward-Oriented Developing Economies Really Do Grow More Rapidly: Evidence from 95 LDCs, 1976–1985', *Economic Development and Cultural Change*, 40.

Drèze, Jean (1990a), 'Famine Prevention in India', in Drèze and Sen (1990), vol. II.

—— (1990b), 'Famine Prevention in Africa', in Drèze and Sen (1990), vol. II.

—— (1990c), 'Widows in Rural India', Discussion Paper No. 26, Development Economics Research Programme, STICERD, London School of Economics.

—— (1990d), 'Poverty in India and the IRDP Delusion', *Economic and Political Weekly*, September 29.

Drèze, Jean, and Gazdar, Haris (1996), 'Uttar Pradesh: The Burden of Inertia', in Drèze and Sen (1996).

Drèze, Jean, Guio, Anne-Catherine, and Murthi, Mamta (1995), 'Demographic Outcomes, Economic Development and Women's Agency', Working Paper No. 28, Centre for Development Economics, Delhi School of Economics.

Drèze, Jean, Lanjouw, Peter, and Sharma, Naresh (forthcoming), 'Economic Development in Palanpur, 1957–94', to be published in P. Lanjouw and N. Stern (eds.), *A Kind of Growth: Palanpur 1957–94* (Oxford: Clarendon Press).

Drèze, Jean, and Loh, Jackie (1995), 'Literacy in India and China', Working Paper No. 29, Centre for Development Economics, Delhi School of Economics.

Drèze, Jean, and Mukherjee, Anindita (1989), 'Labour Contracts in Rural India: Theories and Evidence', in S. Chakravarty (ed.), *The Balance between Industry and Agriculture in Economic Development*, vol. III (London: Macmillan).

Drèze, Jean, Samson, Meera, and Singh, Satyajit (eds.) (forthcoming), *Displacement and Resettlement in the Narmada Valley* (New Delhi: Sage).

Drèze, Jean, and Saran, Mrinalini (1995), 'Primary Education and Economic Development in China and India: Overview and Two Case Studies', in Basu et al. (1995).

Drèze, Jean, and Sen, Amartya (1989), *Hunger and Public Action* (Oxford: Clarendon Press).

—— (1991), 'Public Action for Social Security', in Ahmad et al. (1991).

Drèze, Jean, and Sen, Amartya (eds.) (1990), *The Political Economy of Hunger*, 3 volumes (Oxford: Clarendon Press).

Drèze, Jean, and Sen, Amartya (eds.) (1996), *Indian Development: Selected Regional Perspectives* (Oxford and Delhi: Oxford University Press).

Dube, Leela (1988), 'On the Construction of Gender: Hindu Girls in Patrilineal India', in Chanana (1988b).

Dutta, Bhaskar (1994), 'Poverty in India: Trends, Determinants and Policy Issues', Discussion Paper No. 94–16, Indian Statistical Institute, New Delhi.

Dutta, B., Panda, M., and Wadhwa, W. (1994), 'Human Development in India: An Inter-state Analysis', mimeo, Indian Statistical Institute, New Delhi.

Duvvury, Nata (1989), 'Women in Agriculture: A Review of the Indian Literature', *Economic and Political Weekly*, October 28.

Dworkin, Ronald (1978), *Taking Rights Seriously*, second edition (London: Duckworth).

—— (1981), 'What is Equality? Part 1: Equality of Welfare', and 'What is Equality? Part 2: Equality of Resources', *Philosophy and Public Affairs*, 10.

Dyson, Tim (1979), 'A Working Paper on Fertility and Mortality Estimates for the States of India', mimeo; partly published in *World Health Statistics Quarterly*, 37 (2), (1984).

—— (1987), 'Excess Female Mortality in India: Uncertain Evidence on a Narrowing Differential', in K. Srinivasan and S. Mukerji (eds.), *Dynamics of Population and Family Welfare* (Bombay: Himalaya).

Dyson, Tim, and Moore, Mick (1983), 'On Kinship Structure, Female Autonomy, and Demographic Behavior in India', *Population and Development Review*, 9.

Easterly, William, Kremer, Michael, Pritchett, Lant, and Summers, Lawrence (1993), 'Good Policy or Good Luck? Country Growth Performance and Temporary Shocks', mimeo, World Bank, Washington, DC.

Egerö, Bertil, and Hammarskjöld, Mikael (eds.) (1994), *Understanding Reproductive Change: Kenya, Tamil Nadu, Punjab, Costa Rica* (Cambridge, MA: Harvard Series on Population and International Health).

Ehrlich, Paul (1968), *The Population Bomb* (New York: Ballantine Books).

Ehrlich, P., and Ehrlich, A. (1990), *The Population Explosion* (New York: Simon and Schuster).

Elwin, Verrier (1989), *The Tribal World of Verrier Elwin: An Autobiography* (Delhi: Oxford University Press).

EPW Research Foundation (1993), 'Poverty Levels in India: Norms, Estimates and Trends', *Economic and Political Weekly*, August 21.

—— (1994), 'What Has Gone Wrong with Economic Reforms?', *Economic and Political Weekly*, April 30.

Eswaran, Mukesh, and Kotwal, Ashok (1994), *Why Poverty Persists in India* (Delhi: Oxford University Press).

Ethier, Wilfred, Helpman, Elhanan, and Neary, Peter (1993), *Theory, Policy, and Dynamics in International Trade: Essays in Honor of Ronald W. Jones* (New York: Cambridge University Press).

Fallows, James (1994), *Looking at the Sun: The Rise of the New East Asian Economic and Political System* (New York: Pantheon).

Fernandes, Walter (ed.) (1985), *Social Activists and People's Movements* (New Delhi: Indian Social Institute).

Fields, Gary S. (1980), *Poverty, Inequality and Development* (Cambridge: Cambridge University Press).

—— (1993), 'Changing Labor Market Conditions and Economic Development in Hong Kong, Korea, Singapore and Taiwan', mimeo, World Bank, Washington, DC.

Findlay, Ronald (1993), *Trade, Development, and Political Economy: Selected Essays of Ronald Findlay* (Brookfield, VT: Aldershot, Hants).

Findlay, Ronald, and Wallisz, Stanislaw (eds.) (1993), *The Political Economy of Poverty, Equity, and Growth* (New York: Oxford University Press).

Fishlow, A., Gwin, C., Haggarad, S., Rodrik, D., and Wade, R. (1994), *Miracle or Design? Lessons from the East Asian Experience* (Washington, DC: Overseas Development Council).

Ford Foundation (1992), *Perspectives on India's Development in the 1990s: Symposium Review* (New Delhi: Ford Foundation).

Foster, James (1984), 'On Economic Poverty: A Survey of Aggregate Measures', *Advances in Econometrics*, 3.

Foster, J., Greer, J., and Thorbecke, E. (1984), 'A Class of Decomposable Poverty Measures', *Econometrica*, 52.

Foster, J., and Shorrocks, A.F. (1991), 'Subgroup Consistent Poverty Indices', *Econometrica*, 59.

Frank, C.R., Kim, K.S., and Westphal, L. (1975), *Foreign Trade Regimes and Economic Development* (New York: National Bureau of Economic Research).

Franke, Richard, and Chasin, Barbara (1989), *Kerala: Radical Reform as Development in an Indian State* (San Francisco: Institute for Food and Development Policy).

Frankel, Francine (1978), *India's Political Economy 1947–1977* (Princeton: Princeton University Press).

Frankel, Francine, and Rao, M.S.A. (eds.) (1989), *Dominance and State Power in Modern India* (Delhi: Oxford University Press).

Fuchs, Victor (1986), *The Health Economy* (Cambridge: Harvard University Press).

Furer-Haimendorf, C. von (1982), *Tribes of India: The Struggle for Survival* (Delhi: Oxford University Press).

Gadgil, M., and Guha, R. (1993), 'Ecology and Equity: Steps Towards an Economy of Permanence', mimeo, Delhi School of Economics; to be published as a monograph.

Gaiha, Raghav (1993), *Design of Poverty Alleviation Strategy in Rural Areas* (Rome: Food and Agriculture Organization).

Gaiha, Raghav (1994a), 'Structural Adjustment in India: Rationale and Content', mimeo, Faculty of Management Studies, University of Delhi.

——— (1994b), 'Structural Adjustment, Rural Institutions and the Poor in India: A Comparative Analysis of Andhra Pradesh, Maharashtra and Karnataka', mimeo, Faculty of Management Studies, University of Delhi.

Galenson, Walter (ed.) (1979), *Economic Growth and Structural Change in Taiwan* (Ithaca: Cornell University Press).

Gandhi, Geeta (1994), 'An Economic Evaluation of School Management-Types in Urban India: A Case Study of Uttar Pradesh', unpublished Ph.D. thesis, Faculty of Social Studies, University of Oxford.

Gasper, Des (1993), 'Entitlements Analysis: Relating Concepts and Contexts', *Development and Change*, 24.

George, P.S. (1994), 'Management of Education in Kerala', paper presented at a seminar on 'Management of Education under Panchayati Raj' held at the National Institute of Educational Planning and Administration, 27–8 October, 1994.

George, S., Abel, R., and Miller, B.D. (1992), 'Female Infanticide in Rural South India', *Economic and Political Weekly*, May 30.

Germain, Adrienne (1994), 'Gender and Health: From Research to Action', in M. Das Gupta et al. (1994).

Ghate, Prabhu (1984), *Direct Attacks on Rural Poverty* (New Delhi: Concept).

Ghose, Sanjoy (1993), 'Tryst with Textbooks', *Indian Express*, March 24.

Ghosh, A. (1991), 'Annals of the Literacy Programme: A Scenario from Rajasthan', *Economic and Political Weekly*, October 19.

——— (1992), 'Education for All: The Financing Problem', *Economic and Political Weekly*, April 4.

——— (1994), 'Structural Adjustment and Industrial and Environmental Concerns', *Economic and Political Weekly*, February 19.

Ghosh, A., Ananthamurthy, U.R., Béteille, A., Kansal, S.M., Mazumdar, V., and Vanaik, A. (1994), 'Evaluation of Literacy Campaigns in India', report of an independent Expert Group appointed by the Ministry of Human Resource Development (New Delhi: Ministry of Human Resource Development).

Ghurye, G.S. (1969), *Caste and Race in India*, fifth edition (Bombay: Popular Prakashan).

Gidwani, D. (1994), 'What Population Problem? Sterilisation Targets Achieved with Nepali Help', *India Today*, March 31.

Gillespie, S.R., and McNeill, G. (1992), *Food, Health and Survival in India and Developing Countries* (Delhi: Oxford University Press).

Gokhale, A.M. (1988), 'Panchayati Raj in Nagaland', mimeo, Department of Rural Development, Ministry of Agriculture, New Delhi.

Goodburn, E., Ebrahim, G.J., and Senapati, Sishir (1990), 'Strategies Educated

Mothers Use to Ensure the Health of Their Children', *Journal of Tropical Pediatrics*, 36.

Gopal, Sarvepalli (ed.) (1983), *Jawaharlal Nehru: An Anthology* (Oxford and Delhi: Oxford University Press).

Government of India (1979), *Report of the Committee on Child Labour* (New Delhi: Ministry of Labour).

—— (1981), *Census of India 1981: Series I (India), Part II-A(i), General Population Tables, Tables A-1 to A-3* (New Delhi: Office of the Registrar-General).

—— (1982), *Sample Registration System 1979–80*, (New Delhi: Office of the Registrar General).

—— (1988a), 'Child Mortality Estimates of India', Occasional Paper No.5 of 1988, Demography Division, Office of the Registrar General, Ministry of Home Affairs, New Delhi.

—— (1988b), 'Fertility in India: An Analysis of 1981 Census Data', Occasional Paper No.13 of 1988, Demography Division, Office of the Registrar General, Ministry of Home Affairs, New Delhi.

—— (1989a), 'Child Mortality, Age at Marriage and Fertility in India', Occasional Paper No.2 of 1989, Demography Division, Office of the Registrar General, Ministry of Home Affairs, New Delhi.

—— (1989b), *The Drought of 1989: Response and Management* (New Delhi: Ministry of Agriculture).

—— (1991), *Family Welfare Programme in India: Yearbook 1989–90* (New Delhi: Ministry of Health and Family Welfare).

—— (1992a), *Sample Registration System 1989* (New Delhi: Office of the Registrar General).

—— (1992b), *Annual Report 1991–92 (Part I) of the Department of Education* (New Delhi: Ministry of Human Resource Development).

—— (1992c), *National Policy on Education 1986 (With Modifications Undertaken in 1992)* (New Delhi: Ministry of Human Resource Development).

—— (1992d), *National Policy on Education 1986: Programme of Action 1992* (New Delhi: Ministry of Human Resource Development).

—— (1992e), *Health Information of India: 1991* (New Delhi: Central Bureau of Health Intelligence, Ministry of Health and Family Welfare).

—— (1993a), *Sample Registration System: Fertility and Mortality Indicators 1990* (New Delhi: Office of the Registrar General).

—— (1993b), *Sample Registration System: Fertility and Mortality Indicators 1991* (New Delhi: Office of the Registrar General).

—— (1993c), *Education for All: The Indian Scene* (New Delhi: Ministry of Human Resource Development).

—— (1993d), *Education for All, The Indian Scene: Widening Horizons* (New Delhi: Ministry of Human Resource Development).

—— (1993e), 'Housing and Amenities: A Brief Analysis of the Housing

Tables of 1991 Census', Census of India 1991, Paper 2 of 1993, Office of the Registrar General, New Delhi.

Government of India (1994a), *Economic Survey 1993–94* (New Delhi: Ministry of Finance).

—— (1994b), *Status Report of Literacy and Post Literacy Campaigns* (New Delhi: Directorate of Adult Education).

—— (1994c), 'National Population Policy', draft report of the 'Committee on Population' appointed by the National Development Council.

—— (1994d), *Poverty Eradication through Growth, Employment and Social Development*, (New Delhi: Planning Commission).

—— (1994e), *Learning without Burden: Report of the National Advisory Committee Appointed by the Ministry of Human Resource Development* (New Delhi: Ministry of Human Resource Development).

—— (1994f), *Annual Report 1993–94 (Part I) of the Department of Education* (New Delhi: Ministry of Human Resource Development).

—— (1995), *Economic Survey 1994–95* (New Delhi: Ministry of Finance).

Government of Karnataka (1989), *Report of the Zilla Parishad and Mandal Panchayat Evaluation Committee* (Bangalore: Government of Karnataka).

Goyal, Sangeeta, and Mehrotra, Nidhi (1995), 'Primary Schooling in Rural India: A Field Report', mimeo, Centre for Development Economics, Delhi School of Economics.

Grant, James P. (1978), *Disparity Reduction Rates in Social Indicators* (Washington, DC: Overseas Development Council).

Greenhalgh, S., Zhu Chuzhu, and Li Nan (1993), 'Restraining Population Growth in Three Chinese Villages: 1988–93', Working Paper No. 55, Population Council, New York.

Gribble, James, and Preston, Samuel (1993), *The Epidemiological Transition: Policy and Planning Implications for Developing Countries* (Washintgon, DC: National Academic Press).

Griffin, Keith, and Knight, John (eds.) (1990), *Human Development and the International Development Strategy for the 1990s* (London: Macmillan).

Griffin, Keith, and Zhao Renwei (eds.) (1993), *The Distribution of Income in China* (London: Macmillan).

Grossman, Gene M., and Helpman, Elhanan (1990), 'Comparative Advantage and Long-run Growth', *American Economic Review*, 80.

—— (1991a), 'Quality Ladders and Product Cycles', *Quarterly Journal of Economics*, 106.

—— (1991b), *Innovation and Growth in the Global Economy* (Cambridge, MA: MIT Press).

Guha, Ashok (ed.) (1990), *Economic Liberalization, Industrial Structure and Growth in India* (New Delhi: Oxford University Press).

Guha Ranajit (1983), *Elementary Aspects of Peasant Insurgency in Colonial India* (Delhi: Oxford University Press).

Guha, Ranajit (ed.) (1982), *Subaltern Studies, vol. I: Writings on South Asian History and Society* (Delhi: Oxford University Press).

—— (1986), *Subaltern Studies*, vol. I (Delhi: Oxford University Press).

Guha, R., and Spivak, G. (eds.) (1988), *Selected Subaltern Studies* (New York: Oxford University Press).

Guhan, S. (1981), 'Social Security: Lessons and Possibilities from the Tamil Nadu Experience', Bulletin, Madras Development Seminar Series, 11 (1).

—— (1990), 'Social Security Initiatives in Tamil Nadu 1989', Working Paper No. 96, Madras Institute of Development Studies.

—— (1992), 'Social Security in India: Looking One Step Ahead', in Harriss et al. (1992).

—— (1993a), 'Social Security Options for Developing Countries', paper presented at a symposium on 'Poverty: New Approaches to Analysis and Policy', International Institute of Labour Studies, Geneva, November 1993.

—— (1993b), 'Social Security for the Unorganised Poor: A Feasible Blueprint for India', mimeo, Madras Institute of Development Studies.

Guio, Anne-Catherine (1994), 'Aspects du Sex Ratio en Inde', unpublished M.Sc. thesis, Université de Namur, Belgium.

Gulati, S.C. (1992), 'Developmental Determinants of Demographic Variables in India: A District Level Analysis', *Journal of Quantitative Economics*, 8 (1).

Gupta, D.B., Basu, A., and Asthana, R. (1993), 'Population Change, Women's Role and Status, and Development in India: A Review', mimeo, Institute of Economic Growth, Delhi University.

Gupta, N., Pal, P., Bhargava, M., and Daga, M. (1992), 'Health of Women and Children in Rajasthan', *Economic and Political Weekly*, October 17.

Gupta, S.P., and Sarkar, A.K. (1994), 'Fiscal Correction and Human Resource Development: Expenditure at Central and State Levels', *Economic and Political Weekly*, March 26.

Halstead, S.B., Walsh, J., and Warren, K. (1985), *Good Health at Low Cost* (New York: Rockefeller Foundation).

Hamlin, A., and Pettit, P. (eds.) (1989), *The Good Polity: Normative Analysis of the State* (Oxford: Blackwell).

Hardiman, David (1987), *The Coming of the Devi: Adivasi Assertion in Western India* (Delhi: Oxford University Press).

Hardin, Garrett (1993), *Living Within Limits* (New York: Oxford University Press).

Harriss, Barbara (1990), 'The Intrafamily Distribution of Hunger in South Asia', in Drèze and Sen (1990), vol. I.

—— (1991), *Child Nutrition and Poverty in South India* (New Delhi: Concept).

Harriss, Barbara (1993), 'Economic Reforms and Social Welfare in India', mimeo, Queen Elizabeth House, Oxford.

Harriss, B., Guhan, S., and Cassen, R. (eds.) (1992), *Poverty in India: Research and Policy* (Delhi: Oxford University Press).

Hasan, Zoya (1989), 'Power and Mobilization: Patterns of Resilience and Change in Uttar Pradesh Politics', in Frankel and Rao (1989).

Helleiner, G.K. (ed.) (1992), *Trade Policy, Industrialization, and Development* (Oxford: Clarendon).

Helpman, Elhanan, and Krugman, Paul R. (1990), *Market Structure and Foreign Trade* (Cambridge, MA: MIT Press).

Helpman, Elhanan, and Razin, Assad (eds.) (1991), *International Trade and Trade Policy* (Cambridge, MA: MIT Press).

Heyer, Judith (1992), 'The Role of Dowries and Daughters' Marriages in the Accumulation and Distribution of Capital in a South Indian Community', *Journal of International Development*, 4 (4).

Hirschman, Albert O. (1958), *The Strategy of Economic Development* (New Haven, CT: Yale University Press).

—— (1970), *Exit, Voice and Loyalty* (Cambridge, MA: Harvard University Press).

—— (1992), *Rival Views of Market Society and Other Recent Essays* (Cambridge, MA: Harvard University Press).

Hitchcock, John T. (1975), 'The Idea of the Martial Rajput', in M. Singer (ed.), *Traditional India: Structure and Change* (Jaipur: Rawat Publications).

Hong, W., and Krueger, Anne O. (eds.) (1975), *Trade and Development in Korea* (Seoul: Korea Development Institute).

Howes, Stephen (1992), 'Purchasing Power, Infant Mortality and Literacy in China and India: An Inter-provincial Analysis', Discussion Paper No. 19, Research Programme on the Chinese Economy, STICERD, London School of Economics.

—— (1993), 'Income Inequality in Urban China in the 1980s: Levels, Trends and Determinants', Discussion Paper No. 3, Series on 'Economic Transformation and Public Finance', STICERD, London School of Economics.

Howes, Stephen, and Hussain, Athar (1994), 'Regional Growth and Inequality in Rural China', Discussion Paper No. 11, Series on 'Economic Transformation and Public Finance', STICERD, London School of Economics.

Hubbard, Michael (1988), 'Drought Relief and Drought-Proofing in the State of Gujarat, India', in D. Curtis, M. Hubbard, and A. Shepherd (eds.), *Preventing Famine: Policies and Prospects for Africa* (New York and London: Routledge).

Hull, Terence (1990), 'Recent Trends in Sex Ratios at Birth in China', *Population and Development Review*, 16 (1).

Hussain, Athar (1990), 'The Chinese Enterprise Reform', Discussion Paper No.

5, Research Programme on the Chinese Economy, STICERD, London School of Economics.

Hussain, Athar (1992), 'The Chinese Economic Reforms in Retrospect and Prospect', Discussion Paper No. 24, Research Programme on the Chinese Economy, STICERD, London School of Economics.

—— (1993), 'Reform of the Chinese Social Security System', Discussion Paper No. 24, Research Programme on the Chinese Economy, STICERD, London School of Economics.

—— (1994), 'Social Security in Present-Day China and Its Reform', *American Economic Review*, 84.

Hussain, Athar (ed.) (1989), *China and the World Economy* (London: Suntory-Toyota International Centre for Economics and Related Disciplines).

Hussain, A., and Liu, H. (1989), 'Compendium of Literature on the Chinese Social Security System', Discussion Paper No. 3, Research Programme on the Chinese Economy, STICERD, London School of Economics

Hussain, Athar, and Stern, Nicholas (1992), 'Economic Reforms and Public Finance in China', Discussion Paper No. 23, Research Programme on the Chinese Economy, STICERD, London School of Economics.

Indian Council of Medical Research (1989), *Evaluation of Quality of Maternal and Child Health and Family Planning Services* (New Delhi: ICMR).

Indian Institute of Management (1985), *Study of Facility Utilization and Programme Management in Family Welfare* (Ahmedabad: Public Systems Group, Indian Institute of Management).

Indira Gandhi Institute of Development Research (1994), 'Mid Year Review 1994–95', mimeo, IGIDR, Bombay.

International Institute for Population Sciences (1994), *National Family Health Survey: India 1992–93* (Bombay: IIPS).

Irschick, Eugene (1969), *Politics and Social Conflict in South India: The Non-Brahman Movement and Tamil Separatism 1916–1929* (Berkeley: University of California Press).

Iyengar, Sudarshan, and Bhargava, Ashok (1987), 'Primary Health Care and Family Welfare Programme in Rural Gujarat', *Economic and Political Weekly*, July 4.

Jain, A.K. (1985), 'Determinants of Regional Variations in Infant Mortality in Rural India', *Population Studies*, 39.

Jain, A.K., and Nag, M. (1985), 'Female Primary Education and Fertility Reduction in India', Working Paper No.114, Center for Policy Studies, Population Council, New York.

—— (1986), 'Importance of Female Primary Education for Fertility Reduction in India', *Economic and Political Weekly*, September 6.

Jain, A.K., and Visaria, P. (eds.) (1988), *Infant Mortality in India: Differentials and Determinants* (New Delhi: Sage).

Jain, Devaki, and Banerjee, Nirmala (eds.) (1985), *Tyranny of the Household: Investigative Essays in Women's Work* (New Delhi: Vikas).

Jain, L.R., Sundaram, K., and Tendulkar, S.D. (1988), 'Dimensions of Rural Poverty: An Inter-Regional Profile', *Economic and Political Weekly*, November (special issue); reprinted in Krishnaswamy (1990).

Jalan, Bimal (1991), *India's Economic Crisis* (Delhi: Oxford University Press).

Jalan, Bimal (ed.) (1992), *The Indian Economy: Problems and Prospects* (New Delhi: Viking).

Jalan, J., and Subbarao, K. (1995), 'Adjustment and Social Sectors in India', in Cassen and Joshi (1995).

Jeffery, P., Jeffery, R., and Lyon, P. (1989), *Labour Pains and Labour Power: Women and Child-bearing in India* (London: Zed).

Jeffery, Roger (1988), *The Politics of Health in India* (Berkeley: University of California Press).

Jeffrey, Robin (1987), 'Culture and Governments: How Women Made Kerala Literate', *Pacific Affairs*, 60 (4).

—— (1992), *Politics, Women and Well-Being: How Kerala Became 'A Model'* (Cambridge: Cambridge University Press).

Jejeeboy, Shireen, and Rama Rao, S. (1994), 'Unsafe Motherhood: A Review of Reproductive Health', in M. Das Gupta et al. (1994).

Jena, B., and Pati, R.N. (eds.) (1989), *Health and Family Welfare Services in India* (New Delhi: Ashish).

Jesani, Amar (1990), 'Limits of Empowerment: Women in Rural Health Care', *Economic and Political Weekly*, May 19.

Jha, Prem Shankar (1980), *India: A Political Economy of Stagnation* (Bombay: Oxford Univesity Press).

Jha, Shikha (1994), 'Foodgrains Price and Distribution Policies in India: Performance, Problems and Prospects', Reprint No. 134–1994, Indira Gandhi Institute of Development Research, Bombay; forthcoming in *Asia-Pacific Development Journal.*

Johansen, Frida (1993), 'Poverty Reduction in East Asia: The Silent Revolution', Discussion Paper No. 203, East Asia and Pacific Region Series, World Bank, Washington, DC.

Johansson, Sheila R. (1991), 'Welfare, Mortality and Gender: Continuity and Change in Explanations for Male/Female Mortality Differences over Three Centuries', *Continuity and Change*, 6.

Johansson, S., and Nygren, O. (1991), 'The Missing Girls of China: A New Demographic Account', *Population and Development Review*, 17 (1).

Johnson, D. Gale (1950), 'Resource Allocation under Share Constraints', *Journal of Political Economy*, 58.

Jones, Ronald W., and Kenen, Peter B. (eds.) (1985), *Handbook of International Economics* (Amsterdam: North Holland).

Joshi, Vijay, and Little, Ian (1993), 'Macro-Economic Stabilization in India, 1991–93 and Beyond', *Economic and Political Weekly*, December 4.

——— (1994), *India: Macroeconomics and Political Economy 1964–91* (Washington, DC: World Bank).

Kabir, M., and Krishnan, T.N. (1992), 'Social Intermediation and Health Transition: Lessons from Kerala', paper presented at a workshop on 'Health and Development in India', 2–4 January, 1992; to be published in M. Das Gupta et al. (forthcoming).

Kakar, Sudhir (1979), 'Childhood in India', *International Social Science Journal*, 31.

——— (1981), *The Inner World: A Psycho-analytic Study of Childhood and Society in India* (Delhi: Oxford University Press).

Kakwani, Nanak (1986), *Analyzing Redistribution Policies* (Cambridge: Cambridge University Press).

——— (1993), 'Peformance in Living Standards: An International Comparison', *Journal of Development Economics*, 41.

Kakwani, Nanak, and Subbarao, K. (1990), 'Rural Poverty and Its Alleviation in India', *Economic and Political Weekly*, June 3.

Kanbargi, R. (ed.) (1991), *Child Labour in the Indian Subcontinent* (New Delhi: Sage).

Kanitkar, T. (1991), 'The Sex Ratio in India: A Topic of Speculation and Research', *Journal of Family Welfare*, 37 (3).

Kannan, K.P. (1993), 'Public Intervention and Poverty Alleviation: A Study of the Declining Incidence of Poverty in Kerala', paper presented at a workshop on 'Poverty Alleviation in India' held at the Institute of Development Studies, Jaipur, February 1993.

Kannan, K.P., Thankappan, K.R., Raman Kutty, V., and Aravindan, K.P. (1991), *Health and Development in Rural Kerala* (Trivandrum: Kerala Sastra Sahitya Parishad).

Kapadia, Karin (1992), 'Pauperizing the Rural Poor: Landless Labour in Tamil Nadu', mimeo, London School of Economics.

Kapadia, K.M. (1966), *Marriage and the Family in India,* third edition (Bombay: Oxford University Press).

Kaplan, Robert D. (1994), 'The Coming Anarchy', *Atlantic Monthly*, 273 (February 2).

Karkal, Malini (1985), 'Health of Mother and Child Survival', in K. Srinivasan and S. Mukerji (eds.), *Dynamics of Population and Family Welfare 1985* (Bombay: Himalaya).

——— (1987), 'Diifferentials in Mortality by Sex', *Economic and Political Weekly*, August 8.

——— (1991), 'Progress in Literacy in India: A Statistical Analysis', *Indian Journal of Social Work,* 52 (2).

Karlekar, Malavika (1988), 'Woman's Nature and the Access to Education', in Chanana (1988b).

Karve, Irawati (1965), *Kinship Organisation in India* (Bombay: Asia Publishing House).

Kelkar, Vijay, Kumar, Rajiv, and Nangia, Rita (1990), *India's Industrial Economy: Policies, Performance and Reforms* (Manila: Asian Development Bank).

Khan, A.R., Griffin, K., Riskin, C., and Zhao Renwei (1992), 'Household Income and its Distribution in China', *The China Quarterly*, 132.

Khan, M.E. (1988), 'Infant Mortality in Uttar Pradesh: A Micro-level Study', in A.K. Jain and P. Visaria (eds.), *Infant Mortality in India: Differentials and Determinants* (New Delhi: Sage).

Khan, M.E., Anker, R., Ghosh Dastidar, S.K., and Bairathi, S. (1989), 'Inequalities between Men and Women in Nutrition and Family Welfare Services: An In-depth Enquiry in an Indian Village', in J.C. Caldwell and G. Santow (eds.), *Selected Readings in the Cultural, Social and Behavioral Determinants of Health*, Health Transition Series No.1 (Canberra: Health Transition Centre, Australian National University).

Khan, M.E., Ghosh Dastidar, S.K., and Singh, R. (1986), 'Nutrition and Health Practices among the Rural Women: A Case Study of Uttar Pradesh', *Journal of Family Welfare*, 33 (2).

Khan, M.E., Gupta, R.B., Prasad, C.V.S., and Ghosh Dastidar, S.K. (1988), *Performance of Health and Family Welfare Programmes in India* (Bombay: Himalaya Publishing House).

Khan, M.E., and Prasad, C.V.S. (1983), *Under-Utilization of Health Services in Rural India: A Comparative Study of Bihar, Gujarat and Karnataka* (Baroda: Operations Research Group).

Khan, M.E., Prasad, C.V.S., and Majumdar, A. (1980), *People's Perceptions about Family Planning in India* (New Delhi: Concept).

Khan, M.E., Prasad, C.V.S., and Qaiser, N. (1983), 'Reasons for Under-utilization of Health Services: Case Study of a PHC in a Tribal Area of Bihar', paper presented at the ICMR/Ford Foundation workshop on 'Child Health, Nutrition and Family Planning'.

Khan, M.E., Gupta, R.B., Prasad, C.V.S., and Ghosh Dastidar, S.K. (eds.) (1987), *Performance of Family Planning in India: Observations from Bihar, Uttar Pradesh, Rajasthan and Madhya Pradesh* (New Delhi: Himalaya Publishing House).

Khan, Sharukh R. (1993), 'South Asia', in King and Hill (1993).

Khatu, K.K., Tamang, A.K., and Rao, C.R. (1983), *Working Children in India* (Baroda: Operations Research Group).

Khemani, Stuti (1994), 'Neoclassical vs. Nash-bargained Model of Household Fertility: Evidence from Rural India', undergraduate thesis, Department of Economics, Mount Holyoke College, USA.

Kim, C.K. (ed.) (1977), *Industrial and Social Development Issues* (Seoul: Korea Development Institute).

Kim, Kiwan, and Leipziger, Danny (1993), 'Korea: A Case of Government-Led Development', mimeo, World Bank, Washington, DC.

King, Elizabeth, and Hill, Anne (eds.) (1993), *Women's Education in Developing Countries: Barriers, Benefits and Policy* (Baltimore: Johns Hopkins University Press).

Kishor, Sunita (1993), ' "May God Give Sons to All": Gender and Child Mortality in India', *American Sociological Review*, 58.

—— (1994), 'Gender Differentials in Child Mortality: A Review of the Evidence', in M. Das Gupta et al. (1994).

Kishwar, Madhu, and Vanita, Ruth (eds.) (1991), *In Search of Answers*, second revised edition (New Delhi: Horizon India).

Klasen, Stephan (1994), ' "Missing Women" Reconsidered', *World Development*, 22.

Knight, John, and Song, Lina (1993a), 'The Length of Life and the Standard of Living: Economic Influences on Premature Death in China', *Journal of Development Studies*, 30 (1).

—— (1993b), 'The Spatial Contribution to Income Inequality in Rural China', *Cambridge Journal of Economics*, 17 (2).

Kohli, Atul (1987), *The State and Poverty in India: The Politics of Reform* (Cambridge: Cambridge University Press).

—— (1988), *India's Democracy: An Analysis of Changing State–Society Relations* (Princeton, NJ: Princeton University Press).

Kohli, Atul (ed.) (1990), *Democracy and Discontent* (Cambridge: Cambridge University Press).

Kolenda, Pauline (1983), 'Widowhood among "Untouchable" Chuhras', in A. Ostor, L. Fruzzetti, and S. Barnett (eds.), *Concepts of Person: Kinship, Caste and Marriage in India* (Delhi: Oxford University Press).

—— (1984), 'Woman as Tribute, Woman as Flower: Images of "Woman" in Weddings in North and South India', *American Ethnologist*, 11.

Koopmans, T. (1957), *Three Essays on the State of Economic Science* (New Haven: Yale University Press).

Krishnaji, N. (1987), 'Poverty and Sex Ratio: Some Data and Speculations', *Economic and Political Weekly*, June 6.

—— (1992), *Pauperising Agriculture: Studies in Agrarian Change and Demographic Structure* (Delhi: Oxford University Press).

Krishnakumari, N.S. (1987), *Status of Single Women in India* (Delhi: Uppal).

Krishnan, T.N. (1976), 'Demographic Transition in Kerala: Facts and Factors', *Economic and Political Weekly*, 11 (31–33), special number.

—— (1991), 'Kerala's Health Transition: Facts and Factors', Center for Population and Development Studies, Harvard University.

Krishnan, T.N. (1994), 'Social Intermediation and Human Development: Kerala State, India', a study prepared for the World Summit on Social Development; mimeo, Centre for Development Studies, Thiruvananthapuram.

—— (forthcoming), *Society, State and Economy in Kerala*; to be published.

Krishnaswamy, K.S. (1994), 'Agricultural Development under the New Economic Regime', *Economic and Political Weekly*, June 25.

Krishnaswamy, K.S. (ed.) (1990), *Poverty and Income Distribution* (Delhi: Oxford University Press).

Krueger, Anne O. (1974), 'The Political Economy of the Rent-Seeking Society', *American Economic Review*, 64 (June).

—— (1979), *The Development Role of Foreign Sector and Aid* (Cambridge, MA: Harvard University Press).

—— (1985), 'Trade Policies in Developing Countries', in Jones and Kenen (1985).

Krugman, Paul R. (1979), 'Increasing Returns, Monopolistic Competition, and International Trade', *Journal of International Economics,* 9.

—— (1986), *Strategic Trade Policy and the New International Economics* (Cambridge, MA: MIT Press).

—— (1987), 'The Narrow Moving Band, the Dutch Disease, and the Consequences of Mrs. Thatcher: Notes on Trade in the Presence of Scale Economies', *Journal of Development Economics*, 27.

Krugman, Paul R., and Smith, Alisdair (eds.) (1994), *Empirical Studies of Strategic Trade Policy* (Chicago: University of Chicago Press).

Kulkarni, M.N. (1992), 'Universal Immunisation Programme in India: Issues of Sustainability', *Economic and Political Weekly,* July 4.

Kumar, A.K. Shiva (1991), 'UNDP's Human Development Index: A Computation for Indian States', *Economic and Political Weekly*, October 12.

—— (1992), 'Maternal Capabilities and Child Survival in Low Income Regions: An Economic Analysis of Infant Mortality in India', unpublished Ph.D. thesis, Harvard University.

—— (1994), 'Women's Capabilities and Infant Mortality: Lessons from Manipur', in M. Das Gupta et al. (1994).

Kumar, K. (1991), *The Political Agenda of Education* (New Delhi: Sage).

Kundu, Amitabh, and Sahu, Mahesh (1991), 'Variation in Sex Ratio: Development Implications', *Economic and Political Weekly*, October 12.

Kuo, S. (1983), *The Taiwan Economy in Transition* (Boulder, CO: Westview).

Kurian, N.J. (1989), 'Anti-Poverty Programmes: A Reappraisal', *Economic and Political Weekly,* March 25.

Kurrien, John (1983), *Elementary Education in India: Myth, Reality, Alternative* (New Delhi: Vikas).

Kynch, Jocelyn (1985), 'How Many Women Are Enough?', in *Third World Affairs 1985* (London: Third World Foundation).

Kynch, Jocelyn, and Sen, Amartya (1983), 'Indian Women: Well-being and Survival', *Cambridge Journal of Economics*, 7.

Lakshmamma, T. (1989), 'Underutilization of MCH and Family Planning Services: A Case Study of Andhra Pradesh', in Jena and Pati (1989).

Lal, Deepak (1988), *The Hindu Equilibrium* (Oxford: Clarendon Press).

Lane, Robert E. (1991), *The Market Experience* (Cambridge: Cambridge University Press).

—— (1994), 'Quality of Life and Quality of Persons: A New Role for Government', *Political Theory*, 22.

Langford, Christopher (1984), 'Sex Differentials in Mortality in Sri Lanka: Changes since the 1920s', *Journal of Bio-social Science*, 16.

—— (1988), 'Sex Differentials in Sri Lanka: Past Trends and the Situation Recently', mimeo, London School of Economics.

Langford, Christopher, and Storey, Pamela (1993), 'Sex Differentials in Mortality Early in the Twentieth Century: Sri Lanka and India Compared', *Population and Development Review*, 19.

Leslie, Joanne (1988), 'Women's Work and Child Nutrition in the Third World', *World Development*, 16.

Leslie, J., and Paolisso, M. (eds.) (1989), *Women, Work and Child Welfare in the Third World* (Boulder, CO: Westview).

Lewis, John (1995), *India's Political Economy: Governance and Reform* (Delhi: Oxford University Press).

Lewis, W. Arthur (1955), *The Theory of Economic Growth* (London: Allen & Unwin).

Li Chengrui (1992), *A Study of China's Population* (Beijing: Foreign Languages Press).

Lieten, G.K. (1993), *Continuity and Change in Rural West Bengal* (London: Sage).

Lin, Justin Yifu (1992), 'Rural Reforms and Agricultural Growth in China', *American Economic Review*, 82.

Lipton, Michael, and Ravallion, Martin (1994), 'Poverty and Policy', in Behrman and Srinivasan (1994).

Little, Ian M.D. (1977), 'Development Economics', in Alan Bullock, Oliver Stallybrass, and Stephen Trombley (eds.), *The Fontana Dictionary of Modern Thought* (London: Fontana Press, 2nd edition).

—— (1982), *Economic Development* (New York: Basic Books).

—— (1994), 'Trade and Industrialization Revisited', Iqbal Memorial Lecture, Pakistan Institute of Development Economics, April 2.

Little, Ian M.D., Scitovsky, Tibor, and Scott, Maurice Fg. (1970), *Industry and Trade in Some Developing Countries* (Oxford: Clarendon Press).

Lopez, Alan D., and Ruzicka, Lado T. (eds.) (1983), *Sex Differentials in Mortality: Trends, Determinants and Consequences,* Miscellaneous Series No. 4, Department of Demography, Australian National University, Canberra.

Lucas, Robert E. (1988), 'On the Mechanics of Economic Development', *Journal of Monetary Economics*, 22.

—— (1993), 'Making a Miracle', *Econometrica*, 61.

McGuire, James W. (1994), 'Development Policy and its Determinants in East Asia and Latin America', forthcoming in *Journal of Public Policy*.

McKenzie, Lionel (1959), 'On the Existence of General Equilibrium for a Competitive Market', *Econometrica*, 27.

Maharatna, Arup (1992), 'The Demography of Indian Famines: A Historical Perspective', Ph.D. thesis, London School of Economics; to be published by Oxford University Press, New Delhi, 1996.

Mahendra Dev, S. (1992), 'Poverty Alleviation Programmes: A Case Study of Maharashtra with Emphasis on Employment Guarantee Scheme', Discussion Paper No.77, Indira Gandhi Institute of Development Research, Bombay.

—— (1993a), 'India's (Maharashtra) Employment Guarantee Scheme: Lessons from Long Experience', paper presented at a workshop on 'Employment for Poverty Alleviation and Food Security', October 11–14, 1993, Virginia, coordinated by the International Food Policy Research Institute, Washington, DC.

—— (1993b), 'In Defence of Maharashtra's EGS', mimeo, Indira Gandhi Institute of Development Research, Bombay.

—— (1993c), 'Social Security in the Unorganized Sector: Lessons from the Experiences of Kerala and Tamil Nadu', mimeo, Indira Gandhi Institute of Development Research, Bombay.

Mahendra Dev, S., and Ranade, Ajit (1995), 'Secondary Benefits of Rural Works Programmes', mimeo, Indira Gandhi Institute of Development Research, Bombay.

Mahendra Dev, S., Suryanarayana, M.H., and Parikh, K. S. (1992), 'Rural Poverty in India: Incidence, Issues and Policies', *Asian Development Review*, 10.

Maithani, B.P., and Rizwana, A. (1992), 'Nagaland's Village Development Board Programme', *Journal of Rural Development*, 11.

Majumdar, Tapas (1983), *Investment in Education and Social Choice* (Cambridge: Cambridge University Press).

—— (1992), 'Educational Attainments and Social Security Provisions in the States of India', mimeo, WIDER, Helsinki.

—— (1993), 'The Relation between Educational Attainment and Ability to Obtain Social Security in the States of India', research paper, WIDER, Helsinki.

Malenbaum, W. (1956), 'India and China: Development Contrasts', *Journal of Political Economy*, 64.

—— (1959), 'India and China: Contrasts in Development Performance', *American Economic Review*, 49.

Malenbaum, W. (1982), 'Modern Economic Growth in India and China: The Comparison Revisited, 1950–1980', *Economic Development and Cultural Change*, 30.

Malhotra, K.C., and Poffenberger, M. (eds.) (1989), *Forest Regeneration through Community Protection: The West Bengal Experience*, Proceedings of the Working Group Meeting on Forest Protection Committees, Calcutta, June 21–2, 1989.

—— (1988), *Women's Seclusion and Men's Honor: Sex Roles in North India, Bangladesh and Pakistan* (Tucson: University of Arizona Press).

Mankiw, N. Gregory, Romer, David, and Weil, David (1992), 'A Contribution to the Empirics of Economic Growth', *Quarterly Journal of Economics*, 107.

Marathe, Sharad S. (1989), *Regulation and Development: India's Policy Experience of Controls over Industry* (New Delhi: Sage Publications).

Mari Bhat, P.N. (1994), 'Widows and Widowhood Mortality in India', paper presented at a conference on 'Widows in India', Bangalore, March 1994; to be published in Chen (forthcoming, b).

Mari Bhat, P.N., Navaneetham, K., and Rajan, S.I. (1992), 'Maternal Mortality in India', paper presented at a workshop on 'Health and Development in India', India International Centre, 2–4 January 1992.

—— (1994), 'Maternal Mortality: Model Estimates of Levels, Trends and State Differentials', in M. Das Gupta et al. (1994).

Mari Bhat, P.N. and Rajan, S.I. (1990), 'Demographic Transition in Kerala Revisited', *Economic and Political Weekly*, September 1–8.

—— (1992), 'Demographic Transition in Kerala: A Reply', *Economic and Political Weekly*, June 6.

Marx, Karl (1857–8), *Grundrisse: Foundations of the Critique of Political Economy*, English translation, M. Nicolaus (Harmondsworth: Penguin Books, 1973).

—— (1867), *Capital*, vol. I (London: Allen and Unwin).

Mata, L., and Rosero, L. (1988), 'National Health and Social Development in Costa Rica: A Case Study of Intersectoral Action', Technical Paper No. 13, Pan American Health Organization, Washington, DC.

Mathur, K., and Bhattacharya, M. (1975), *Administrative Response to Emergency: A Study of Scarcity Administration in Maharashtra* (New Delhi: Concept).

Matson, Jim, and Selden, Mark (1992), 'Poverty and Inequality in China and India', *Economic and Political Weekly*, April 4.

Matsuyama, Kiminori (1991), 'Increasing Returns, Industrialization and Indeterminacy of Equilibrium', *Quarterly Journal of Economics*, 106.

Maurya, K.N. (1989), 'An Analysis of Causative Factors Responsible for Low Utilisation of Health and Family Welfare Services', in Jena and Pati (1989).

Mazumdar, Vina (1985), *Emergence of Women's Questions in India and the Role of Women's Studies* (New Delhi: Centre for Women's Development Studies).

Mencher, Joan (1980), 'The Lessons and Non-Lessons from Kerala', *Economic and Political Weekly*, Special Number, 1781–1802.

Mendis, P. (1992), 'The Debate on Size and Productivity in Developed and Developing Countries', *Journal of Contemporary Asia*, 22.

Mehrotra, Nidhi (1995), 'Primary Schooling in Rural India: Determinants of Demand', paper presented at a workshop on 'Applied Development Economics' held at the Delhi School of Economics, January 1995; forthcoming as a Ph.D. thesis, University of Chicago.

Middleton, John, et al. (1993), 'Uttar Pradesh Basic Education Project: Staff Appraisal Report', report No. 11746-IN, Population and Human Resources Operations Division, World Bank, Washington, DC.

Mill, John Stuart (1848), *Principles of Political Economy* (London: Parker; republished Fairfield: Augustus Kelley, 1976).

—— (1859), *On Liberty* (republished, Harmondsworth: Penguin, 1954).

—— (1861), *Utilitarianism* (republished, London: Dent, 1929).

—— (1869), *The Subjection of Women*, (London); republished in S. Alice Rossi (ed.), *Essays on Sex Equality* (Chicago: University of Chicago Press, 1970).

Miller, Barbara (1981), *The Endangered Sex* (Ithaca: Cornell University Press).

—— (1989), 'Changing Patterns of Juvenile Sex Ratios in Rural India, 1961 to 1971', *Economic and Political Weekly*, June 3.

—— (1993a), 'On Poverty, Child Survival and Gender: Models and Misperceptions', *Third World Planning Review*, 15.

Miller, Barbara (ed.) (1993b), *Sex and Gender Hierarchies* (Cambridge: Cambridge University Press).

Minhas, B. (1991), 'On Estimating the Inadequacy of Energy Intakes: Revealed Food Consumption Behaviour versus Nutritional Norms', *Journal of Development Studies*, 28(1).

—— (1992), 'Educational Deprivation and its Role as a Spoiler of Access to Better Life in India', in A. Dutta and M.M. Agrawal (eds.), *The Quality of Life* (Delhi: B.R. Publishing).

Minhas, B.S., Jain, L.R., and Tendulkar, S.D. (1991), 'Declining Incidence of Poverty in India in the 1980s', *Economic and Political Weekly*, July 6–13.

Mitra, A. (1979), *Implications of Declining Sex Ratio in India's Population* (Bombay: Allied Publishers).

Mookherjee, Dilip (1992), 'Indian Economy at the Crossroads', *Economic and Political Weekly*, April 11–18.

Morris, Morris D. (1979), *Measuring the Condition of the World's Poor* (Oxford: Pergamon Press).

Mukherjee, Amitava (1993), 'Structural Adjustment Programme and the Common Man', mimeo, Lal Bahadur Shastri National Academy of Administration, Mussoorie.

Mukherjee, Sudhansu Bhusan (1976), *The Age Distribution of the Indian Population:*

*A Reconstruction for the States and Territories, 1881–1961* (Honolulu: East–West Centre).

Mundle, Sudipto (1993), 'Unemployment and the Financing of Relief Employment in a Period of Stabilisation: India 1992–94', mimeo, National Institute of Public Finance and Policy, New Delhi.

Murthi, Mamta, Guio, Anne-Catherine, and Drèze, Jean (1995), Mortality, Fertility and Gender Bias in India: A District Level Analysis', *Population and Development Review*, 21.

Murthy, Nirmala (forthcoming), 'Issues in Health Policies and Management in India', paper presented at a workshop on 'Health and Development in India', 2–4 January 1992; to be published in M. Das Gupta et al. (forthcoming).

Muscat, Robert (1994), *The Fifth Tiger: A Study of Thai Development Policy* (Tokyo: United Nations University Press).

Myrdal, Gunnar (1968), *Asian Drama* (New York: Pantheon).

Nadarajah, T. (1983), 'The Transition from Higher Female to Higher Male Mortality in Sri Lanka', *Population and Development Review*, 9.

Nag, Moni (1983), 'Impact of Social Development and Economic Development on Mortality: Comparative Study of Kerala and West Bengal', *Economic and Political Weekly*, 28 (annual number, May).

—— (1989), 'Political Awareness as a Factor in Accessibility of Health Services: A Case Study of Rural Kerala and West Bengal', *Economic and Political Weekly*, February 25.

Naidu, U.S., and Kapadia, K.R. (eds.) (1985), *Child Labour and Health: Problems and Prospects* (Bombay: Tata Institute of Social Sciences).

Naik, J.P. (1975a), *Elementary Education in India: A Promise to Keep* (Bombay: Allied).

—— (1975b), *Policy and Performance in Indian Education, 1947–74* (New Delhi: Dr K.G. Saiyidain Memorial Trust).

—— (1975c), *Equity, Quality and Quantity: The Elusive Triangle in India* (Bombay: Allied).

—— (1982), *The Education Commission and After* (New Delhi: Allied).

Nair, K.N., Sivanandan, P., and Retnam, V.C.V. (1984), 'Education, Employment and Landholding Pattern in a Tamil Village', *Economic and Political Weekly*, June 16–23.

Nair, P.R.G. (1981), *Primary Education, Population Growth and Socio-Economic Change: A Comparative Study with Particular Reference to Kerala* (New Delhi: Allied).

Nanda, Amulya Ratna (1992), 'Final Population Totals: Brief Analysis of Primary Census Abstract', Census of India 1991, Series-1, Paper-2 of 1992, Office of the Registrar-General, New Delhi.

—— (1993), 'Union Primary Census Abstract for Scheduled Castes and Scheduled Tribes', Census of India 1991, Series-1, Paper-1 of 1993, Office of the Registrar-General, New Delhi.

Narain, I. (1972), 'Rural Local Politics and Primary School Management', in Rudolph and Rudolph (1972).

National Council of Educational Research and Training (1992), *Fifth All-India Educational Survey*, 2 volumes (New Delhi: NCERT).

National Institute of Public Cooperation and Child Development (1992), *Statistics on Children in India: Pocket Book 1992* (New Delhi: NIPCCD).

Nautiyal, K.C. (1989), *Education and Rural Poor* (New Delhi: Commonwealth Publishers).

Nayyar, Deepak (1976), *India's Exports and Export Policies in the 1960s* (Cambridge: Cambridge University Press).

Nayyar, Deepak (ed.) (1994), *Industrial Growth and Stagnation: The Debate in India* (Oxford: Oxford University Press).

Nayyar, Rohini (1991), *Rural Poverty in India: An Analysis of Inter-state Differences* (New York: Oxford University Press).

Newbery, D.M.G. (1977), 'Risksharing, Sharecropping and Uncertain Labour Markets', *Review of Economic Studies*, 44.

NIEPA (1994), 'Management of Education under Panchayati Raj: A Review of Literature', report prepared for a seminar on 'Management of Education under Panchayati Raj' held at the National Institute of Educational Planning and Administration, New Delhi, 27–8 October 1994.

Ninan, K. (1994), 'Poverty and Income Distribution in India', *Economic and Political Weekly*, June 18.

North, D.C. (1981), *Structure and Change in Economic History* (New York: Norton).

Nozick, Robert (1974), *Anarchy, State and Utopia* (Oxford: Blackwell).

Nuna, Sheel C. (1990), *Women and Development* (New Delhi: National Institute of Educational Planning and Administration).

Nussbaum, Martha (1992), 'Human Functioning and Social Justice', *Political Theory*, 20.

—— (1993), 'Non-relative Virtues: An Aristotelian Approach', in Nussbaum and Sen (1993).

Nussbaum, Martha, and Sen, Amartya (eds.) (1993), *The Quality of Life* (Oxford: Clarendon Press).

O'Hanlon, Rosalind (1985), *Caste, Conflict, and Ideology: Mahatma Jotirao Phule and Low Caste Protest in Nineteenth-century Western India* (Cambridge: Cambridge University Press).

Olson, Mancur (1965), *The Logic of Collective Action* (Cambridge, MA: Harvard University Press.

—— (1982), *The Rise and Decline of Nations* (New Haven: Yale University Press).

—— (1993), 'Dictatorship, Democracy and Development', *American Political Science Review*, 87 (3).

Omvedt, Gail (1980), *We Will Smash This Prison! Indian Women in Struggle* (London: Zed).

—— (1989a), 'Rural Women Fight for Independence', *Economic and Political Weekly*, April 29.

—— (1989b), 'India's Movements for Democracy: Peasants, "Greens", Women and People's Power', *Race and Class*, 31.

—— (1990), 'Women, Zilla Parishads and Panchayati Raj: Chandwad to Vitner', *Economic and Political Weekly*, August 4.

—— (1993), *Reinventing Revolution: New Social Movements and the Socialist Tradition in India* (London: M.E. Sharpe).

—— (1994), *Dalits and the Democratic Revolution: Dr. Ambedkar and the Dalit Movement in Colonial India* (New Delhi: Sage).

Oommen, M.A. (1993a), *The Kerala Economy* (New Delhi: Oxford & IBH).

—— (1993b), 'Bhagwati–Srinivasan Report on Economic Reforms', *Economic and Political Weekly*, October 2.

Osmani, Siddiq R. (1990), 'Nutrition and the Economics of Food: Implications of Some Recent Controversies', in Drèze and Sen (1990), vol. I.

—— (1991), 'Social Security in South Asia', in Ahmad et al. (1991).

—— (1995), 'The Entitlement Approach to Famine: An Assessment', in Basu et al. (1995).

—— (forthcoming), *Growth and Poverty in South Asia* (Oxford: Clarendon Press).

Osmani, Siddiq R. (ed.) (1992), *Nutrition and Poverty* (Oxford: Clarendon Press).

Otsuka, K., and Hayami, Y. (1988), 'Theories of Share Tenancy: A Critical Survey', *Economic Development and Cultural Change*, 36.

Otsuka, K., et al. (1992), 'Land and Labor Contracts in Agrarian Economies: Theories and Facts', *Journal of Economic Literature*, 30.

Pack, Howard (1993), 'Industrial and Trade Policies in the High-Performing Asian Economies', mimeo, World Bank, Washington, DC.

Paddock, William, and Paddock, Paul (1968), *Famine—1975!*(London: Weidenfeld and Nicolson).

Pal, Sarmistha (1994), 'Choice of Casual and Regular Labour Contracts in Indian Agriculture: A Theoretical and Empirical Analysis', Ph.D. thesis, London School of Economics.

Panigrahi, Lalita (1972), *British Social Policy and Female Infanticide in India* (New Delhi: Munshiram Manoharlal).

Panikar, P.G.K., and Soman, C.R. (1984), *Health Status of Kerala: The Paradox of Economic Backwardness and Health Development* (Trivandrum: Centre for Development Studies).

—— (1985), *Status of Women and Children in Kerala* (Trivandrum: Centre for Development Studies).

Parikh, Kirit (1992), 'Privatisation and Deregulation: Irrelevant Hypotheses', *Economic and Political Weekly*, February 29.

—— (1994), 'Who Gets How Much from PDS: How Effectively Does It Reach the Poor?', mimeo, Indira Gandhi Institute of Development Research, Bombay.

—— (1995), 'The Lost Decades, 1971–91: Population, Development and Poverty', mimeo, Indira Gandhi Institute of Development Research, Bombay.

Parikh, Kirit, and Sudarshan, R. (eds.) (1993), *Human Development and Structural Adjustment* (Madras: Macmillan).

Parkin, Robert (1992), *The Mundas of Central India: An Account of their Social Organization* (Delhi: Oxford University Press).

Patel, I.G. (1992), 'New Economic Policies: A Historical Perspective', *Economic and Political Weekly*, January 4–11.

Patel, Surendra J. (1985), 'India's Regression in the World Economy', *Economic and Political Weekly*, September 28.

—— (1994), *Indian Economy Towards the 21st Century* (Bombay: Orient Longman).

Pati, R.N. (1991), *Rehabilitation of Child Labourers in India* (New Delhi: Ashish Publishing).

Patil, B.R. (1984), *Problem of School Drop-outs in India: An Annotated Bibliography* (New Delhi: Council for Social Development).

Patnaik, Prabhat (1991), *Economics and Egalitarianism* (Oxford: Oxford University Press).

—— (1994), 'International Capital and National Economic Policy: A Critique of India's Economic Reforms', *Economic and Political Weekly*, March 19.

Peng, Xizhe (1987), 'Demographic Consequences of the Great Leap Forward in China's Provinces', *Population and Development Review*, 13.

—— (1991), *Demographic Transition in China: Fertility Trends since the 1950s* (Oxford: Clarendon Press).

—— (1994), 'Recent Trends in China's Population and Their Implications', Discussion Paper No. 30, Research Programme on the Chinese Economy, STICERD, London School of Economics.

Perkins, Dwight (1983), 'Research on the Economy of the People's Republic of China: A Survey of the Field', *Journal of Asian Studies*, 42.

—— (1988), 'Reforming China's Economic System', *Journal of Economic Literature*, 26.

Persson, Torsten, and Tabellini, Guido (1991), 'Is Inequality Harmful to Growth? Theory and Evidence', mimeo.

Platteau, Jean-Philippe (1991), 'Traditional Systems of Social Security and Hunger Insurance', in Ahmad et al. (1991).

Platteau, Jean-Philippe, and Baland, Jean-Marie (1994), 'A Broad Framework for Analysis of Evolving Patron–Client Ties in Agrarian Economies', mimeo, Faculté des Sciences Economiques, Université de Namur, Belgium.

Poitevin, Guy, and Rairkar, Hema (1985), *Inde: Village au Féminin* (Paris: Harmattan).

Prakasamma, M. (1989), 'Analysis of Factors Influencing Performance of Auxiliary Nurse Midwives in Nizamabad District', Ph.D. thesis, Centre for Social Medicine and Community Health, Jawaharlal Nehru University, New Delhi.

Prakash, B.A. (1994), *Kerala's Economy: Performance, Problems and Prospects* (New Delhi: Sage).

Prasad, K.V. Eswara (1987), *Wastage, Stagnation and Inequality of Opportunity in Rural Primary Education: A Case Study of Andhra Pradesh* (New Delhi: Ministry of Human Resource Development).

Preston, Samuel H. (1976), *Mortality Patterns in National Populations* (New York: Academic Press).

Priya, Ritu (1987), 'Family Planning and Health Care: A Case Study from Rajasthan', paper presented at the 12th Annual Meeting of Medico Friends Circle.

—— (1990), 'Dubious Package Deal: Health Care in Eighth Plan', *Economic and Political Weekly*, August 18.

Psacharopoulos, G. (1985), 'Returns to Education: A Further International Update and Implications', *Journal of Human Resources,* 20.

—— (1988), 'Education and Development: A Review', *The World Bank Research Observer*, 3 (1).

—— (1993), 'Returns to Investment in Education: A Global Update', Working Paper, World Bank, Washington, DC.

Putnam, Robert D., with Leonardi, Robert and Nanetti, Raffaella Y. (1993), *Making Democracy Work: Civic Traditions in Modern Italy* (Princeton, NJ: Princeton University Press).

Qadeer, I., and Priya, R. (1992), 'Planning for Health in Independent India', paper presented at a seminar on 'Understanding Independent India', Jawaharlal Nehru University, March 1992.

Quibria, M.G., and Rashid, S. (1984), 'The Puzzle of Sharecropping: A Survey of Theories', *World Development*, 12.

Quibria, M.G. (ed.) (1994), *Rural Poverty in Asia: Priority Issues and Policy Options* (Oxford: Oxford University Press).

Rahman, Omar, Foster, Andrew, and Menken, Jane (1992) 'Older Widow Mortality in Rural Bangladesh', *Social Science and Medicine*, 34.

Raghunandan, D., Baru, Rama, Lakshmi, G., and Sengupta, A. (1987), 'Health Seeking Behaviour and the Primary Health Care System: Case Study of a Backward Village in Andhra Pradesh', report submitted to the United Nations University, Tokyo; mimeo, Society for Economic and Social Studies, New Delhi.

Raj, K.N., and Sen, A.K. (1961), 'Alternative Patterns of Growth under Conditions of Stagnant Export Earnings', *Oxford Economic Papers*, 13.

Raj, K.N., and Tharakan, M. (1983), 'Agrarian Reform in Kerala and Its Impact on the Rural Economy', in A. Ghose (ed.) *Agrarian Reform in Contemporary Developing Countries* (London: Croom Helm).

Rajan, S.I., Mishra, U.S., and Navaneetham, K. (1991), 'Decline in Sex Ratio: An Alternative Explanation?', *Economic and Political Weekly*, December 21.

—— (1992), 'Decline in Sex Ratio: Alternative Explanation Revisited', *Economic and Political Weekly*, November 14.

Rajivan, Anuradha K. (1991), 'Weight Variations among Preschoolers: An Analysis of Evidence from Rural Tamil Nadu', unpublished Ph.D. thesis, University of Southern California.

Raju, S., and Premi, M.K. (1992), 'Decline in Sex Ratio: Alternative Explanation Re-examined', *Economic and Political Weekly*, April 25.

Rakshit, Mihir (1992), 'Issues in Structural Adjustment of the Indian Economy', paper presented at the Tenth World Congress of the International Economic Association, Moscow.

Ram, N. (1990), 'An Independent Press and Anti-Hunger Strategies: The Indian Experience', in Drèze and Sen (1990), vol. I.

Ramachandran, V.K. (1990), *Wage Labour and Unfreedom in Agriculture: An Indian Case Study* (Oxford: Clarendon Press).

—— (1996), 'Kerala's Development Achievements', in Drèze and Sen (1996).

Ramalingaswami, V., Deo, M.G., Guleria, J.S., Malhotra, K.K., Sood, S.K., Om, P., and Sinha, R.V.N. (1971), 'Studies of the Bihar Famine of 1966–1967', in G. Blix et al. (eds.), *Famine: Nutrition and Relief Operations in Times of Disaster* (Uppsala: Swedish Nutrition Foundation).

Rao, C.H.H. (1966), 'Alternative Explanations of the Inverse Relationship Between Farm Size and Output Per Acre in India', *Indian Economic Review*, 1.

Rao, Nitya (1993), 'Total Literacy Campaigns: A Field Report', *Economic and Political Weekly*, May 8.

Rao, S.L. (1994), 'Labour Adjustment as Part of Industrial Restructuring', *Economic and Political Weekly*, February 5.

Ravallion, Martin (1987), *Markets and Famines* (Oxford: Clarendon Press).

—— (1994), *Poverty Comparisons* (Chur, Switzerland: Harwood Academic Press).

Ravallion, Martin, and Datt, Gaurav (1995), 'Growth and Poverty in Rural India', Policy Research Working Paper 1405, World Bank, Washington, DC.

Ravallion, M., Datt, G., and Chaudhuri, S. (1993), 'Does Maharashtra's Employment Guarantee Scheme Guarantee Employment? Effects of the 1988 Wage Increase', *Economic Development and Cultural Change*, 41 (2).

Ravallion, M., and Subbarao, K. (1992), 'Adjustment and Human Development in India', *Journal of the Indian School of Political Economy*, January–March.

Rawls, J. (1971), *A Theory of Justice* (Cambridge, MA: Harvard University Press).

—— (1993), *Political Liberalism* (New York: University of Columbia Press).

Raz, J. (1986), *The Morality of Freedom* (Oxford: Clarendon Press).

Raza, M. (1990), *Education, Development and Society* (New Delhi: Vikas Publishing House).

Raza, M., and Ramachandaran, H. (1990), 'Responsiveness to Educational Inputs: A Study of Rural Households', *Indian Journal of Social Science*, 3 (1).

Reddy, Sanjay (1988), 'An Independent Press Working Against Famine: The Nigerian Experience', *Journal of Modern African Studies*, 26.

Riskin, Carl (1987), *China's Political Economy: The Quest for Development since 1949* (Oxford: Oxford University Press).

—— (1990), 'Feeding China', in Drèze and Sen (1990), vol. III.

—— (1993), 'Income Distribution and Poverty in Rural China', in Griffin and Zhao Renwei (1993).

Rodrik, Dani (1992), 'The Limits of Trade Policy Reform in Developing Countries', *Journal of Economic Perspectives*, 6.

—— (1994a), 'King Kong Meets Godzilla: The World Bank and *The East Asian Miracle*', Discussion Paper No. 944, Centre for Economic Policy Research, London.

—— (1994b), 'Trade and Industrial Policy Reform in Developing Countries: A Review of Recent Theory and Evidence', in Behrman and Srinivasan (1994).

Roemer, John (1982), *A General Theory of Exploitation and Class* (Cambridge, MA: Harvard University Press).

Rogaly, Ben (1994), 'Rural Labour Arrangements in West Bengal, India', unpublished Ph.D. thesis, University of Oxford.

Rokadiya, B.C., Mehta, C.S., Jain, A.K., and Tripathi, V. (1993), 'The Final Evaluation of the Total Literacy Campaign of Ajmer District', mimeo, National Institute of Adult Education, New Delhi.

Romer, Paul M. (1986), 'Increasing Returns and Long-Run Growth', *Journal of Political Economy*, 94.

—— (1987a), 'Growth Based on Increasing Returns Due to Specialization', *American Economic Review*, 77.

—— (1987b), 'Two Strategies for Economic Development: Using Ideas and Producing Ideas', in World Bank, *Proceedings of the World Bank Annual Conference on Development Economics 1992* (Washington, DC: World Bank).

—— (1990), 'Endogenous Technical Change', *Journal of Political Economy*, 98.

—— (1993), 'Idea Gaps and Object Gaps in Economic Development', *Journal of Monetary Economics*, 32.

Rose, Kalima (1992), *Where Women are Leaders: The SEWA Movement in India* (London: Zed Books).

Rosen, George (1992), *Contrasting Styles of Industrial Reform: China and India in the 1980s* (Chicago: University of Chicago Press).

Rosenzweig, Mark R., and Evenson, R. (1977), 'Fertility, Schooling, and the Economic Contribution of Children in Rural India: An Econometric Analysis', *Econometrica*, 45 (5).

Rosenzweig, Mark R., and Schultz, T. Paul (1982), 'Market Opportunities, Genetic Endowments, and Intrafamily Resource Distribution: Child Survival in Rural India', *American Economic Review*, 72.

Rothschild, Emma (1992a), 'Adam Smith and Conservative Economics', *The Economic History Review*, 45 (February).

—— (1992b), 'Commerce and the State: Turgot, Condorcet and Smith', *Economic Journal*, 102.

Rowley, Charles, Tollison, R., and Tullock, Gordon (eds.) (1988), *The Political Economy of Rent-Seeking* (Boston: Kluwer).

Roy, D.K.S. (1992), *Women in Peasant Movements: Tebhaga, Naxalite and After* (New Delhi: Manohar Publications).

Roy, S.B. (1992), 'Forest Protection Committees in West Bengal', *Economic and Political Weekly*, July 18.

Roy Choudhury, Uma Datta (1993), 'Inter-state and Intra-state Variations in Economic Development and Standards of Living', *Journal of the Indian School of Political Economy*, 5 (1).

Rudolph, S.H., and Rudolph, L.I. (1987), *In Pursuit of Lakshmi: The Political Economy of the Indian State* (Chicago: University of Chicago Press).

Rudolph, S.H., and Rudolph, L.I. (eds.) (1972), *Education and Politics in India: Studies in Organization, Society, and Policy* (Cambridge, MA: Harvard University Press).

Rudra, Ashok (1991), 'Privatisation and Deregulation', *Economic and Political Weekly*, December 21.

Sachau, E.C. (ed.) (1992), *Alberuni's India*, originally published in 1910 (New Delhi: Munshiram Manoharlal Publishers).

Sachs, Ignacy (1990), 'Growth and Poverty: Some Lessons from Brazil', in Drèze and Sen (1990), vol. III.

Saha, Anamitra, and Swaminathan, Madhura (1994), 'Agricultural Growth in West Bengal in the Eighties', *Economic and Political Weekly*, March 26.

Sahn, David, and Alderman, Harold (1988), 'The Effects of Human Capital on Wages, and the Determinants of Labor Supply in a Developing Country', *Journal of Development Economics*, 29.

Sainath, P. (1993), 'A Teacher Too Many, A Student Too Few', *The Times of India*, 28 October.

Saith, Ashwani (1990), 'Development Strategies and the Rural Poor', *Journal of Development Studies*, 17.

Saldanha, Denzil (1994), 'Literacy Campaigns in Maharashtra and Goa: Issues, Trends and Policy Implications', mimeo, Tata Institute of Social Sciences, Bombay.

Santha, E.K. (1994), 'Local Self-Government in Malabar (1800-1960)', Occasional Paper No. 12, Institute of Social Sciences, New Delhi.

Satia, J.K., and Jejeebhoy, S.J.(eds.) (1991), *The Demographic Challenge: A Study of Four Large Indian States* (Delhi: Oxford University Press).

Sau, Ranjit (1994), 'World Capitalism and Globalisation', *Economic and Political Weekly*, October 8.

Schultz, T. Paul (1988), 'Education Investments and Returns', in Chenery and Srinivasan (1988).

Schultz, Theodore W. (1962), 'Reflections on Investment in Man', *Journal of Political Economy*, 70.

—— (1963), *The Economic Value of Education* (New York: Columbia University Press).

—— (1971), *Investment in Human Capital* (New York: Free Press and Macmillan).

—— (1980), *Investing in People* (San Francisco: University of California Press).

Scott, Maurice Fg. (1979), 'Trade', in Galenson (1979).

Seetharamu, A.S. (1994), 'Structure and Management of Education in Karnataka State', paper presented at a seminar on 'Management of Education under Panchayati Raj' held at the National Institute of Educational Planning and Administration, New Delhi, 27–8 October, 1994.

Seetharamu, A.S., and Ushadevi, M.D. (1985), *Education in Rural Areas: Constraints and Prospects* (New Delhi: Ashish).

Sen, Amartya (1970), 'Aspects of Indian Education', Lal Bahadur Shastri Memorial Lecture at the Institute of Public Enterprises, Hyderabad; reprinted in S.C. Malik (ed.), *Management and Organization of Indian Universities* (Simla: Institute of Advanced Study, 1970), and partly reprinted in P. Chaudhuri (1971).

—— (1973), 'On the Development of Basic Income Indicators to Supplement GNP Measures', *Economic Bulletin for Asia and the Far East*, United Nations, 24.

—— (1976a), 'Real National Income', *Review of Economic Studies*, 43.

—— (1976b), 'Poverty: An Ordinal Approach to Measurement', *Econometrica*, 44.

—— (1980), 'Equality of What?', in S. McMurrin (ed.), *Tanner Lectures on Human Values*, vol. I (Cambridge: Cambridge University Press); reprinted in Amartya Sen, *Choice, Welfare and Measurement* (Oxford: Blackwell, and Cambridge, MA: MIT Press, 1982).

—— (1981), *Poverty and Famines* (Oxford: Clarendon Press).

Sen, Amartya (1982), 'How Is India Doing?', *New York Review of Books.*

—— (1983a), 'Development: Which Way Now?', *Economic Journal,* 93.

—— (1983b), 'Poor, Relatively Speaking', *Oxford Economic Papers,* 35.

—— (1984), *Resources, Values and Development* (Oxford: Blackwell, and Cambridge, MA: Harvard University Press).

—— (1985a), *Commodities and Capabilities* (Amsterdam: North-Holland).

—— (1985b), 'Well-being, Agency and Freedom: The Dewey Lectures 1984', *Journal of Philosophy,* 82.

—— (1985c), 'Women, Technology and Sexual Divisions', *Trade and Development* (UNCTAD), 6.

—— (1987), *The Standard of Living,* Tanner Lectures with discussion by J. Muellbauer and others, ed. G. Hawthorn (Cambridge: Cambridge University Press).

—— (1988), 'India and Africa: What Do We Have to Learn from Each Other?', in K.I. Arrow (ed.), *The Balance between Industry and Agriculture in Economic Development,* vol. I (London: Macmillan).

—— (1989), 'Women's Survival as a Development Problem', *Bulletin of the American Academy of Arts and Sciences,* 43; shortened version published in *The New York Review of Books,* Christmas number, 1993.

—— (1990), 'Gender and Cooperative Conflict', in Tinker (1990).

—— (1992a), *Inequality Reexamined* (Oxford: Clarendon Press, and Cambridge, MA: Harvard University Press).

—— (1992b), 'Life and Death in China: A Reply', *World Development,* 20.

—— (1992c), 'Missing Women', *British Medical Journal,* 304 (March).

—— (1993a), 'Markets and Freedoms', *Oxford Economic Papers,* 45.

—— (1993b), 'Markets and the Freedom to Choose', paper presented at the Kiel Institute of World Economics; published in a volume on 'The Ethical Foundations of the Market Economy'.

—— (1993c), 'Positional Objectivity', *Philosophy and Public Affairs,* 22.

—— (1994a), 'Population and Reasoned Agency', in K. Lindahl-Kiessling and H. Landberg (eds.), *Population, Economic Development, and the Environment* (Oxford: Oxford University Press).

—— (1994b), 'Population: Delusion and Reality', *New York Review of Books,* September 22.

Sen, Amartya, and Sengupta, Sunil (1983), 'Malnutrition of Rural Children and the Sex Bias', *Economic and Political Weekly,* 19 (annual number).

Sen, Geeta, Germain, Adrienne, and Chen, Lincoln (eds.) (1994), *Population Policies Reconsidered: Health, Empowerment, and Rights* (Harvard Series on Population and International Health).

Sen, Ilina (1986), 'Geography of Secular Change in Sex Ratio in 1981: How Much Room for Optimism?', *Economic and Political Weekly,* March 22.

Sen, Sunanda (1994), 'Dimensions of India's External Economic Crisis', *Economic and Political Weekly*, April 2.

Sengupta, Chandan (1992), 'Sociological Impact of Total Literacy Campaign: The Case of Midnapore', unpublished report, Tata Institute of Social Sciences, Bombay.

Sengupta, S. (1991), 'Progress of Literacy in India during 1983 to 1988', *Sarvekshana*, April–June.

Sengupta, Sunil (1981), 'West Bengal Land Reforms and the Agrarian Scene', *Economic and Political Weekly*, Review of Agriculture, 16 (25–6).

Sengupta, Sunil, and Gazdar, Haris (1996), 'Agrarian Politics and Rural Development in West Bengal', in Drèze and Sen (1996).

Shah, Ghanshyam (1990), *Social Movements in India: A Review of the Literature* (New Delhi: Sage).

Shah, M.H. (1989), 'Factors Responsible for Low Performance of Family Welfare Programme', in Jena and Pati (1989).

Shah, Nasra M. (ed.) (1986), *Pakistani Women: A Socioeconomic and Demographic Profile* (Islamabad: Pakistan Institute of Development Economics).

Shah, Tushaar (1987), 'Gains from Social Forestry: Lessons from West Bengal', mimeo, Institute of Rural Management, Anand.

Shankari, Uma (1993), 'A Story from the Field', *Lokayan Bulletin*, 10.

Sharma, Ursula (1980), *Women, Work and Property in North-West India* (London: Tavistock).

—— (1986), *Women's Work, Class, and the Urban Household: A Study of Shimla, North India* (New York, Tavistock).

Sibbons, Maureen (1992), 'Health for All by the Year 2000: The Good Example of Kerala?', Papers in International Development, No. 5, University of Wales, Swansea.

Singh, A.K. (1993), 'Social Consequences of New Economic Policies with Particular Reference to Levels of Living of Working Class Population', *Economic and Political Weekly*, February 13.

Singh, A.N. (1990), *Child Labour in India: A Socioeconomic Perspective* (New Delhi: Shipra Publications).

Singh, H.N. (1993), 'Social Background and Role Performance of Village Pradhans', Occasional Paper Series, No. 10, Institute of Social Sciences, New Delhi.

Singh, Inderjit (1990), *The Great Ascent: The Rural Poor in South Asia* (Baltimore: Johns Hopkins).

Singh, K.B.K. (1988), *Marriage and Family System of Rajputs* (New Delhi: Wisdom Press).

Singh, K.S. (1975), *The Indian Famine, 1967* (New Delhi: People's Publishing House).

—— (1985), *Tribal Society in India* (New Delhi: Manohar).

Singh, K.S. (1993), *The Scheduled Castes* (Delhi: Oxford University Press).

Singh, K.S. (ed.) (1983), *Tribal Movements in India*, 2 volumes (New Delhi: Manohar).

Singh, Manmohan (1964), *India's Export Trends and Prospects for Self-Contained Growth* (Oxford: Clarendon Press).

Singh, R.R. (1994), 'Impact of Nutritive Meal Programme on Enrolment and Health of Girls in Tamil Nadu Primary Schools', mimeo.

Singha, H.S. (1992), *School Education In India: Contemporary Issues and Trends* (New Delhi: Sterling Publishers).

Smith, Adam (1776), *An Inquiry into the Nature and Causes of The Wealth of Nations*; republished in R.H. Campbell and A.S. Skinner (eds.), *Adam Smith: An Inquiry into the Nature and Causes of The Wealth of Nations* (Oxford: Clarendon, 1976).

—— (1790), *The Theory of Moral Sentiments,* revised edition (republished, Oxford: Clarendon Press, 1975).

Solow, Robert M. (1956), 'A Contribution to the Theory of Economic Growth', *Quarterly Journal of Economics*, 70.

—— (1957), 'Technical Change and Aggregate Production Function', *Review of Economics and Statistics,* 39.

Somanathan, E. (1991), 'Deforestation, Property Rights and Incentives in Central Himalaya', *Economic and Political Weekly*, January 26.

Sopher, David (1980a), 'The Geographical Patterning of Culture in India', in Sopher (1980b).

Sopher, David (ed.) (1980b), *An Exploration of India: Geographical Perspectives on Society and Culture* (Ithaca, NY: Cornell University Press).

Srinivas, K. (1991), 'The Demographic Scenario Revealed by the 1991 Census Figures', *Journal of Family Welfare*, 37 (3).

Srinivas, M.N. (1962), *Caste in Modern India and Other Essays* (Bombay: Allied).

—— (1965), *Religion and Society among the Coorgs of South India* (Bombay: Asia Publishing House).

—— (1967), 'The Cohesive Role of Sanskritization', in P. Mason (ed.), *India and Ceylon: Unity and Diversity* (London: Oxford University Press).

—— (1989), *The Cohesive Role of Sanskritization and Other Essays* (Delhi: Oxford University Press).

Srinivasan, T.N. (1991a), 'Reform of Industrial and Trade Policies', *Economic and Political Weekly*, September 14.

—— (1991b), 'Indian Development Strategy: An Exchange of Views', *Economic and Political Weekly*, August 3–10.

—— (1993), 'Indian Economic Reforms: Background, Rationale and Next Steps', mimeo, Economic Growth Center, Yale University.

Srinivasan, T.N. (ed.) (1994), *Agriculture and Foreign Trade in China and India since 1950* (San Francisco: International Center for Economic Growth).

Srinivasan, T.N., and Bardhan, Pranab (eds.) (1974), *Poverty and Income Distribution in India* (Calcutta: Statistical Publishing Society).

Srinivasan, T.N., and Bardhan, Pranab (eds.) (1988), *Rural Poverty in South Asia* (New York: Columbia University Press).

State Statistical Bureau of the People's Republic of China (1985), *1982 Population Census of China*, Chinese edition (Beijing: Population Census Office).

—— (1992), *China Population Statistics Yearbook 1992* (Beijing: Population Census Office).

—— (1993a), *Tabulation of the 1990 Census of the People's Republic of China*, vol. II, Chinese edition (Beijing: Population Census Office).

—— (1993b), *China Statistical Yearbook 1993* (Beijing: China Statistical Information and Consultancy Service Center).

Stevenson, H., and Stigler, J. (1992), *The Learning Gap* (New York: Summit).

Stewart, Frances (1985), *Basic Needs in Developing Countries* (Baltimore: Johns Hopkins).

Stiglitz, Joseph (1974), 'Incentives and Risk Sharing in Share-cropping', *Review of Economic Studies*, 61.

—— (1993), 'Some Lessons from the Asian Miracle', mimeo, World Bank, Washington, DC.

Stockholm International Peace Research Institute (1994), *SIPRI Yearbook 1994* (Oxford: Oxford University Press).

Stokey, Nancy L. (1988), 'Learning by Doing and the Introduction of New Goods', *Journal of Political Economy*, 96.

—— (1991a), 'Human Capital, Product Quality and Growth', *Quarterly Journal of Economics*, 106.

—— (1991b), 'The Volume and Composition of Trade between Rich and Poor Countries', *Review of Economic Studies*, 58.

Stree Shakti Sanghatana (1989), *'We Were Making History': Women and the Telangana Uprising* (London: Zed Books).

Streeten, Paul, with Burki, S.J., Mahbub ul Haq, Hicks, N., and Stewart, F. (1981), *First Things First: Meeting Basic Needs in Developing Countries* (New York: Oxford University Press).

Subbarao, K., and Raney, L. (1994), 'Social Gains from Female Education: A Cross-National Study', Discussion Paper No. 194, World Bank, Washington, DC.

Subramaniam, V. (1975), *Parched Earth: The Maharashtra Drought 1970–73* (Bombay: Orient Longman).

Summers, Lawrence H. (1992), 'Investing in *All* the People: Educating Women in Developing Countries', Working Paper, World Bank, Washington, DC.

Sundaram, K., and Tendulkar, S.D. (1994), 'On Measuring Shelter Deprivation in India', Discussion Paper No. 23, Centre for Development Economics, Delhi School of Economics.

Sundari, T.K. (1993), 'Women and the Politics of Development in India', *Reproductive Health Matters*, 1.

—— (1994), 'Women's Health in a Rural Poor Population in Tamil Nadu', in M. Das Gupta et al. (1994).

Swaminathan, Madhura (1990), 'Village Level Implementation of IRDP: Comparison of West Bengal and Tamil Nadu', *Economic and Political Weekly*, March 31.

Swaminathan, Mina (1991), 'Child Care Services in Tamil Nadu', *Economic and Political Weekly*, December 28.

Swamy, G.V. (1991), 'Common Property Resources and Tribal Economy', paper presented at the Ninth Annual Conference of the Andhra Pradesh Economic Association, Vijaywada; published in the proceedings of the conference.

Swamy, V.S., and Sinha, S.K. (1994), 'A Note on Disaggregation of Data Below State Level from Sample Registration System', *Sample Registration Bulletin*, 28 (1).

Taylor, Lance (ed.) (1993), *The Rocky Road to Reform: Adjustment, Income Distribution, and Growth in the Developing World* (Cambridge, MA: MIT Press).

Tendulkar, S.D., Sundaram, K., and Jain, L.R. (1993), 'Poverty in India, 1970–71 to 1988–89', Working Paper, ILO-ARTEP, New Delhi.

Tharu, S., and Lalita., K. (eds.) (1991), *Women Writing in India*, 2 volumes (Delhi: Oxford University Press).

Thirlwall, A.P. (1994), *Growth and Development*, fifth edition (London: Macmillan).

Thomas, D., Strauss, J., and Henriques, M.H. (1991), 'How Does Mother's Education Affect Child Height?', *Journal of Human Resources*, 26.

Tilak, Jandhyala B.G. (1989), 'Centre–State Relations in Financing Education in India', *Comparative Education Review*, 33.

—— (1990), 'Expenditure on Education in India: A Comment', *Journal of Education and Social Change*, 4 (2).

—— (1993), 'Costs and Financing of Education in India: A Review of Issues, Problems and Prospects', mimeo, National Institute of Educational Planning and Administration, New Delhi; forthcoming as a Discussion Paper of the Centre for Development Studies, Trivandrum.

—— (1994a), 'South Asian Perspectives', *International Journal of Educational Research*, 21.

—— (1994b), 'Elementary Education in India in the 1990s: Problems and Perspectives', mimeo, National Institute of Educational Planning and Administration, New Delhi.

Tinker, Irene (ed.) (1990), *Persistent Inequalities* (New York: Oxford University Press).

Tod, James (1929), *Annals and Antiquities of Rajasthan*, 2 volumes, reprinted 1972 (London: Routledge and Kegan Paul).

Tomkins, Andrew, and Watson, Fiona (1989), *Malnutrition and Infection: A Review* (London: London School of Hygiene and Tropical Medicine).

Toye, John (1993), *Dilemmas of Development*, second edition (Oxford: Blackwell).

Tulasidhar, V.B. (1993), 'Expenditure Compression and Health Sector Outlays', *Economic and Political Weekly*, November 6.

Tulasidhar, V.B., and Sarma, J.V.M. (1993), 'Public Expenditure, Medical Care at Birth and Infant Mortality: A Comparative Study of States in India', in Berman and Khan (1993).

Tyagi, P.N. (1991), *Education for All: A Graphic Presentation*, first edition (New Delhi: National Institute of Educational Planning and Administration).

—— (1993), *Education for All: A Graphic Presentation*, second edition (New Delhi: National Institute of Educational Planning and Administration).

Uberoi, P. (ed.) (1993), *Family, Kinship and Marriage in India* (Delhi: Oxford University Press).

United Nations (1993), *The Sex and Age Distribution of the World Populations: The 1992 Revision* (New York: Department of Economic and Social Development, United Nations).

UNDP (1990), *Human Development Report 1990* (Oxford: Oxford University Press).

—— (1993), *Human Development Report 1993* (Oxford: Oxford University Press).

—— (1994), *Human Development Report 1994* (Oxford: Oxford University Press).

UNICEF (1994), *The State of the World's Children 1994* (New York: UNICEF).

van Bastelaer, T. (1986), 'Essai d'Analyse des Systèmes de Paiements de Mariage: Le Cas de l'Inde', unpublished M.Sc. thesis, Faculté des Sciences Economiques et Sociales, Université de Namur, Belgium.

van Parijs, P. (1990), 'Equal Endowments as Undominated Diversity', *Recherches Economiques de Louvain*, 56.

—— (1991), 'Why Surfers Should be Fed: The Liberal Case for an Unconditional Basic Income', *Philosophy and Public Affairs*, 20.

Vanaik, Achin (1991), *The Painful Transition: Bourgeois Democracy in India* (London: Verso).

Venkatachalam, R., and Srinivasan, V. (1993), *Female Infanticide* (New Delhi: Har-Anand).

Verma, Jyoti (1989), 'Women Education: A Media of Social Change', *Social Change*, 19.

Verma, V.S. (1988), *A Handbook of Population Statistics* (New Delhi: Office of the Registrar General).

Visaria, Leela, and Visaria, Pravin (1995), 'Acceleration of Fertility Decline in Tamil Nadu since 1981: Some Hypotheses', Working Paper, Gujarat Institute of Development Research, Ahmedabad.

Visaria, Pravin (1961), *The Sex Ratio of the Population of India*, Monograph No. 10, Census of India 1961, Office of the Registrar General, New Delhi.

—— (1967), 'The Sex Ratio of the Population of India and Pakistan and Regional Variations during 1901–1960', in A. Bose (ed.), *Pattern of Population Change in India 1951–1961* (Bombay: Allied Publishers).

—— (1993), 'Demographic Aspects of Development: The Indian Experience', *Indian Journal of Social Science*, 6 (3).

Visaria, P., Gumber, A., and Visaria, L. (1993), 'Literacy and Primary Education in India, 1980–81 to 1991', *Journal of Educational Planning and Administration*, 7 (1).

Visaria, Pravin, and Visaria, Leela (1994), 'Demographic Transition: Accelerating Fertility Decline in 1980s', *Economic and Political Weekly*, December 17–24.

Vlassoff, Carol (1980), 'Unmarried Adolescent Females in Rural India: A Study of the Social Impact of Education', *Journal of Marriage and the Family*, 42 (2).

—— (1993), 'Against the Odds: The Changing Impact of Education on Female Autonomy and Fertility in an Indian Village', paper presented at a workshop on 'Female Education, Autonomy and Fertility Change in South Asia', New Delhi, 8–10 April 1993.

Vyas, V.S., Sagar, V., and Bhargava, P. (1993), 'Nature and Direction of Poverty Alleviation Efforts in India: An Overview', mimeo, Institute of Development Studies, Jaipur.

Vyasulu, Vinod (1993), 'Management of Poverty Alleviation Programmes in Karnataka: An Overview', paper presented at a workshop on 'Poverty Alleviation in India' held at the Institute of Development Studies, Jaipur, February.

Wade, Robert (1989), 'What Can Economies Learn from East Asian Success?', *Annals of the American Academy of Political Science*, 505.

—— (1988a), *Village Republics: Economic Conditions for Collective Action in South India* (Cambridge: Cambridge University Press).

—— (1988b), 'Why Some Indian Villages Co-operate', *Economic and Political Weekly*, April 16.

—— (1990), *Governing the Market: Economic Theory and the Role of the Government in East Asian Industrialization* (Princeton: Princeton University Press).

—— (1992), 'How to Make "Street Level" Bureaucracies Work Better: India and Korea', *IDS Bulletin,* 23 (4).

Wadley, S., and Derr, B. (1989), 'Karimpur 1925–1984: Understanding Rural India Through Restudies', in P.K. Bardhan (ed.), *Conversations between Economists and Anthropologists* (Delhi: Oxford University Press).

Ware, H. (1984), 'Effects of Maternal Education, Women's Roles, and Child Care on Child Mortality', in W.H. Mosley and L.C. Chen (eds.), *Child Survival: Strategies for Research* (New York: Population Council).

Weiner, Myron (1991), *The Child and the State in India: Child Labor and Education Policy in Comparative Perspective* (Princeton: Princeton University Press).

Weiner, Myron (1994), 'Compulsory Education and Child Labour', lecture delivered at the Rajiv Gandhi Foundation, New Delhi, 8 January 1994; mimeo, Massachussetts Institute of Technology.

Weitzmann, Martin L., and Chenggang Xu (1993), 'Chinese Township and Village Enterprises as Vaguely Defined Cooperatives', Discussion Paper No. 26, Research Programme on the Chinese Economy, STICERD, London School of Economics.

Westphal, Larry E. (1978), 'The Republic of Korea's Experience of Export Led Development', *World Development*, 6.

Westphal, L.E., Kim, L., and Dahlman, C. (1985), 'Reflections on Korea's Acquisition of Technological Capability', in N. Rosenberg et al. (eds.), *International Technology Transfer: Concepts, Measures and Comparisons* (New York: Praeger).

Westphal, Larry E., Rhee, Yung Whee, and Pursell, Garry (1988), *Korean Industrial Competence: Where It Came From* (Washington, DC: World Bank).

Wong, L. (1994), 'Privatization of Social Welfare in Post-Mao China', *Asian Survey*, 34.

Wood, A. (1991), 'China's Economic System: A Brief Description, with Some Suggestions for Further Reform', Discussion Paper No. 29, Research Programme on the Chinese Economy, STICERD, London School of Economics.

World Bank (1983), *China: Socialist Economic Development* (Washington, DC: World Bank).

—— (1989), *India: Poverty, Employment, and Social Services* (Washington, DC: World Bank).

—— (1992a), *China: Strategies for Reducing Poverty in the 1990s* (Washington, DC: World Bank).

—— (1992b), 'India: Health Sector Financing', Report No. 10859-IN, World Bank, Washington, DC.

—— (1993a), *The World Food Outlook* (Washington, DC: World Bank).

—— (1993b), *World Development Report 1993* (New York: Oxford University Press).

—— (1993c), *The East Asian Miracle* (New York: Oxford University Press).

—— (1994a), 'India: Policy and Finance Strategies for Strengthening Primary Health Care Services', mimeo, World Bank, Washington, DC.

—— (1994b), *World Development Report 1994* (New York: Oxford University Press).

Young, Alwyn (1991), 'Learning by Doing and the Dynamic Effects of International Trade', *Quarterly Journal of Economics*, 106.

—— (1992), 'A Tale of Two Cities: Factor Accumulation and Technical Change in Hong Kong and Singapore', NBER *Macroeconomics Annual 1992*.

Yu Dezhi (1992), 'Changes in Health Care Financing and Health Status: The

Case of China in the 1980s', Innocenti Occasional Papers, Economic Policy Series, No. 34, International Child Development Centre, Florence.

Zachariah, K.C., Rajan, S.I., Sarma, P.S., Navaneetham, K., Nair, P.S.G., and Mishra, U.S. (1994), *Demographic Transition in Kerala in the 1980s* (Trivandrum: Centre for Development Studies).

Zeng Yi, Tu Ping, Gu Baochang, Xu Yi, Li Bohua, and Li Yongping (1993), 'Causes and Implications of the Recent Increase in the Reported Sex Ratio at Birth in China', *Population and Development Review*, 19 (2).

# NAME INDEX

# SUBJECT INDEX